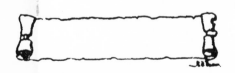

Text, ConText, and HyperText

MIT Press Series in Information Systems
Michael Lesk, editor

Nested Transactions: An Approach to Reliable Distributed Computing,
by J. Eliot B. Moss, 1985

Advanced Database Techniques, by Daniel Martin, 1986

Text, ConText, and HyperText: Writing with and for the Computer,
edited by Edward Barrett, 1988

Text, ConText, and HyperText
Writing with and for the Computer

edited by
Edward Barrett

The MIT Press
Cambridge, Massachusetts
London, England

Publisher's Note

This format is intended to reduce the cost of publishing certain works in book form and to shorten the gap between editorial preparation and final publication. Detailed editing and composition have been avoided by photographing the text of this book directly from the author's prepared copy.

Third Printing, 1989

Library of Congress Cataloging-in-Publication Data

Text, ConText, and HyperText.

(MIT Press series in information systems)
Bibliography: p.
Includes index.
1. Electronic data processing documentation. 2. Electronic data processing—Authorship.
3. Text processing (Computer science) I. Barrett, Edward.
QA76.9.D6T48 1988   808'.066004   87-36157
ISBN 0-262-02275-3

Contents

Series Foreword

Even computer programs that process only numbers come with a good deal of English. Written messages prompt for input, explain errors in the output, and instruct the user in the commands needed to make the program do anything. Documentation usually weighs more than the program itself, is sometimes as much of a trouble to prepare, and is crucial to the "user-friendliness" of the overall system. What kind of documentation is needed for programs, and how can it be written?

The traditional book is read from the beginning to the end, so the author can write each page knowing that the reader has just finished the previous page. Electronic documentation, however, is not read as much as referred to. The readers can skip around, and usually just look up one item and then another. Often the documentation for a program is available on paper as well as online; the online description comes in pages of a different size than the paper copy, can be opened in different ways, and doesn't have coffee stains to indicate the well-used pages.

The new concepts of "hypertext" and "hypermedia" describe this new kind of material, which is not so much disorganized as multiply organized: there are many ways to read the material, and many orders in which the pages can be turned. Each reader can have a different experience with the same material and learn different things from it. There is a new opportunity to tailor text simultaneously for many readers. This book tells us a bit about how to do it, and about the psychological and linguistic background to understand why to do it, and what can be achieved.

In its three sections it talks about computers, communication, and culture. The first section explains computer techniques for implementing hypertext and natural language processing, and addresses other topics involving the processing of language on computers. The second section is about explaining computer systems, and communicating their descriptions to the users. Usually the documentation is written after the code, and the writer must often present as coherent a system that actually has the logic and consistency of the tax laws. We'd be better to write the documents first, many times. In the final section the cultural context of the documentation is discussed. The linguistic and psychological models of people using computers and instructional materials are presented, along with some thoughts about the overall job to be done, rather than just the style of the manuals.

As a result this book breaks new ground in discussions of documentation. There are plenty of writing manuals. This book tells you why we write manuals the way we do, and what we might do instead. If it works, maybe the second edition will be provided on hypercard.

Acknowledgments

Working versions of some chapters in this book were first presented at the Annual Conference on Writing for the Computer Industry at MIT. For his generous support of this conference I wish to thank Frederick J. McGarry, Director of the Office of the Summer Session. I am also grateful to Kenneth R. Manning, Head of the MIT Writing Program, for his support of this conference and his kind encouragement. For their help in organizing this conference I am grateful to Richard Chisholm, John Kirkman, John Kirsch, and Muriel Zimmerman.

I have benefited from many discussions about computers and writing with members of the Committee on Writing Instruction and Computers at MIT. I wish to thank Kate Burnett, William Cattey, Janet Murray, Bonnie Walters, Rosalind Williams, and from IBM, Frank Bequaert. My thanks also to Dave Custer for our discussions about computers and education.

From the MIT Press, I wish to thank Frank Satlow, Larry Cohen, and Terry Ehling for their support and generous assistance in bringing this volume to print.

Finally, I am most pleased to express my gratitude to James Paradis of the MIT Writing Program who acted as co-director of the Annual Conference on Writing for the Computer Industry and with whom I served as co-principal investigator for the Athena Writing Project. With respect and admiration I dedicate this volume to him.

Introduction: A New Paradigm for Writing *with* and *for* the Computer

Text, ConText, and HyperText presents a unique conceptualization of the role of computing in documentation and the role of documentation in the development of computing technology. Part One, *Artificial Intelligence, Document Processing, and Hypertext* addresses the future of writing for the computer industry with reference to automated publishing and expert systems, document databases, natural language processing systems, and the uses of hypertext in documentation. Part Two, *Management, Training, and Corporate Culture* examines the training and management of documentation groups and the effects of documentation on product development. Part Three, *Designing On-line Documentation* analyzes the organization, style, and cultural contexts of on-line documentation. In essence, this volume argues a first synthesis of three related areas of technical communication: writing, management, and computer technology. *Text, ConText, and HyperText* calls for a revisioning of the roles of writer, manager, and engineer, and in doing so, offers a topography of ideas about the future.

Inventing futures, however, is also a process of deconstructing the present: of seeing the shape of the wave just before it breaks. The field of technical communication views itself in two ways. On the one hand, it defines itself in relation to a rhetorical tradition concerned with the dialectic between style and content. This approach views "writing" in relation to well established forms and genres (usually in print formats) and offers an analysis of how to structure writing within those genres. This approach to technical communication has traditionally occupied an ancillary position in the development of computer technology. By definition, writers offer skills that can be exploited to explain a product once it has been developed. From this perspective, it is easy to see a gap between writing and the development of computing.

On the other hand, the field of technical communication is also driven by a technological avant-garde that seeks new ways of presenting information and constructing knowledge with various on-line tools for writing and problem-solving. As more documentation goes on-line, and as computing technology is increasingly used to support the processes that have traditionally defined writing, the gap between writing and computer research is narrowed. But does that narrowing change the position of writing in respect to development?

The tensions created by these two poetics of technical communication can serve as a starting point for another synthesis. As the gap between writing and computing narrows, the future of writing and the computer industry will be more complicated than ever before. Writing will be perceived not as an ancillary support function, but rather as the larger context within which development proceeds. The technological avant-garde and the traditions of rhetoric are not necessarily opposed, if we can see them from another perspective. But achieving this other perspective requires a revisioning of the fields of computer research and writing--a new definition of ends and means. *Text, Context, and Hypertext* initiates this difficult process of self-examination and integration.

The Structure of this Volume

Text, ConText, and HyperText is divided into three major parts, with each part commenting upon and developing ideas from the other two. The structure of this book is musical rather than linear: chapters looks forward or back to other chapters, and ideas are deepened in this way. Individual chapters, therefore, are part of a larger dialogue among authorities from industry and the university in the fields of computer science, writing, and management. The subtitle of this volume, "writing *with* and *for* the computer," is a statement of the organic relationship among these three areas.

The natural audience for this book, therefore, includes technical writers, managers of documentation groups, and software engineers. In addition, researchers into artificial intelligence will see how their work has problematized the field of technical communications, and just as importantly, how writing as conceived by writers impacts upon the design of expert systems. Teachers of technical writing in both industry and the university will find important discussions of the definition of competence in technical communication, as well as new tools for training writers. Finally, composition researchers can use this volume to analyze theory in light of real-world practice.

It makes sense, then, to discuss individual contributions to this volume in terms of several overarching themes. Those themes include the definition of writers and writing in the computer industry in light of artificial intelligence and automated publishing systems; hypertext and hypermedia; documentation and product development; and management and training of writers in industry. After a brief discussion of these themes as they are reflected in *Text, ConText, and HyperText* I offer the conceptual basis upon which I have structured this volume and upon which I feel we can begin to integrate the fields of writing, management, and computer science.

What is Writing in the Computer Industry? What is a Writer?

The crucial question for technical communicators and designers of computer systems should be the assessment of the effects of automation on writing and its cognate, thinking. What are we giving up by bringing the machine into the cognitive garden? Mark Haselkorn sets the context for this volume by discussing the application of artificial intelligence to document processing and its effect on the future of writing in the computer industry. An impressive example of such an application is provided by Boris Katz who discusses text processing with the START natural language system he developed at MIT. Yet, as the exchange between Geoffrey James and R. John Brockmann demonstrates, these advances in technology are also problematic. Artificial intelligence and automated publishing systems can augment as well as diminish the process of writing, and, therefore, the role of the writer as traditionally conceived. In the discussion of an on-line training system we developed for the Athena Writing Project at MIT, James Paradis and I express the basis for this conflict as a dialectic between the views of Skinner and Papert in systems design.

Hypertext, Hypermedia and the Design of On-line Documentation

Another aspect of the re-definition of writing and writer dictated by on-line documentation systems is the assault on a central concept of Western culture--the book itself: a linear narrative moving in time, occupying real space, with a beginning, middle, and end. Hypertext and hypermedia environments permit self-authoring texts and non-linear documents, creating a mirage of depth in the collapse of space and time within the computer. Developers of hypertext systems are inspired by a highly Romantic, Coleridgean concept of writing: an infinitely evolving text that tracks momentary cognitive processes within the individual reader-author. In this volume, Geri Younggren offers one possible scenario for creating such an audience-driven hypermedia environment, while Patricia Ann Carlson and John Slatin propose specific applications of hypertext for incorporating user feedback into documentation and for teaching writing, respectively. In broader conceptual terms, Philip Rubens and Robert Krull analyze the design of on-line documentation, while Jonathan Price addresses the rhetoric of on-line help systems. The challenge presented by this new form of knowledge representation leads Henrietta Shirk to re-define the writer as computer scientist. John Kirkman, on the other hand, offers a tonic reminder of the real-world environment such documentation inhabits, and returns us to a consideration of fixed language systems and cultural values in documentation.

Management, Training, and Corporate Culture: Writing as Context and Social Construction

When Roger Grice states that information development is part of product development, he radicalizes the role of the writer in the computer industry. Grice's deceptively quiet re-assessment of "writing" can be used to define a new perspective on the relationship between writing and development: writing as the larger context in which product development takes place. Thus, Muriel Zimmerman's analysis of how people learn in the computer industry forces her to ask if writers are obsolete only because "writing" is the invisible tegument of the entire industry: everyone is a writer all the time. For Edmond Weiss, theoretician of process, a slightly different perspective on this question of context and development results in a revisionist statement of the value of usability testing as an element of closure in product development. It is a point of view that resonates in the cognitive process model for information design developed by Elizabeth Keyes, David Sykes, and Elaine Lewis, and in the conceptual approach to training writers as desktop publishers discussed by Patricia Sullivan.

Finally, a concept of context and its effect on documentation and product development is the basis for a "diagnosis" of "corporate culture" by Lawrence Levine. The vaguely medical tincture of his language quoted here serves to indicate two important points: first, Levine sees documentation and management as organically related to product development; second, he suggests the patient is in need treatment. John Kirsch offers two highly detailed case studies in which he analyzes the effects of varying degrees of investment in computer-product documentation; and Richard Ziegfeld, Ruth Hawkins, Wilson Judd, and Robert Mahany present an unusually candid insider's view of preparations for a large-scale courseware development project. These case studies serve as useful commentary on the Grice-Levine-Weiss axis of context analysis.

Such a brief summary, however, cannot do justice to the individual chapters in this volume, nor to the dialogic nature of their relationship to one another. I also fear that I may have put more interpretation on them than their authors would allow. In the final section of this introduction, therefore, I sketch out the conceptual basis upon which I have structured *Text, ConText, and HyperText*.

Computer Science, Cognitive Science, and the Social Construction of Knowledge

There exists a natural affinity between writing and computers, almost a *genetic* relationship. They are used as tools for representing and discovering knowledge and as instruments for communication between people. As mechanisms for knowledge representation they allow thought to achieve an historical projection so that ideas can be presented for discussion. Both writing and computers offer means for reviewing, altering, and developing those ideas. Finally, writing and computers both employ symbolic languages to fix meanings for individual and social purposes. Thus, there is a family of relationships that unites thinking, writing, and computers.

Yet, without an adequate conceptual basis for the development of computing technologies to support writing and thinking, we risk dealing only in metaphors, anthropomorphizing the machine and mechanizing the uniquely human. When we misapply computing technologies, we waste the resources they carry with them. Moreover, we falsify the functions they were meant to serve, and instead of augmenting human power, we diminish it. Two scenes illustrate the sorts of functions I believe we expect the computer to support.

First Scene

In November of this year I visited with Boris Katz at the Artificial Intelligence Laboratory at MIT. Boris was going to demonstrate START, a natural language processing system he had developed. We sat before the computer and typed in English language sentences which were instantaneously compiled to form a knowledge base. We then queried this knowledge base with other conversational English sentences to retrieve information. It was an impressive performance. For over an hour we engaged in a "dialogue" with the computer. Boris also mentioned a program he wrote just before he left the Soviet Union, a sort of poetry compiler that generated verse. I was going to say something about Ted Nelson and *Xanadu*, but Boris was showing me his copy of Pasternak which was tucked in between two massive user manuals: English poetry was still beyond his reach, he said, even though he has lived in this country for nine years.

Second Scene

From my notebook, February 1987, jottings of a conversation with James Paradis after our third class in the electronic classroom developed for the Athena Writing Project:

the traditional classroom unglued--new image for functions of teaching. on-line system
as a sequence of interruptions, interaction speeded up, puts you inside the process.
from critic to collaborator. Display shows mind in process. Changing the time-scale to
get closer to the creative act in composition

Exterior and Interior Processes in Computing and Writing: Translation,
Semiosis, Dialogue, and Cognition

These two scenes represent a matrix of issues at the heart of writing for
the computer industry. The first scene dramatizes the functions we seek to
model in the computer: translation and creation of ideas (with associations of
contingency and compiling: storing, classifying); semiosis, or presentation of
information in symbolic forms; and finally, dialogue and exchange (between
self and others; self and machine; self, machine, and others). The first scene
presents these functions in light of real cultural and language dependencies:
contexts the individual both relies upon and seeks escape from. The second
scene, however, is essentially interior: seeking the vanishing point of thinking
in the context of writing, with associations of commentary, drafting, and revising: processes that also offer an historical projection of that interior domain.

Of course, this vanishing point is a mirage of perspective, a place created
only when we look for it--nowhere and everywhere. The image of a vanishing
point, however, changes the language of thinking about thinking: thought becomes a place now, a theater of pure meanings interacting with each other,
masked, speaking with different voices. My notebook entry shows I was using
the computer to de-center that place away from the individual: objectifying, or
at least tracing the activity of thought in writing, using the computer to archive
each perspective as it was created, so that it could be reviewed, speculated
upon, and facilitate in turn another tentative entrance of an idea, a revision.
The computer, then, was a stage for acting out ideas. A place to audition.

Information archiving and retrieval, document display, dialogue or communication with self and others, and the generation of further ideas: these are
the processes that have traditionally defined thinking in writing. How can the
computer be used to support these processes?

Papert, Piaget, Skinner, and Vygotsky

Research into computer support for thinking and writing can be characterized in terms of three broad conceptual approaches. One approach is given

expression in the work of Seymour Papert; another derives from the work of
Jean Piaget; and the third is best described in terms of Skinnerian behaviorism.
In this section I sketch out the general outlines of each of these conceptual
models and offer an analysis of their effect on research into computer support
for writing and problem-solving. I conclude with a suggestion of a new
paradigm for systems development derived from the work of Lev Vygotsky.
This new model, I feel, offers an especially useful perspective on computer
support for writing and thinking--and, equally important, the application of
writing to the development of computer technology.

Papert

In his book, *Mindstorms*, Seymour Papert wrestles with the use of computers in education. His analysis of the cognitive basis for computer-mediated
instruction provides us with a unique conceptualization for computer systems
in any training or conferencing environment--corporate or academic. Papert
analogizes the power of the computer to the Greek god, Proteus: he says the
computer is unique in its ability to simulate. And this protean ability for
simulation means that the computer should be used to provide us with "an object to think with." Papert, therefore, aligns himself with Weizenbaum and
Turkle in warning against unthinking anthropomorphism of the computer: it
is not a thinking object, but a means for objectifying, or displaying the cognitive processes of the learner. As he states, ideally the user learns to program
the machine rather than being programmed by it.

Papert and Hypertext

Although Papert's ideas on the proper use of computers to stimulate
thinking were applied to mathematical reasoning primarily, they have
relevance for designers of hypertext environments as well. Hypertext systems
can provide us with robust objects to think with: self-authoring texts that body
forth the movements of a mind focused on a particular topic. *Intermedia*, an
impressive hypermedia environment at Brown University, is an example of
this kind of object to think with. But *Intermedia* also demonstrates a critical
limitation of hypertext: as linkages grow more complex the learner becomes
trapped in an associative web that threatens to overwhelm the incipient logic
of discovery that created it. The user is presented with a collage of
contingencies--information, not necessarily understanding. This tangle of
linkages becomes an even more critical limitation to the user when navigation
in hypertext is unmediated by an instructor or experienced guide. A user may

just glance over the surface of a body of knowledge without integrating it into a personal knowing. And if pathways are too firmly established, then the point of hypertext is lost.

A second crucial element in the design of hypermedia environments must be the quality of the database. What is the use of a system that provides supple pathways through material that is not worth digesting in the first place? And how does the uninitiated learner distinguish between wheat and chaff if access to the system is purely solitary? How will hypertext help the learner "think with" on-line information? Or are we to be satisfied with mere "knowledge representation" instead of knowing? Our own experience with the design and implementation of a modified version of a hypertext document in an on-line training environment (Barrett and Paradis, this volume) suggests that the effectiveness of hypertext for instructional purposes is limited by the monolithic presence of the machine itself. Students (and instructors) tie information together (that is, learn and teach) in far more socially structured ways. As Papert says, learning is syntonic--responsive, and a response to, the environment of shared concepts in which it occurs. How hypertext contributes to syntonic learning should be a consideration in assessing its value for training contexts in industry and the academy.

Finally, research into hypertext and hypermedia must also address the application of these systems to writing. The representation of information under the control of an leading idea has traditionally defined one aspect of knowledge in our culture. The text objectifies ideas, beliefs, and reasoning not only for the reader but also for the writer. Writing, therefore, becomes an instrument of knowing as well as communication. The danger in hypertext applications to technical communication is that they may unduly stress a mere aggregation of discrete planes of information, rather than the unique structuring of ideas for a particular purpose: in other words, boilerplate writ large.

Piaget

In contrast to Papert, who conceptualizes computers as generic objects to think with, the work of Jean Piaget has had impact on the more specific application of computers to writing instruction. Piaget's "genetic epistemology" interprets language development as an activity of mind. "Language," he states, "is indispensable to the elaboration of thought." And language plays a central role in cognitive development because "it is elaborated socially and contains a notation for the entire system" of cognitive functions. His views on "individual semiosis," semiotic thought, and the development of the child's command of language from egocentic speech to an awareness of socially accepted conventions for addressing others, have become the conceptual basis of popular educational software for training writers.

Piaget, therefore, is relevant to the field of writing "with and for" the computer because he directs our attention to the cognitive uses of language--language as a structure of, and for, knowing. Writing becomes a path out of and into the domain of knowing and learning: and clearly, technical documentation--its creation and uses--falls within this area of research. Yet the cognitive process model for the application of computers to writing is problematic because of the limitations of the machine itself.

Cognitive Process, Computing, and Skinner

How cognitive theories of learning get implemented in computer systems is a difficult subject to analyze. Most contemporary software packages for writing instruction align themselves with a "process" theory of learning. Typically, they are designed to lead a user through a well established series of steps for producing a document. As the user interacts with these programs, he or she begins to internalize these fixed prompts. In essence, the user is being programmed by the machine.

How well can a machine "simulate," to use Papert's term, the inner life, the matrix of cognitive processes that go on in any individual? Hypertext, as a concept, does not really attempt any such simulation; rather, it is essentially a muscular note-taking, or note-gathering, mechanism. It permits the user to assemble an integration of texts partly through dictating structures of meanings (by pathways or windows) and partly through an absence of direction: it offers a suspension of meanings on various levels that the user can string and restring under the impulse of a developing idea. Hypertext has heuristic value in so far as it pulls away from trying to command any structure other than the one that is audience-driven.

But when the computer is used to simulate an essentially interior process, one that is uniquely human and personal--as in software that offers to teach a process of writing or problem-solving--it inevitably models only the behaviors that are the outcome of such an interior process. In fact, B.F. Skinner lauded "teaching machines" for that reason alone: they were extremely effective mechanisms for reinforcing selected behaviors. They could be used in private settings, directed solely by one user interacting with a "frame" that "chunked" material for review at a variable pace. The user was programmed for a behavior; therefore, thinking, or even "knowing," could be dispensed with as operative terms. The "protean ability" of the computer for simulation is a function of what is being simulated.

Vygotsky, Social Construction, and a New Paradigm for Using the Computer

How, then, should we think about the design and implementation of computer systems in documentation, conferencing, problem-solving, and management contexts? How can we best write "with and for" the computer? Hypertext and related systems offer important tools for use. But we need a more comprehensive "environment" that integrates systems with traditional human *connivances* for understanding, teaching, and writing. Papert's language is important here: the computer is "an object to think with," not a thinking object. It can be used to support the matrix of ineffable processes that go into any writing or learning situation--processes that I have identified in those two earlier scenes: dialogue or exchange, display, creation, and review. Such an environment would support an "ecology" (Cooper) of interactive systems to facilitate thinking and writing; it would not dictate a process or imply a necessary methodology.

Papert's ideas receive strong theoretical backing in the work of Lev Vygotsky, the mid-twentieth century Russian socio-linguist. Vygotsky's views on knowledge as a social construction offer a new model for conceptualizing how to use computers in conferencing, problem-solving, documentation, and training contexts. His work is central to contemporary discussions of discourse and learning and, therefore, has relevance to any discussion of writing "with and for" the computer.

Vygotsky asserts that we use language instrumentally. The Piagetian notion of "inner speech" is de-centered: we "talk through" our task with someone else and then internalize this conversation as thought; writing re-externalizes this language of internalized conversation (Bruffee, 1986). Thinking and writing are processes fixed in history: a series of dialogues and revisions punctuating an inner text. Learning, therefore, is collaborative and social, a text of interactions among peers. And the knowledge that results from these interactions is a social construct, too--a construct of language. Text is *con-textual*, a knowing with. Language systems are knowledge systems.

Obviously, this perspective provides a unique conceptual basis for using the computer as "an object to think with." Now the computer is not needed to model the inner working of a "mind." Language and the use of language for discovering and structuring knowledge become the focus, with the computer supporting the social processes that define language use. Learning with the computer in this way obviates simplistic behaviorism since the computer is only employed to enhance the "social conversation" of knowledgeable peers. The power of the computer facilitates this exchange of "texts" in context--it permits review and re-creation of ideas as part of an historical process of discovery.

What does this new model mean for developers? The computer becomes an means for supporting a *hyper-context* of collaboration and dialogue--in Vygotskian terms, a social construction of knowledge. Mind and interior cognitive processes are not intruded upon: not modeled in the design of a system. The role of writing in the development of computing technology, therefore, is revisioned. Writing--the textual, contextual process of externalizing thought--becomes the fundamental ground of development.

This re-conceptualization of writing for the computer industry, however, demands a rigorous re-examination of our ideas about writing and automation. Language is knowledge constantly re-creating itself; when writing is fixed within an automated schema, then it is no longer a flexible instrument for constructing cognition. Hypertext attempts to face up to this dilemma; how well it answers the demands of a social constructionist model of knowledge is difficult to ascertain and deserves fuller treatment than the brief scope of an introduction.

Another approach can be found in the discussion of an on-line system for conferencing and training in this volume (Barrett and Paradis). Basically, we posit using the computer to model the mechanisms of the social construction of knowledge rather than the presumed cognitive processes that underlie those mechanisms.

Peter Denning, Director of the Research Institute for Advanced Computer Science at the NASA Ames Research Center, writes that "science is not only the knowledge in various disciplines and the processes for producing that knowledge; it is groups of people working together in each discipline. They are the institutional memory, the selection mechanism, deciding what science is and is not. The knowledge of science and the expertise of science live in the people of science." He suggests that computer networks used to model the social processes or mechanisms of constructing knowledge offer a "new paradigm for science."

This new paradigm for science should extend to the design and implementation of computer systems to support documentation, conferencing, and training programs--all intrinsically social, process-driven contexts. Vygotsky offers critical language for conceptualizing how knowledge is constructed, and his ideas should be brought into our analysis of writing with and for the computer.

References

Bruffee, Kenneth A. "Social Construction, Language, and Knowledge." *College English* 48 (1986): 773-90.

_____. "Writing and Reading as Collaborative or Social Acts: The Argument from Kuhn and Vygotsky." *The Writer's Mind: Writing as a Mode of Thinking.* Ed. Janice N. Hays, et al. Urbana:NCTE, 1983.

Cooper, M. "The Ecology of Writing." *College English* 48 (1986):364-375.

Denning, Peter J. "The Science of Computing: A New Paradigm for Science." *American Scientist* 75 (1987):572-73.

Foster, David. *A Primer for Writing Teachers: Theories, Theorists, Issues, Problems.* Upper Montclair: Boynton/Cook, 1983.

Papert, Seymour. *Mindstorms: Children, Computers, and Powerful Ideas.* New York: Basic Books, 1980.

Piaget, Jean. *Six Psychological Studies.* Trans. Anita Tenzer and Davis Elkind. New York: Random House, 1967.

Piaget, Jean and B. Inhelder. *The Psychology of the Child*, trans. Helen Weaver. New York: Basic Books, 1969.

Skinner, B.F. "Why We Need Teaching Machines." *Harvard Educational Review* 3 (1961):377-398.

Turkle, Sherry R. *The Second Self: Computers and the Human Spirit.* New York: Simon and Schuster, 1984.

Vygotsky, L.S. *Mind in Society.* Ed. Michael Cole. Cambridge, MA: Harvard UP, 1978.

_____. *Thought and Language*, trans. Eugenia Hanfmann and Gertrude Vakar. Cambridge, MA: MIT Press, 1962. Rev. ed. 1986.

Weizenbaum, Joseph. *Computer Power and Human Reason: From Judgement to Calculation.* San Francisco: W. H. Freeman, 1976.

Wertsch, James V. *Vygotsky and the Social Formation of Mind.* Cambridge, MA: Harvard UP, 1986.

I

Artificial Intelligence, Document Processing, and HyperText

1

The Future of "Writing" for the Computer Industry

Mark P. Haselkorn

Program in Scientific & Technical Communication
College of Engineering
University of Washington

Writers in the computer industry are becoming responsible for tasks that, while logical extensions of their present work, go far beyond the traditional notions of writing. These future "writing" tasks are in response to trends in the computer industry which call for greater attention to user needs and perspectives, greater integration of documentation into the design process, greater use of the computer as a delivery medium, increased dissatisfaction with the cost of effective documentation, increased efforts to formally link user demands and system design, and increased application of natural language processing, expert system development, and vision research to system and user support. This article briefly explores these newly developing roles of "writers" in the computer industry, pointing out that while today's writers must be prepared to augment their skills in a number of ways to meet these new demands, it is precisely their current specialization in communication techniques and in understanding the user's perspective which will make them even more valuable to the industry in the future.

This year I've worked on a relatively narrow aspect of the future of writing for the computer industry--a flavor of smart online documentation I call "Smart Documentation Systems" (SDS).[1] Here, however, I look forward to taking a broader, less abrupt view of the future. SDS are only one of many developments that will make "writing" for the computer industry very different in the future than it has been in the past. (So different, that quotes are necessary.)

Changes to the computer industry's "writing" tasks are being stimulated by a number of current trends and developments. These changes will involve those who currently write user and product documentation in tasks that go far beyond traditional notions of writing. Nevertheless, these future "writing" tasks will be logical extensions of their present work--providing help and information to those who own, operate, and maintain computers.

Before looking at these changes in the "writing" task, let's first briefly mention some of the trends and developments which are stimulating them.

(a)   The growing realization by executives that the computer industry must not only be engineering driven, but user driven as well

This point is extremely broad; so broad, in fact, that almost every other point made here can be seen as a manifestation of it. Most industries are marketing driven (e. g. it is the marketing division which authorizes new product development), but until quite recently, the computer industry has been driven by engineering developments and breakthroughs (e. g. new chips lead to new products). Now, however, the computer industry is realizing that while engineering advances are essential, they must be tied to helping people do something they want to do. Thus more and more attention is being paid to marketability and customer service, while the lament of failed enterprises in the Silicon Valley is "we didn't understand the end-user."

(b)   The increasing dissatisfaction with documentation created as an isolated, final stage of product development

As concern for the end-user grows, so does the industry's awareness of the ineffectiveness of past practices in the area of user support. The impracticality of documentation created as an isolated, final stage of product development is fast becoming one of the fundamental truths of writing for the computer industry.[2] It is impractical not to incorporate documentation development onto the critical path of product development for many reasons, not the least of which is that documentation efforts with a late, low priority, must deal with products that keep changing both during and after the creation of documentation. Even if this doesn't happen, the documentation must be rushed to achieve the earliest possible market release, leaving no time for usability testing. Thus there is no way to assure that the documentation accurately reflects the finished product.

But even more importantly, late documentation eliminates the possibility of incorporating the insights of documentation developers and testers into product development. No time for usability testing means no time to test the complete product from the perspective of the end-user; no time to change the product to better provide the user with what he or she wants. Instead, there is time only to document some bug or aspect of poor design and label it a feature.

Of course changes in this area have been occurring for some time. Over two years ago when Burroughs came to recruit graduates from our program, they promised that documentation specialists would get paid on the same scale as programmers and that documentation would appear on the critical path of product development. I am not aware of how this stated policy has worked in practice.[3] Nevertheless, change in this area is clearly well on the way if not already implemented.

(c)   The increasing use of computer systems as the primary device for delivering documentation

This is another trend that is already well on the way, in fact, most of what has just been said about documentation can be said about user interface design and development as well. We don't yet have HAL, but we do have menu-driven help screens, interactive online tutorials, context sensitive help systems that track the context in which an error occurs and provide instructions relevant to that context, and even the initial application of AI techniques to create intelligent online help. Wherever this trend takes us, it is clear that in the near future (if not already), online computer documentation will be the first line of defense while paper will be used as a backup, if at all.

(d)   The increasing awareness of and dissatisfaction with the high cost of effective documentation

The previous points begin to illustrate just how expensive it can be to provide effective user support and to incorporate user needs and perspectives into product design and development. Usability testing is a good example. Without a well-designed, formal testing program implemented sufficiently early in the product development process, it is impossible to be sure either that documentation efforts have been successful or that insights into user patterns have been incorporated into the product. Yet usability testing generally requires a larger effort than most companies are able or willing to afford. Even large companies such as Xerox, Hewlett Packard, U.S. West and Microsoft currently employ consultants to supplement their capabilities in this area. In addition, there are still many large questions of testing methodology and application which cannot be efficiently tackled by a single company. Such questions will need to be addressed as industry-wide problems. The required overall effort for effective usability testing is huge. For this reason, user documentation and support is often not as effective as it might be simply because it is not yet cost-effective to do it right.

If we move beyond user documentation to include all required product information, sheer size can be the overwhelming factor. This is especially true in the case of complex computer-based products for the government. In such cases, it is not unusual for up to half the budget to be spent on documentation.[4] (This leaves aside the issue of the proposal writing effort required to obtain these projects.) Recently, studies at Boeing were made to determine what areas needed to be improved so that the same product (in this case airplanes) could be produced for less. Not surprisingly, documentation was found to be in the top three, leading to the initiation of an automated documentation project at Boeing's Advanced Technology Center.

Another reason that documentation can be uncomfortably expensive is that some environments place special constraints on effective documentation. The Space Station project is a good example of this since huge manuals are likely to be useless in space. Instead, highly sophisticated user interfaces will need to be designed and developed; interfaces capable of delivering complex assistance in a quick and natural manner. The high cost of effective documentation today may become even more expensive tomorrow.

(e)   **The growing search for formal methods to integrate system design with issues of user perspective such as interface and documentation ("designing for usability")**

The trends discussed before this one are already in the almost mature, "state of the art " phase. This point, however, takes us a bit further. Formal methods for integrating system design with user perspective are not yet well understood. In fact, the main reason there is often more lip service than actual effort put into user needs at the design level is that the methodologies for implementing user driven design aren't yet clear. We know we need to design from both ends, that is, both from the user's perspective "in" and the system's specifications "out," but how is this to be done?

The search for formal methods to link user issues with system design is underway.[5] In work at the University of Washington, we take an approach based on natural language processing. By this approach, a formal representation of the language by which a user specifies a task is mapped to the specification module which defines the functionality of lower level software. This may sound like a far cry from technical writing, but remember that documentation writers are specialists both in the user's perspective and in language. As "designing for usability" becomes a technique rather than a research area, "writers" will become involved earlier and earlier in product design and development.

(f)   **The increasing applicability of artificial intelligence techniques to system and user support**

Like many others, I am not comfortable with the ambiguity of the phrase "artificial intelligence." Specifically, there are three bodies of work, generally lumped under the AI label, that are having an impact on documentation efforts: (a) natural language processing (b) vision and (c) expert system development. Natural language processing has already been introduced in the previous point and will be discussed further in the final point of this paper. Computer vision and scanning techniques have a clear application in the documentation production process.[6] Here I will briefly discuss expert systems.

Expert systems have a unique applicability to user support. In some cases, technical writers are becoming expert system developers.[7] In other cases, there is the potential for a truly symbiotic relationship between expert system developers and technical writers. Not only can expert systems do much for technical writers, but technical writers can do much for expert systems.

Expert systems provide technical "writers" with a new medium. After all, expert systems which advise, help troubleshoot, and help diagnose **are** documentation. Many technical "writers" already deliver their documentation through the terminal; expert systems simply take online documentation one step further.

On the other hand, technical "writers" have much to contribute to expert system development. Perhaps the two major challenges in creating an expert system are 1) getting knowledge from the expert into the system and 2) providing the appropriate knowledge to the expert system user in an appropriate form. Who will be our future "knowledge engineers"--the developers of expert systems?

At the first Artificial Intelligence Satellite Symposium on knowledge-based systems and their applications (November 13, 1985), the panel of expert system experts[8] was asked where the knowledge engineers of tomorrow would come from... The panel agreed that training and experience in computer science or electrical engineering is not of primary importance. Rather, they said, knowledge engineers will need to be able to take complex processes and break them down into discrete components, to organize those components into logical sequences, to understand the nature of problem solving. Above all, knowledge engineers must be curious. They must like to poke around in other people's business and figure out what makes them tick. But these have been and will remain the essential skills of anyone who makes a living explaining scientific and technical ideas to others. These are the skills of today's technical communicator.[9]

Technical "writers" will contribute as much to expert system development as they will gain from the availability of this new medium for documentation.

The trends and developments discussed thus far are already having an impact on the nature of user support and product documentation efforts. What will be some of the specific changes to the future tasks of computer industry "writers?"

(1)   "Writers" will be involved earlier and earlier in the process.

This is not an earth shaking statement. It is already happening, in fact even our undergraduate interns working at Microsoft tell me they are working on documentation for a product that "doesn't exist yet." In the future, the entry point of "writers" into the product development process will continue to push earlier and earlier, all the way back to research and product conception. As experts in the users' perspectives and needs, "writers" will play the role of "user advocate" throughout the processes of product research, design, development, and support.

(2)   "Writers" will test for usability, not only to adjust documentation, but to feed results back into design and development.

This change, which has also already begun to occur, further amplifies the growing "user advocate" role of the technical "writer." In order to create and test effective documentation, writers must become specialists in user needs and perspectives (as well as in meeting those needs in print, online, video, or whatever form is required). Thus, writers view the product not from the technology "out" but from over the user's shoulder "in." As specialists in user perspective, "writers" are needed at all stages of product development, not just at the end.

One reason for "writers" earlier involvement in the process of product development will be to allow usability testing to adjust not only documentation but design and production as well. When usability tests show that the available user support is insufficient to enable people to perform computer tasks, it is not always the fault of the documentation and support effort. Often it is the fault of an inconsistent design philosophy which creates expectations in the user which are not fulfilled, or a failure to anticipate the demands of the task in a real world environment. Early tests can show what the user wants, needs, and expects, and this information can be incorporated into design philosophy and implementation.

At this conference, Geoffrey James began his presentation by stating he had "defected" from technical writing to system design. Actually, his job change was not so much a defection as it was a logical extension of what all technical "writers" do.

(3)   "Writers" will become more technically sophisticated (without sacrificing their special knowledge of user perspectives and communication skills)

The demand for increased technical sophistication on the part of "writers" is a necessary extension of the previous two points. If "writers" are to become functioning members of project teams throughout the design and development process, they must become more technically sophisticated. Even more than today, "writers" will need to interact comfortably with engineers and computer scientists on technical questions that will impact not only on documentation, but on machine architecture and program design as well. Those "writers" who can gain the necessary sophistication without sacrificing their present skills will have roles on interdisciplinary teams making decisions, not only about product support, but about the nature of the product itself.

However, documentation specialists must not emphasize technical training to the point of losing their expertise in user perspective and communication skills. It is, after all, precisely their ability to function as "user advocates" that will make "writers" more and more valuable to the technical specialist absorbed in the complexities of machine specification and code.

(4)   "Writers" will play a major role in the design and development of user interfaces.

In addition to interacting with engineers and computer scientists, another impetus for the increased technical sophistication of documentation "writers" is the increased complexity of delivery mediums. As more and more documentation is delivered through the user interface, the line between user support and interface design will blur.

"Writers" involvement in user interface research, design, and development is a natural one. The interface provides the means by which a user specifies a task. Clearly the "writer" who looks at the product through the user's eyes and also is a communication specialist has much to contribute in this area. More specifically, as usability testing impacts more on design issues, it will often become easier and more effective to incorporate "help" implicitly in the design itself rather than to provide it explicitly, even online.

For example, a user study might show that a particular pull-down menu is difficult to use. Perhaps it is difficult to understand the linear list of choices as representing directional alternatives. One solution might be to allow the user to select the menu, hit a "help" key, and receive instructions on how to best use the menu, with amplification of what the choices mean. A superior solution, however, would be to redesign the menu so that the directional alternatives were physically represented in the shape of the menu. Here we can see the narrow line between design and documentation. In the future, "writers" will often find it easier to integrate help into interface design rather than to write and deliver text.

(5)   "Writers" will help develop formal methods for linking program functionality with corresponding interface and documentation.

This role, which is yet in its infancy, is also based on the "writers" special awareness of the user's perspective, in this case, the language by which the user specifies a task. "Writers" who can help formally describe the language of human/machine interaction will play a role on interdisciplinary research teams attempting to match these linguistic formalisms with those that drive the machine. In other words, they will help establish a formal link between the world asserted by the user's commands and the internal procedures by which the machine goes from its current state to that desired by the user.

When techniques for linking user specification with machine implementation are established, then system and product developers will truly be able to "design from both ends," and "writers" will have a direct means of incorporating their understanding of user needs and perspectives into the design process. Thus, in addition to reacting to product design through usability testing, "writers" will be able to contribute directly to the initial design phase of product development.

Of course "writers" will want to acquire new skills (e.g. computational linguistics and other formal language training) to help them in this new role, but it is important to emphasize that these new skills will be useless without the "writers" current expertise in user perspective and communication situations.

(6)   "Writers" will apply work in natural language processing and knowledge engineering to help develop smart, online documentation systems.

Like the previous role, this one is yet in its infancy and will require "writers" to augment their current skills. But also like the previous role, it is the fundamental skills of today's writers that will be the basis of this new effort. Smart online documentation differs from today's online help, but like today's online documentation, the construction of smart documentation requires, first and foremost, an understanding of the user's needs and of the communication situation between user and machine.

As with "standard" documentation, the complexity of smart online documentation (and the necessity for a natural language interface) depends partly upon the nature of what is being documented. One page can provide sufficient help to assemble a toy while a series of books may be required for a complex computer system. Similarly for smart documentation; in some cases, such as the space station, the cost, complexity, and special user circumstances call for extremely complex, natural language based smart online documentation. In more usual cases, the central issue in deciding the extent of a smart documentation effort revolves around whether or not the user is faced with an *analytic* or *synthetic* problem solving situation.

An analytic problem is one with a finite set of possible solutions. The issue, in this case, is to help the user select the appropriate solution from the set of possible ones. In such cases, the primary technique is the use of conditional logic statements. *If the prompt reads 'DESTINATION:' and you want to use the IBM/CMS operating system, then type '4381/CMS' after the prompt.* While the techniques still require further exploration, augmenting online documentation with expert system based "smarts" is actually a fairly well defined game for analytic situations. The more strictly analytic the situation, the more straightforward the documentation effort.

In analytic situations, not only is the representation of knowledge more straightforward than in synthetic situations, but the interface techniques used to elicit information from the user are more straightforward as well. Since strictly analytic situations have a well defined set of possible solutions, there are also a well defined set of possible types of information needed to drive the decision procedure. In this case, interfaces based on pattern techniques such as key words, menus, and "canned" conversations will prove sufficient. To worry about a true natural language interface while constructing documentation to help someone hook up their printer would be the equivalent of killing a fly with a howitzer.

Synthetic problem solving situations, however, are different. A synthetic problem has an infinite number of possible solutions. In this case, the challenge is to derive a solution based on the current state of affairs, an awareness of the desired state of affairs, and knowledge of the procedure for getting from the former to the latter. Presently, the techniques for synthetic problem solving are far less agreed upon than those for analytic problem solving.

In addition, since a synthetic situation has infinite possibilities, it will be impossible to anticipate every possible question the user may have, every possible path the system may take to construct a solution, or every type of user input required to drive the problem solving procedure. Thus, the documentor of a complex computer system cannot know beforehand every use to which the system will be put, every problem that could arise, or every type of information needed to respond to a user's query. In this case, pattern matching is insufficient. Instead, the user needs to be able to naturally yet precisely describe a problem space while the system needs the ability to understand that description, interact with the user to acquire additional information, and generate a solution in terms that are natural to the user. It is this type of documentation effort, based on work in natural language processing and knowledge representation, that I call Smart Documentation Systems (SDS).

The future, then, will see "writers" involved in major efforts to develop SDS primarily in the realm of documentation for large, complex computer systems. While these efforts will require considerable expertise in higher level logics, formal grammars, and machine languages, equally crucial will be expertise in analysis of documentation situations and user perspectives. These last two are, of course, the areas of expertise of today's writers.

Given these developments, the job of "writers" in the computer industry will undergo some basic changes, though an understanding of the user's perspective and the ability to create clear, usable help will remain, as today, the fundamental skills of tomorrow's technical communicator. I don't think we'll call them "writers" anymore, but they will have the same basic responsibilities--to assure that the user is able to complete those tasks which he or she wants to do and which the machine is designed to accomplish.

It is important that today's writers do not reject new roles and augmented skills from fear or lack of understanding. Instead, writers should recognize the increasing value of the fundamental skills they currently employ, and build on them.

Notes

1 Haselkorn, M.P. (1986a). Smart documentation systems. <u>Proceedings of the 1986 IEEE International Professional Communication Conference</u>, October, 77-80.

Haselkorn, M.P. (1986b). Computational linguistics, expert systems, and the future of documentation. Special issue of <u>Technical Writing Teacher</u> (Linguistics and Technical Communication), <u>13</u>(3), 243-253.

2 Roger Grice's paper at this conference, "Information Development is Part of Product Development--Not an Afterthought," is only one of many recent statements of this truism.

3 Unfortunately, it is not uncommon for companies to pay considerable "lip service" to user needs but do little in practice.

4 A recent Boeing space station project, for example, had a 2 billion dollar budget with approximately 1 billion dollars of that for documentation.

5 See, for example, Harrison and Monk, eds., <u>People and Computers: Designing for Usability</u>, Cambridge University Press, 1986.

6 This was discussed at this conference in "Artificial Intelligence and Document Processing" presented by Geoffrey James of Honeywell Bull.

7 While Thomas Burke's paper, presented at this conference, is not represented in this collection, his subject, "Knowledge-Based Expert Systems: A New Role for Technical Writers?," was an exploration of this very point.

8 Edward A. Feigenbaum, Stanford; Randall Davis, MIT; Bruce G. Buchanan, Stanford; Mark S. Fox, Carnegie-Mellon; and Harry Tennant, Texas Instruments.

9 Haselkorn, M.P. (1986a), p. 80.

2

Artificial Intelligence and Automated Publishing Systems

Geoffrey James

Honeywell Bull Inc.
5250 West Century Blvd.
Los Angeles, CA, 90045

1 Introduction

As a designer of automated publication systems, I am often called upon to discuss new technologies and how they apply to the technical communications environment. Few subjects generate more controversy than artificial intelligence. Between unrealistic expectations on the one hand and fears of job security on the other, the practical applications of the technology often gets lost in the shuffle. This article takes a practical look at how artificial intelligence is used in the design of automated publications systems.

What is artificial intelligence? Sometimes it seems that there are as many definitions as there are computer scientists working in the field. Below are two samples:

> *Artificial Intelligence (AI) is the endeavor of automating particular tasks that have been traditionally regarded as requiring intelligence...any task that humans can or do perform routinely and which requires intelligence is a candidate AI application.*[14]

> *Artificial intelligence is an umbrella term encompasses fields like robotics (programming machines to perform specific functions); language processing (programming machines to simulate human communication); vision and speech (programming machines to recognize and respond to an object); and expert systems (programming machines to provide advice and solve problems in a specific area).*[17,3]

In publications systems, the two most important artificial intelligence techniques are object recognition programs (called "vision and speech" above) and expert systems.

Object recognition programs recognize and respond to objects. These objects can be anything from parts moving down an assembly line to characters on a page. Expert systems simulate the behavior of an expert, reproducing the logic that the expert applies to a routine situation. An often-cited example is a program that asks questions about various symptoms and then reaches a conclusion about the nature of the patient's malady.

Object recognition programs and expert systems apply to four areas of publishing system design:

Optical Character Recognition — The conversion of characters printed on paper into editable text files.

Vectorization — The conversion of drawings printed on paper into editable object files.

Declarative Formatting — The automatic pagination of structured documents based upon a predefined set of rules.

Online Retrieval — The location and display of documents contained in a document database.

This article describes each area in detail and then speculates upon the future of artificial intelligence and automated publications systems.

2   Optical Character Recognition

Optical Character Recognition (OCR) is the conversion of characters printed on paper into editable text files. The operator feeds a page of text into a scanner. The OCR program stores each character on the page as a cluster of black dots. The OCR program compares each stored cluster against a library of character shapes, locating the character that most closely matches each cluster. The resulting file of characters can then be edited on a word processor.

It is often difficult for OCR programs to differentiate between the characters of a font. As a result, the first OCR programs only processed special fonts, such as OCR-A and OCR-B, whose individual characters are as different as possible.[18] However, even with special fonts, error rates of three or more per page were common.[16]

As object recognition software became more sophisticated, OCR programs began to handle standard typewriter fonts and even typeset copy. However, because each font required its own object recognition program, scanning text from a variety of sources was expensive.[16]

This problem is overcome by adding expert systems to the OCR process. The resulting programs are "self-learning." The operator makes corrections during the scanning process. The program stores these corrections as rules for distinguishing between characters. The program then recalls these rules during subsequent scanning operations.

Low quality originals can confuse even a "self-learning" OCR program. Because each smudge or blemish is unique, the operator gains nothing by training the OCR to ignore it. This remains true as long as the computer only views the text as a disconnected series of characters. Accurate scanning of low quality original requires another layer of intelligence, either human or artificial.

Human intelligence usually suffices. An operator runs a spelling check program that compares each word in the OCR-produced file against a dictionary file of valid words. The program flags words that are not in the dictionary file and asks the operator for the correct word. Most programs also provide a list of possible corrections. Some even remember prior corrections, though these corrections are not stored from session to session.[10,31]

Researchers remain fascinated by the possibility of fully automatic spelling correction, which would permit (among other things) direct inclusion of OCR files without human intervention. One experimental program used thesaurus comparison and multiple dictionary searches to compute the likelihood of a given word appearing at any given place. This program succeeded in an 87 percent correction of a scanned, hand-written page, without human intervention.[19,84] This technology has not, however, resulted in any publicly available products.

3 Vectorization

Vectorization is the conversion of drawings printed on paper into editable object files.

Vectorization is similar to optical character recognition, except that the recognized images are graphical shapes rather than characters. As with OCR, vectorization is a two-step process. First the drawing is scanned and stored as a series of pixels or dots, similar to the dots on a television screen. Then the vectorization program compares the positions of those dots, deciding which constitute lines and shapes. The resulting file can then be edited using an object-oriented graphics editing program.

To understand the value of vectorization, one must first understand the difference between pixel-oriented and object-oriented graphics editing programs. With a pixel editor, the artist edits dots on a screen. With an object editor, the artist edits the relationships between objects. This is an important distinction.

Imagine a screen display of a circle intersecting a square. Now imagine that the artist wants to separate the circle from the square. If the artist uses a pixel editor, he or she must make a copy of the two shapes, and then use an "eraser" to remove the circle from the original area of the screen and the square from the copy. This is necessary because the computer cannot tell the difference between the dots that make up the circle and the dots that make the square.

If the artist uses an object editor, he or she selects the circle and moves it away from the square. This is possible because the computer can differentiate between the two objects – they are not just dots on a screen.

Another disadvantage of pixel-oriented graphics editors is resolution. Since the drawing consists of dots, the only way to make it bigger is to increase the size of the dots. This results in "jaggy" output when the drawing is printed on a device that has a higher resolution than the screen. Object editors provide editing capabilities beyond those that pixel editors provide.

Vectorization programs vary in price and function. PC-based packages, for example, can discern lines, areas, and simple symbols.[3,8] By contrast, some sophisticated stand-alone vectorization systems support layer separation, geometry recognition, and optical character recognition.[21,4]

4 Declarative Formatting

Declarative formatting is the automatic pagination of structured documents based upon a predefined set of rules.

Formatting programs fall into two classes: procedural and declarative. With procedural formatting program, the user tells the program what to do with the document. With a declarative formatting program, the user tells the program what the document *contains*.

A procedural formatter treats the presentation of data as the most important element. The user tells the system how the document is to appear. Procedural formatters range from simplistic "dot command" formatters such as RUNOFF and SCRIPT to word processing programs to elaborate What-You-See-Is-What-You-Get (WYSIWYG) workstations.

A declarative formatter treats the content of the data as the most important element. The user tells the system about the structure and content of the document. The system then applies a set of previously defined rules to the structured document, producing pages automatically. By using a different set of rules, a declarative formatter creates documents of differing appearances. In addition, declarative formatting makes it possible to create tables of contents and indexes automatically, as well as resolve internal cross references.[8,87-106]

Declarative formatters are a simple form of expert system. The predefined rules represent the document designer's expertise about how the document should appear. This frees the writer to concentrate on writing:

> *The hard part about writing is writing... WYSIWYG systems don't help matters by forcing writers to think about how their documents look when most of their attention should really be focused on how their material reads. In an ideal world, writers would be left to concentrate on writing, while computers would handle all the necessary formatting... Where text is the principal object, a mouse-driven graphical interface doesn't necessarily improve anything—and may, in fact, slow writers down because of all the mouse movements that are required.[13,38]*

Designers of publications systems have long understood the value of declarative formatting.[4,251] Even Interleaf, the foremost producer of WYSIWYG software, admits that:

> *If the document is more than a set of images of individual pages—if it is a structured document, in other words—there is much useful information about its structure and the relationships between its components that users can be shown, even though doing so will break the "Thou shalt be WYSIWYG" commandment.[2,34]*

A declarative formatting program is implemented using a procedural formatting program as a base. The document designer programs macros that define how the procedural formatting program will react to the structures that the user specifies in the editable document. Since this process is really one of building an expert system, it is surprising that so many procedural formatting programs contain only rudimentary programming constructs. Even the highly rated NROFF/TROFF contains fewer string manipulation functions than most BASIC interpreters.[6,passim]

Perhaps it is because of these limitations that declarative formatters are perceived as more difficult to use than WYSIWYG systems.[2,30] The first procedural formatter to overcome these limitations is Donald Knuth's TEX. The TEX formatting language includes recursion, string functions, boolean logic, recursion, asynchronous output routines and other programming constructs missing from other procedural format-ters.[9,passim] This opens up the possibility of declarative formatters with significantly more powerful expert systems than those available to-day. For example, the Computer Aided Publication development group at Honeywell Bull Inc. has recently demonstrated a prototype of an advanced TEX-based formatting expert system.

5 Online Retrieval

Online retrieval is the location and display of documents contained in a document database.

In *Document Databases*, I predicted the future importance of online retrieval and its connection with declarative formatting.[8,80] Since online document databases have become a significant force in the computer business,[1] it is appropriate to revisit this technology.

The usefulness of a document database is limited by the number of ways that a reader can access it. Most document databases have predefined access points. Typically an editor or data entry clerk creates these access points by entering the author's name, affiliations, the document title, etc., along with any significant keywords that might appear relevant. The limitation of editor-defined keywords is that they may not reflect all aspects of a document. The editor cannot anticipate all the reasons that a reader might want to view a given document.

This is one reason why declarative formatting is well suited for online retrieval. Not only does declarative formatting make the production of the database easier,[8,80] but the chapter titles, subsection headings, flagged index terms, etc. can function as additional access points. This is because they identify the structural elements of a document and therefore provide a contextual window into the author's intentions.

But is this enough? An author may choose to emphasize one aspect of a document while letting another slip into the background. To be really useful, the document database should provide access points "on the fly", based upon what the reader wants, rather than the preconceptions of the author or editor.

This is where artificial intelligence comes into the picture. Textual database search programs such as STATUS build cross-reference indexes of all the words in a document, recording the location of each word and its proximity to other words. This cross-reference index allows the reader to treat ideas as objects constructed of words and word patterns. Although phrasing will differ from writer to writer, the program assumes that certain characteristics will be recognizable, such a vocabulary and proximity.[7] This allows the reader to make very general queries such as:

```
LOCATE: 'THEORY' WITHIN 20 WORDS OF 'SYSTEM' AND 'PUBLISH'
or
LOCATE: 'LANGUAGE' WITHIN 10 PARAGRAPHS OF 'IDEAS'
```

The reader is now free to view the document database according to his or her own interests.

Another recently-developed technique may make online retrieval even more powerful. In most document database systems, a query that is too general will locate too many documents, while a query that is too specific will fail to locate enough documents. This problem can be overcome with a "seed document." The seed document is a document that the reader believes most closely matches the subject matter that he or she wished to know about. The reader first locates the seed document by making a very specific query. Another search of the database is made, using the vocabulary and word patterns in that seed document as search criteria.[20,1233]

6 The Future

So far, I have been talking about technology that is available today, although seldom presented as part of a single system. Now I'd like to take a brief look at the future.

There are two software areas where I expect artificial intelligence to play a significant role: text conversion and style file generation.

Text conversion is the transference of textual information from one formatter or formatting system to another. Since there are so many conflicting standards in markup languages, there is a real need for programs that perform such conversions.[12,408] Constructing such programs would be easier if there were a means to recognize objects in the text and correct the conversion process as it proceeds. A combination of an object recognition program and self-learning expert systems might prove valuable.

A style file is a collection of predefined formatting rules used by a declarative formatter. Currently, the process of building style files is labor intensive, making it time-consuming to support many different styles and standards. Perhaps with advanced vectorization and optical character recognition programs, it might someday be possible to scan a sample document and obtain a style file that reflects that layout.

A breakthrough already taking place in the computer industry has enormous implications for the role of artificial intelligence and document processing – parallel computer architectures. A parallel computer architecture uses multiple computers acting in coordination rather than a single computer performing multiple tasks. Parallel architectures are particularly effective for applications that have large sets of similar data items.[5,1170]

Parallel architectures are well suited to artificial intelligence applications,[11] not to mention certain types of document processing. Graphics and image processing are already being moved to parallel architectures;[15,65] optical character recognition and vectorization are probably not far behind.

Some designers have theorized about publications workstations that are both declarative and interactive.[2,30] Since an extremely fast processing speed is required for such a system, it is possible that parallel architectures may be the appropriate platform. Declarative formatters already break documents into logical "chunks", a technique that might lend itself to parallel processing. Parallel architectures are already used for advanced online retrieval systems. During one experiment, a parallel computer architecture ran substantially faster than existing search systems.[20,1238]

7 Conclusion

Artificial intelligence plays an important role in the design of automated publishing systems. Optical character recognition, vectorization, declarative formatting, and online retrieval streamline the publication process. Future applications, hosted on parallel architectures, will continue to free the writer from clerical and repetitious labor. What this means to the writer and to industry at large is a technical publications environment that is more responsive and productive, better able to provide the valuable service of keeping people informed.

[1] Belitsos, B. "Plug Into the World of Public Data Bases". *Computer Currents*. Volume 4, Number 7. August 26, 1986.

[2] Bohn, L. and Weinberger, D. "Why Not Have It All?" *Unix Review*, July 1987.

[3] *CAD/camera 2.0 User Guide*. Mountain View: Autodesk Inc., 1985.

[4] Chamberlin, D. et al. "Janus: An interactive document formatter based on declarative tags". *IBM Systems Journal*. Volume 12, #3, September 1982.

[5] Hillis, Daniel W. and Steele Guy L. "Data Parallel Algorithms", *Communications of the ACM*. Volume 29, Number 12. December 1986.

[6] Holub, A. *NR: An Implementation of the Unix NROFF Word Processor*. Redwood City: M&T Publishing Inc., 1987.

[7] *Introduction to STATUS*. Oxford: Harwell University Computer Science and Systems Division, March 1982.

[8] James, Geoffrey. *Document Databases*. New York: Van Nostrand Reinhold, 1984.

[9] Knuth, D. *The TeX Book*. New York: Addison Wessley, 1986.

[10] Korenthal Associates, Inc. *Webster's New World Spelling Checker*. New York: Simon & Schuster, Inc., 1985.

[11] Lewyn, M. "Danny Hillis: Computer scientist makes Connection with brainy Machine". *USA Today*. August 31, 1987

[12] Mamarak, S.A. et al. "A Software Architecture for Supporting the Exchange of Electronic Manuscripts." *Communications of the ACM*. Volume 30, Number 5. May 1987.

[13] McGilton, H. and Tuthill, B. "Progress Through Accretion" *Unix Review*, July 1987.

[14] Modesitt, K. *Lecture Notes*. Northridge: California State University, 1985

[15] Piol, A. "Parallel architecture tackles graphics and image processing". *Computer Design*. September 1, 1987.

[16] Pugiese, A.J. "OCR – A Solution or Another Problem". *Proceedings of the 28th International Technical Communications Conference*. Society for Technical Communication, 1981.

[17] Puelo, Steve. "Artificial Intelligence – The Sexy Side of the Computer Business". *Worldlink*. Minneapolis: Honeywell Bull, 1987.

[18] Sachs, I. "Automated Composition for the Small-Budget Publications Department". *Proceedings of the 28th International Technical Communications Conference*. Society for Technical Communication, 1981.

[19] Srihari, S.N., Jull, J.J. and Choudhari, R. "Integrating Diverse Knowledge Sources in Text Recognition". *ACM Transactions in Office Automation Systems*. Volume 1, Number 1, January 1982.

[20] Stanfill, C. and Kahle, B. "Parallel Free-Text Search on the Connection Machine". *Communications of the ACM*. Volume 29, Number 12. December 1986.

[21] *Vectorscan Brochure*. Annapolis: InterCAD Corporation, 1986.

3

Exploring the Connections Between Improved Technology—Workstation and Desktop Publishing and Improved Methodology—Document Databases

R. John Brockmann
Concentration in Business and Technical Communication
English Department
University of Delaware

Summary

The new desktop and workstation publishing technology presents documenters with three hurdles to overcome. First, it has been difficult to identify a comprehensive organization to integrate all the relevant hardware and software products [1]. Second, the marketing of this new technology has paid scant attention to the supporting skills in typography, design, layouts, etc. which alone make the new technology effective [2]. Although considerable attention is now paid to overcoming these two hurdles, a third hurdle has not yet been overcome. Little attention has been paid to creating and understanding the publishing **methodologies** needed to drive this publishing **technology** to its fullest potential.

Geoffrey James' *Document Databases* (New York: Van Nostrand Reinhold, 1985) offers a candidate for such an innovative publishing methodology to match the new desktop and workstation publishing technology[3, 4]. However, few have connected the desktop or workstation publishing technology with his methodology because his book seems to focus exclusively on mainframe computer applications, most especially Honeywell's *Computer Assisted Publication* (C.A.P.). But, it is possible to achieve the same effects he describes in a microcomputer environment by combining a number of innovative off-the-shelf microcomputer software and hardware packages .

In his book, James, of course, envisions the positive aspects of such a methodology's use. Yet although he says in his book that "a new methodology combined with a new technology always changes the culture," he does not begin to prepare documenters to deal with the problematic aspects involved with implementing his new methodology. And, it seems especially important that three problems be resolved:

I would like to thank Xyvision Inc. for permission to reproduce the first two figures and Texet Corp. for their permission to reproduce the third. I would also like to thank Mr. Kevin Brock for his aid in rendering these three graphics. The text example in Appendix A is from *The Writer's Pocket Almanack* by R. John Brockmann and Bill Horton (Santa Monica, Ca.: Info Books, 1988)

- how to prevent this new publishing methodology from impoverishing the rhetorical appropriateness of text and graphics;

- how to prevent the separation of content and format of "declarative structuring" from hobbling the development of text and graphics or from leading to an over centralization of corporate document design; and

- how to ensure that this methodology does not lead to a decrease in the skills or professionalism of documenters.

Only when these problematic aspects of the document database **methodology** are resolved will documenters be able to successfully implement the new desktop and workstation publishing **technology** to its fullest potential.

Setting the Stage

> *"Production is not the application of tools to material, but logic to work."*
> Peter Drucker[5]

Geoffrey James is absolutely right when he points out that our profession will be using more and more electronic publishing technology. The technology allows the documenter to have more control over document design features of text—features which were formerly the province of typographers, text designers, and compositors. Thus the technology, at first glance, seems to require documenters to handle new responsibilities and to develop new areas of expertise.

The technology also allows the writer to create graphics using electronic clip art, paint and draw packages, or high density scanners. With even minor additions of hardware, this capability can yield great savings in time and cost [6]. Here again the technology seems to require documenters to handle new responsibilities and to develop new areas of expertise.

However, most organizations and most documenters only use the new desktop and workstation technology to speed up the traditional document production methodology by eliminating steps or conjoining responsibilities. The figures on the next two pages from a Xyvision marketing brochure, "Computer Integrated Publishing Systems," exemplify such step elimination. The first figure illustrates the traditional publishing work flow in an aerospace company. The elapsed time to produce a document in this traditional publishing workflow required 26 steps and 18 days. The second figure illustrates the production of a similiar document using a publishing system produced by Xyvision. With this new system the company produced the similar document using an "integrated" publishing work flow requiring only 6 steps and 3 days. This change in efficiency with a shift in technology seems very dramatic.

But as Marshall McLuhan noted "We live in the rear-view mirror;" [7] that is, we always seem to use new technologies to do what we did yesterday—only now, a little faster. For example, Michael Kleper points out that until recently,

instead of computer technology providing better-appearing output than has been available in the home and office since the

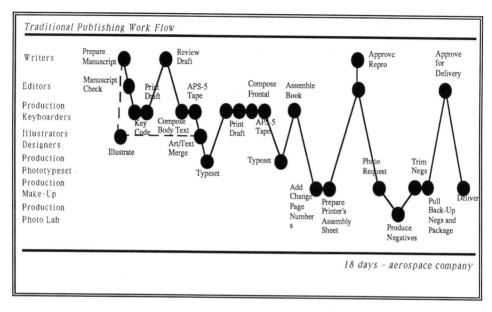

Traditional Publishing Work Flow

Writers · Editors · Production Keyboarders · Illustrators · Designers · Production · Phototypeset · Production · Make-Up · Production · Photo Lab

Prepare Manuscript · Review Draft · Approve Repro · Approve for Delivery · Manuscript Check · Print Draft · APS-5 Tape · Compose Frontal · Assemble Book · Key Code · Compose Body Text · Print Draft · APS-5 Tape · Illustrate · Art/Text Merge · Typeset · Typeset · Photo Request · Trim Negs · Typeset · Add Change Page Numbers · Prepare Printer's Assembly Sheet · Produce Negatives · Pull Back-Up Negs and Package · Deliver

18 days - aerospace company

introduction of the typewriter, the goal has been the imitation of standard typewriter output—letter quality or correspondence quality output[8].

One reason for this rear-view mirror mentality is "the inertia of human thinking and a limited imagination unable to forsake the old manual methods when trying to mechanize them"[9].

We are seeing this problem of inertia and limited imagination in the applications of desktop and workstation publishing technology. Aldus *PageMaker* and its software cousins, for example, simply allow electronic pasteup using grids on a screen. Although the digital technology *PageMaker* uses is new, the process it implements is generations old,

> The use of the computer to produce printed matter has changed the tools we use, but not the way in which we use them. One of the reasons *PageMaker* is the most successful page composition software is that it mimics the traditional tools of production—straight-edges, rulers, pasteboards, toolboxes—that have been so familiar to keyliners. The main difference is that the wide variety of old tools have been combined into a single new one: the personal computer[10].

Another instance of rear-view mirror progress is the current typical method of using different publishing processes for different media or for different publications. Text for offline paper manuals and for online Help

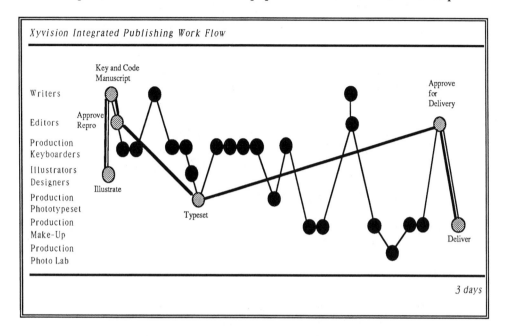

screens must often be entered, designed, and published in two different processes. In other cases, text is re-entered or even re-written even though there are perfectly useable text modules available within the organization to fit the situation. For example, in one company's manuals a half page section entitled "What is a Menu" with the identical content and intended audience was written three times over the span of two years by three different writers in the same documentation group.

If we are to beat this traditional problem of mental inertia and limited imagination which shackles new technologies to old methodologies, we need to consider the role of the document database methodology in our workplace. James notes an historical precedent in this instance:

> Every time a new widget is introduced to the publishing
> industry, somebody compares it to Gutenberg's press. This type
> of remark is ironic, because the effect of Gutenberg's invention
> on Western Civilization is often overemphasized. A hundred

years before Gutenberg, the largest library in Europe was around
a thousand manuscript volumes. A hundred years after
Gutenberg, the largest library in Europe contained only four
thousand volumes one-fourth of which were handwritten
manuscripts. Libraries of more than five hundred volumes were
still extremely rare; as late as 1582 the University Library at
Cambridge numbered only 451 books and manuscripts.
Gutenberg's improvement in technology did not by itself cause a
revolution in communications. The full impact of his invention
was delayed by limitations in the method by which books were
produced. Each book was hand-crafted to resemble a hand-
lettered manuscript. Only the wealthy could afford the luxury of
the written word. The real revolution took place when early
forms of mass-manufacturing were applied to publications. **The
change in methodology** [emphasis mine] made books available
to a wider range of readers. (9)

The Link Between Document Databases Methodology and Desktop or Workstation Publishing Technology

James defines document database methodology in the following way:

A document database is the use of appropriately scaled data
processing and publications hardware and software to record,
store, format, distribute, maintain, synthesize, and reutilize
textual and graphic information of a referential and/or technical
character, which, due to it subject matter, must be accurate and
complete, as well as dynamic and flexible. (11)

And the seven key elements of a document database according to James are:

- declarative formatting to ensure the re-usability of text and graphics,

- segmenting up text into screen size modules for later assembly into pages or screens,

- making text modules easily accessible throughout an organization,

- ensuring that documents are available for concurrent tasks,

- allowing on-demand printing of customized documentation,

- using mass storage devices, and

- safeguarding data integrity.

Within a microcomputing context, the first five of these elements can be implemented using software, whereas the final two seem best to be implemented using hardware.

The key to James's document database concept is that to increase the reusability of text, text should be stored separately from its formatting, referencing, and organizational characteristics. This type of storage he calls "declarative formatting." Thus when a text or graphic has to be produced, the text or graphic can simply be linked up with a format appropriate to the required output medium (offline or online[11]), as well as to the new reference or organizational characteristics of the new document into which it is to be assembled.

This theoretical concept of "declarative formatting" can be seen in currently available microcomputer products where one "tags" text (as used in Xerox's *Ventura Publishing* software or in Texet's workstation software), or where one uses stylesheets (as used in *Microsoft Word*'s word processing software). An example of such "declarative formatting" can be seen in the graphic on the next page which was taken from a presentation by the President of Texet[12]. The graphic illustrates how "text with I.D. tags"—declarative formatting—can be processed through the Design A format to produce a page with two columns or through Design B format to produce another page with a single column format. (An example of using "stylesheets" from *Microsoft Word 3.0* to achieve this "declarative formatting" can be seen in Appendix A "Example of Text Before and After The Inclusion of Declarative Formatting."

Another key element to James's methodology is that text modules are designed by the "screen size"—the amount of text appropriate for prersentation on one VDT screen—rather than by the page, paragraph, or by the document. Once these "screen size" size modules are created, they can later be combined to assemble a paper page or can be directly transmitted to the screen as online information. Thus a "whole page" is

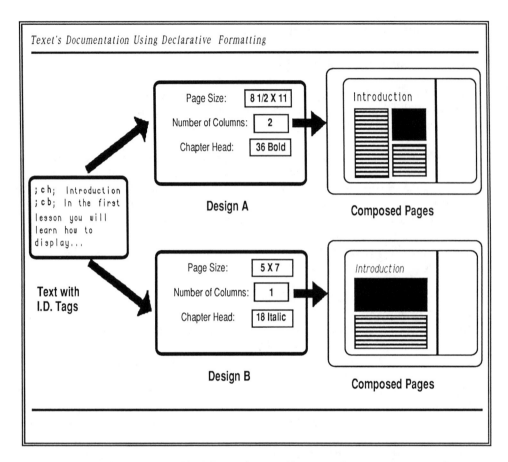

never written but is assembled from the smaller stored "screen sizes" of text. As David Hancock points out, "Doing this gives you more options in combining information units"[13]. Mr. Hancock was thinking primarily in terms of combining them into paper pages, but using "screen sizes" also "gives you more options" in combining them effectively into online documents. Breaking down information in this way and later reassembling it into pages is currently available in most microcomputer word processing packages which have Merge features[14].

Another key element to James's methodology is that, once created, these modules must be accessible to everyone throughout an organization. Again this is possible in microcomputer applications using database products such as *PictureBase, Helix,VisionFile,* and *Hypercards* on local area networks.

James also requires that the document database have the text available for concurrent activities. Again microcomputer products such as Borderbund's *For Comment* can make this happen—on a Local Area Network, the text is available to a number or reviewers who can simultaneously comment on the text during the review process.

James suggests that one of the advantages of a document database is increased accuracy because everything is entered once, reviewed once, and tested once. And he argues document databases would also increase usability because readers can independently access the database and decide for themselves the required depth and organization of the material. The reader then would be able to print-on-demand this customized document. Thus document databases using "just-in-time" production (as the innovative Japanese system of manufacturing suggests) would cut down on warehousing costs and also cut down on the need to update information. Each document when printed on demand would be the most up-to-date document possible. Again, this is simply no longer a theoretical possibility; the Macintosh software package *Guide* currently enables readers and authors to do this [15].

Moving to the hardware implications of his methodology, James suggests that a key element of a document database system is a mass storage device sufficiently large enough to hold all the text and graphic modules incorporating many hundreds of pages. Again this is no longer just a theoretical possibility. Hughes Aircraft is offering just this sort of database in their CDROM FOMM (Functionally Organized Maintenance Manuals) for onboard ship use by the U.S. Navy—these CDROM disks replace hundreds of paper manual pages. And, the FOMM documents are accessible on a laser disk reader, which allows hundreds of different accessing paths to the information [16].

Finally, James suggests that the security and quality assurance of the document database must be maintained through the use of a Read Only mode. By allowing only a Read Only mode, the integrity of the text can be protected from user tampering. This is a practical possibility, as again demonstrated by the CDROM FOMM documents which can only be accessed by read-only laser disk readers. And in updating, there are no more tens of pages to delete from manuals nor tens of replacement pages to be inserted. Whenever a CDROM FOMM document needs updating, a new CDROM disk is sent out, and the old CDROM disk is returned. Updating has never been simpler [17].

We can see, then, that document database methodology is no longer just a theoretical possibility nor any longer just a mainframe opportunity. It can be implemented right now through clever use of off-the-shelf microcomputer software and hardware. And the time is coming very quickly when management will jump at the opportunities that such a methodology will provide. James notes that the opportunities include the following (157-164):

- the cost for a document, even ones produced by desktop or workstation publishing, will be cut in half,

- the speed at which documents can be produced will increase dramatically, and

- the number of tasks a documenter can handle will increase.

The Problems of the New Methodology

"Lo! Men have become tools of their tools."
Henry David Thoreau[18]

James's book carries within it a warning concerning the new methodology: " a new methodology combined with a new technology always changes the culture" (172). A most telling example of such a change is the effect that the horse and the gun (technologies) and horseback hunting (methodology) had on the Plains Indians. Those technologies and that methodology changed the Indian's religion, their economy, and their way of life. And all the changes were not necessarily good. The horse and the gun allowed formerly subservient marginal tribes to dominate well established tribes by increasing the frequency and ferocity of the internecine wars; it increased the dependence of the tribes on the white man for guns and bullets which in turn led to the over-trapping of fur-bearing animal species and a decrease in self-sufficient farming[19]. If past marriages of innovative technology and methodology produced such dramatic cultural changes, documenters should carefully consider not only the benefits of a union between desktop publishing and document databases, but also the problems it may bring.

Three questions need to be answered: will the methodology encourage documenters to serve the needs of the reader? Will the methodology make document production easier for the documenters? And, will the methodology increase or diminish the professional status of documenters?

One of the major expected contributions of the document database methodology is that it will greatly improve productivity by the re-using of text and graphic modules. But exactly how re-useable are such modules [20]? One study that may shed some light on the question of re-usability is a study of computerized business letter libraries done by John Penrose [21]. These computerized business letter libraries include dozens of stock business letters; a businessperson only needs to find one on his or her diskette, insert the appropriate names and addresses, print it, sign it, and mail it. Penrose asked a group of "expert business communication teachers" to review the letters for readableness, tact, personal quality, and quality of message. Considering the group asked, one would have expected them to castigate such canned communication. Instead, the experts declared the letters to be "readable and slightly tactful." The experts agreed that the letters "were not seen as being personal," but disagreed as to whether "the messages were of high quality." (29 - 30) If one were to translate such qualified words into a commonly understood metric, the net result for such stock canned letters would be a grade of a B—not a bad grade from experts. Thus this study seems to show that although not perfect, "canned" communications are adequate for some purposes.

However, can "canned" text and graphic modules truly respond to different complex rhetorical contexts? An analogous situation can be seen in the use of automated readability guides. Automated readability guides[22] began as tools to help writers and editors. But such products all too often suggest—to those less knowledgeable about the communication process—that these tools can replace the human editor. Will the temptations of production speed and reusable-ness cause those less able to understand the process of creating effective computer documentation to undercut or entirely forego audience analysis or field testing? Will it lead to scenarios such as re-using segments of an engineer's operating specifications for a clerical department's user manual—two situations which call for different text modules responding to different backgrounds, approaches to the task, and reading levels?

Efficacy of production could overwhelm the quality of output; the means, in fact, confounding the end. Will managers and other schedule-obsessed administrators allow documenters the time to customize modules if modules can be assembled quickly into something that looks pretty good on a page and adds up to a hefty manual? Perhaps the very slowness of current production methods gave documenters the time to think, and to analyze the manual's audience and context? Won't the methodology's very efficiency encourage those ubiquitous mis-management maxims such as "It's the deadline alone that counts," or "Content doesn't matter so long as it looks good" (one surely to become more predominant in the age of laser printers)? Won't the methodology lead even more documenters to say, "I don't have the time to understand it, I have a manual to write" . . . or in our new situation, "I don't have the time to understand it, I have a document to assemble?"

Second, aside from the speed of the entire methodology, will the methodology actually make it easier for documenters to do their work? Shifting the emphasis of documenters from creating documents to creating re-usable modules looks positive at first glance. As David Hancock notes

> all this should be liberating to writers: they are freed from niggling worries about format, appearance, pagination, and product name changes. They are free to concentrate on the information they are producing. Time once spent poring over galley proofs making repetitive changes . . . can instead go to quality writing[23].

However, if documenters totally cut off the text and graphic composition from layout and format qualities—qualities which will be "declaratively structured"—then they may have a difficult time. They may, in fact, find it more, not less, difficult to create the text in the first place.

Stephen Bernhardt[24] points out that part of what allows writers to produce text and to control their thoughts on paper is the format/headings/indentations they make in their texts on the page. In other of words, verbal production of text is crippled without the accompanying visual presentation of its organization. In fact, Bernhardt suggests that a visually informative presentation of information (the way documenters now produce manuals) is composed by writers in a qualitatively different way than non-visually informative text—the type of format-stripped text that may make up the screen size frames of the document database (see Appendix B - Table 1 from Stephen Bernhardt's "Seeing the Text" for a comparison of the two ways of writing). Won't "declarative formatting," in fact, be blindfolding the documenter just as the knife thrower in the sideshow is blindfolded? Both need to be applauded because neither *should* be able to perform successfully. And, perhaps, one shouldn't be surprised when the knife thrower's assistant, (or a documenter's audience), is pierced on a misplaced throw.

In addition to undermining the documenters traditional method of composition, "declarative formatting" could possibly put documenters in a new political problem—a political problem analogous to the current European VAT taxes. In Europe, one of the the reasons politicians like VAT's (Value Added Taxes) is because the taxes generate funds in ways less visible to a taxed population—the taxing all takes place within the manufacturing process itself, behind the walls of the factory and in the counting rooms of the corporate accountants. Because the taxes are thus less visible to the taxed public, the taxes seem less onerous and are subject to fewer voter backlashes. The politicians realize that the taxes will have fewer repeals because no one in the public realizes what the tax is doing . . . or that it even exists. Couldn't "declarative formatting" be like VAT's to documenters? After all, the individual documenters will probably not be the ones who develop the "declarative structures," rather such structures will probably be generated by those same people at the corporate headquarters who presently hand out the corporate style guidelines and formats . . . or perhaps even those outside hardware, software, or consultant companies who are presently developing canned formats for desktop publishing [25]. At least now documenters feel the corporate guideline's bit in their mouths. They know what it is they are complaining about, and, perhaps, what it is they must change. When these corporate guidelines disappear into the digital ether of "declarative formatting," the corporate bit in documenters' mouths will become less visible, less questioned, and less open to innovation and improvement. If it has occasionally been revealed that those old corporate guidelines were simply linguistic prejudices of management rather than guidelines derived from studies of readers in a business context [26] , couldn't "declarative formats" simply be new mistaken linguistic prejudices whose errors are simply less visible[27]?

Thus the centralization of the document creation process that "declarative formatting" makes possible, and almost certainly makes inevitable, can cripple documenters because they lose the visual qualities of their composition process, and the possibility of recognizing the limitations and need for improvement of corporate guidelines.

Finally, the third question to ask of document databases is whether they will improve or undermine the professional stature of documenters. Documenters are already embarrassed by the managers who, in responding to pressure for more documentation, simply go to the word processing pool and promote a keyboard operator to software documenter. Won't this methodology lead to, and even encourage this kind of action because the methodology leads to a de-skilling of the documentation profession? By taking away decisions regarding format, layout, design, typeface and size, and even reference aid design, won't this methodology, when married to desktop or workstation publishing technology, lead to a contraction of professional responsibilities and to less of a need to increase documenters' expertise?

A similar process of de-skilling in programmer ranks was well described by Phillip Kraft[28]:

> De-skilling is a deliberate effort to transform work made up of separate but interdependent tasks into a larger number of simpler routine and unrelated tasks. Such routinized subtasks can be parceled out to workers who do only one, or at most, a few, of them over and over, and nothing else. Such workers obviously need less skill than the workers who performed all the tasks of the more complex original work.

Thus, William Houze's prediction [29] that 75% of current technical communication positions will be obsolete by 1990 could be coming true. Fewer people will be needed to produce many more manuals. And the people that remain to churn out the manuals will be divided almost along class lines into those who assemble and develop the generic text and graphic "screen size" modules and those handful of "super-documenters" at the home office designing all the "declarative formats."

Thus Geoffrey James is right to point out that the printers's culture changed a hundred years after Gutenberg when they began using a new methodology. So too will the documenters experience a culture change when using these new technologies of desktop and workstation publishing married to a document database methodology. And all documenters need to consider both the positive as well as the negative aspects of such a marriage.

Appendix A
Example of Text Before and After The Inclusion of Declarative Formatting

The following pages taken from *The Writer's Pocket Almanack* (Santa Monica, CA.: INFO Books, 1988) illustrate the concept of declarative formatting using the style sheets of *Microsoft Word 3.0.*. Page one is a page where the text has been entered without any formatting. Pages two, three and four are the **stylesheet** (a file of separately stored format instructions) which will be applied to the unformatted text on page one. Page five shows the finished formatted text produced on a *Laser Writer Plus* with the location of stylesheet applications noted.

Before Application of Stylesheets—Text and Graphic Parts

Broken Quill Award

Applicant is employed by a car dealership. He does no manual-type work, no mechanical work, no delivery work, and no sales. He is the manager.
- Report by insurance investigator

Audience
If you really want to help the American theater, don't be an actress, darling. Be an audience.
- Tallulah Bankhead

In Hollywood the woods are full of people that learned to write but evidently can't read. If they could read their stuff, they'd stop writing.
- Will Rogers

The only unchanging rule in technical communication is that the audience is always right.
- R. John Brockmann

```
┌─────────────────────────────────────────────────────┐
│ ╔═════════════════════════════════════════════════╗ │
│ ║  A Listing of the Stylesheets Applied To The Text and ║ │
│ ║         Graphics of the Previous Page             ║ │
│ ╚═════════════════════════════════════════════════╝ │
└─────────────────────────────────────────────────────┘
```

author
> Normal + Font: Goudy 16 Point. Keep With Next.
> Border: Thick. Tab stops: 4.63in Right Flush

author2
> author +   Keep Lines Together. Border: Single.
> Tab stops: 1 in; 1.38in; Not at 4.63in

Bfooter
> boxed text + Font: 12 Point. Hidden

boxed text
> Normal + Font: Goudy 18 Point. Indent: Left
> 0.25in First -0.25in. Space Before 20 pt After
> 20 pt. Keep Lines Together. Border: Double Box.
> Tab stops: 2.38in Centered; 4.5in Right Flush

footer
> Normal + Italic.   Tab stops: 3 in Centered; 6 in
> Right Flush

footnote reference
> Normal + Font: 9 Point. Superscript 3 Point

footnote text
> Normal + Font: 10 Point

graphic
> Normal + Font: Goudy 18 Point. Centered. Space
> Before 10 pt After 15 pt. Keep With Next

header
> Normal +   Tab stops: 3 in Centered; 6 in Right
> Flush

index
> **Normal + Font: Geneva. Hidden. Keep With Next.**
> **Keep Lines Together**

A Listing of the Stylesheets Applied To The Text and Graphics of the Previous Page

index 1
Normal + Font: Times

index 2
Normal + Font: Times, Indent: Left 0.25in

index 3
Normal + Font: Times, Indent: Left 0.5in

index 4
Normal + Indent: Left 0.75in

index 5
Normal + Indent: Left 1 in

index 6
Normal + Indent: Left 1.25in

index 7
Normal + Indent: Left 1.5in

index1
Normal + Font: 14 Point

index2
Normal + Font: 14 Point

level 1
Normal + Font: Goudy 24 Point, Bold, Space
Before 20 pt After 15 pt, Keep With Next

level 2
Normal + Bold, Space Before 6 pt

level 3
Normal + Bold

level 4
Normal + Bold

level 5
Normal + Bold

A Listing of the Stylesheets Applied To The Text and Graphics of the Previous Page

level 6
Normal + Bold

level 7
Normal + Bold

level 8
Normal + Bold

level 9
Normal + Bold

line number
Normal +

Normal
Font: New York 12 Point. Flush left

page number
Normal +

para
Normal + Font: Goudy 18 Point. Keep With Next

rule
Normal + Font: Bookman 10 Point. Indent: Right 0.88in. Space After 3 pt. Border: Line Below

toc 1
Normal + Font: Times 14 Point. Indent: Right - 0.44in. Space After 4 pt. Tab stops: 2.38in Right Flush ...

The Final Composed and Printed Page

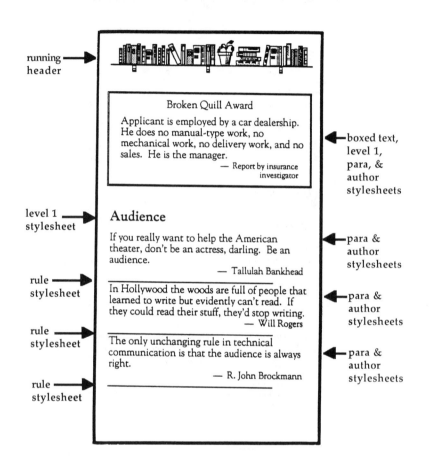

running header

level 1 stylesheet

rule stylesheet

rule stylesheet

rule stylesheet

boxed text, level 1, para, & author stylesheets

para & author stylesheets

para & author stylesheets

para & author stylesheets

Appendix B - Table 1
from Stephen Bernhardt's "Seeing the Text,"
College Composition and Communication 37 (1) February 1986,
pp. 66 - 78.

Visual Organization of Written Texts

Visually Informative		Non-Visually Informative
	Rhetorical Control	
varied surface offers aesthetic possibilities; can attract or repel reader through the shape of the text; laws of equilibrium, good continuation, good figure, closure, similarity.	**Visual Gestalt**	homogeneous surface offers little possibility of conveying information; dense, undistinguished block of print; every text presents the same face; formidable appearance assumes willing reader.
localized; each section is its own locale with its own pattern of development; arrests reader's attention.	**Development**	progressive: each section leads smoothly to the next; projects reader forward through discourse-level previewing and backwards through reviewing.
iconic: spacing, headings reveal explicit highly visible divisions; reader can jump around, process the text in a non-linear fashion access information easily, read selectively.	**Partitioning**	integrated: indentations give some indication of boundaries, but sections frequently contain several paragraphs and sometimes divisions occur within paragraphs; reader must read or scan linearly to find divisions.
emphasis controlled by visual stress of layout, type size, spacing headings.	**Emphasis**	emphasis controlled semantically through intensifiers, conjunctive ties; some emphasis achieved by placement of information in initial or final slots in sentences or paragraphs.

subordinate relations signaled through type size, headings, indenting.	**Subordinate Relations**	controlled semantically within linear sequence of paragraphs and sentences.
signalled through listing structures, expanded sentences, parallel structures, enumerated or iconically signally by bullets, or other graphic devices.	**Coordinate Relations**	controlled semantically through juxtaposition, parallel structure and cohesive ties, especially additive ties.
linkage controlled visually; little or no use of semantic ties between sentences or sections; reliance on enumerative sequences or topicalization of series.	**Linking/ Transitional/ Intersentential Relations**	liberal use of cohesive ties, especially conjunctives and deictics; frequent interparagraph ties or transitional phrases.
variety in mood and syntactic patterning; much use of Q/A sequences, imperatives; fragments and minor forms; phrases used in isolation.	**Sentence Patterns**	complete sentences with little variation in mood; sentences typically with full syntax.

[1] See R. John Brockmann, "Desktop Publishing—Beyond GEE WHIZ, Part 1: A Critical Overview," *IEEE Transactions on Professional Communication* (March 1988).

[2] R. John Brockmann. "Desktop Publishing—Beyond GEE WHIZ, Part 2: A Critical Bibliography of Materials" *IEEE Transactions on Professional Communication* (March 1988). In this second article of the "Beyond GEE WHIZ" series reviewing the dozen books, two demonstration videotapes, and three magazines focused on the topic of desktop publishing, I also tried to point out the fallacies in the blasé do-it-yourself attitude permeating the desktop publishing industry. This attitude is exemplified in a major vendor's demonstration videotape, "Introduction to Desktop Publishing" (1986) in which one of the speakers says "Look, at the flick of a button I can achieve what it used to take years of experience and education to achieve." However, as Erick Sandberg-Diment wrote in his "On Computers" column of *New York Times*, "The majority of layout and design examples I've seen by such software under the guidance of nonprofessionals . . . make a freshly poured bowl of alphabet soup seem by comparison a masterpiece of clarity and design" (September 7, 1986).

3 James concept of document databases is not to be confused with the printing of reports from databases performed by software such as *Incredible Jack* (Pecan Software Systems, Brooklyn, N.Y.).

4 Another candidate for an innovative methodology which could unleash the desktop and workstation technology is "hypertext" as described in Ted Nelson's 1983 book *Literary Machines* (available from the author at Box 128, Swathmore, Pa. 1980, ISBN 0-89347-052-X), embodied in the software package *Guide* (O.W.L. Software Inc.) and the 1987 Apple Macintosh system software *Hypercard*. (The Hypercard software is discussed quite well in the *Complete Hypercard Textbook* by Danny Goodman (New York, N.Y.: Bantam, 1987), and in a series of editorials by David Bunnell in *Macworld*: "Hypervisions" (March 1987, 21-30) and "The Challenge of Hypermedia" (November 1988, 17-23).

5 Peter Drucker, *Peter's Quotations: Ideas for Our Times* (New York: Bantam Books,1980), p. 60.

6 See David Colburn "Inexpensive Text/Graphic System: A Step Forward for Writers," in*Proceedings of the 33rd International Technical Communication Conference, 1986. (Detroit. Michigan).* p. 21 - 29 and Terry Urlick, *Personal Publishing on the Macintosh* (Indianapolis, In.: Hayden Books, 1986), p. 26.

7 Marshall McLuhan, *Counterblast* (New York: Harcourt Brace, 1969), p. 22.

8 Michael L. Kleper, *The Illustrated Book of Desktop Publishing and Typesetting* (Blue Summit, Pa.: TAB Books, 1987), p. 3.

9 V. Stibic, *Tools of the Mind: Techniques and Methods for Intellectual Work* (Amsterdam: North Holland Publishing Co., 1982), pp. 10 - 11.

10 Michael Waitsman, "The Future of Page Production" *ThePage* (October 1987): 10.

11 The differences between offline and online media is discussed in R. John Brockmann,*Writing Better Computer User Documentation: From Paper to Online* (New York: Wiley Interscience, 1986), pp. 208 - 216.

[12] Al R. Ireton. "Liberating the Corporate Publishing Process," in *Proceedings of the Corporate Electronic Publishing Systems IV: A Conference/Show, World Trade Center, Boston, Massachusetts, September 9 - 11, 1986*, p. 32.

[13] David Hancock, "Document Databases Can Save You Money" in *Proceedings of the 33rd International Technical Communication Conference,1986* (Detroit, Michigan), pp. 65 - 68.

[14] The concept of writing "screen size" frames and later reassembling them has long been advocated in the Information Mapping ™ writing style. See Robert Horn, *How to Write Information Mapping* (Lexington, Ma.: Information Resources, Inc. 1969), "Structured Writing and Text Design" in *The Technology of Text: Principles for Structuring, Designing, and Displaying Text* edited by David Jonassen (Educational Press: Englewood Cliffs, New Jersey, 1982), or Robert E. Horn and John N. Kelley "Structured Writing—An Approach to the Documentation of Computer Software" *SIGDOC Asterisk Newsletter*, 7 (4), (July 1981): 4 - 25.

[15] *Guide* is produced by OWL International Inc. 14218 NE 21st Street, Bellevue, Washington 98007.

[16] Raymond Q. Little "An Interactive FOMM" *Technical Communication* 32 (3) (1985): 11 - 12; "Improving FOMM Troubleshooting" *Technical Communication* 30 (1) (1983): 20 - 24; also personal communication.

[17] This can also be accomplished by the Write Once Read Many (WORM) CDROM units now being implemented in a microcomputer environment.

[18] Peter Drucker, *Peter's Quotations: Ideas for Our Times* (New York: Bantam Books, 1980), p. 35.

[19] "Indians in the Land: A Conversation Between William Cronon and Richard White," *American Heritage* 37 (5) (August/September 1986): 18 - 25.

[20] Of course James is not suggesting swopping a bit of Henry James and Edgar Allen Poe and inserting the new combination into Erica Jong. He is talking about technical or referential documents that are highly structured.

[21] John Penrose, "A Qualitative Comparison of Three Microcomputer Business Letter Libraries," *Journal of Business Communication,* 23 (2) (Spring 1986): 23 - 30. The three P.C. software products studied were *Gold Letters, Business Letter Library* and *Letterform 1000.*

[22] For example the Fog Index or the Gunning Index included on ATT's *Writer's Workbench* , Aspen Software's *Grammatik,* or Aegis Development Corp.'s *Don Clapp's Word Tools.*

[23] David Hancock, "Document Databases Can Save You Money" in *Proceedings of the 33rd International Technical Communication Conference,* 1986 (Detroit, Michigan): p. 67

[24] Stephen Bernhardt, "Seeing the Text," *College Composition and Communication* 37 (1) (February 1986): 66 - 78.

[25] For example, New Riders Publishing *Tec Doc Collection* for the Xerox Ventura Publisher package, or Aldus Corporation's forthcoming *PageMaker Portfolio: Designs for Manuals* .

[26] See "Rules of Editing Best Left Forgotten" in Jonathan Price, *How to Write a Manual: A Handbook of Software Documentation* (New York: Addison Wesley, 1984), p. 226 - 229.

[27] For example, the New Riders Publishing *Tec Doc Collection* for the Xerox · Ventura Publisher package offers "automatic section numbering." Thus just as the documentation profession is getting away from paragraph numbering such as "1.1.1.1.1.1.1.," the built-in canned document templates will automatically be inserting them.

[28] Phillip Kraft, *Programmers and Managers: The Routinization of Computer Programming in the United States* (New York: Springer-Verlag, 1977). See also Joseph E. van Oss, "Documentation Systems: Changing Products, Tools, and Theory," in *Proceedings of the 31st International Technical Communication Conference, 1984,* pp. WE-150 - WE-153.

[29] William C. Houze. "Today's Technical Writer/Editor in Tomorrows 'Electronic Mega-Cottage Industry' World of Work: Will They Survive?" *Proteus: A Journal of Ideas* 1(1) (1983): 23 - 28.

The Ethics of Automated Publishing Systems
(A response to Dr. Brockmann)

Geoffrey James

Honeywell Bull Inc.
5250 West Century Blvd.
Los Angeles, CA, 90045

1 Introduction

Ideally, an advance in technology and methodology is accompanied by an advance in responsibility. History tells us that all too often the opposite is true. It is essential to examine the ethical issues of powerful and new techniques that are now available to the technical communicator. That is why I welcome commentaries such as the one provided by Dr. Brockmann elsewhere in this volume. Dr. Brockmann is well known as an industry spokesman and it is significant that he should turn his perceptive eye on potential problems long before others realize that problems might occur.

Brockmann's article can be considered in two parts. The first part provides a valuable update to the book *Document Databases*, pointing out the applicability of the document database methodology to the desktop environment. It is true that *Document Databases* has a mainframe orientation. This is because the manuscript was submitted in final form in September of 1983. At that time, there was no such term as "desktop publishing" and the only publications systems available were based upon mainframe or minicomputer architecture.

The methodology described in *Document Databases* is, as Brockmann rightly points out, applicable to a wide range of hardware and software vehicles. I have sometimes been criticized for the theoretical slant of the book. In retrospect it seems that this stance was correct, as the basic principles remain true even though the technology has gotten less expensive and more sophisticated. This is not to say that I believe that mainframes don't have a place in the future of publications systems. Some projects are just so large that they don't adapt well to isolated or networked workstations. Complex documentation projects still require the centralization of a large computer.

The second part of Brockmann's article deals with the ethical implications of the document database methodology. These concerns can be grouped into five areas and paraphrased as follows:

Reusability - Canned text is of limited usefulness, therefore reusability is of limited usefulness.

Quality - Management may use the methodology to sidestep proper audience analysis thereby degrading document quality.

User Friendliness - Writers are better served by systems that provide visual cues to textual organization and flow; i.e., WYSIWYG.

Standardization - Corporations might find it easier to squelch creativity through the enforced application of inappropriate and restrictive writing and production standards.

Job Security - Writers will be de-skilled by automated document production, thus becoming vulnerable to layoffs and work reductions, or at least the "de-professionalization" of their jobs.

I would like to examine each of these areas to see whether or not Brockmann's concerns are justified.

2 Reusability

Canned text is of limited usefulness, as Brockmann rightly points out. However, the inclusion of canned or boilerplate material is not the primary purpose of reusability.

The real power of reusability is the ability to update subdocuments (text and graphics) without concern for formatting issues. For example, one major aerospace company uses Honeywell Bull's CAP product to generate reports for missile flight tests. Raw data is gathered from real-time sensors and then partitioned to various engineers, who reduce the data to graphs and explanations. CAP then formats a document skeleton that points at the various files that the engineers have created, producing the final report overnight without human intervention.

Thus the structure of the document is reused, as well as the subdocuments not changed during the current iteration. In other words, reusability primarily is for producing successive versions of the same document, rather than using boilerplate material across many documents.

Of course, a highly modular system or product can be described with reusable documentation blocks. For example, there is little reason to rewrite the description of "How to Log On" to a mainframe system if the process is identical for all users. The point here is that the technology must be applied in appropriate circumstances.

3 Quality

There is little question that the inclusion of inappropriately-targetted engineering specifications lowers the quality of user manuals. However, plenty of this activity goes on in traditional publications environments.

This is not a technological or methodological issue. It is a management issue. Management must ultimately decide how it wants to use the additional resources that are generated through a raise in productivity. These resources can be used to produce higher quality documents, or they can be used to produce a larger number of low quality documents. The same thing is true if management hires more people rather than automating the publication system. Quality costs, regardless of how a document is produced.

On the other hand, a document database can substantially raise quality by making possible what was once impossible. For example, online access to documents promote an interactive environment where communication between writer and reader can be more responsive and spontaneous. Similarly, the compression of the production cycle permits a document to be ready concurrently with the product. This goal is usually unattainable with traditional production methods, however well intentioned and quality-minded management might be.

4 User Friendliness

While it is true that some writers use format, headings, pages and indentations as thinking aids, it is not true that declarative structuring is without visual cues. A well-designed markup language can provide visual cues that are superior to those provided by a WYSIWYG system.

The key phrase here is "well-designed", a concept open to numerous interpretations. In my opinion, many markup languages have a definite tendency to fill a document with overly-complex constructs. In the case of SGML, it is my feeling that the markup addresses too many formatting elements, making the language little better than a procedural formatter. In the case of LaTeX, the English-like form of the instructions presents the eye with visual flack that is difficult to differentiate from the words that make up the document's content.

Again in my opinion, a well-designed markup language should use only a small handful of structural elements that match the structures in the document itself. These structures must be consistent in appearance and location so that they provide the visual cues that the writer needs to organize material properly. A well-designed markup language also requires a full-featured "pretty-printer" that presents the marked-up document source in a readable and consistent manner. Since few markup languages have these characteristics, it is not surprising that some writers prefer a WYSIWYG interface. Thus Dr. Brockmann's criticism is not one inherent to markup languages but only to their current implementations.

5 Standardization

While it is true that declarative formatting is often used to enforce standards, it also opens the door to the support of multiple standards.

Since a document's appearance is determined by an exterior definition, it is trivial to change from one standard to another. This tends to make document appearance *more* rather than less fluid. In other words, there is less possibility of a standard becoming ossified if the standards (and the documents) can be altered at will.

In my opinion, the worst manifestation of standardization takes place when a writer is constrained to learn arbitrary formatting sequences merely to get the job done. This forces the writer to remain cognizant of extraneous issues such as margins and fonts, when he or she should be concentrating on the content of the document. In other words, declarative formatting frees the writer from worrying about standards while simultaneously making it possible to support many different document styles.

6 Job Security

I agree that the document database methodology will result in readjustments in the publications labor force. This has already happened to some degree – when was the last time you had a conversation with a hot-lead typographer?

However, the methodology does not pose a threat to the professional technical communicator. To understand why this is so, one must first understand the difference between computerization and automation.

Computerization is the process of moving a physical action onto a computer. WYSIWYG workstations are good examples of computerization. Automation is the process of removing a physical action from a workflow. Honeywell Bull's CAP system is a good example of automation.

Both computerization and automation promote a union between human and computer. To quote a very wise man, "the question is—which is to be the master—that's all."

With computerization, the human is the slave of the computer, and is forced to learn arbitrary techniques to perform the same clerical tasks as before. With automation, the human is the master, commanding the computer to perform clerical functions without the necessity for constant supervision. This frees the human to perform intellectual rather than clerical labor.

Brockmann worries that the document database methodology will deskill the writing profession. He bases this worry in part upon the belief that programmers have been de-skilled. I question that perception. As a project leader for a complex software product and as a former technical writer, I have had the opportunity to work with programmers from a variety of backgrounds. If anything, the average programmer (and the average technical writer) of today is more skilled than he or she was ten years ago.

Automation lessens the requirement for *clerical* labor, not for *professional* labor. As the automation process removes clerical labor from the publishing process, it raises the professional status of the writer. I have seen this at Honeywell Bull's Los Angeles Development Center (LADC), where the entire technical publications organization (which use a document database) is paid on an equivalent scale to the software programming staff. In addition, when layoffs occurred at LADC, several programmers were terminated while the technical writing staff remained intact.

7 Conclusion

All of this comes down to a question of writer identity. Is a writer somebody who understands high-school grammar and knows which button calls up a twelve point Zapf dingbat font? Or is a professional writer somebody who can synthesize ideas and then express them with clarity? In my opinion, it is demeaning to the writing profession to believe that good writing is intimately tied up with the petty details of document production. The intellectual effort of writing—communication from human to human—is the real skill. It is a skill that can never be automated.

4

Text Processing with the START Natural Language System

Boris Katz

Artificial Intelligence Laboratory
Massachusetts Institute of Technology
Cambridge, MA 02139

This paper describes a natural language processing system START (SynTactic Analysis using Reversible Transformations). The system analyzes English text and automatically transforms it into an appropriate representation, the *knowledge base*, which incorporates the information found in the text. The user gains access to information stored in the knowledge base by querying it in English. The system analyzes the query and decides through a matching process what information in the knowledge base is relevant to the question. Then it retrieves this information and formulates its response also in English.

Researchers at MIT, Stanford University, and the Jet Propulsion Laboratory have used the START system for creating knowledge bases from English text in domains as diverse as medicine, politics, space, vision, and commonsense physics. (See, for example, Winston [1982], [1984], Winston, Binford, Katz, and Lowry [1983], Doyle [1984], Katz and Brooks [1987]). In section 11 of this paper we give an example of a technical document which specifies the experiments to be performed onboard an interplanetary spacecraft. We show how this document, prepared for the Mars Observer mission, is transformed into a knowledge base. Finally, we present an actual dialog with START based on the Mars Observer knowledge base.

1. Understanding Language

Before we provide a detailed description of the START system we should make clear what we mean by "understanding." What does it mean for a machine to understand language?

Let us consider a situation where a mother gives instructions or tells a story to her daughter Jill. Hopefully, the child has "stored" the new information/knowledge in her memory. In this case, we say that the child understood her mother.

How can this be verified?

- If Jill heard a story, her mother can ask questions relevant to the story. If after searching her memory, Jill is able to utilize the acquired knowledge and answer the questions correctly, then she understood the story.

- Suppose instead of a story Jill heard a set of instructions for a task she is supposed to perform. If Jill is able to retrieve the knowledge given by the instructions and accomplish the task, then she understood the instructions.

We will use these two criteria as "Turing tests" to help us define what it means for a computer to understand English:

A. English text is typed into the computer and a knowledge base is created on the basis of this text. The user queries the knowledge base in English. If the computer's responses are correct, then we can say the computer understood the text.

B. A sequence of English commands or instructions is entered in the computer. If the computer carries out appropriate actions in response to them, then we can say the computer understood the instructions.

Remarkably, START passes these two tests in a variety of situations although it incorporates no explicit theory of meaning.

As suggested by these two criteria, knowledge bases created by START can either be used in question-answering situations or they can provide input data for other computer systems. The START knowledge base is employed by both modules that comprise START: the *understanding* module and the *generating* module. These two modules also share the same Grammar (see Katz [1980], Katz and Winston [1982]).

2.   Kernel Sentences

Most English sentences break up into units that we will call *kernel sentences*. Before we can formally define these units let us examine how START represents sentence elements internally. The system uses three types of building blocks for constructing a kernel sentence, the *noun-template*, the *verb-template*, and the *adverb-template*:

noun-template (NT) = [prep det mod adj* noun]

verb-template (VT) = [aux1 neg aux2 aux3 verb]

adverb-template (AT) = [mod adverb]

Here *prep, det, mod, adj, aux, neg* are, respectively, abbreviations for preposition, determiner, modifier, adjective, auxiliary, and negation. The asterisk * indicates that a string of one or more symbols or their conjunction is allowed. All the elements in the templates are optional. Noun phrases and prepositional phrases in English can be constructed by reading off the slot values in instantiated noun-templates. In a similar way, verbs and their auxiliaries can be obtained by reading off slot values in verb-templates. For example, the instantiation of the noun-template, NT = [(noun **Mary**)], where most elements of the NT are omitted, produces a simple noun phrase *Mary*, while the same template with all its elements filled,

$$NT = [(\text{prep } \textbf{after}) \ (\text{det } \textbf{a}) \ (\text{mod } \textbf{very}) \ (\text{adj } \textbf{long}) \ (\text{noun } \textbf{flight})]$$

generates a full-fledged prepositional phrase *after a very long flight*. Similarly, the verb-template may produce either one main verb, *launch*, when using VT = [(verb **launch**)], or a more complex string like *could have been watching*:

$$VT = [(\text{aux1 } \textbf{could}) \ (\text{aux2 } \textbf{have}) \ (\text{aux3 } \textbf{been}) \ (\text{verb } \textbf{watching})]$$

Now let us define a *kernel structure* as the following sequence of templates:

(1) $NT^{initial} \ NT^{subject} \ VT \ NT^{object} \ NT^{final}$

Here $NT^{subject}$ and NT^{object} are noun-templates that represent the subject and the object in the sentence; $NT^{initial}$ and NT^{final} represent its initial and final prepositional phrases; VT is a verb-template.

We should point out that most of the elements in the kernel structure are optional. Also for simplicity the adverb-templates have been omitted although they may appear in (1) in a number of places. In addition, transformational rules, introduced in section 5, are allowed to modify the kernel structure and change the order of templates.

A *kernel sentence* is an English sentence obtained by reading off from left to right all slot values in all templates in (1). We define *parsing* as a process of syntactic analysis which, given an English kernel sentence as input, produces the corresponding kernel structure as output.[1] For example, given the sentence below:

After the launch the commander will give additional instructions to the astronaut

---

[1] In sections 5 and 6 this notion of parsing is extended to a wider class of English sentences.

the *parser* produces the following instantiated kernel structure where the order
of templates follows that of (1):

$NT^{initial}$	[(prep **after**) (det **the**) (noun **launch**)]
$NT^{subject}$	[(det **the**) (noun **commander**)]
VT	[(aux1 **will**) (verb **give**)]
NT^{object}	[(adj **additional**) (noun **instructions**)]
NT^{final}	[(prep **to**) (det **the**) (noun **astronaut**)]

Many natural language understanding systems restrict themselves to the parsing process just defined and stop there. However, this is clearly not enough
to satisfy our definition of understanding. It is not enough to teach the computer to recognize different syntactic categories and fill in the slots in the
kernel structure. Our goal is to enable the computer to use the knowledge
encoded in the kernel structure; in other words, to *index* and *retrieve* this
knowledge efficiently.

3.   From Kernel Structures to T-expressions

Recall that in order to understand her mother, Jill had to perform two important operations. When listening to the story, Jill had to store (or *index*)
the new knowledge in her memory. When answering the questions, she had
to search her memory and *retrieve* the knowledge. These two operations, indexing and retrieving, are crucial in our model of understanding language. In
this section we will describe the indexing procedure of START. The retrieval
task is carried out by a matching procedure described in section 10.

Suppose we type the following English sentence on a computer terminal:

(2) Jane will recognize Paul tomorrow

and the parsing procedure constructs the appropriate kernel structure. Now,
there are many things about this sentence that the computer should remember: that *Jane* is the subject of the sentence, *Paul* is the object, that *recognize*
is the relation between them. There is more to remember: the tense and the
aspect of the sentence, its auxiliaries, its adverbs. Was this sentence embedded in a larger sentence? Does it have a relative clause? Was the verb in
the active or passive form? We certainly want all this information about the
sentence to be stored in the computer's memory. However, we also want to
be able to retrieve this information efficiently.

We could store all these sentence features in one long list. This approach, however, would not account for the fact that some of the features in a sentence seem more salient than others. A simple list of features in sentence (2) would also fail to capture its structural affinity with the following two sentences:

(3) Yesterday Jane could have recognized Paul.

(4) Paul wasn't recognized by Jane.

And finally, this approach would turn the matching/retrieval task into a computational nightmare.

We could try to emphasize the hierarchical nature of the English sentence by using the kernel structure representation. However, since most elements of the kernel structure are optional, its shape is too unpredictable to allow the system to match the kernel structures efficiently.

Our system, START, rearranges the elements of the kernel structure into embedded *ternary expressions (T-expressions)* by tying together the three most salient parameters of a sentence, the subject, the object, and the relation between them, ⟨**subject relation object**⟩. All three sentences (2, 3, 4) will yield the same T-expression

(5) ⟨**Jane recognize Paul**⟩.

Certain other parameters are used to create additional T-expressions in which prepositions and several special words serve as relations. The remaining parameters, adverbs and their position, tense, auxiliaries, voice, negation, etc., are recorded in a representational structure called *history*. The history has a *page* pertaining to each sentence which yields the given T-expression. When we index the T-expression in the knowledge base, we cross-reference its three components and attach the history H to it. The resulting entry in the knowledge base, denoted ⟨**subject relation object**⟩$_H$, will be called a *T-entry*. For example, the T-entry ⟨**Jane recognize Paul**⟩$_H$ corresponding to T-expression (5) has a three-page history, assuming that all three sentences (2, 3, 4) appeared in the input text. One can thus think of a T-entry as a "digested summary" of the syntactic structure of English sentences.

The T-entry is the cornerstone of the representational hierarchy of the START system. It is the level of the hierarchy where the understanding and the generating modules meet. The understanding module analyzes English sentences and creates a set of T-entries. The generating module, in turn, retrieves these T-entries from the knowledge base and produces English text.

4. Referents for Noun Phrases

The subject and the object of T-expression ⟨**Jane recognize Paul**⟩ are proper names which are taken directly from sentence (2). However, the process is more complex if, for example, the subject of a sentence is not a proper name but a complex noun phrase:

(6) Jane's good friend from Boston recognized Paul.

In sentence (6) the system needs to establish the referent for the head noun, *friend*. The system has to come up with a *unique name* for this noun in case a different instance of *friend* appears later in the analyzed text. In order to do this, START computes the *name environment* E_1 for this occurrence of *friend*. We define E_1 as a list of adjectives (in this case, *good*), possessive nouns (*Jane's*), prepositional phrases (*from Boston*), etc. modifying that noun in the present sentence. Then START associates with this environment a unique name, say *friend-1*, which we will call a *referent*[2] for the noun *friend* in the environment E_1. The main T-expression for sentence (6) will therefore take the form ⟨**friend-1 recognize Paul**⟩.[3]

The analyzed noun, *friend*, its name environment E_1, and its referent, *friend-1* are then recorded in the computer's memory. This bookkeeping gives the system the ability to compute the referent of a noun given its name environment. If, for instance, the same noun phrase,

Jane's good friend from Boston

occurs again in a different sentence later in the text, then its name environment would coincide with E_1 and hence the same referent, *friend-1*, would be retrieved and utilized in the T-expressions constructed for this sentence.

Suppose now that START encounters a new sentence where the noun *friend* appears in a slightly different noun phrase like

(7) Miriam's good friend from Pasadena.

The environment E_2 associated with the new noun phrase is different from E_1 and is not to be found in the computer memory. This means that there is no referent readily available for the noun *friend* in this sentence and the system

---

[2] In calling a unique name a referent we deviate from standard usage, which reserves the term for an object in the world.

[3] The analysis of the subject noun-phrase in sentence (6) will produce three additional T-expressions (see section 6).

needs to generate a new unique name, *friend*-2, to be associated with E_2.

START recursively employs the procedure just described to find a referent for *every* noun in the sentence. Thus, given the noun phrase

The young woman's good friend from the big city

the system first determines the referents of the nouns *woman* and *city*. Only after that, once the computation of its name environment becomes possible, does the head noun, *friend*, get its referent.[4]

Sometimes, however, the information in the name environment is not sufficient to find referents for noun phrases. For instance, if a noun phrase is modified by a relative clause (see section 6) the entire knowledge base has to be consulted in order to determine the appropriate referent.

5. Transformational Rules

The standard kernel structure introduced in section 2,

(1) $NT^{initial} \ NT^{subject} \ VT \ NT^{object} \ NT^{final}$

allows the system to generate or parse only a limited variety of English sentences. To account for other kinds of sentences, START employs commuting *transformational rules* (see Chomsky [1957], Akmajian and Heny [1975], Katz [1980]). For instance, consider how the kernel sentence

The probe reached Venus

is modified by several transformational rules, where each transformation is applied to the outcome of the previous one:

Transformation	Sentence
	The probe reached Venus.
Question	Did the probe reach Venus?
Negation	Didn't the probe reach Venus?
Passive	Wasn't Venus reached by the probe?

The transformations shown are executed by the generating module of START. In the understanding mode, the system's goal is to recognize which transfor-

---

[4]In the remainder of this paper, for reasons of simplicity, we will use the nouns themselves in *T*-expressions rather than their referents.

mations were applied. In some cases, for instance, *Negation*, START simply. makes the appropriate additions to the histories of the resulting *T*-entries. In other cases, the system must actually *reverse* the effect of the transformation.

All the examples of English sentences considered so far have been very simple. We can make them a little more complex by allowing simpler sentences to be embedded in larger sentences, as shown below:

(8) Spock wanted the computer to print the message

(9) For Spock to ignore the command would anger Kirk.

The transformational rules responsible for sentence embedding form a special class called *connective transformations* (see Katz [1980]). Each connective transformation takes two kernel sentences as input; these correspond to the *matrix* clause and the *embedded* clause in the resulting English sentence. For example, sentence (8) above consists of a matrix clause, *Spock wanted it*, and an embedded clause, *the computer printed the message*. We assume that one of the noun-templates in the kernel structure of the matrix clause always contains *it* as a *joining point* for glueing the two kernels together. Table 1 shows examples illustrating the application of several different connective transformations.

Matrix clause	Embedded clause	Resulting Sentence
It angered Kirk	The computer ignored the message	That the computer ignored the message angered Kirk
Spock suggests it	McCoy is silent	Spock suggests that McCoy be silent
Spock watched it	Kirk read the message	Spock watched Kirk read the message
Kirk asked it	The computer repeated the message	Kirk asked the computer to repeat the message
Spock claims it	Spock has written the message	Spock claims to have written the message
It shocked Kirk	Spock ignored the command	Spock's ignoring the command shocked Kirk
Spock saw it	McCoy read the message	Spock saw McCoy reading the message
It angered Kirk	Kirk read the message	Reading the message angered Kirk
Kirk knew it	The computer ignored the message	Kirk knew whether the computer ignored the message

Table 1. Examples of applications of connective transformations.

Recall that in section 2 we defined *parsing* only for kernel sentences. Connective transformations allow us to extend this notion to a wider class of English sentences which includes embedded sentences. After START determines the connective transformation involved it reverses the connective transformation and splits the sentence into kernel sentences. Then it parses each kernel sentence separately and produces kernel structures. And finally, the indexing procedure utilizes the lexical material provided by kernel structures to build T-expressions and index them as T-entries.

In order to handle embedded sentences, START allows any T-expression to take another T-expression as its subject or object. Thus, sentence (8) leads to *right embedding*:

(10) ⟨**Spock want** ⟨**computer print message**⟩⟩

while the sentence (9) leads to *left embedding*:

(11) ⟨⟨**Spock ignore command**⟩ **anger Kirk**⟩.

Connective transformations may be recursively applied without any restrictions on the depth of embedding. This means that START can analyze and generate sentences with arbitrarily complex embedded structures.

6. Complex Noun Phrases and Relative Clauses

We have seen how START analyzes a sentence and produces a T-expression whose corresponding T-entry "summarizes" the syntactic structure of the sentence. Let us examine now how complex noun phrases result in the construction of several additional T-expressions. Consider sentence (6):

(6)   Jane's good friend from Boston recognized Paul.

The head of the noun phrase, *friend*, is premodified by *Jane's* and *good* and postmodified by the prepositional phrase *from Boston*. As a result, along with the main T-expression, ⟨**friend-1 recognize Paul**⟩, the system will construct three additional T-expressions: ⟨**friend-1 is good**⟩, ⟨**friend-1 related-to Jane**⟩, and ⟨**friend-1 from Boston**⟩. In fact, every adjective or possessive noun in the sentence, as well as every prepositional phrase or relative clause, will cause new T-expressions to be built and stored in the knowledge base.

START can handle different types of relative clauses:
(12) The girl *who wants to become an astronaut* is young.
(13) The planet *which Voyager photographed yesterday* was shrouded in clouds.
(14) The man *we admire* walked on the Moon.
(15) The planet *the spacecraft flew behind* has a strong magnetic field.
(16) The satellite *to which the antennas were pointing* had an impact crater.
(17) The spacecraft *orbiting the Earth* photographed its surface.
(18) The satellite *launched by NASA* handles telecommunications.
(19) The space shuttle *whose protective tiles were damaged* underwent repairs.

Let us analyze sentence (13), which involves a full relative clause with an object relative pronoun. First, the system has to find the relative clause boundaries and identify the location of the *gap* (denoted by *e*) which is coreferent to the head noun phrase:

> The planet$_i$ [which Voyager photographed e_i yesterday] was shrouded in clouds.

Then the relative clause is "removed" from the sentence, the gap is filled with its antecedent and the modified clause is processed independently. As a result, the sentence (13) will be split into the following two sentences:

(20) Voyager photographed the planet$_i$ yesterday

(21) The planet$_i$ was shrouded in clouds.

Relative clauses do not need to be simple kernel sentences (see example (12), for instance). In fact, any two sentences that may be analyzed by START, with arbitrarily complex embedded structures, can be combined into main and relative clauses of a larger sentence as long as they have a common noun phrase. Moreover, several relative clauses may be recursively embedded inside one another.

7. Lexical Ambiguity

Every word in the sample sentences discussed so far was assumed to belong to a unique part of speech. Thus, *Jill, friend*, and *man* are nouns, *read, write*, and *tell* are verbs, and *old* and *good* are adjectives. This assumption however is not always correct. Most words in English can receive several alternative category assignments (that is, can serve as different parts of speech); the particular choice depends on the context. For instance, in the following sentence from a detective story

(22) The gangsters *can supply uniform* alibis

the word *can* is used as a modal auxiliary, but it could also serve as a noun; the word *supply* is a verb, but it could also be a noun or a modifier in a noun-noun modification sequence; the word *uniform* is an adjective that could be used as a noun in a different context. Sentence (22) will be analyzed correctly only if the system selects the right category assignments for each word; any other assignment will result in an error.

Lexical entries in START (see section 9) are allowed to specify more than one category assignment. The system is equipped with a mechanism for category disambiguation which uses error feedback from the parser (including context information and type of error) to efficiently resolve ambiguities. As a result, along with sentence (22), START is able to process successfully another sentence from the same detective story:

(23) But the policeman found the *uniform* in the *supply can.*

Notice that each of the three ambiguous words in sentence (23) is a different part of speech from what it was in (22).

8.   Forward and Backward S-rules

In sections 3 and 5 we showed how START builds *T*-expressions using the pattern **⟨subject relation object⟩** at every level of embedding. As a consequence, *T*-expressions closely follow the syntax of analyzed sentences. This property incidentally is one reason why the language generator is frequently able to reconstruct the original English sentence almost verbatim. Unfortunately, this property also implies that sentences which have different surface syntax but are close in meaning will not be considered similar by the system.

An example will clarify this point. Given as input the sentence (24) START will create an embedded *T*-expression (25):

(24) Jane presented Paul with a gift

(25) ⟨⟨**Jane present Paul**⟩ **with gift**⟩

whereas the almost synonymous sentence (26) will generate expression (27):

(26) Jane presented a gift to Paul

(27) ⟨⟨**Jane present gift**⟩ **to Paul**⟩.

Speakers of English know that sentences (24) and (26) both describe a transfer of possession. They also know that *the gift* is the transferred entity and *Paul* is its recipient in both sentences, in spite of different syntactic realizations of these noun phrases. The problem is, however, that the START system, as described so far, does not consider expressions (25) and (27) similar. As a result, given only sentence (24) as input, the system will not be able to answer the following question:

(28) To whom did Jane present a gift?

This is a serious problem since interactions between the syntactic and semantic properties of verbs such as these pervade the English language and cannot be ignored when constructing a natural language system.

START's solution to this problem requires us to introduce the concept of an *S-rule*. *S*-rules (where *S* stands for both *Syntax* and *Semantics*) are implemented as a rule-based system where the antecedents and consequents are schemata of *T*-expressions (blueprints in which the elements of *T*-expressions may be replaced by variables) of the knowledge base. *S*-rules operate in two modes: *forward* and *backward*.

When triggered by certain conditions, *S*-rules in the forward mode allow the system to intercept *T*-expressions produced by the understanding module, transform or augment them in a way specified by the rule, and then incorporate the result into the knowledge base. For instance, the following *S*-rule can be used to solve the problem posed by a verb such as *present*:

If   ⟨⟨subject **present** object1⟩ **with** object2⟩
Then   ⟨⟨subject **present** object2⟩ **to** object1⟩.

As soon as this *S*-rule encounters expression (25) produced by START,

(25) ⟨⟨**Jane present Paul**⟩ **with gift**⟩

it creates a new *T*-expression

(27) ⟨⟨**Jane present gift**⟩ **to Paul**⟩

and then adds the corresponding *T*-entry to the knowledge base.

S-rules have several functions. They may represent simple lexical information about the possible ways a verb can realize its arguments, as in (24) and (26). *S*-rules can also express more complex knowledge about the real world. Notice that all additional facts produced by the forward *S*-rules are instantly entered in the knowledge base. This forward mode is especially useful when the information processed by START is put into action by another computer system because in this situation START ought to provide the interfacing system with as much data as possible.

In contrast, the backward mode is employed when the user queries the knowledge base. Often, for reasons of efficiency, it is advantageous not to incorporate all inferred knowledge into the knowledge base immediately. The backward *S*-rules trigger only when a request comes in which cannot be answered directly. Then the rules initiate a search in the knowledge base to determine if the answer can be deduced from the available information.

In a more complex situation, S-rules are allowed to trigger each other and to ask each other for help. At any given moment hundreds of rules may be hidden in the computer's memory examining the output flow generated by START and waiting for their turn to participate in the deduction process. S-rules fundamentally expand the power of our language understanding system; they open a window into the intricate world of syntax-semantic interactions.

9. Lexicon

In order to understand an English sentence, the system needs to have certain morphological, syntactic, and semantic information about the words that form the sentence. All the words that the system is aware of, along with the appropriate information about part of speech, inflection, gender, number, etc. are stored in the *Lexicon*. Virtually every branch of our system resorts to the Lexicon to accomplish its task. In the understanding mode, the Lexicon is used to recognize embedded clauses, to construct kernel structures, to build *T*-expressions. In the generating mode, the Lexicon is consulted when a noun or verb phrase is built, when a connective transformation is applied, when a question is answered.

Let us examine how lexical information about verb classes may be utilized by the S-rules. Suppose we typed the following sentence into the computer:

(29) Paul surprised the audience with his performance.

An English speaker knows that sentence (29) can be paraphrased as:

(30) Paul's performance surprised the audience.

According to Van Oosten [1980] and Levin [1987], *surprise* is not the only verb which exhibits these different syntactic realizations of its arguments. This property also holds for many other verbs including

amuse, anger, disappoint, embarrass, frighten, please, worry ...

An astute reader will notice that these verbs share a certain semantic property as well: they all denote *emotional reactions*. For this reason we identify a class of *emotional-reaction* verbs and say that the syntactic property of the verb *surprise* responsible for the alternations shown in (29) and (30) holds for all verbs that comprise the *emotional-reaction* class (see Katz and Levin [1988]).

S-rules allow START to take advantage of these regularities in the Lexicon. Knowing that sentence (29) results in the *T*-expression

(31) ⟨⟨**Paul surprise audience**⟩ **with performance**⟩

one can write a simple *S*-rule which will trigger not only on the verb *surprise* but on any verb from the *emotional-reaction* class:

If   ⟨⟨subject verb object1⟩ **with** object2⟩
Then   ⟨object2 verb object1⟩
Provided   verb ∈ *emotional-reaction*

After typing sentence (29), we may now ask the system:

Did Paul's performance surprise the audience?

The *S*-rule described above (used in the backward mode) will trigger, since the *T*-expression

⟨**performance surprise audience**⟩

produced by the question matches the THEN-part of the rule and the Lexicon tells it that the verb *surprise* belongs to the *emotional-reaction* class. The correct answer to the question is deduced when the IF-part of the rule is matched to *T*-expression (31) found in the knowledge base.

This example shows how the transparent syntax of the *S*-rules coupled with the semantic information about verb classes provided by the Lexicon facilitates fluent and flexible dialog between the user and the language understanding system.

The process of *lexical acquisition* (adding new words to the Lexicon, with all relevant information about them) is very simple. In fact, introducing a new lexical item in START amounts to little more than appending it to a list of similar words, adding a few idiosyncratic features when necessary. All this makes the system portable, i.e. easily adaptable from one domain to another.

10. Answering Questions

Recall our two criteria *A* and *B* of section 1 which define whether the computer understood English text. We have already seen how START creates knowledge bases employed by other AI programs (Test *B*). In this section we will concentrate on the question-answering machinery in START (Test *A*). Suppose the system has analyzed and indexed a text containing the sentence

(32) Spock wanted the computer to print the message.

The knowledge base now contains the following T-entry:

(33) ⟨**Spock want ⟨computer print message⟩**⟩$_H$.

Suppose now that a user asks:

(34) What did Spock want the computer to print?

First the system needs to *reverse* the effect of the *Question* transformation applied in (34). In order to accomplish this, the system must find the place in the sentence that the *wh*-word *what* came from. This situation is very similar to the treatment of *relative clauses* discussed in section 6; the system again needs to find the *gap e* that is coreferent with *what*:[5]

(35) Spock wanted [the computer to print e]

Once the location of the gap has been found, the language understanding system leads the sentence (35) through the same flow of control as any other declarative sentence and produces the following T-expression:

(36) ⟨**Spock want ⟨computer print e⟩**⟩.

Treating e as a matching variable the system then feeds T-expression (36) through a matcher in order to determine whether there is anything in the knowledge base that matches (36). The matcher finds the T-entry

(33) ⟨**Spock want ⟨computer print message⟩**⟩$_H$,

retrieves it from the knowledge base, and hands it over to the language generation system which produces the English response to question (34):

Spock wanted the computer to print the message.

Other types of English questions, including *Yes/No*-questions, *when*-questions, *where*-questions, *why*-questions, etc. are treated in a similar fashion.

In this example we implicitly assumed that the tense and the aspect of question (34) were identical to the tense and aspect of sentence (32) in the text. We also assumed that sentence (32) was used in the text only once and that it was not embedded in another sentence. All these assumptions need not necessarily hold, however. For instance, one might ask:

(37) Does Spock want the computer to print the message?

---

[5]The same computational machinery is used to handle these two phenomena.

or

(38) Did the computer print the message?

A person answering these questions in the context of (32) would probably say
"I don't know" since sentence (32) just states that Spock wanted a certain
action to happen at one time in the past. Sentence (32) does not imply that
Spock wants this action to happen in the present nor does it imply that this
action actually happened.

To illustrate a different case, suppose that it is known from the text that

(39) The telescope is orbiting the Earth.

Now someone may ask the following questions:

(40) Has the telescope been orbiting the Earth?

(41) Can the telescope orbit the Earth?

In spite of the fact that in the original sentence (39) the auxiliaries and the
form of the main verb are different from those in questions (40) and (41), a
person would most likely answer *Yes* in both cases. Somehow people know
when they can or cannot answer such questions.

What about computers, then? Although clearly world knowledge plays
an important role here, the text itself may often provide sufficient data to
determine whether the information in the system's knowledge base implies
a definitive (*yes* or *no*) answer to the question. Matching the embedded *T*-
expressions described earlier is only a "rough" first step in answering a question. The next step requires a more subtle analysis of the histories attached
to the *T*-entries returned by the matcher. Additional sentence features stored
in the histories, such as tense, auxiliaries, embedding, voice, etc. allow the
system to determine whether the *T*-entries from the knowledge base and from
the question refer to the same time interval and whether the meaning of the
modal auxiliaries used in the text imply the meaning of the question asked.
For a *Yes/No*-question, for instance, there are three types of responses: *Yes,
No,* and *Unknown.* The *Unknown* category is further broken down to reflect
the reason for this response — certain types of embedding, wrong time interval, or disagreement in corresponding modal auxiliaries. All this information
is employed to answer the user's question. Our experiments show that the
system's final responses, made on the basis of this analysis, echo people's
judgments in answering such questions.

11. Spacecraft Sequencing

In this section we demonstrate the application of the START system in a real-world situation: interplanetary exploration. The scientists and engineers who plan to perform experiments aboard an interplanetary spacecraft compete for a limited amount of time and resources. Their requests are coordinated and integrated into a sequence of activities for the spacecraft through a *spacecraft sequencing* process. This process involves designing, scheduling and programming the onboard activities of a spacecraft as well as controlling its functions. It is a complex, tedious, and time consuming process which is carried out by a team of experts called the *Sequence Team*. In order to perform this task, the Sequence Team uses a set of computer programs, the *Mission Sequence Software (MSS)*. These programs do everything from simulating the geometry of the encounter to detailed constraint checking of the proposed sequence and actual command simulation and generation. Unfortunately, this software is very difficult to use. Producing MSS which is more "user friendly" could reduce the costs of a mission dramatically.

In Katz and Brooks [1987] we have identified three possible roles that the START system could play in improving the MSS performance. First, START could function as a translator from English conceptual descriptions of activities into inputs for the MSS, providing the long-needed link between early design work and integration of the sequence. Secondly, START could act as an interface between a user and the various components of the MSS during integration, allowing, but not requiring, the user to operate the MSS by means of English commands instead of the cryptic operands used presently. And finally, START could be employed as a query tool. The researchers could ask questions in English about the spacecraft or the state of its submodules and the system would analyze the query, retrieve the relevant information from the knowledge base and formulate its response also in English.

The Mars Observer Mission plans to employ small modular sequence components called Sequence Segments. These segments, which are based on the geography of Mars, will be used during mission operations to build the sequences of activities to be executed onboard. Shown below is a sample of the types of observations which will be specified in a typical segment. This document is automatically transformed by the START system into a knowledge base which incorporates the information found in the text. Following that, we show how the user obtains the information about the events which are taking place in the sequence by querying the knowledge base in English.

MOC, VIMS, TES, and PMIRR are all scientific instruments on the Mars Observer spacecraft. IR is an abbreviation for Infra-red. All other capitalized words (ALBA PATERA, ASCRAEUS MONS, TANTALUS FOSSAE, etc.) are names of targets on the planet's surface.

Mars Observer Sequence Segment
(as entered in the computer)

00:04:20 ASCRAEUS MONS is at Nadir.
00:04:35 MOC takes 5 pictures of ASCRAEUS MONS.
00:04:35 TES performs experiment number 16 on ASCRAEUS MONS.
00:04:35 PMIRR performs IR study of ASCRAEUS MONS.
00:04:35 VIMS takes 1 picture of ASCRAEUS MONS.
00:08:20 Entering CERAUNIUS FOSSAE region from south side.
00:10:25 PMIRR performs IR study of CERAUNIUS FOSSAE.
00:12:30 Exiting CERAUNIUS FOSSAE region from north side.
00:14:30 Entering TANTALUS FOSSAE region from south side.
00:14:35 MOC takes 4 pictures of TANTALUS FOSSAE.
00:16:40 +40-deg latitude crossing pulse occurs northbound.
00:17:00 Entering ALBA PATERA region from south-east side.
00:17:00 Exiting TANTALUS FOSSAE region from north side.
00:18:40 Entering ALBA FOSSAE region from south side.
00:18:40 Exiting ALBA PATERA region from north-east side.
00:18:45 Take 5 pictures of ALBA FOSSAE with MOC.
00:20:40 Entering VASTITAS BOREALIS region from south side.
00:20:40 Exiting ALBA FOSSAE region from north side.
00:22:55 Take 2 pictures of VASTITAS BOREALIS with MOC.
00:22:55 VIMS takes 1 picture of VASTITAS BOREALIS region.
00:27:05 +65-deg latitude crossing pulse occurs northbound.
00:29:10 MOC takes 3 pictures of the North-polar region.
00:29:10 Take 1 picture of North-polar region using VIMS.
00:31:15 PMIRR begins continuous IR study of North-polar region.
00:33:20 TES begins study of North-polar region.
00:34:10 Entering North-polar region.
00:37:30 +90-deg latitude crossing pulse occurs.
00:37:30 MOC takes 6 pictures of the North Pole.
00:37:30 PMIRR performs internal experiment # 21 on North Pole.
00:37:30 TES does internal experiment #11 on North Pole.
00:37:30 VIMS executes internal experiment number 1 on North Pole.
00:41:40 TES ends study of North-polar region.
00:43:45 Exiting VASTITAS BOREALIS region from north side.
00:43:45 Exiting North-polar region.
00:43:45 PMIRR ends study of North-polar region.
00:47:55 +65-deg latitude crossing pulse occurs southbound.
00:52:05 Entering UTOPIA PLANITIA from north side.
00:54:10 Use MOC to take 2 pictures of VASTITAS BOREALIS.

00:54:10 VIMS takes 1 picture of VASTITAS BOREALIS.
00:58:20 +40-deg latitude crossing pulse occurs southbound.
01:00:25 Entering NILOSYRTIS MENSAE from north side.
01:00:25 Exiting UTOPIA PLANITIA from south side.
01:01:15 Take 1 picture of NILOSYRTIS MENSAE using MOC.
01:01:15 Take 1 picture of NILOSYRTIS MENSAE with VIMS.
01:04:35 Entering NILI FOSSAE region from north side.
01:04:35 Exiting NILOSYRTIS MENSAE from south side.
01:06:40 Entering SYRTIS MAJOR PLANITIA region from north side.
01:06:40 Exiting NILI FOSSAE region from south side.
01:06:40 PMIRR begins IR study of SYRTIS MAJOR PLANITIA.
01:06:40 VIMS takes 1 picture of NILI FOSSAE.

Querying the Mars Observer Knowledge Base
(actual dialog with START)

How many pictures of ASCRAEUS MONS does MOC take?

At 00:04:35, MOC takes 5 pictures of ASCRAEUS MONS.

When is the spacecraft entering CERAUNIUS FOSSAE region from south side?

At 00:08:20, spacecraft enters CERAUNIUS FOSSAE from the south side.

When does PMIRR begin continuous IR study of North-polar region?

At 00:31:15, PMIRR begins the North-polar region's continuous IR study.

When does VIMS take pictures of VASTITAS BOREALIS region?

At 00:54:10, VIMS takes 1 picture of VASTITAS BOREALIS.
At 00:22:55, VIMS takes 1 picture of VASTITAS BOREALIS.

When is ASCRAEUS MONS at Nadir?

At 00:04:20, ASCRAEUS MONS is near Nadir.

Which instruments take pictures of ASCRAEUS MONS?

At 00:04:35, MOC takes 5 pictures of ASCRAEUS MONS.
At 00:04:35, VIMS takes 1 picture of ASCRAEUS MONS.

When does PMIRR execute the experiment #21 on North Pole?

At 00:37:30, PMIRR performs experiment21 on North Pole.

What does PMIRR do?

At 00:04:35, PMIRR performs ASCRAEUS MONS' IR study.
At 00:10:25, PMIRR performs CERAUNIUS FOSSAE'S IR study.
At 00:31:15, PMIRR begins the North-polar region's continuous IR study.
At 00:37:30, PMIRR performs experiment21.

At 00:43:45, PMIRR ends the North-polar region's continuous IR study.
At 01:06:40, PMIRR begins SYRTIS MAJOR PLANITIA'S IR study.

When do latitude crossing pulses occur?

At 00:58:20, the +40-deg latitude crossing pulse occurs southbound.
At 00:16:40, the +40-deg latitude crossing pulse occurs northbound.
At 00:47:55, the +65-deg latitude crossing pulse occurs southbound.
At 00:27:05, the +65-deg latitude crossing pulse occurs northbound.
At 00:37:30, the +90-deg latitude crossing pulse occurs.

Does the spacecraft enter the NILI FOSSAE region?

Yes—you have told me that:
At 01:04:35, spacecraft enters NILI FOSSAE from the north side.

From which side is MARS OBSERVER exiting the regions?

At 00:12:30, spacecraft exits CERAUNIUS FOSSAE from the north side.
At 00:17:00, spacecraft exits TANTALUS FOSSAE from the north side.
At 00:18:40, spacecraft exits ALBA PATERA from the north-east side.
At 00:20:40, spacecraft exits ALBA FOSSAE from the north side.
At 00:43:45, spacecraft exits VASTITAS BOREALIS from the north side.
At 01:00:25, spacecraft exits UTOPIA PLANITIA from the south side.
At 01:04:35, spacecraft exits NILOSYRTIS MENSAE from the south side.
At 01:06:40, spacecraft exits NILI FOSSAE from the south side.

When does MO enter VASTITAS BOREALIS?

At 00:20:40, spacecraft enters VASTITAS BOREALIS.

Which targets does VIMS look at?

At 01:06:40, VIMS takes 1 picture of NILI FOSSAE.
At 01:01:15, VIMS takes 1 picture of NILOSYRTIS MENSAE.
At 00:29:10, VIMS takes 1 picture of the North-polar region.
At 00:54:10, VIMS takes 1 picture of VASTITAS BOREALIS.
At 00:22:55, VIMS takes 1 picture of VASTITAS BOREALIS.
At 00:04:35, VIMS takes 1 picture of ASCRAEUS MONS.

How many pictures does MOC take?

At 00:37:30, MOC takes 6 pictures of North Pole.
At 00:29:10, MOC takes 3 pictures of the North-polar region.
At 00:54:10, MOC takes 2 pictures of VASTITAS BOREALIS.
At 00:22:55, MOC takes 2 pictures of VASTITAS BOREALIS.
At 00:18:45, MOC takes 5 pictures of ALBA FOSSAE.
At 00:14:35, MOC takes 4 pictures of TANTALUS FOSSAE.
At 00:04:35, MOC takes 5 pictures of ASCRAEUS MONS.
At 01:01:15, MOC takes 1 picture of NILOSYRTIS MENSAE.

Total number of pictures is 28.

Conclusion

We presented an overview of a natural language understanding system START. The system translates English text into a knowledge base which is used as a repository of information contained in the text. Users can retrieve this information by querying the knowledge base in English and the system will then generate the appropriate English answers. If needed, the knowledge base can provide input data to other computer systems. We introduced forward and backward S-rules which allow us to express more complex knowledge about the real world and thus expand the power of our system. A very simple process of lexical acquisition makes START truly *portable*—the system can easily be adapted to many different domains. Finally, we demonstrated the use of START in a real-world situation, in the spacecraft sequencing domain.

Acknowledgments

From the beginning Patrick H. Winston has been actively involved in the process of designing and developing START. He has also been a very active user of the system.

A number of MIT students have participated in the project, in particular, David A. Chanen, Robert Frank, Jill Gaulding, and Jeff Palmucci contributed significantly to various parts of the system.

I am grateful to Mikhail Katz and Beth Levin for their time and numerous helpful suggestions concerning this paper. In addition, useful comments were provided by Ed Barrett, Robert Frank, Jill Gaulding, Michael Kashket, David Kirsh, Thomas Marill, and William I. McLaughlin.

Robert N. Brooks from JPL developed the data for the Mars Observer mission which is used in section 11.

This paper describes research done at the Artificial Intelligence Laboratory of the Massachusetts Institute of Technology. Support for the Laboratory's Artificial Intelligence research is provided in part by the Advanced Research Projects Agency under Office of Naval Research contract N0014-85-K-0124.

References

1. A. Akmajian and F. Heny, *An Introduction to the Principles of Transformational Syntax*, MIT Press, Cambridge MA, 1975.

2. N. Chomsky, *A Theory of Syntactic Structures*, Moulton & Co., 1957.

3. R.J. Doyle, "Hypothesizing and Refining Causal Models," M.I.T. Artificial Intelligence Laboratory Memo No. 811, December 1984.

4. B. Katz, "A Three-step Procedure for Language Generation," M.I.T. Artificial Intelligence Laboratory Memo No. 599, December 1980.

5. B. Katz and R. Brooks, "Understanding Natural Language for Spacecraft Sequencing," *JBIS*, vol. 40, no. 10, 1987.

6. B. Katz and B. Levin, "Exploiting Lexical Regularities in Designing Natural Language Systems," to appear, 1988.

7. B. Katz and P.H. Winston, "A Two-way Natural Language Interface," in *Integrated Interactive Computing Systems*, edited by P. Degano and E. Sandewall, North-Holland, Amsterdam, 1982.

8. B. Levin, "Approaches to Lexical Semantic Representation," in *Automating the Lexicon*, edited by D. Walker, A. Zampolli, and N. Calzolari, to appear, 1987.

9. J. Van Oosten, "Subjects, Topics and Agents: Evidence from Property-factoring," *Proceedings of the Berkeley Linguistics Society* 6, Berkeley CA, 1980.

10. P.H. Winston, *Artificial Intelligence*, Addison-Wesley, Reading MA, 1984.

11. P.H. Winston, "Learning New Principles from Precedents and Exercises," *Artificial Intelligence*, vol. 19, no. 3, 1982.

12. P.H. Winston, T.O. Binford, B. Katz, and M.R. Lowry, "Learning Physical Descriptions from Functional Definitions, Examples, and Precedents," *National Conference on Artificial Intelligence*, Washington, D.C., 1983.

5

Using an Object-Oriented Programming Language to Create Audience-Driven Hypermedia Environments

Geri Younggren

Software Technical Publications
Apple Computer, Inc.
20525 Mariani Ave.
Cupertino, CA 95014

Hypermedia systems will continue to evolve toward an ideal environment for the communication of technical information. In the future, rather than relying on linear forms of communication, technical educators will use these new systems to create ideal environments for information delivery. These new environments will incorporate software elements from a variety of sources, including authoring systems, data base management systems, and traditional programming environments.

This paper explores how a scripting language, based on the principles of object-oriented programming, can be used in a hypermedia environment.

The Evolution of the Technical Writer

For the past 40 years, professional writers within the computer industry have been working on the problem of conveying complex technical concepts on paper. They are faced with the task of explaining multi-dimensional processes using traditional linear exposition and narrative, paired with relatively simple illustrations.

Meanwhile, education professionals working in other areas of the computer industry have approached this problem from a variety of other perspectives. Training departments design traditional standup classroom training. Instructional designers create computer-aided instruction, using tools ranging from sophisticated authoring systems to standard procedural programming languages. With the advent of relational databases and applications generators, even novice programmers have in a sense become instructional designers. These people all share a common goal: Finding a medium and a method that are optimally suited for conveying technical information.

While the writers and educators in the trenches have worked with whatever tools are available, a few visionaries have stepped back to take a look at what an ideal educational environment might look like. How can interactive educational media be adapted to meet the needs of complex reference material? One of the most interesting ideas has been the notion of hypertext — a form of "non-sequential" writing. A hypertext system allows information to be divided into "chunks," and those chunks to be linked together in any way that serves a writer's purpose — or that of the audience.

Audience-Driven Information Systems

The central theme here is the idea of representing technical information in a way that corresponds to the needs of every audience level. The structure of information must be geared toward the needs of the audience, not based on the arbitrary structure of the medium itself. Traditional books present a linear, two-dimensional path through information. Chapter-by-chapter organization offers a possibility for alternative paths through the content, but the linear paradigm remains. A hypertext system provides the possibility of many paths through content, with the system user deciding the path. The idea of hypertext can be taken one step further, to the idea of *hypermedia*. Rather than simple links between chunks of text, hypermedia becomes an interconnected net of information in all forms, from text to static graphics, animation, and other types of media that can be accessed by the computer system. Using such a system, a "reader" would have the ability to move easily between introductory and advanced material, or between text explanation and graphic representations. Novice users would be given one possible route to use, experienced users another.

What's needed is an environment for learning and accessing information that truly incorporates the idea of *n dimensions* — the ability to move in any direction that seems appropriate within the information at hand. This environment would allow a piece of information to be linked to any other piece of information — including information that resides across phone lines or on videodiscs. Such a system will allow writers and educational designers to become *information architects*: professionals who build the *n-dimensional information space*. We can think of this environment as an "information application" — a network of knowledge that can be accessed in a personal way, and annotated to suit the user's needs.

New Tools for New Times

During the next few years a variety of computer-based tools will become available that will give writers and other technical educators the ability to create systems that approach this ideal medium for teaching and referencing technical information. These systems will include elements from many of the systems mentioned above: hypertext systems, applications generators, database management, and authoring systems. One common element must be a powerful, yet easy to use, programming language for automating and extending the system. Typically, powerful application generators, database managers, and authoring systems all include some sort of programming language that allow users to customize information.

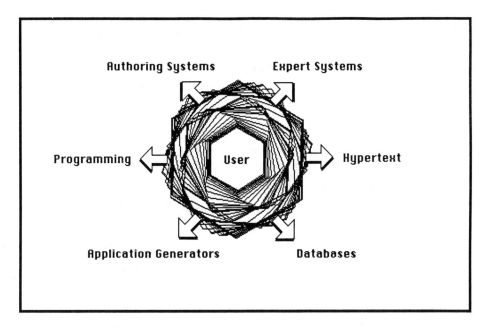

Figure 1: Contributors to the n-Dimensional Information Space

One of the goals for creating a powerful medium for designing information applications should be to make the necessary programming chores either transparent or relatively simple and painless. The goal must be to allow people to program without making them become programmers.

One of the shortcomings of sophiscated programs for education, like authoring systems, is that they isolate the subject-matter expert from the core tasks in developing educational software. Designing computer-based educational programs in the past has been a team effort, in which the design and implementation phases were carried out by different people. A well-designed system for creating information applications must find a way to allow curriculum designers, who might be unwilling to learn traditional programming techniques, the ability to create their own software.

Before we can take a look at an example of such a programming language, let's begin with a general overview of how an ideal system might be structured. The key to understanding how an object-oriented language fits into this type of system is to look at how hypertext and graphics-based systems combine to create applications uniquely suited to the concepts behind object-orientation.

When Graphics Predominate
Many of the advances in computer interfaces that benefit technical educators are based on new breakthroughs in the use of graphics. Bitmapped displays offer a wide range of graphic possibilities, including intensive use of icons and other graphic metaphors to convey information to the user. In a well-designed system, the user quickly becomes

used to the idea that processes can be represented as graphic objects. Manipulating these objects, which is a central part of the experience of learning to use the interface, becomes a natural process.

Hypermedia systems are particularly suited to graphic interfaces. Hypermedia revolves around the idea of partitioning information into discrete "chunks." Each chunk can be linked in a variety of ways to any other piece of information in the system. A chunk of information is by default defined by the size of the display on the computer running the system.

One of the original metaphors used to describe a hypertext system is the idea of 3x5 index cards. One chunk is analogous to the information that could be contained on one card. Several hypertext systems employ this metaphor as the basis of their interface. Chunks are then linked together to form a unique body of information. In a graphics-based system it's possible to move beyond the index card metaphor by using any image relevant to a subject.

For example, in Figures 2a and 2b, the same display area is treated in two very different ways. One way to contrast the information content possible using each of these images is to consider the idea that a picture could be worth a thousand links to other informational chunks The image in Figure 2a, with its obvious 3x5-card format, suggests only text-based access to information. The image in Figure 2b, with its rich graphic content, suggests a graphic index to a multi-dimensional information base represented by a variety of familiar objects (a filing cabinet, a telephone, a reference library, a calculator, and so on).

Figure 2a: The Index Card Metaphor

Figure2b: An Alternate Image.

Within a hypertext system, paths through information are defined as links between chunks. In a predominately text-based network of information, which might contain a node like the one shown in Figure 2a, a link might be presented as a word that could be selected. The process of selection would activate the link to another chunk, which would contain information pertaining to the word selected.

In a graphics-based hypermedia system, links can be defined graphically, using the idea of *buttons*. A button is any area of the screen — text or graphic — that initiates an action when a user selects it with a device, such as a mouse, controlling an on-screen pointer. In Figure 2b, any area of the image could be defined as a button.

In a simple system, buttons might serve only as links between cards. Within a system that can fully develop an n-dimensional information space, buttons would initiate a variety of actions: linking to other chunks of information, queueing animation sequences, controlling a videodisc player, playing a musical sequence. For example, in figure 2b, a button represented by the image of the world globe could, when selected, initiate a videodisc display of geographic images. Each button action would be defined, behind the scenes, by "scripts" written in an object-oriented programming language designed specifically for this purpose.

The Anatomy of a Link

The next step in understanding the place of an object-oriented programming language in a hypermedia system is to take a closer look at the button mechanism. The modified card shown in Figure 3 contains a button labeled "Go to Inventory." The task of this button is to link to another node in this information base. How does this happen?

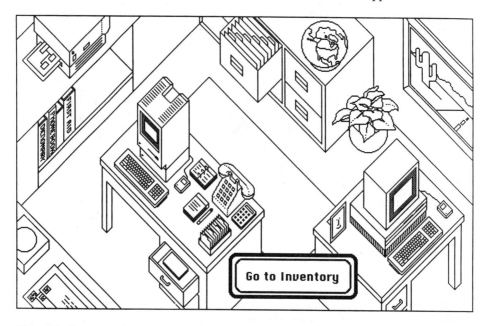

Figure 3: Inventory button

In this case, the "Go to Inventory" button, which can be viewed as an object, would contain a short program, or script, requesting a jump to the node designated as inventory. In the world of user-driven software, it is the system's job to monitor input devices continually for information from the user. In the case of a hypermedia system in which a mouse is used as an input device, pressing and releasing the mouse button, called a "mouseup," is a message to the system itself.

When the system detects a mouseup (that is, that the mouse button has been clicked), it immediately relays the mouseup message to the current object displayed on the screen. In this case, the current object is the "Go to Inventory" button because the mouse click occurred there. In the world of object-orientation, any object can contain routines that can be activated when messages are received. The "Go to Inventory" button, in this case, would have a script that would respond to the "mouseup" message. Here's what this script would look like:

```
on mouseUp
        go to card "inventory"
end mouseUp
```

Short scripts, such as the one above, are called "message handlers." This script, when activated by the mouseup message from the system, would immediately cause the "inventory" node to be displayed on the screen.

The idea of objects communicating via messages is easy to grasp, even for people who are not programmers familiar with arcane concepts of data abstraction. The beauty of a scripting language designed using a visual object-oriented paradigm is that it can be readily understood and used by people other than professional programmers.

An Aside: Must Writers Program?

Although the visual object-oriented paradigm makes scripting within such a system simpler and easier to learn than many programming languages, there is still a need for systems in which curriculum designers can design systems without writing a line of code. One of the features of a fundamentally graphics-oriented system is that the scripting itself can be completely invisible, residing as part of an object. Designers can customize their own information without being involved in coding by simply "cutting and pasting" a graphic object, along with its scripts, using standard computer graphic editing functions.

As an example, consider a designer who wants to create a link in her own set of cards to an inventory list. Given a button like the "Go to Inventory" button that is part of another set of cards, she could cut that button and paste it onto one of her own cards. This would create the link she wanted (if her inventory list were on a card named "Inventory" — an easy matter to arrange).

In the same way cards themselves could be copied along with their scripts, and the information contained on them could simply be modified. This gives even novice programmers the ability to create their own information systems with a minimum learning curve.

The convergence of hypermedia and visual programming environments will provide many of these capabilities for instructional designers. The answer to the hypothetical question, "Must writers program?" is a qualified "No."

The qualification refers to the fact that anyone working with such a system who learns how to use the system's programming capabilities will be able to create even more sophisticated and effective environments. Many of the barriers that have prevented subject-matter experts and professional technical communicators from creating interactive systems are dissolving.

Why Object-Orientation?

Visualizing a system based on a graphic interface is a good introduction to the subject of object-oriented programming. The original "object-oriented" languages — Simula, Smalltalk, and so forth, created objects on only an abstract level. The data structures used by each of these languages and the routines that operated on that data were the "objects." With the rise in popularity and the availability of graphics-oriented systems, the original concept of object-orientation has evolved to become the idea of "visual" programming. In a visual system, the objects being manipulated are often actual graphic images that are displayed on the screen. The underlying structures that implement these images are often objects in the original sense of the word.

Any language that can be loosely defined as "object-oriented" applies three primary concepts:

- It binds data and the routines that work with that data.
- It supports the idea of message passing between objects.
- It supports some form of the idea of inheritance: the ability to define objects in terms of pre-existing objects, and as part of a hierarchy of objects.

Each of these ideas is illustrated by the simple example of the "Inventory" button. In a graphics-oriented hypermedia system, each graphic object may contain its own scripts. In the example, the button contained a script that linked to a node containing inventory information. The card itself, which "contains" the button, might also own scripts that would perform other actions. The objects and the scripts they contain are inseparable.

Message-passing between objects and the system creates a flexible universe that can be truly user-driven. The system constantly looks for messages from the outside world by monitoring the user's actions. Objects can send messages to other objects, triggering sequences of events. A system constructed of objects — most of which have an actual graphic form — communicating with one another is less abstract than alternate methods of data abstraction used in non-object-oriented languages and is easier for non-programmers to envision.

The idea of inheritance comes in when we consider what might happen if the button in the example didn't contain a script that could handle the "mouseup" message. In a graphics-based object-oriented system, a logical implementation of this idea would be to make each graphic object a part of a hierarchy that would determine how messages are to be passed. In the case of the button without a script to handle a "mouseup" message, the next object in the hierarchy would be the card. If the card contained a script that could handle the "mouseup" command, that message handler would be activated when the mouse was clicked.

Object-oriented languages that embody these concepts are particularly valuable in systems that can be used to construct hypertext or hypermedia applications. Writers, or other subject-matter experts, find that languages based on a metaphor that is readily apparent through the use and manipulation of graphic objects are easier to learn and to use than are languages in which data abstraction is less concrete.

Final Requirements

In addition to implementing the features of an object-oriented language, there are three final requirements for any language that can be used easily by technical educators to create information applications:

- It must draw on English for its terminology and syntax. Any language that is designed for use by non-programmers must be easy to learn and use. Employing English as a model contributes to this design goal.

- It must incorporate the powerful control structures found in high-level languages like Pascal. Although an ideal scripting language will be English-like enough for easy use, it must use the key elements of any structured language to allow powerful applications to be built.

- It must incorporate a wide variety of built-in commands that are geared toward the creation of information applications. The key here is to provide enough power via the built-in commands to allow the designer of an application to write a short script that is nonetheless extremely powerful.

Now that we've seen an example of how a scripting language can be used to create a simple link, and become conversant with the concepts behind object-oriented lanaguages, we can look at how such a language can be used to create versions of the n-dimensional information space.

Using Scripts to Create the n-Dimensional Information Space

Each "card," or set of "cards," in the previous examples can be thought of as one node in such a space. Each button on each card can activate scripts to perform a variety of actions, each of which represents one possible branch on a learning path chosen by the user. In a system designed around a scripting language, the environment can be extended in many ways by the use of scripts. The types of actions that can be defined with scripts are limited only by the imagination of the designer. The following sections give an overview of typical ways in which one might extend a learning environment using scripts.

Navigation

One of the problems in having a large body of information to access providing an effective method by which someone can easily "navigate." Any technical writer faced with documenting a major hardware or software project has been up against the problem of creating a linear organization that serves a variety of audiences. What kind of assumptions can the author make about the knowledge the audience will bring to the subject? How can the author best serve an audience that may be composed of people with differing learning styles: people who want to scan examples, people who learn best by seeing graphic representations of conceptual material, people who have no interest in conceptual material, but who want detail-level information quickly?

There are a variety of solutions to these problems available to a writer working on a traditional book. The writer can begin the book with a detailed list of which chapters must be read, or should not be read, depending upon the reader's interests. This essentially circumvents the linear nature of books, but in an unwieldy physical way.

When a body of information can be put into a computer-based hypermedia format, these standard organizational problems disappear. A scripting language, used to implement the idea of buttons, provides an ideal method for defining paths through information — not just paths defined via an awkward spatial metaphor, but conceptual paths that correspond to the the needs of the user. In a system that has been designed to be truly audience-driven, it's possible to create an environment in which a user can move about by selecting different paths through the information, each path designed from a particular audience "viewpoint." The person looking for information will always perceive himself to be in the center of an information universe designed specifically for his needs.

How can a script language support this paradigm? A behind-the-scenes view of interconnected nodes will reveal that each node is named, in keeping with the idea of referring to objects via messages. A script writer can define an arbitrary path through these nodes by creating simple links, using the names of nodes as destinations. Each node would have a button that, when activated, would jump to the next node in that conceptual path. The script for such a button would look something like this:

```
on mouseUp
    go to card "overview 6"
end mouseUp
```

In this case, the button would reside on a card called "overview 5," which would be the fifth in the overview series. The button would immediately link to the next card in the series. This example is quite linear, and assumes that the path thorough overview information is defined as a strict sequence of nodes. But this is simply a naming convention. It would be just as simple to create an overview path by linking to nodes that are already part of another path. An analogous idea would be to create a book by taking the introductory paragraphs of each chapter and binding them together.

The important idea here is that a script language can provide the author with true random access. Links can be defined in any way that suits the needs of the audience, as opposed to the nature of the medium.

For a script language to be useful as a tool for navigation, someone browsing through information must be able to use the language on-the-fly to move about between nodes. This use of the language brings us back to the idea of message passing, and how that concept is implemented in an information system.

Not only must the designer of an information application be able to create buttons that perform particular actions — for example, providing immediate links between nodes — but the user must have access to the language to pass messages to the system. This idea can be seen in the use of a "message box": an input convention that someone browsing through information can use to navigate through the system, by passing commands directly to the system itself.

In the previous example we saw how a button script would use the "Go" command to link to another node in the system. In a system that uses the "message box" concept to allow message passing to the system, a user would be able to directly send the "Go" command to the system, and specify any location within the current set of information.

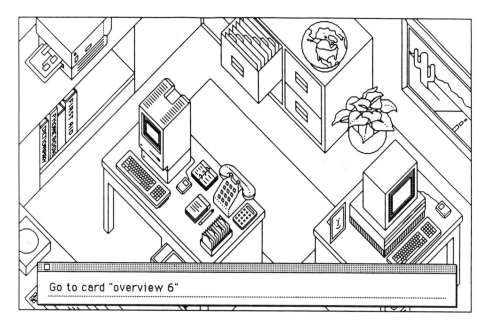

Go to card "overview 6"

Figure 4: Message Box

The idea of a message box suggests another navigational use of a script language: providing the user with the ability to exit the current information application, move to a different program, and then return to the information system. A built-in command, "Open," might be included for this use. A typical scenario might find a user browsing thorough information while performing a particular task in another environment. For example, a programmer might go to an information application to find a particular piece of information. When she found the information she wanted, she could use the message box to issue an "Open" command, which would take her to her software development environment.

Providing a method that allows the user to use the scripting language for navigation in essence gives the user the ability to define her own optimal learning experience. It also provides a method that can be used to integrate information applications into the wider world of software.

Animation

Another technique that adds new dimensions to an information environment is the use of animation to illustrate concepts, or to simply add variety and interest value to the presentation of information. A script language can be used to create simple animation sequences, by automatically displaying a sequence of cards, or by moving entities within cards. Another possible feature that can be used for animation is that of "visual effects": the way in which the visual transition is made when moving from one card to the next. A script language that supports built-in visual effects brings the power of animation to anyone who can write a simple script.

Figure 5 shows a set of cards that display in sequence to create a simple animation. The action begins when the user clicks the "Start Orientation" button. The other four cards are then displayed, one after another, using built-in visual effects.

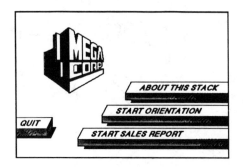

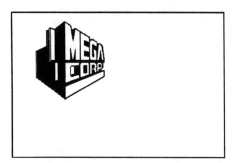

Figure 5: Cards Displayed in Animation Sequence

Here is the script that prompts the animation sequence. Notice the use of built-in commands to create visual effects, paired with automatic linking using the "Go" command:

```
on mouseUp
    visual effect dissolve fast
    go to card "second"
    visual effect dissolve fast
    go to card "third"
    visual effect dissolve fast
    go to card "fourth"
    visual effect iris open slow
    go to card "fifth"
end mouseUp
```

In addition to adding simple entertainment value, animation can be used to demonstrate processes and interrelationships in a way that two-dimensional illustrations cannot. A graphic overview can be assembled, component by component, on the screen. Advanced users can view detailed processes. Animation provides another method for customizing paths through information to the needs of individual users.

Extending the Environment with a Videodisc
One of the most exciting possibilities for designers using a hypermedia environment is that of driving a videodisc player. The use of a scripting language that supports this type of peripheral means that a designer can integrate information from a videodisc into an information application as easily as integrating any other node that would normally appear on the computer display.

Figure 6 is an example of a node that would act as a control panel for a videodisc player.

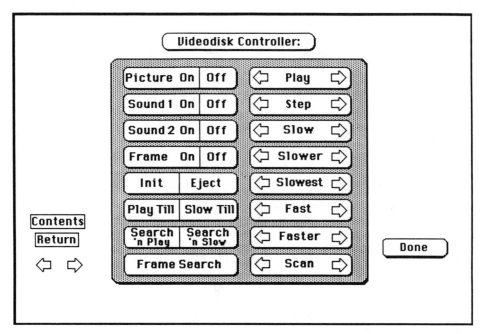

Figure 6. Videodisc Control Node

Each control illustrated is a button that contains a script that performs the action specified. The scripts that would activate these buttons would not have to be elaborate, if the scripting language were customized to include built-in commands to support this peripheral. Rather than implementing the actual interface to the videodisc, the designer working with the system would approach the videodisc player as simply another tool available through the scripting language. The designer would be able to write additional scripts to access information from a videodisc and integrate it into an information application. Each frame on the videodisc would appear to the system as simply another node, and could be accessed with the same combination of the "Go" command and a "card name" that we saw in an earlier example.

Adding Sound

Another useful extension to an information environment is sound. A script language that supports sound gives the designer of an information application the ability to use sound in a variety of ways: as a simple cue device, to add interest value, to augment an animation sequence, or to provide information via human voice simulation.

This is a script that illustrates the use of built-in sound commands within a system. This script simulates the sound of a harpsichord playing:

```
on mouseUp
    play "Harpsichord" tempo 380 b3 c#4 d e f# g a#3 g4 f# e d c# d r f# r b r c# r b r a#
end mouseUp
```

The name "Harpsichord" refers to the data used to simulate the actual sound of the instrument. The data is stored in a disk file that is accessible to the information application. "Tempo" is a parameter that specifies the speed at which the notes will be played. The notation for specifying notes is fairly simple: "b3" is a b in the octave above the middle (4 specifies the middle octave). The time value for each note can be specified after the octave: "c#5q" specifies a c sharp quarter note in the octave below the middle octave.

Technical Documentation Meets the n-Dimensional Information Space

Given an ideal authoring system that incorporates the features we've described, how would today's technical writer design reference material for a new computer system? What part would a scripting language play in the design and implementation of such a system?

The first step in designing information to be presented on such a system would be to define the potential audiences for the material. Traditionally, multiple audiences meant multiple volumes. Using a computer-based system based on a scripting language, one information base can serve the needs of several audiences. Rather than focus on partitioning information into books, a designer working with this system can focus on how to best serve the needs of each audience, using tools described earlier.

Because the system is graphics based, a logical first step might be to design an overview block diagram of the system. Each component could be described with text, and then animation could be used to place each component on the screen to create the complete picture.

Such an overview diagram might be a jumping-off point for audiences with many perspectives. A person who wanted an overview of all system components might choose to proceed from a hardware block diagram to an introduction to system software components. Another person might see the hardware diagram as the first step to an in-depth understanding of the system, and would follow a different path through ever more detailed explanation of the hardware components.

Each of these audiences could be easily served by using the scripting facilities. A button marked "In-Depth Hardware Information" would be the first step on a path designed for a particular audience.

One of the paths designed for a systems programmer might lead to a node that included an animation sequence illustrating data flow through memory. Or a data communications engineer might find an animation that illustrated various information channels through particular network configurations.

Another overview path might lead to a video presentation of interviews with the engineers responsible for designing the system to be documented. A node that provided information about a particular feature might also include a button that lead to background implementa- tion information. A video presentation by the engineer who designed the feature might provide additional insight and data for a programmer attempting to use the system.

Each of these scenarios would be implemented using scripts like the ones shown in earlier sections. A writer who had learned how to write these simple programs would be in a position to design an information system that incorporated a variety of media and provided a variety of perspectives for the users of the system.

Summary
The use of tools like object-oriented scripting languages within hypermedia systems provide technical educators with the opportunity to greatly enhance the training and reference materials they design. As tools evolve that give writers capabilities once available only through programming, the resulting information applications will use the techniques described in this paper to meet the needs of audiences of all levels.

Acknowledgments
The concepts discussed in this paper have been illustrated using the HyperCard™ program and the HyperTalk™ script language by Apple Computer, Inc. Figure 1 was created by Jody Larson. Screen displays shown in other figures are copyright 1987 by Apple Computer, Inc. and are reprinted with their permission. Special thanks to Bill Atkinson, creator of HyperCard, and Dan Winkler, creator of HyperTalk. Thanks to Alan Kay for the idea of the "n-dimensional information space."

References

Apple Computer, Inc. *HyperCard User's Guide.* Cupertino, CA: Apple Computer, Inc., 1987.

Apple Computer, Inc. *HyperCard Script Language Guide.* Cupertino, CA: Apple Computer, Inc., 1987.

Conklin, Jeff. "A Survey of Hypertext." MCC Technical Report Number STD-356-86, October 23, 1986 (Microelectronics and Computer Technology Corporation, Austin, Texas).

Finzer, William, and Laura Gould. "Programming by Rehearsal." *Byte Magazine.* June 1986.

Goodman, Danny. *The Complete HyperCard Handbook.* New York: Bantam Books, 1987.

Kaehler, Ted, and Dave Patterson. *A Taste of Smalltalk.* New York: W. W. Norton & Company, 1986.

Nelson, Ted. *Literary Machines,* fifth edition. Swarthmore, PA: Theodor Holm Nelson (author), 1983.

Young, Jeffrey S. "Hypermedia." *Macworld*, March 1986.

6

Hypertext: A Way of Incorporating User Feedback into Online Documentation

Patricia Ann Carlson

Humanities
Rose-Hulman Institute of Technology
Terre Haute, Indiana 47803

We are seeing an increasing trend toward online documentation. However, because of the change in medium, the lack of fully-understood design principles, and in many cases the sheer amount of information being integrated, user overload in online systems is a significant concern. The traditional solution to this problem of presenting complex information in a timely fashion is to design a consistent display format and to employ standard control commands. At a deeper level, however, questions of information integration become issues of information engineering and the nature of knowledge structures. The hypertext concept considers a body of knowledge as a database--potentially, a highly organized, compressed structure of richly interconnected "chunks"--and allows for flexible indexing and retrieval by implementing a "smart" interface (a programmable "idea processing" mechanism). Hypertext as the backbone for an online documentation system permits advanced design features--such as enhanced functionality, customized views, and improved knowledge synthesis and representation--which, in turn, increase the user's ability to interact productively with information. Using a hypertext approach to online documentation also provides the documentation manager with a set of "tools" to facilitate prototyping a document, profiling an audience, and analyzing both the logic structure and content of an online user support system.

1. Introduction

The industry trend is toward more online documentation, and many installations have begun converting offline materials to online. However, simply putting existing text online is not satisfactory because accessibility and ease-of-use are seriously impaired [4]. Two general approaches help to overcome these limitations. First, design and rewrite the manual text so that substance, structure, style, and syntax meet the requisites of electronic presentation. Second, treat existing documentation as a database and develop sophisticated retrieval mechanisms allowing the user to access appropriate portions of the text in a timely manner.

This paper describes a hybrid of the two methods--based on the concept of *hypertext* (or document database) and suggests a scenario for implementing a user interface which simulates the functionality of a book while collecting meaningful information for revision and restructuring of the text in the database. This type of system documentation allows for individual tailoring of a document by a specific user or group of users. In addition, the approach offers the documentation manager some of the design concepts used in software engineering and some of the management tools available to a system manager. For example, a hypertext systems provides the capability to "field test" an online document. Secondly, the documentation manager can "profile" a large user community to determine critical needs and areas for improvement in system support. Finally, better management "tools"--such as online questionnaires, automated collection of user responses, and comparative data on usage patterns-- help to develop and maintain quality online support materials.

2. Hypertext and Individualized Interfaces

Ideas on how to transform paper documentation libraries to electronic support systems vary. A relatively simple approach is to use the word processor files from the paper delivery system and run them through a reformatting program to create screen presentation. A more complex approach--known generically as hypertext--makes use of sophisticated database management techniques and requires the information designer to deconstruct the paper text into a collection of fragments embedded in a knowledge base which can then be accessed by specially designed retrieval software [31].

"Hypertext"--a model based on the assumption that human idea processing occurs through association--receives increasing attention as a framework for effective and efficient communication of knowledge [12, 13]. A hypertext system uses electronic capabilities to overcome the limitations of the linear nature of printed text. Paper text (or flat text) provides only two dimensions of information processing: linear and hierarchical. (See Fig. 1.)

LINEAR TEXT

HIERARCHICAL INFORMATION FLOW

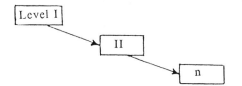

Figure 1: 2-D Information Processing

A hypertext system more closely models the deep structure of human idea processing by creating a network of nodes (modules) and links (webs), allowing for three-dimensional navigation through a body of information. (See Fig. 2.) Modules are defined as pools of information collected in one anthology, labelled or typed, and electronically stored as nodes in a database. Webs consist of the pattern or links among the nodes. The links can be predefined by the hypertext system designer, or the user(s) can establish the links as part of walking through the information domain [12, 13].

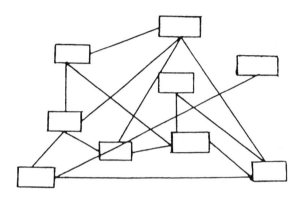

Figure 2: 3-D Information Processing

By treating text as a collection of nodes--interconnected by links, and displayed as windows on a screen--the information designer adds layers of functionality and flexibility to the traditional, paper-based method of text delivery. For example, information may be ordered hierarchically or in association networks, based on the reader's preference or upon the requisites of the task being supported. Customized filters can preprocess information based on level of detail desired or on specified content. Readers can quickly navigate through a large body of material using graphic browsers which show ideas as icons or as block diagrams [39, 65, 66, 67]. Additionally, the "webs" or patterns of links established among the nodes provide researchers with a "trace" device for analyzing how individuals (or groups in a particular user community) use documentation [61, 64].

2.1 The Rhetoric of Hypertext

The rhetoric of conventional, linear text has a long history. The Greeks (as exemplified by Aristotle's <u>Rhetoric</u>) made careful, analytical studies both of the art and science of composition and delivery. While the teaching of classical rhetoric may have waned over the years, an accepted set of conventions about style, syntax, and structure still exists. For example, even though there is not complete agreement, we operate with a relatively similar concept of what constitutes a paragraph.

Modern rhetoric and discourse analysis have produced refined theories of writing (encoding) and reading (decoding) based on the principles of cognitive psychology. Applications of this knowledge are apparent in the design of documentation and instructional materials. User/task-orientation, structured writing and text-as-diagram, the function of advanced organizers, multiple layers of explanation, and improved access devices are but a few ways in which research has influence modern information design [32, 33].

No such "rhetoric" exists for hypertext. To the contrary, it would seem that few of the notions of classical rhetoric an be used in constructing a hyperdocument. Important questions emerge and can be answered only as the profession gains more experience with specific hypertext environments. For example:

o Modularization: A true hypertext is a database made up of information-rich "chunks." Determining boundaries and slicing text into sets and subsets require knowledge of the information domain. Additionally, since nodes may be "threaded" into different paths, they must be reusable, requiring research into the requisites (as well as the effects) of free-standing, rhetorically "neutral" prose.

o Node Size: Most theoreticians of hypertext feel that a node should consist of a single concept or idea. This fine-grained approach improves the potential to thread the same node into different paths. However, it also creates many nodes, requires more keystroking to access information, and increases the likelihood that the user will get lost in the system. This trade-off between node size and ease of navigation needs to be examined in a case study.

o Composition Guidelines: Traditional rhetoric considers the sentence and the paragraph as the basic units of composition. Answers to the issues of modularization and node size may help to isolate the basic units in the rhetoric of hypertext; however, further analysis and description of prose in hypertext systems must take into account the medium of display. In short, the "grammar" of hypertext intersects issues of screen design and user interface.

2.2 Application Issues

Additional questions have to do with applications and implementation.

o Minimal Requisites: The basic elements of hypertext are nodes and links (chunks of text threaded together, either on an ad hoc bases by the user(s) or in predefined patterns by information designers). However, is the presence of a database and a retrieval mechanism enough to constitute a hypertext system? How much functionality must the system incorporate in order to reach critical mass? Additionally, if the chunks have been rigorously threaded in predefined webs, has the hypergraph (the pattern of links between the nodes) become just another form of flat text processing?

o Effects of Preprocessed Text: Proponents of hypertext point out that the hypergraph captures the deep structure of a body of information. This is especially useful in situations where the information is complex or where the relationship of its parts either is not clear or cannot be agreed upon. However, is hypertext a useful approach when the web (or knowledge structure) of a text has already been defined (as in, for example, a set of procedural instructions)?

o Variations in Task Environment: Hypertext helps in dealing with open-ended problems where creativity, spontaneity, and large bodies of information are involved, but how useful is hypertext to a task domain where documentation is intended for cueing/prompting purposes (such as it is in maintenance manuals)?

o Optimal Time for Integration: As the above questions suggest, not all treatments of documentation as a database need result in a genuine hyperdocument. The advantages of hypertext are flexibility (especially the ability to create individual views of a body of information) and functionality (for example, rapid traversal through pools of data, marking text for different levels of user, and increased potential for knowledge synthesis and improved representation). However, not all applications require all these features. At what point does the additional functionality become a useful dimension? A what point does the increased power offset the cost of development and the overhead of implementation?

3.0 Implementation Scenario

Because so many issues regarding hyperdocuments are still unsettled, the following scenario suggests an incremental approach using three stages of development. Not all transitions to online documentation will include each stage. This paper will present them in a sequential fashion, but it is entirely possible that a specific implementation may remain at stage one or that another implementation will begin at stage two. Appropriate levels are determined by the nature of the system, the needs of the audience, the characteristics of the environment, and the purpose of the document.

The basic model for an online document consists of two parts: the text (which should be treated as a database) and an assistance processor (a program which determines what "view" the user has of the information in the database). The database must be a collection of texts that have meaningful boundaries of sets and subsets and logical relationships among elements. Taking the text of a hardcopy manual and refining it into a database which is a highly organized, compressed structure of small, richly interconnected "chunks" is a problem in rhetoric. On the other hand, designing a retrieval mechanism for effective access to and management of the text is a software issue.

The three phases of implementation described in the following segments depend on simultaneously creating smarter interfaces and improving the rhetorical quality and internal logic of the text files. Stage One emulates a hypertext application, but uses a sequential file rather than a true database structure [24, 30]. Stage Two adds more sophistication to the basic model by upgrading the retrieval mechanism to include "individual views" and a true database representation of the text. Also, tracking procedures are added to help collect information on how easily people can use and understand the online documents. Stage Three builds on the insights learned from the previous stage. Guided by a clear model for both the usage patterns and the information structure of an online document, the designers can employ "knowledge engineering" strategies to further improve information delivery.

3.1 Stage One: A Pseudo-Hypertext

This stage takes a sequential file--such as the tape of a pre-existing document-- and automates the information in a hierarchical tree, creating a usable online document with a limited amount of restructuring of the paper text. The designer of the screen display writes the file exactly as it is to appear on the display frame when the manual is read at the terminal. In addition to text, the file contains "directives" (gen-code) which allow the retrieval program to treat the screen images as nodes in a database [14].

Features and functionality are minimal. Only two "views" of the information base are available: an inverted tree structure and an index of keywords. However, the system frees the user from the strictures of linear text and page numbers. In addition, support utilities aid in creating and maintaining text. The system provides a reasonable user interface to online materials at a fairly low cost in terms of system resources.

3.2 Stage Two: Individual Views and User Response

Every document, whether it be offline or online, has three features which determine user satisfaction:

o Contents: What Does the Document Say?   Incorrect, ambiguous, out-of-date, or inappropriate content obviously lessens the effectiveness of the manual for a user community.

o Representation: How is the Information Organized and Stored? Poor structure (weak internal logic, missing segments, inadequate sectioning and sequencing) limits the document's usefulness.

o View: How is the Data Accessed? Insufficient or confusing access points caused by poor information mapping (for example, ineffective table of contents, inadequate indexing, illogical chapter breaks, lack of segment headings, flawed paragraph patterns) inhibit the user's ability to find and understand information in a timely fashion.

The aspects of content, representation, and sequencing designed into the document to benefit all users constitutes a "generic view" of the information. Varying degrees of effort may have gone into assessing the needs or the user community and designing the document to fit the resultant profile. However, a generic view remains just that: a fixed text whose structure and substance are intended to meet the needs of the majority of the user, most of the time.

3.2.1 Interface Enhancements: Individualized "Views"

Currently, "documentation" tends to be synonymous with the "generic view" concept. In other words, in both offline and online support, the favored approach is to design a single document for use by many. Collecting user feedback and tailoring documents for individuals are recognized as useful activities, but the methodology for each--in its current state--is ad hoc, costly, or ineffective [5, 30].

Nevertheless, individuals--especially those with a long history of learning from paper documents such as textbooks--have developed a number of strategies and tactics for establishing an "individual view" to a generic document.

Notice that your own techniques for manipulating paper text are dependent upon the text and task and that you have various methods of perusal--e.g. thumbing, glancing, skimming, and browsing. In addition, text is made more accessible through individual markup techniques--e.g. writing in the margins or on the end papers, making corrections, summaries, or mnemonic devices, commentary, conversion of prose to tables and graphs, lists, cross-references, key terms, diagrams, and indexing aids. Placing bookmarks or "dog ears" and marking trails in various ways help to sequence and reference materials in a personalized pattern. Intuiting "place" in a body of information through various visuo-spatial cues improves navigation and access. And, as a last example, we all make use of the subtle psychological benefit of tactile contact with paper documentation (a form of reification not yet fully researched).

Furthermore, modern methods of document design greatly increase ease-of-use, timeliness of information, and accessibility in a paper delivery system. For example, modern design techniques allow for alternatives to the paragraph as the basic unit of prose (e.g. structured writing and other devices of information compression). Improved printing and graphics technology, including the emergent capabilities of desktop publishing promise additional benefits for paper documentation. More sophisticated techniques for indexing, referencing, and branching provide rapid pathways and multiple tracks through paper text. Integrated graphics which signal knowledge structure (e.g. visual table of contents and logos as signposts) serve as landmarks and aid in navigation. Increased sensitivity to matching a presentation to user needs (e.g. task orientation versus reference function) enhances the ease-of-use of hardcopy.

Any electronic information delivery system must be able --at a very minimum-- to duplicate the capabilities provided by the combination of an experienced reader and a well-designed text. Anything less degrades the system: leaving, at best, an electronic page-turner; at worst, even less than the paper version. Furthermore, in order to justify abandoning the conventional method and medium, an electronic system should offer improvements, such as increased flexibility, reduction in storage, and convenient document development and maintenance.

As a framework for a hypertext application, the designer should consider the natural analogy between the two elements of the traditional paper system (skilled reader and structured text) and the two elements of a hypertext system (assistance processor and "designed"--or modularized--text). Hypertext's innate flexibility and ability to support individualized views allow the system to duplicate the skilled reader's capabilities (both strategic and tactical) for coping with paper text. "Trails" are marked automatically; markup techniques are electronically supported; and rapid traversal from node to node is accommodated by the web of the hyperdocument.

Hypertext also increases the functionality over paper-based information delivery systems in particular applications environments. For example, maintenance procedures for military aircraft require that all systems on the unit be shut down prior to repair work. The check list for stabilizing the craft is in alphabetical order, which aids in information control and update for the author but does not reflect the task sequence that would facilitate moving about the plane. With a database document, the sequence can be altered to accommodate the situation or personal preference. For instance, a particular aircraft mechanic may prefer to work by categories--electronics, hydraulics, and the like. Another may prefer to complete tasks based upon which specific set of tools are needed. Hypertext allows the user to interact with documentation in a way that best suits his needs, at any given time.

Along these same lines, a hyperdocument can support various constituencies in the user community (e.g., technicians, trainers, documentation managers, systems vendors, etc.). Additionally, a hyperdocument can accommodate modes (types of information delivered--technical, logistical, training), facilitate graceful transition among modes, and integrate into an easily used synthesis (meta modes).

As an example, management information systems (MIS) collect data from many sources. For this data to become useful information, it must be assimilated into meaningful patterns. A hypertext system allows for both hierarchical and non-hierarchical organizations of unstructured information. The same data may even exist in alternative structures, depending on the needs of the user. Also, global views (such as graphic browsers which visually present the web of links in any given hyperdocument) aid in the top-down processing of information and increase comprehension. Such "meta-views" of data help the user to see logic patterns in a body of information and thus more easily assimilate meaning.

Equally significant is that fact that a hyperdocument points toward the integration of expert systems and other AI functions. Even now, the designer may incorporate--perhaps on a rudimentary level--filters based on content analysis and navigational devices based on logic representations. For example, if the links between nodes can be typed, the user may call up a specified category, and thus "view" the data through a pre-established filter (e.g. all links attached after a certain date and by a specific individual). Other enhancements to a hyperdocument include procedural attachments (where executable executable becomes the content of a node) and "nested" webs (where a node becomes a gateway into another knowledge structure).

One feature of a hypertext deserves special notice: the user can annotate sections of a document by creating a new node and linking it to the appropriate portion of the text. This commentary could include notes to the general user community, to the document designer, or to the user himself. In addition, a "mail" function allows the user to send a message directly to the document manager or to the document's author(s). In this way, content errors can be identified and corrected; the author of the document has immediate access to user responses; and the documentation manager can collect data on which materials (and even which portions of materials) need a revision in the "general view."

While the features of the tailored interface duplicate the functionality of a paper text, the results are more than an "electronic book" [63]. User satisfaction improves because of greater control over the environment; increased speed of access; positive contribution to the general view; outlet for frustration; incremental usability. Higher order features of the system include the capabilities to effectively "field test" a document and to profile a specific user community.

3.2.2 Document Prototyping

"Prototyping" is a well-know concept in the development of software systems. Software engineers attest to the use of pre-release versions of a system. In particular, a "skeleton" version of a system provides a concrete conceptualization and demonstrates a new system's ability to function and grow. Additionally, through prototyping, end users can interact with the system and suggest changes to the interface (screen design) or to session management before the costs of reconfiguration make redesign impossible.

Yet "Prototyping"--or field testing--is not widely used in the development of hardcopy documentation for two reasons. First, testing is very expensive and lengthens the production cycle. Second, the methods now used for collecting user response are neither valid nor reliable. Readability scales are questionable as to what they actually measure. Protocol analysis (case studies of how a text is read and used) are time consuming, expensive, and idiosyncratic. User questionnaires generally have low return rates. And Beta test sites tend to have too intimate a relationship with the software developer to say that the users are learning the system through the documentation [30].

Document prototyping is especially appropriate for present-day trends in online documentation. Many installations attempt simply to put the content of their paper library online without an adequate assistance processor. This is a natural tendency, considering that most new manuals are prepared using word processors, so the text is available on diskette or tape. While this approach may improve the site's ability to update and distribute manuals, it can also severely decrease access and functionality.

The product of this approach is--in essence--an online reflection of an offline document. And the electronic support is only as good as the hardcopy's organization. Many paper manuals--from the user's point of view--have unrefined, flawed, or illogical categorization of major text segments and are not adequately indexed. These limitations make the electronic reflection far too "grainy" to give a view to the fine points of the information. By automating the collection of user response to these first-cut implementations, the document designer can achieve the same benefits from "prototyping" as does the software developer.

A hypertext approach allows the documentation manager to collect and incorporate user feedback in two ways. First, the mail messages are a source of direct commentary. Second, the documentation manager has access to all the individualized "views," as well as a set of software tools to analyze and to construct a composite from these idiosyncratic interfaces. After constructing such an overview and determining areas of user consensus, the manager can--at announced intervals--revise either the general view, the text in the database, or both, to better suit the user community. In essence, responses from the user community generate the manual in its final form.

3.2.3 User Community Profiles

Like prototyping, user profiles are not a new notion in the development of software. Human engineering experts predict what problem-solving capabilities a user will bring to a piece of software and attempt to match the end user interface with these abilities. For most documentation projects, at least some effort goes into assessing the audience for the manual. However, the larger and the more dispersed the user community the more likely that the assessment will be based on intuition, political pressures, or the more vocal in the user group, rather than real data. Yet a reasonably accurate profile of the entire user community is essential for effective documentation.

Stage two contains programs for automatically and unobtrusively collecting statistical data on a large or dispersed user community and for abstracting information from this data. In addition, these analytical tools can be constructed so that the documentation manager uses the whole array or defines a particular subset to focus on. Much in the way a system manager collects data on general system usage, particular application packages, error logs, and the like, the documentation manager can find out which portions of the document are accessed most frequently over a given period of time, number of users, "paths" most frequently taken through the document, and the like. From this, the manager can determine how, when, and why the user community consults the documentation.

In addition to this automatic gleaning of data, other information could be collected by a direct appeal to the user. Brief questionnaires at the beginning of a session could ask for a self-report on level of expertise, type of information sought, success in finding the answer, general satisfaction, and the like. Or, the entire user community could be polled to determine central questions of revision and reorganization. And, as a third illustration of this direct collection of data, small experiments could be set up so that users who "visited" certain portions of a text previously identified as difficulty would be asked to select the best from a set of revised versions.

3.3 Stage Three: Approximation of an Expert System

Breakthroughs in artificial intelligence and the increasing feasibility of "modeling" problem-solving strategies in a specific domain will propel online documentation into the realm of expert systems in the future. Such growth, however, cannot occur overnight. Nor can it take place in an uncontrolled fashion. Enhancements in the retrieval mechanism (the document processor) must be in response to the facility's specific needs--not driven by available technology. Improvements in the database (the manual's text) must be in response to the user community's needs--not solely determined by the document's author(s).

This three-part scenario facilitates incremental growth, aids in establishing development policy, provides a mechanism for evaluating effectiveness, matures with the local environment, and keeps pace with advances in computing technology.

The power and effectiveness of electronic user support has yet to be realized by the industry. However, with guidance and development, online support will surpass its current model--that of an "electronic book." Improvements predictable in the near-term include--

o Query-in-depth capabilities: Levels of help allow the user to access additional online assistance beyond that provided in the first query. For example, a system might be devised so that the user enters "?" to get an expanded version of a quick reference. A second "?" would produce a full page from the manual. Yet another "?" would give an information rich tutorial [53].

o Enhanced navigational aids: Chaining through an online document becomes difficult because the reader is apt to lose the way. Additional "tracking" devices--such as landscape markers, graphical representations of knowledge structure (for example, visual table of contents and decision tables), and other visuo-spatial coding help the user to maneuver through a text.

Far-term advancements include:

o Contextual or fluid assistance: Eventually, online support will have enough built-in intelligence to offer system-initiated assistance. Sophisticated interfaces will monitor frequency of use, patterns of use, expertise, and types of errors to determine when documentation should be consulted and at what level.

o Question-answering capabilities: Patterned after an expert system, the interface allows users ask a question--in natural language-and receive either a specific answer or a dynamically generated listing of places in the documentation where the topic is treated.

4.0 Conclusion

Planning the graceful transition from offline to online user documentation is exacerbated by the lack of proven implementation models, the changing environment, and the complexity of user expectations. Clearly, when making decisions for online support systems, a manager should look for a dynamic rather than a static approach. A hypertext system has the advantage of not only tolerating change, but of actually encouraging development toward the optimal system--based upon available resources, facility requirements, and user needs.

Beginning with a baseline system--a reflection of the printed document--the package allows individuals to structure their own interface to a document. In essence, users can create their own document and remedy whatever flaws they see in the generic manual. This feature--no matter how much the environment, the system, or the facility changes--provides an immediate and individualized solution to whatever problem a user perceives in the online support. Perhaps more importantly, the approach ensures a controlled evolution of online support, guided by the responses of individual users and by the informed judgment of the documentation manager.

Through the individualized "view" feature, users can duplicate the functionality of paper documentation. Old patterns of learning, reading, and reviewing need not be discarded because the documentation medium has changed. In fact, these cognitive strategies can be enhanced by the automatic features of an electronic medium. Users face far fewer frustrations in making the transition from paper to screen because they have a mechanism both for controlling the document and for fashioning a manual suitable to their individualized needs.

"User response" can be defined as the various strategic and tactical procedures readers come up with to deal with a document. These may include "artifacts" (e.g. user-written performance aids, summary sheets, and notes) and "local legend" (e.g. grapevine commentary on locating information). Currently, a very small percentage of this feedback ever gets collected, collated, or used by the "official" channels of communication. Automating response mechanisms increases the likelihood that this crucial feedback becomes a part of the considerations that guide the revision process.

In fact, the "bootstrapping" model for automated user response sees revision as a recursive process of incorporating user-generated improvements into the general document. For example, since gripe forms are automated, complaints are more likely to be transmitted and thereby acted upon. Updates to the general view can then be made, resulting in an immediate improvement for the entire user community. Collection of the personal views for a particular document over a course of time enables an unbiased assessment of the content, representation, and entry points of the material.

The biggest timesaving bonus may result from the collection of personal indices. Rather than having to construct from scratch the chunking and indexing of the volume, the document maintainer can, in a sense, put a "raw" document into the system and let the users do the necessary refining. Parts which are heavily used will be thoroughly indexed, providing immediate benefits to new users. This "incremental usability" lies in stark contrast to a dumb keyword index because the former indexes not only words but ideas, which no current automated system approaches.

Although the concept of hypertext was discussed by H.G. Wells (1938) and more fully expounded by Vannevar Bush, President Roosevelt's Science Advisor (1945), the term itself originated with Ted Nelson (1974). Despite their radically different intellectual backgrounds, all three men describe hypertext as an electronic means for enhancing primary categories of idea processing:

o Reading: goal-oriented (information seeking) navigation through a large, unstructured library of information or casual browsing through a pool of text and graphics.

o Annotating: recording ideas dynamically generated while reading text (including critiquing); explicating difficult passages; storing user-produced mnemonic aids; communicating with other users.

o Collaborating: electronic conferencing and/or multiple authoring of complex documents.

o Learning: accommodating varying learning styles, varying speeds of ingesting materials, and personalized structuring of bodies of information.

We are now seeing only the beginning of hypertext reflected in commercial products, but it seems safe to predict that the notion of three-dimensional idea processing will capture the imagination of the software industry the way top-down programming dominated software engineering a few years ago. In a hypertext survey report done for MCC, Jeff Conklin asks his readers to ". . . come away from this paper excited, eager to try using hypertext for yourself, and with the sense that you are there at the beginning of something big, something like the invention of the wheel, but something that still has enough rough edges that no one is really sure that it will fulfill its promise" [13].

References

[1]   R. M. Akscyn and D. L. McCracken, "Zog and the *USS Carl Vinson*: Lessons in Systems Development," Technical Report CMU-CS-84-127, Department of Computer Science, Carnegie-Mellon University, Pittsburgh, PA., March 1984.

[2]   M. L. Bariff and E. J. Lusk, "Cognitive and Personality Test of the Design of Management Information Systems," *Management Science*, Vol. 23, April 1977, pp. 820-829.

[3]   S. J. Boies, "User Behavior on an Interactive Computer System," IBM *Systems Journal*, Vol. 13, 1974, pp. 253-257.

[4]   Annette Norris Bradford, "Conceptual Differences Between the Display Screen and the Printed Page," *Technical Communication*, Vol. 31, Third Quarter 1984, pp. 13-16.

[5]   Bob Bramwell, "BROWSE: An On-line Manual & System Without an Acronym," ACM SIGDOC *Asterisk*, Vol. 9, December 1983, pp. 7-11.

[6]   R. J. Brochmann, "A Structural Paradigm for Representing Knowledge," Doctoral Dissertation, Harvard University, 1979.

[7]   Vannevar Bush, "As We May Think," *Atlantic Monthly*, Vol. 176:1, July 1945, pp. 101-108.

[8]   Vannevar Bush, "Memex Revisited," in *Science is Not Enough.* V. Bush and William Morrow, Eds. 1967, pp. 63-88.

[9]   J. R. Carbonell, "On Man-Computer Interaction: A Model and Some Related Issues," IEEE *Transactions on Systems Science and Cybernetics*, Vol. SSC-5, January 1969, pp. 16-26.

[10] D. D. Chamberline, "SEAUEL 2: A Unified Approach to Data Definition, Manipulation, and Control," IBM *Journal of Research and Development*, Vol. 20, November 1976, pp. 560-574.

[11] I. A. Clark, "Software Simulation as a Tool for Usable Product Design," IBM *Systems Journal*, Vol. 20, Third Quarter 1981, pp. 273-293.

[12] J. Conklin, "A Survey of Hypertext," MCC Technical Report STP-356-86, MCC Software Technology Program, Austin, TX, January 1987.

[13] J. Conklin, "Hypertext: An Introduction and Survey," *Computer*, Vol. 20, 1987, pp. 17 - 41.

[14] Control Data Corporation. "CONTEXT: Online Manuals System--Reference Manual," online description for building a manual using this tool.

[15] Richard E. Cullin, Myron W. Krueger, Mallory Selfridge, and Marie A. Bienkowski, "Automated Explanations as a Component of a Computer-

aided Design System," IEEE *Transactions on Systems, Man, and Cybernetics*, Vol SMC-12, March/April, 1982, pp. 168-181.

[16] Robert S. Fenchel and Gerald Estrin, "Self-describing Systems Using Integral Help," IEEE *Transactions on Systems, Man, and Cybernetics*, Vol. SMC-12:2, March/April 1982, pp. 162-176.

[17] Mike Fitter, "Towards More 'Natural' Interactive Systems," *International Journal of Man-Machine Studies*, Vol. 11, 1979,pp. 339-350.

[18] E. Foster, "Outliners: A New Way of Thinking," *Personal Computing*, May 1985, p. 74.

[19] Carl H. Frederiksen and Joseph F. Dominic, "Writing: The Nature, Development, and Teaching of Written Communication," Vol. II: *Process, Development and Communication.* Hillsdale, New Jersey: Lawrence Erlbaum, 1981.

[20] George W. Furnas, "Experience with an Adaptive Indexing Scheme," *Proceedings*, CHI 1985 Human Factors in Computing Systems, San Francisco, CA, April 14-18, 1985, pp. 131-135.

[21] T. R. Girill and Clement H. Luk. "Documentation: An Interactive Online Solution to Four Documentation Programs," *Communications of the AMC*, Vol. 26, May, 1983, pp. 328-337.

[22] Mario C. Grignetti, Catherine Hausmand, and Laura Gould, "An 'Intelligent' On-line Assistant and Tutor--NLS-Scholar," *Proceedings* of the 1975 National Computer Conference, pp. 775-781.

[23] Lee W. Gregg and Erwin R. Steinberg, eds. *Cognitive Processes in Writing.* Hillsdale, New Jersey: Lawrence Erlbaum, 1980.

[24] *Guide User's Manual*, Owl International, Inc. 14218 NE 21st Street, Bellevue, WA 98007.

[25] F. Halasz, T. Moran, and R. Trigg, "NoteCards in a Nutshell," *Proceedings*, ACM +GI '87 Conference, Toronto, Canada, April 5-9, 1987, pp. 1-9.

[26] D. J. Hart, "The Human Aspects of Working with Visual Display Terminals," INCA-FIEJ Research Report No. 76/02, Washingtonplatz, Darmstadt, West Germany (1976), pp. 1-61.

[27] D. J. Hart, "Idea Processors," *BYTE*, June 1985, p. 337.

[28] William Hershey, "ThinkTank," *BYTE*, May 1984, p. 189.

[29] H. D. Holt and F. L. Stevenson. "Human Performance Considerations in Complex Systems," *Science*, 1978, pp. 195.

[30] Raymond C. Houghton, Jr., "Online Help Systems: A Conspectus," *Communications of the ACM*, Vol. 27:2, February 1984, pp. 126-133.

[31] Geoffrey James, *Document Databases*. New York: Van Nostrand Reinhold Company, 1985.

[32] David H. Jonassen, *The Technology of Text: Principles for Structuring, Designing, and Displaying Text*, New Jersey: Educational Technology Publications, 1982.

[33] David H. Jonassen, *The Technology of Text: Principles for Structuring, Designing, and Displaying Text*, Vol. II, New Jersey: Educational Technology Publications, 1985.

[34] Steven Jong, "Issues in Online Documentation," *Proceedings* of the 29th ITTC, Boston, Massachusetts, 1982, T36-T39.

[35] A. Kay and A. Goldberg. "Personal Dynamic Media," *Computer*, Vol. 10, March 1977, pp. 31-34.

[36] John I. Kiger, "The Depth/Breadth Tradeoff in the Design of Menu-Driven User Interfaces," *International Journal of Man-Machine Studies*. Vol. 20, 1984, pp. 210-213.

[37] Celeste S. Magers, "An Experimental Evaluation of On-line HELP for Non-Programmers," *Proceedings*, CHI '83 Human Factors in Computing Systems, Boston, Massachusetts, December 12-15, 1983, pp. 277-281.

[38] Margaret Martlew, ed. *The Psychology of Written Language: Developmental and Educational Perspectives*. New York: John Wiley & Sons, 1983.

[39] N. Meyrowitz, "Intermedia: The Architecture and Construction of an Object-Oriented Hypertext/Hypermedia System and Application Framework," *Proceedings of OOPSLA '86*, Portland, Oregon, September 29 - October 2, 1986.

[40] G. A. Miller, "Needed: A Better Theory of Cognitive Organization." IEEE *Transactions on Systems, Man, and Cybernetics*, Vol. SMS-4, January 1974, pp. 95-97.

[41] N. Negroponte, "Books Without Pages," IEEE *International Conference on Communications*, Vol. IV, 1979, pp. 1-8.

[42] T. H. Nelson, "Dream Machines: New Freedoms through Computer Screens--A Minority Report." Issued with "Computer Lib: You Can and Must Understand Computers Now." Hugo's Book Service, Chicago, IL 1974.

[43] D. A. Norman, "Design Principles for Human-Computer Interface," *Proceedings* of the CHI 1983 Conference on Human Factors in Computer Systems. Boston, December, 1983.

[44] L. A. Price, "Representing Text Structure for Automatic Processing," unpublished doctoral dissertation, University of Wisconsin-Madison, 1978.

[45] *Producing Quality Technical Information*, IBM System Information, Santa Teresa Laboratory, nd.

[46] Nathan Relles, "The Design and Implementation of User-Oriented Systems," unpublished doctoral dissertation (University Microfilms #79-24,190), University of Wisconsin-Madison, 1979.

[47] Nathan Relles, Norman K. Sondheimer, and Giorgio Ingargiola. "A Unified Approach to Online Assistance," *Proceedings*, 1981 National Computer Conference, pp. 383-388.

[48] Nathan Relles and Lynne A. Price. "A User Interface for Online Assistance," *Proceedings* for the 5th International Conference of Software Engineering, 1981, pp. 400ff.

[49] Roger Roberts, "HELP--A Question Answering System," *Proceedings*, 1970 Fall Joint Computer Conference, pp. 547-554.

[50] G. Robertson, D. McCracken, and A. Newell, "The Zog Approach to Man-Machine Communication," *International Journal of Man-Machine Studies*, Vol. 14, p. 461.

[51] Saul Rosenberg, "Computer-aided Documentation," *Proceedings*, National Computer Conference, 1982, pp. 287-291.

[52] J. Rothenburg, "An Intelligent Tutor: Online Documentation for the SIGMA Message Service," *Proceedings* AFIPS, 1979 NCC, pp. 863-867.

[53] Mary-Beth Santarelli, "It's Not the Same Old 'Help' Anymore," *Software News*, April 1984, pp. 45-46.

[54] Mary-Beth Santarelli, "Expert Database Systems," *Proceedings*, First International Conference on Expert Database Systems, Charleston, South Carolina, 1986, pp. 109 - 120.

[55] Dennis Shasha, "NetBook: A Data Model to Support Knowledge Exploration," *Proceedings of VLDB*, Stockholm, 1985, pp. 418-425.

[56] Ben Shneiderman and Janis Morariu, "The Interactive Encyclopedia System (TIES)," Department of Computer Science, University of Maryland, College Park, MD 20742, June 1986.

[57] Ben Shneiderman, *Software Psychology: Human Factors in Computer and Information Systems*. Cambridge, MA: Winthrop Publishers, 1980.

[58] Kathleen Snowberry, Stanley R. Parkinson, and Norwood Sisson. "Computer Display Menus," *Ergonomics*, Vol. 26, 1983, pp. 699-712.

[59] G. C. Stevens, "User-friendly Computer Systems? A Critical Examination of the Concept," *Behavior and Information Technology*, Vol. 2, 1983, pp. 3-16.

[60] Richard G. Teilbaum and Richard E. Granda, "The Effects of Positional Constancy on Searching Menus for Information," *Proceedings*, CHI '83 Human Factors in Computing Systems, Boston, Massachusetts, December 12-15, 1983, pp. 150-153.

[61] R. Trigg, "A Network-based Approach to Text Handling for the On-line Scientific Community," unpublished Ph.D. Thesis (University Microfilms #8429934), University of Maryland, College Park, MD 1983.

[62] H. G. Wells, *World Brain*, Garden City, New York, Doubleday, Doran & Co., 1938.

[63] S. A. Weyer, "The Design of a Dynamic Book for Information Search," *International Journal of Man-Machine Studies*, Vol. 17, 1982, pp. 87-107.

[64] A. S. Woodhall, "Kamas," *BYTE*, April 1986, p. 241.

[65] W. A. Woods, "What's in a Link: Foundations for Semantic Networks," *Representation and Understanding: Studies in Cognitive Science*, D. G. Bobrow and A. Collins, Eds. New York: Academic Press, 1975.

[66] N. Yankelovich, G. P. Landow, and D. Cody, "Creating Hypermedia Materials for English Literature Students," Institute for Research in Information and Scholarship, and Department of English, Brown University, Providence, RI, October 1986.

[67] N. Yankelovich, G. P. Landow, and D. Cody, INTERMEDIA: A System for Linking Multimedia Documents," IRIS Technical Report 86-2, Institute of Research in Information and Scholarship, Brown University, Providence, RI, 1986.

[68] N. Yankelovich, N. Meyrowitz, and A. van Dam, "Reading and Writing the Electronic Book," *Computer*, Vol. 18, October 1985, pp. 15-30.

[69] J. S. Young, "Hypermedia," *MacWorld* Vol. 3, March 1986, pp. 16-21.

7

Hypertext
and the Teaching of Writing

John M. Slatin

Department of English
University of Texas at Austin
Austin, TX 78712

*The features that make hypertext a valuable
tool for organizing large bodies of technical information make it an equally powerful medium for use
in the college environment, especially in the humanities. Rhetorical principles provide a framework for
addressing problems of reference and intertextual
relationships which stem from the effort to integrate
large bodies of material and which are inherent to
hypertext. Software developers, technical writers,
and educators should work together to develop ways of
using hypertext effectively in the college setting.*

1.0 Introduction

In a recent paper, Jeff Conklin of Microelectronics and Computer Technology Corporation's Software
Technology Project describes the current direction of
hypertext-development as follows:

> One of the most promising applications for
> hypertext is in structuring on-line access
> to the large number of documents currently
> involved in the system development process,
> e.g. requirements, specifications, designs,
> standards, policies, memos, notes, etc.
> Not only can hypertext provide more rapid
> and natural access to these documents, but
> it can smoothly integrate the official
> public documents with personal notes and
> memos. [3]

Conklin's view is clearly correct. But the promise of
hypertext as a medium for *thought* is not limited

to such technical applications, and it may be that they only begin to scratch the surface. I want to try something different here, and suggest another promising application for hypertext, and another promising environment for it.

1.1 Hypertext and the college campus

The environment I have in mind is the college campus, and particularly those areas that house the humanities and the social sciences; the application I'm thinking of is writing in general; and the problem I want eventually to come to is the question of how we might go about teaching people to write in a hypertext environment.

I teach English at a large public university. My training is in literary criticism and scholarship with a specialization in 20th century American poetry, but much of what I teach falls under the heading of general literature. I also teach freshman composition, and I want to explore some of the implications of hypertext for work in both literature and composition.

1.2 Three propositions

I have several propositions that I want to talk about. The first is in two parts. Part 1 says that hypertext is an essentially literary concept, and Part 2 says that the problems hypertext poses for the reader are very similar to though not precisely identical with the problems posed by poetry-- especially 20th-century poetry. (These are problems having to do with reference, and with the nature of the relationships between one text and another.) My next proposition, which complicates the first, is that the "true hyperdocument"-- one that meets Jeff Conklin's criteria for high-speed, machine-supported linkage between nodes organized in a nonhierarchical data structure [3]-- exists and can exist only on-line, and only in the process of being constructed by a reader who chooses which of the available references to pursue and which to ignore.

The third proposition pertains to the composing process rather than the reading process. Precisely because the hyperdocument contains a number of *possible* documents, each of which may (or may not) be constructed (and so made actual) by an individual reader, the creator of a hyperdocument has to pay even more conscious attention to small details *and* to general structure than does the author of a more conventional document, and must do so at an earlier stage in the composing process; moreover, the details that must be attended to are qualitatively different. I want to emphasize this last point, though it is not especially new, because the discussions of hypertext I am familiar with have been written primarily by designers of hypertext systems for designers of hypertext systems, and I am speaking from the perspective of the end-user. Finally, I want to urge the importance of collaboration between designers and educators-- and again I'm thinking especially of educators in the humanities.

I will try to take these points in some sort of rational (i.e. linear) sequence. Reading and writing are interdependent processes; better readers make better writers, and vice versa. So I'll begin as I would in the classroom, with the problem of reading; then I will go on to talk about the related problems of writing, and end with some pedagogical issues.

2.0 Hypertext as a literary concept

Let's start with the proposition that hypertext is an essentially literary concept. It's no accident that Ted Nelson, who first coined the term *hypertext,* called his own hypertext system *Xanadu,* in honor of the magical realm in the poem "Kubla Khan," written a little less than two hundred years ago by the English Romantic poet Samuel Taylor Coleridge:

In Xanadu did Kubla Khan
A stately pleasure dome decree,
Where Alph, the sacred river, ran
Through caverns measureless to man...[2]

As Nelson must have known, Coleridge was a real mag-
pie--he read an enormous amount, and his reading covered an extraordinarily wide range of material, everything from natural history to theology to political
economy to the popular press. He also took detailed
and copious notes as he read, and, as the critic John
Livingston Lowes demonstrated in a classic work of
literary scholarship and criticism called *The Road
to Xanadu* (1927), many of those notes became the basis for lines or phrases or conceptions in his poems.
In fact, Coleridge's reading was such an integral part
of his writing that some later critics, laboring under
a naive misconception of what originality entails, accused him of being little more than a plagiarist.

But it was the modernist poets of this century, a
hundred years after Coleridge, who really began to
challenge the strict linearity of print as they re-defined the art of poetry. Here is an excerpt from Ezra
Pound's Canto CXII:

The firm voice amid pine wood,

many springs are at the foot of

Hsiang Shan

By the temple pool, Lung Wang's

the clear discourse

as Jade stream

玉 Yü⁴

河 ho²

Artemisia

Arundinaria

Winnowed in fate's tray

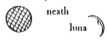 neath

luna

Like all of Pound's work, this poem makes multiple
linguistic and cultural references (English, Chinese,
Latin), and, as you can see, combines text and graphics as well. This is a late poem, dating from the

1960s; but the principles that govern its composition were essentially in place by 1916. By that time, Pound had devised an aesthetic based on the unexplained (not unmotivated) juxtaposition of discrete images-- the image being, as he put it in terms strikingly appropriate to the discussion of hypertext, "not an idea" but rather "a radiant *node* or cluster...from which, and through which, and into which, ideas are constantly rushing" [6].

2.1 Intertextuality

Such poetry makes extreme demands on the reader. Those demands are at least partly a function of what literary critics now call *intertextuality*, which might be crudely defined as the notion that a text (any text) is really a collectivity of texts, so intimately and intricately bound to one another that they have to be described as mutually constituting each other; the text one is looking at is composed of and by other texts. It is in its embodiment of intertextuality that hypertext is most closely analogous to poetry; and one implication of this analogy, I think, is that there is likely to be an irreducible element of difficulty about hypertext, as there is in poetry-- neither form being *meant* to be easy. It is in the nature of hypertext to be complex and difficult, and we ought to respect that and work with it, rather than treating it as a flaw to be overcome. And this may be one area where academics and writers outside the academy can help one another.

2.2 The poem as a hyperdocument

To illustrate the point I have just been making, I want to try treating a particular poem as an exemplary hyperdocument. I have chosen a poem called "Poetry," by one of Pound's contemporaries, the American poet Marianne Moore, who died (as Pound did) in 1972. I've chosen Moore's poem for two complementary reasons:

(1) Unlike Pound's *Cantos* or T.S. Eliot's *Waste Land* (to take another example), Moore's poem *looks* conventionally linear, both in its arrangement on the page and in its syntax. In this respect

it resembles the individual nodes of a hyperdocument,
which also tend to be organized along fairly conventional lines (though there is of course no necessity
to follow such patterns).

(2) But Moore's poem is like Pound and Eliot's
work in that it too has (in Eliot's words) "an extremely wide spread of association," and those associations are not extrinsic to the poem, not nonessen-
tial: they *constitute* the poem.

2.2.1 Marianne Moore's "Poetry" (print version)

Here, then, is the text of Marianne Moore's poem
"Poetry" as you might encounter it in a book or some
other printed form.

I too, dislike it: there are things that
            are important beyond all this
            fiddle.
    Reading it, however, with a perfect con-
            tempt for it, one discovers
            that there is in
    it after all, a place for the genuine.
        Hands that can grasp, eyes
        that can dilate, hair that can rise
            if it must, these things are im-
            portant not because a

high sounding interpretation can be put up-
            on them but because they are
    useful; when they become so derivative
            as to become unintelligible,
            the
    same thing may be said for all of us--
            that we
        do not admire what
        we cannot understand. The bat,
            holding on upside down or in quest
            of something to

eat, elephants pushing, a wild horse taking
            a roll, a tireless wolf under
    a tree, the immovable critic twinkling
            his skin like a horse that

                         feels   a   flea,   the   base-
            ball   fan,   the   statistician--case   after
                         case
                 could   be   cited   did
                 one   wish   it;   nor   is   it   valid
                         to   discriminate   against   "business
                         documents   and

            school-books";   all   these   phenomena   are   im-
                         portant.   One   must   make   a
                         distinction
                 however: when   dragged   into   prominence   by
                         half   poets,   the   result   is   not
                         poetry,
                 nor   till   the   autocrats   among   us   can   be
                         "literalists   of
                 the   imagination"--   above
                         insolence   and   triviality   and   can
                         present

            for   inspection,   imaginary   gardens   with   real
                         toads   in   them,   shall   we   have
            it.   In   the   meantime,   if   you   demand   on
                         one   hand,   in   defiance   of
                         their   opinion--
            the   raw   material   of   poetry   in
                 all   its   rawness   and
                 that   which   is   on   the   other   hand,
                         genuine   then   you   are   interested   in
                         poetry.   [5]

"Poetry"   begins   in   essayistic   fashion   with   a
strongly   stated   position   about   its   subject;   it   then
goes   through   a   certain   amount   of   argument,   and   ends   by
partially   modifying   the   original   position.   The   apparent   linearity   of   this   procedure   is   reinforced,   too,   by
the   nearly   geometrical   appearance   of   the   poem   on   the
page,   an   appearance   which   suggests   regularity,   preci-
sion,   strict   logical   control;   the   only   disruptions   are
caused   by   the   two   phrases   in   quotation   marks.

An   individual   reading   the   on-line   version   of   this
discussion,   which   was   prepared   using   the   Authoring
system   provided   by   HyperTIES   ver.   2.2,   and   which   can
be   read   by   persons   using   the   HyperTIES   Browser,   would

see something very different.[4] The title, "Poetry,"
would appear in boldface (on a monochrome monitor),
indicating a link between the highlighted term and another element, or node, in the hypertext database.
The reader would select the entry by moving the cursor
to the highlighted term and pressing the return key;
this would result in the appearance at the bottom of
the screen of a two-line message explaining that the
linked node contains the text of Moore's poem as originally published in 1919 and inviting the reader to
call up the text by pressing the return key again.

2.2.2 Moore's "Poetry" as hypertext

The first of three HyperTIES "pages" containing
the text of "Poetry" would then appear on screen, like
this:

```
Marianne Moore, "Poetry".                      PAGE 1 OF 3
                          POETRY
    I too, dislike it: there are things that are important beyond all
                              this fiddle.
          Reading it, however, with a perfect contempt for it, one
                              discovers that there is in
          it after all, a place for the genuine.
              Hands that can grasp, eyes
              that can dilate, hair that can rise
                  if it must, these things are important not because a

    high sounding interpretation can be put upon them but because they are
          useful; when they become so derivative as to become
                              unintelligible, the
          same thing may be said for all of us--that we
              do not admire what
              we cannot understand.  The bat,
    ----------------------------------------------------------------

    NEXT PAGE                                                  INDEX
```

*Fig. 1. The first HyperTIES screen of Moore's
"Poetry"*

Each of the phrases in boldface is a pointer, a link
to another node (or article) in the HyperTIES
database. Here, for example, is what we get if we
select the node attached to the word **fiddle**:

```
"All this fiddle"                                      PAGE 1 OF 2

        Two thirds  of the way down the left-hand side of a page in Moore's

Reading Notebook, the following entry appears:


        There are things important beyond all
        this fiddle -

        May 4 1919-
        there are signs of evolution in
            Hardy's work which
        encourage me -- In his early
        work there are certain flaws
        and evidences of inexperience-- I
        am not sorry,  I should rather that
        ----------:---------------------------- [new notebook page begins]
                he should
        ----------------------------------------------------------------


    NEXT PAGE                        RETURN TO "POETRY" (MOORE)     INDEX



"All this fiddle"                                      PAGE 2 OF 2
        have evolved than that he should
        have come out like something [crossed out]
        young drag [crossed out] the dracontine cockatrice
        "perfect and poisonous" from
        the beginning

        The appearance of the phrase "beyond all this fiddle" so

close to an entry in which Moore is trying out some of her ideas about

Thomas Hardy suggests that she may have been working on "Poetry" and

"Picking and Choosing" at very nearly the same time.



    --------------------------------------------------------------------



        BACK PAGE                    RETURN TO "POETRY" (MOORE)     INDEX
```

*Fig. 2.   HyperTIES screens showing the node attached
   to the word "fiddle" in Moore's "Poetry."*

This node contains the text of a notebook entry which puts that phrase right next to a passage in which Moore is working out her thoughts about the imperfections in the early work of a writer she admires very much. That entry in turn incorporates *another* link; selecting the highlighted phrase about the "dracontine cockatrice 'perfect and poisonous from the beginning'" would take us to another poem written four years later, in which these lines find a home.

It should thus be evident that the apparent linearity of Moore's text is at best an illusion; like other texts, this one is made up of other texts, of several different types. The finished text of Moore's poem reaches out to include her own notebooks, which furnish raw material for later reworking; they also reveal an aspect of Moore's engagement with other writers.

That subterranean (or perhaps I should say sub- and intertextual) conversation continues throughout the poem, coming to the surface in the two phrases which Moore herself highlighted with quotation marks-- "business documents and// school-books," and "literalists of/ the imagination." The first of these is a quotation from a diary entry in which the Russian novelist Tolstoy complains about the difficulty of defining the essential difference between poetry and prose; the second is an adaptation (not a quotation) of a phrase by the Irish poet W.B. Yeats, who described his Romantic predecessor, William Blake, as "a too literal realist of imagination, as others are of nature"--a judgment with which Moore disagreed, as her alteration of Yeats's words indicates.

The fit between the methods of the poet and the capabilities of hypertext is very close, as I hope this brief discussion has indicated; but it should also be clear that this cuts two ways. The very capabilities that make hypertext such a useful tool for revealing the intricate intertextuality of Moore's poem, also make negotiating the hyperdocument a rather complicated process.

3.0 Creating hypertext

The complexities of that process will perhaps be more readily evident from a complementary angle, so I turn now to the matter of creating hypertext. I begin with an observation about the difference between hypertext and conventionally linear composition, of the sort that I engage in when I'm writing for publication.

3.1 A problem of placement

While I was writing the last portion of this paper, it seemed perfectly natural to go back and forth between Marianne Moore's text and my own text. I ran into a problem, however, when I came to this point in my effort to compose a hypertext presentation about the same material. The current version of HyperTIES (2.2) limits nodes to approximately 10,000 characters [4], and I was coming close to that limit; partly for that reason but by no means only for that reason, it made sense to put the text of "Poetry" into a different node (at one point I had considered making the poem itself what HyperTIES calls the lead article, and trying to make everything else branch off that; but that became unwieldy very quickly). That was not a difficult decision, but once I'd made it I was faced with a much tougher one: where should I put my commentary on the poem, and how could I ensure that my reader would *find* it?

This may seem to be a familiar organizational problem, the kind of thing anyone has to deal with when writing anything at all; and to some extent it is. But I have found again and again that the computer transforms familiar problems in unexpected ways, and hypertext is certainly no exception-- it may in fact represent the most powerful and far-reaching transformation yet. The degree of specificity required in the present instance is an example of such a transformation, at least for me; I don't ordinarily work through this sort of problem as consciously as I have had to here. This is part of what I meant when I said earlier that the creator of a hyperdocument must attend to details of a different *kind* than those

that concern the author of a more conventional document (in addition to the latter, that is); and we'll
see in a moment that a different sense of general
structure is required as well.

3.1.1 Evaluating possible solutions

There were, I thought, three choices. I could
(1) incorporate the commentary in the node containing
the text of the poem, or (2) include my discussion of
the poem in the node from which I intended to call up
the text of the poem-- that is, the one I was composing at the moment; or (3) I could set up an independent node specifically for the commentary. Each of
these choices involves certain advantages and disadvantages.

3.1.1.1 Incorporating commentary in the node
containing the text of the poem

The advantages of incorporating commentary in the
node containing the text of the poem appear considerable. Such a procedure seems logical and commensensi-
cal, first of all, because it keeps the poem and the
analysis of the poem together, as in the conventional
written text. Second, the commentary is readily accessible: the reader need only follow a single link
from what HyperTIES defines as the "lead" article.
And finally, this method requires no additional links,
since a reader following the links in the text of the
poem will probably return eventually to his or her
point of departure. In other words, handling it this
way resembles conventional writing and is therefore
familiar, comfortable.

But this choice involves several disadvantages as
well. First, it will be difficult to link the
commentary with other elements of the hyperdocument;
second, the reader who wants only to examine the text
of the poem will nonetheless be required to read
through the commentary each time he or she looks at
the poem. The difficulty of creating appropriate
links, and the constant having to wade through
commentary when it's not necessary outweigh the

advantages of convenience (convenience for the writer) and render this alternative an unsatisfactory one.

3.1.1.2 Incorporating commentary in the node from which the text of the poem is to be called

Incorporating commentary into the node *from* which the text of "Poetry" is called also has certain attractions. Since it requires only one link, to the text of "Poetry" itself, it allows the author to maintain the flow of his or her ideas; i.e., it seems to resemble the traditional linear pattern of organization even more closely than the first alternative. The disadvantages, however, are even more considerable.

The procedure risks incomprehensibility because the principal text now includes commentary on material which is not actually in the text. Furthermore, the reader has to return to the calling article after reading the text of the poem. This is a real problem. As we have already seen, the text of the poem itself contains many links to other nodes in the hypertext database, and there is no way of knowing how many of the possible links the user will actually follow or ignore.

It is necessary, then, to make provision for a reader who follows all possible links to the ultimate possible point. There will have to be a way back to the starting point; there will also have to be some inducement to return to the starting point; and, finally, there will have to be some means of reminding the reader about the concerns to which s/he is returning. Once again, therefore, the disadvantages for the reader far outweigh the apparent ability to sustain the flow of ideas or the resemblance to conventional writing.

3.1.1.3 Creating a node specifically for commentary

The final alternative is to create an independent node specifically for the commentary. The disadvantages of this move seem quite formidable. First of all, you create an isolated, context-less chunk of text which, as in the second alternative discussed above, concerns material it does not actually include; this violates the principles that govern coherence in traditional composition. Second, you will have to create more links with other nodes, including at least (a) the main text; (b) the text of the poem it comments on; and (c) nodes containing other material to which the commentary refers.

The advantages are equally significant, however. The text of the poem is now left unencumbered; thus the poem can be called from other nodes (existing or yet to be created) for purposes that do not require the commentary. Similarly, the reader may choose to examine the commentary, or not, at any time. And, lastly, the commentary itself may contain links to the text of the poem, and to any other appropriate node in the database.

Initial appearances to the contrary, then, this last method may actually make it easier for both the author and the reader to maintain continuity than either of the two previous alternatives; it is therefore the best of the three available choices--though it is also the one that least resembles conventional linear writing.

3.2 Further questions: nodes, links, and structure

The question of where to put the commentary on Moore's "Poetry" raises two fundamental questions about creating hypertext, and a third question comes up indirectly as well. These questions are: (1) what constitutes a node? (2) which nodes should be linked to one another, how should they be linked, and how many nodes and links should there be? (In other words, how does one decide when to stop?) These two questions point to a third. This is the question (3) of the general structure constituted by individual nodes and their linkages, and which helps to determine the nature and number of the nodes, and the manner in which they are linked..

3.3 Hypertext and rhetoric

These are questions about which rhetoric, the theory and practice of effective communication, has a good deal to say. Whether or not a given hypertext node has been adequately defined will depend on the answers to several questions, which are much the same as the questions one would ask about any other piece of writing.

In a very helpful textbook called *The Informed Writer*, Charles Bazerman urges us to consider writing as a socially-embedded activity--as, in effect, an extended conversation between the writer and persons living and dead, known and unknown, near and remote. [1] Thus we can ask, of any text or assignment, what is the (social) situation under which this text is to be produced? The answer to this question includes as complete a listing as possible of the participants in the "conversation" and a description of their relation to the writer--those to whom the writer is responding, those who will be responding to the writer, etc. The answer to this question may also include such things as a specific assignment or task (e.g., write a guide for users of hypertext), as well as various constraints such as time or length, or a specific format, and so forth.

From the specification of the writing situation, there should emerge a clearer sense of what Bazerman calls the writing problem, that is, the specific thing that is to be accomplished by a given piece of writing. And, finally, an adequate description of the writing problem should lead to the development of a writing strategy, a method of solving (or at least approaching) the problem.

Bazerman is of course not speaking of hypertext, any more than Ezra Pound or Marianne Moore were speaking of hypertext when they wrote. But just as hypertext converges with poetry when both require the reader to negotiate complex referential and logical chains and networks, so Bazerman's rhetoric of social embeddedness converges with both hypertext and poetry in placing the writer and the text at a nodal point in a complex system. Bazerman does not say so in so many words, but for him an essay is clearly a node, a point where many voices converge, only one of them being the present writer's.

This is, I think, a fruitful way of approaching the questions we looked at a few moments ago. There is no set, pre-determined answer to the question of what constitutes a node, for the simple reason that a node is by definition a knot, a complication, an entanglement--in short, a node is always embedded in a system, and the whole system must be taken into account. A node is something through which other things pass, and which is created by their passage.

This is a way of saying that one cannot really say what should or should not be a node until one has addressed the question of linkage as well. What are the components of the system to which the node in question will belong? What is the situation to which the hyperdocument responds? What is the problem that is to be solved in and by the creation of the hyperdocument? Then, and only then, will an adequate strategy emerge for determining the boundaries of specific nodes and the number and nature of the links connecting them.

4.0 Hypertext and the university environment

The questions of detail we've just been examining will have to be worked out in specific settings and situations; and that brings me back full circle. I began with a quotation from Jeff Conklin's fine survey of hypertext, and I'd like to end by emending it a little. Conklin says, "One of the most promising applications for hypertext is in structuring access to the large numbers of documents currently involved in the system development process." I'd like to alter this so that it reads, simply, "One of the most promising applications for hypertext is in structuring access to large numbers of more or less closely related documents," no matter what the purpose for which those documents may have been assembled.

This is why the college campus affords such a promising field for hypertext. Most of what goes on at a college or university involves large numbers of documents which have to be dealt with on their own and in relation to one another (although the latter concern often falls by the wayside). The texts for courses have to be read, understood, mastered if possible as things-in-themselves; but they also have to be placed in relation to one another and understood *in* their relations; that's what a liberal education is supposed to be for. It's also what hypertext and hypermedia systems are for.

Hypertext and hypermedia systems are of such signal importance precisely because they permit us to assemble large collections of discrete materials composed in different media (text, image, sound), and to *link* them usefully and powerfully together in a variety of ways, without destroying the integrity of the individual components, the nodes of the system.

We have heard again and again in recent years that most people can expect to change careers several times during their working lives; such projections have enormously important implications for the nature of education. In such a world, the educational system cannot serve primarily to train individuals for particular jobs. Education has to mean, instead, providing people with the analytical and synthetic abilities which will enable them to recognize and understand and adapt to changes in the environment and in the demands posed by the environment; education must aim at teaching people to gather information from a wide variety of sources and to integrate what they have gathered into a coherent whole, so that it becomes knowledge.

4.1 Hypertext as instructional medium

The computer revolution has begun to transform the processes of gathering, analyzing, and integrating information, much as the Gutenberg revolution did a few hundred years ago. As they are already doing at places like Brown and Stanford Universities, instructors all over the country will soon be using hypertext as a powerful means of presenting students with large,

very complex bodies of material, say on the Italian
Renaissance or the American Civil War, through which
students can proceed at their own pace. But of course
hypertext is not just for instructors to write and
students to read.

4.2 Hypertext as a medium for learning

Hypertext can also be a powerful, and perhaps a
motivating medium for students to use. There are
situations in which the power of a hypertext system
might be just too much. But hypertext is ideally
suited to many types of student writing, especially to
the research paper which is an important component of
most freshman composition courses, and of many more
advanced courses as well.

As hypertext is also beautifully appropriate for
collaborative work [7], it might be possible to have
an entire class working together to create a hyperdocument, using hypertext as a means of structuring not
only their own *individual* access to multiple
sources of information, but access by fellow-students
as well. An American history class, for example,
might take on a project about the Revolutionary War; a
literature class might produce a hyperdocument about a
particular period in literary history, or a particular
literary form, or even about a major writer. The
class would be divided into groups or teams, with each
group being assigned responsibility for a particular
subtopic, and individual students being assigned to
handle still smaller components. The class as a whole
would decide (within limits set by the instructor) the
scope of the project and how to subdivide it; each
group would have to compose and link its separate
nodes; the class as a whole would have to meet to map
out the hyperdocument. individual students would receive grades for their individual contributions; and
they might also be graded according to the importance
of their group's contribution to the larger hyperdocument.

Such projects would raise different kinds of
problems, both intellectual and managerial, than we
are accustomed to. This is where educators need the

help of software developers, technical writers, and others in the computer industry-- and where those in the computer industry need help from those in the academy. The university classroom is a specialized environment, just as the high-technology laboratory and the corporate office are specialized environments; if educators in the humanities are to make full use of advanced technology, it will be because that technology meets *and is perceived as meeting* their specific needs. The humanities stand to benefit a great deal from the use of advanced technology; so, too, the development of that technology stands to gain considerably from the advice and the expertise of scholars and educators in the humanities.

References

[1] Bazerman, Charles. *The Informed Writer: Using Sources in the Disciplines*, 2d edition. Boston: Houghton Mifflin, 1985.

[2] Coleridge, S.T. "Kubla Khan; or, a Vision in a Dream." In *English Romantic Writers*, ed. David Perkins. New York: Harcourt, Brace and World, 1967.

[3] Conklin, Jeff. *A Survey of Hypertext*, MCC Technical Report Number STP-356-86. Austin, Texas: MCC, 1986.

[4] *HyperTIES Authoring System User's Manual*, version 2.2. College Park, Maryland: Human-Computer Interaction Laboratory/Cognetics Corporation, 1987.

[5] Moore, Marianne. "Poetry." In *Others* 5 (September 1919), 5.

[6] Pound, Ezra. *Gaudier-Brzeska: A Memoir* (1916). Rpt. New York: New Directions, 1970.

[7] *Proceedings of the Third Annual Conference on Computer-Supported Collaborative Work*, Austin, Texas, December 3-5 1986. Austin, Texas: MCC, 1986.

II

Management, Training, and Corporate Culture

8

Information Development Is Part of Product Development—Not an Afterthought

Roger A. Grice
IBM Corporation
Kingston, New York

Introduction

Users of the high-tech products produced by the computer industry require information if they are to use those products effectively. We might observe that today's computer products consist of three components: hardware (the computers and peripheral devices), software (the programs that run on the hardware), and information (the directions for understanding and using the hardware and software).

It follows, or at least it should, that any product-development effort requires the efforts of the corresponding three groups of people: hardware development (engineers), software development (programmers), and information development (technical communicators), and from this it follows—perhaps less obviously—that these three groups must follow similar, parallel development processes if they are to produce an integrated, usable product.

Gone are the days when writing was done after a product was complete and writers were given the product specification and told to "pubs it up!" Today's information developers must work as equal partners with other product developers.

The lines between hardware, software, and information are getting blurred with the advent of interactive programming, firmware, new input devices, and displayable manuals. For this reason cooperation and collaboration across disciplines will become even more important, and people should start practicing it now. Information developers must follow a process that involves collaboration and interaction with other information developers and a great deal of interaction with other product developers.

The Increased Importance of Information

Based on the value of goods and services produced, American society has passed from an era of being an agrarian society (1860-1906) to an industrial society (1906-1954) to today's information society (Porat 1978, 72). Porat charts the fluctuations of four sectors of the American economy over the 120-year period from 1860 to 1980. During this time, the number of people engaged in agriculture and industry declined. The number of information and service workers, on the other hand, has increased significantly.

The resources—material and human—needed to produce the required amount of agricultural and industrial products will continue to decline. An increasing amount of time, energy, and thought will be spent in letting consumers know about these products and their use. Porat states:

> By 1970 close to half of the U.S. workforce was classified as "information workers," holding a job in the production, processing, or distribution of symbols as its main activity. This group of workers earned over 53 percent of the total income of *all* American workers. This growth will continue (Porat 1978, 70).

John Naisbitt describes this change from an agrarian/industrial society to an information society as the first of the megatrends shaping our society. Of these megatrends, he states, "None is more subtle, yet more explosive, than the megashift from an industrial to an information society" (Naisbitt 1984, 1).

Dizard characterizes this information society as having "increasing emphasis on the production, storage, and distribution of information as its major activities" (Dizard 1958, 1). What makes up the information society? The answer is a complex one because the components are so diverse that there is some reluctance to group them all together. But it is this grouping that characterizes the information society, a society that is radically different from the past. One obvious component is the information itself—facts and figures—describing and shaping the way we live. Another component is the computing machinery and computer programs that store, retrieve, and manipulate the information which is stored in such diverse media as computer "memory banks," tapes, disks, and even little diskettes that people can carry in brief cases or their pockets. The last, and probably most important component of the information society is people—the people who generate, store, retrieve, and use the data as part of their daily activities.

Use of computers to handle these large volumes of information is not an easy task. The inherent complexity of the computers and the sheer volume of information processing that needs to be done have thrust many information-processing activities into the forefront of society. One of these activities is providing information to those who must use computers and computer programs as part of their everyday lives. This surge of interest in, and dependence on, technical information has placed those who develop the information—technical communicators—into a position of considerable importance. As an increasing amount of society's resources is expended on the production and use of information, attention will continue to focus on this information—and the ways that industrial concerns organize and prepare themselves to produce and use it.

The Demands for an Effective Information-Development Process

Increased emphasis on using computers, with the attendant emphasis on the information needed to use them, has resulted in growth of technical communication as a discipline in both industry and academia. Davis (undated) states that information development—the profession of technical communication within IBM—is an emerging discipline. Whitburn refers to technical communication as "an emerging revolution in English departments" and asserts that the requirements of the information revolution could well move rhetoric (the classical base for professional rhetoric) from its present position in the academic curriculum to its very heart (Whitburn 1984).

This expanded role for technical communicators places them in a position that can be likened to that of industrial workers in the early decades of this century. Just as developing manufacturing concerns required a new industrial process rather than mere modifications of existing processes and methods, so, too, do today's technical communicators require an information-development process of their own—one that draws on the knowledge and strengths of earlier processes, but one that is defined as a process in its own right. Today's technical communicators need a process that not only enables them to produce the required results, but also one that can be monitored and controlled to ensure the quality of the information produced *while* it is being produced, not after. Such a process should enable them to identify the inputs to and outputs from each step of the process and should make specific people or groups responsible for each step of the process.

The Effects of Process on Quality

The quest to overcome mediocrity and achieve excellence today is perhaps nowhere more visible than in the field of computers and computer documentation. In professional forums, in advertisements, in everyday conversation—quality is a very popular topic. The search for quality becomes the main theme of *Zen and the Art of Motorcycle Maintenance* (Pirsig 1976), perhaps the most widely read book by a technical writer who identifies himself as such in the text.

According to Michaelson, "A realistic view of quality [of scientific and engineering manuscripts] must include all of its elements: technical content, organization, literary style, validity, and significance" (Michaelson 1986, 2). Crosby claims that quality can be built into products at no additional cost by ensuring from the very start of product development that quality is a major concern of all product developers and by monitoring product quality at each stage of its development (Crosby 1980). Building on Crosby's definition of quality as "meeting all requirements (Crosby 1980)," Vreeland asserts that to meet all requirements, we must "follow a perfect process perfectly" (Vreeland 1986).

According to this view, the perfect process is one that catches defects (such as missing or incorrect information) as early in the product-development process as soon possible. To track and measure the quality of information produced, then, requirements must be set for each phase of information development, and quality must be tracked for the objectives, specifications, outlines and prototypes, drafts, and published information, so that information developers—as well as other product developers—will know how well the information is being produced and how well the process is being followed.

Growth and Redefinition of a Profession

In 1979, an IBM Human Factors Task Force met in Atlanta, Georgia to discuss and chart future actions. One of the results of this task force was a newly defined role for technical communicators within the IBM corporation. The job title was changed from "technical writer" to "information developer," reflecting the widening scope of the writers' responsibilities. Describing the way information was produced and used, the task force concluded that information development had become integral to product development and that the emphasis in judging the information had shifted from completeness to technical accuracy to ease of use. "Information" in 1960 consisted of a set of individual books written after a product was designed (or developed) to describe the product. Writers were concerned primarily with producing information that was as complete as possible; as documenters, the main skills required were the ability to write and edit.

In the 1970s, the need for information continued to grow and writers produced libraries of related and coordinated books that were designed at the same *time* as the product they described but not as a part of the same process. The information described functions that products could perform rather than just describing the products themselves. Concern moved from completeness to technical accuracy, and development costs and schedules became important as the information-development and product-development cycles began to coincide. More skills were required as writers began to do the planning necessary to produce libraries of information on schedules specified primarily by hardware and software development groups. Automated text processing became a necessary skill, and the demand for graphics and attractive (and functional) packaging of information changed the character of information development.

In the 1980s, increasing demands were placed on information developers. No longer documenters of product functions, they were called upon to provide the information that customers needed to perform the tasks associated with their jobs. Rather than development cost, emphasis shifted to the total cost associated with placing information in the field; it made good business sense to spend more on producing information if it could be shown that the expense would ultimately save money. Ease-of-use became a primary concern, and the information package grew to include more than books—online information, films and videotapes, and training packages. As it grew, so did the number and depth of skills required by information developers: editing, testing, use of more powerful tools, human factors skills, and financial accountability, to name only a few.

Redefinition of the Profession

This increase in responsibilities has caused the profession to be redefined to make the activities more like those of the professionals with whom technical communicators deal. As was stated earlier, writers can, and should, work as part of the product-development team. It is important, however, that writers "take the initiative during this time of expansion [so that they can] discover challenging and satisfying opportunities" (Stohrer 1984, WE-29).

Within IBM, the profession of technical communication is called information development; "it deals with all aspects of communicating technical information about IBM products. Information development can be thought of as one of three equal parts of a total IBM product" (IBM 1983, 4).

Thomas V. Connolly, Manager of Information Development and Product Support in IBM Kingston, sees this view as necessary for the proper functioning of a product-development group.

When I speak of what engineers do, I refer to it as "hardware development"; when I speak of what programmers do, I refer to it as "programming development"; when I speak of what we do, I call it "information development." We are a part of the same process as they are, and all three development efforts are necessary if our products are to be successful (Connolly 1982).

The case is stated even more strongly in an NCR corporate policy: "If we do not have publications to support a product, we do not have a product" (Manni 1984, 152).

Nelson Johns, while president of IBM's Information Development Council, described the change from "technical writers" to "information developers" as a change that recognizes the new responsibilities, career growth, and organizational job positions and that helps to foster a sense of unity within the information-development community (Johns 1986). The change recognizes that "technical writing is just one of our capabilities" (Hibbard 1986). Raynor Moore, director of IBM's Information Programming Services in Atlanta, sees the change as significant because the change in job title and job description "embraces the great range of jobs, skills, and techniques involved in this area today, over and above technical writing" (quoted in Hilyer 1985, 34). Saar, commenting on her observations as an academic associate in IBM-Kingston's Information Development group, notes five differences between "information development" and traditional "technical writing" (Saar 1986, 133):

1. The developer tends to get information from people rather than from books.
2. The developer works as part of a team.
3. The developer tests the information for its usability.
4. The developer may put the final written product into a variety of forms.
5. The developer is responsible for the form of the presentation of the final product (layout, graphics, binding, etc).

Information Development as Part of a Product Development Organization

The information-development process must be considered in the context of an overall product-development process; information developers are a part of the product-development team in the same way as hardware developers (engineers) and software developers (programmers). As part of a product-development team, they "develop information products that support ... business goals by improving customer, marketing, and service productivity across the product line" (IBM undated). Thus, it is important to understand how the information-development group fits into the overall product-development group's organization and how the information-development group's structure and goals coincide with the overall organization's structure and goals.

Information development is one part of the organization that develops products, and it can occupy a variety of positions in the organization's structure. Its position in the organization determines, in large measure, how the group as a whole operates and what tasks and responsibilities individual writers may have. "Where the writing function sits in an organization can have a significant impact on its performance, and on how it is viewed by the group it supports. Over the past 25 years (in IBM), writing groups have functioned as part of development organizations, part of 'product support' organizations, part of an independent administrative organization, and sometimes a little of each. There are advantages and disadvantages to every type" (Debs 1985).

Two structures that will be discussed are:

1. A centralized group with the information-developers in a self-contained, separate organization within the product-development organization, and
2. A distributed group with information developers associated with individual groups spread throughout the entire product-development organization.

Information Development as a Separate Organization

Placing all information developers in a single, combined organization provides many opportunities for synergism among the information developers, leading to improved processes and techniques for doing their jobs. Opportunities for career growth increase for information developers, since the separate organization provides the hierarchy of managerial and staff jobs inherent in any large organization. And, there is the attendant increase in recognition of information development as a profession and a career choice.

On the other hand, having all the information developers in a single organization may isolate the information developers organizationally (and perhaps physically) from the hardware and software developers with whom they work and create a greater potential for "us-them" view of the organization in situations when resources must be competed for, which is a common occurrence.

Organizations in which it may be best to have information development in a separate organization include those that have a large number of information developers (large enough to warrant the overhead associated with any organizational hierarchy) and those that have a dynamically and rapidly changing workload. In these situations information development work can be parceled out and moved around within the existing information development organization rather than moving the information developers around to the different hardware and software development groups with which they work.

Information Development Integrated into Overall Organization

Integrating the information developers into the overall organization increases the opportunities for synergism among the project's development groups (hardware, software, and information) because they are all parts of the same organization. Since they are part of the same organization, information developers have opportunities to work more closely with other product developers and have a greater chance of becoming technically expert on the products for which they develop information. Because all belong to the same organization, the aims of information-development and other product-development may become more closely related.

On the other hand, integrating the information developers into the overall organization may decrease the contact that information developers have with other information developers; this lack of contact may slow and limit the growth of the profession and limit career growth potential for information developers. If the information developers are only one part of an integrated product-development organization, their growth within the organization can be limited unless they change from information developers to hardware or software developers. As an integrated part of the organization, they may tend to be viewed as "support" personnel, not as leaders of the organization. Information developers may also shift their focus too far in the direction of product development, thus losing or weakening the unique perspective they could otherwise provide.

Organizations in which it may be best to have information development integrated into the overall organization include small organizations with few information developers and stable organizations in which the need for information developers for a particular project remains relatively stable over the life of a project, so that information developers do not have to be moved from organization to organization frequently.

Parallel Development Process

Since engineering development, program development, and information development all function as *development* groups, their activities are of a similar nature, even though the objects they work with (hardware, software, and information) differ. By following parallel processes, with steps occurring on approximately the same schedule, all of the development groups working on a project can focus their attention on the same aspect of their portion of the project (for example, its design or implementation) and thus help to ensure that the pieces of the project will relate to each other.

Product Review Phase

At the beginning of a development project, all those who will work on some aspect of the product must first learn about the product being developed—its functions, audience, schedule, and developers.

During this phase, engineering and programming developers must learn about the product, understand the schedules under which they must work and make arrangements to meet those schedules or have them changed, and agree with other developers on what must be done and who must do it.

At the same time, information developers must do very similar tasks. They, too, must learn about the product and understand the schedules under which they must work. It is as important for the information developers to be able to meet their schedules as it is for the other developers, since a product cannot be released until all areas of product development have completed their portion of the development. They, too, must reach agreement with the other developers on what must be done and who will do it.

Planning (Objectives and Specifications) Phase

Time and effort spent in planning at the beginning of product development help to ensure the orderly development of the product. It is during this phase that each development group specifies the objectives that it plans to meet for its portion of the product.

During this phase, product developers gather and analyze the requirements for this product to meet the needs of its intended audience. From these requirements, the developers make objectives for the product to meet.

Engineering and programming developers identify the functions that are needed in the product, the types of users who will ultimately use the product, and the needs of those users for service from the product. The objectives will match the product functions to the needs of the intended groups of users.

Information developers also must set objectives for the information that they will produce. To do this, they must identify the types of users for the product and the tasks that those users will perform. Based on these user characteristics and the functions provided by the product, they set objectives to be met.

The specification for the design of the product are made in response to the product objectives. A clear understanding and statement of objectives is thus a necessary prerequisite to the successful design of a product.

Engineering developers must specify such hardware parameters as size, shape, and functional capability of the products they design. They must design the users' interface to the hardware portion of their product. Programming developers must specify such software parameters as storage requirements, processing capability, and functions of the software portion of their product. They also must design a user interface—to the software portion of their product.

Similarly, information developers must specify the parameters of their information packages. They must identify the information units (for example, books, reference cards, and videotapes) and produce outlines and prototypes for those information units.

Development (Writing) Phase

During this phase, product developers develop, or implement, a preliminary version of the product based on the specifications set forth in the previous phase.

Engineering developers build hardware devices that meet the product specifications. They also provide source material to information developers and review drafts of customer information. Programming developers code their programs to meet specifications. Like the engineering developers, they also provide source material to information developers and review drafts of customer information.

Information developers write drafts of their information units and arrange for inspecting, testing, and editing those information units.

Verification Phase

During the project's verification phase, each development group designs and executes tests of the product components that they have designed. An overall test plan must be developed to ensure that the entire product will be tested thoroughly. Tests are then conducted—first for individual pieces of the product, then for groups of pieces, and finally for the product as a whole.

Engineering and programming developers must verify (or test) their products to ensure that they work properly, effectively, and efficiently and that they perform the functions that were originally specified during the product design. Verification occurs at several discrete levels. A "unit test" is performed for individual components (for example, a program module) to ensure that each component operates as it should. Components that operate together to perform a function (for example, the group of program modules that handle input and output of data) are tested in a "function test." The product as a whole is tested in a "system test," and then the product is submitted to the ultimate test—"user test," during which users or user surrogates use the product for its intended purpose and determine if it meets their needs (for example, to determine if it is easy to learn or to operate).

Information developers also verify the information they produce at each step of its development—from objectives phase to printed copies. Verification methods used are inspection (during which those responsible for the accuracy and completeness of the information gather to discuss comments arising from their review of the information), editing (during which an editor examines the information for clarity and style), and testing (during which users or user surrogates perform tasks using the information to determine the suitability of the information for its intended audience.)

Post-Verification (Production, Maintenance, and Quality Assessment) Phase

Production (or manufacturing) activities ensure the products that have been designed, developed, and tested are produced in sufficient quantities to meet the expected needs of customers.

Products created by engineering and programming developers are sent into the production phase. The products are assembled, packaged, and shipped to customers. The information produced by the information developers receives a final editing, has artwork prepared, is set into its finished format, and is sent to a printer for printing and distribution to customers.

After a product has been released and is being used by customers, it must be maintained—that is, adjusted for its actual use in customers' working environments. Product developers receive feedback from customers and respond to that feedback.

Engineering and programming developers receive feedback from customers and marketing representatives, make changes to the product, and test the changes and the changed product.

Information developers receive feedback on the information they have produced and may need to make changes in response to it. They may also need to make changes to the information in response to changes made to the product. Changes to the information—from whatever origin—must be inspected and tested, the same as was done for original information.

If the quality of products is to remain high, those who develop them must always maintain awareness of quality—how to measure it and how to improve it. Engineering, programming, and information developers must determine what to measure and how to measure. They must then measure the quality of their product in the way or ways that most contribute to quality and strive constantly to improve that level of quality.

Implications

Viewing information development as an integral part of product development has some interesting and far-reaching implications for those who teach courses in technical communication, engineering, or computer science (the information developers and product developers of the future) as well as for those who are now actively involved in technical communication. This view affects not only how we look at the profession, but also the activities that the profession encompasses.

Implications for Teachers of Technical Communication

This process description contains many implications for those who teach technical communication.

- This process description could serve as subject matter for a course or a portion of a course so that technical-communication students can understand the way that information is developed in industrial organizations.

- It could also serve as a base for modeling writing assignments, starting with source material and the need to set objectives and working through the process to produce a final document that may require modification and maintenance.

- The process description emphasizes the fact that the writing phase is just one portion of the information-development process; the pre-writing and post-writing phases constitute a large portion of the total information-development effort and do much to shape the form, content, and effectiveness of the final information product.

- The process description also emphasizes the fact that information development is not a one-person job. Collaboration and cooperation are needed if the job is to be done right.

- Information development is an integral part of product development. Technical communicators must see themselves as professional equals with the hardware and software developers with whom they work. And the hardware and software developers must also see them as professional equals. significant contributions to the products on which they work—not only by developing information but also by contributing to product design and development.

- Activities not always associated with technical communication must be made an integral part of technical communicators' education; they are vital to the success of an information-development effort. For example, the ability to set objectives and to know if and when those objectives have been met is key to the success of any information-development effort. Similarly, the ability to analyze audiences, user tasks, and available media must be mastered before an optimum information package can be developed.

Implications for Teachers of Engineering and Computer Science

The information-development process relies on the technical people with whom technical communicators work—engineers (hardware developers) and programmers (software developers)—to supply much of the source material necessary to ensure that documents are thoroughly and properly reviewed. It is important, therefore, that their education cover *all* aspects of their future professions, and for many of them, writing and reviewing the writing of others may well be a significant portion of their professional lives.

Implications for Today's Technical Communicators

This process description provides information for industrial practitioners of technical communication, but, at the same time, it presents some challenges. The process considers the needs of the intended audience, the media to be used to convey the information, and the constraints of the product-development cycle. Following this process also ensures that the information-development effort remains synchronized with the other product-development efforts. As technology and our ability to make use of technology advance, the process can be adapted to these new media.

Similarly, new and diverse audiences for computer products will make new and greater demands on information developers charged with meeting the information needs of these audiences. But the same, or a similar, process can still be used to develop that information.

Technical communicators who implement this process would probably want to change parts of it to suit the conditions under which they work. For example, those working on a small project with a short schedule, might produce one instead of two review drafts. On the other hand, those working on a large, complex product with a longer development cycle might produce a greater number of drafts and conduct usability tests on each draft.

Some technical communicators have the freedom to explore the issues raised, such as use of standard outlines, content guidelines, or new production and distribution techniques. On the other hand, others may not. The real challenge facing technical communicators is to do the best that they can with the resources available and work to change for the better those things that prevent achieving excellence.

The process does need to be examined at all times to ensure that those who follow it are best serving the needs of their audience and those with whom they work to develop products.

Conclusions

The process just described is a dynamic one, one that must grow and change to meet the needs of our society and the profession of technical communication. Rather than fixing this process in time so that it will always be done as described, my purpose is to describe the process so that it can be studied, analyzed, used, and improved. Just as industrial concerns cannot meet the needs of tomorrow using yesterday's technologies (or, in some cases, even today's), so must those engaged in teaching or practicing technical communication continue to study and improve the communication process so that society's increasing needs for technical information can be met.

The viewpoint taken throughout this description is that this information forms an integral part of the product—not an add-on or a fringe benefit. This viewpoint is important for *all* to understand if those who develop information are seen as, and work like, the professionals with whom they work—those who develop the hardware and software components of computer products.

References

1. Connolly, Thomas V. At a meeting of IBM information developers at IBM's Kingston, New York, laboratory, 1982.

2. Crosby, Philip B. 1980. *Quality is Free*. New York: Mentor.

3. Davis, Steve, past president of IBM Corporation's Information Development Council. Talk at a Council meeting.

4. Debs, William. 1985. "The Information Development Heritage." unpublished paper prepared for IBM Information Development Education class.

5. Dizard, Wilson P. 1985. *The Coming Information Age*. New York: Longman Inc.

6. Hibbard, Jeffrey L. 1986. "If I Do Come Out of my Cave, Will You Promise not to Throw Rocks?" *Technical Communication*, Second Quarter 1986. Washington, D.C.: Society for Technical Communication: 61.

7. Hilyer, Peter. 1985. "Going by the Book." *Think Magazine*. Armonk, NY. International Business Machines Corporation: 34-37.

8. IBM Corporation. 1983. *Information Development*, GX23-0303. Kingston, NY.

9. IBM Corporation. (undated 1). *Information Development: Through Teamwork, Meeting the Demands of Pride.*

10. Johns, Nelson E. 1986. "Information Development: A Strategic Name Change." *Proceedings of 33rd International Technical Communication Conference*, Detroit, Michigan. Washington, DC: Society for Technical Communication: 85-86.

11. Manni, Michael E. 1984. "Technical Writing - A Profession That Has Arrived." *The Practical Aspects of Engineering Writing: Conference Record of 1984 Professional Communication Conference*, Atlantic City, New Jersey. New York: The Institute of Electrical and Electronics Engineers, Inc.: 151-152.

12. Michaelson, Herbert B. 1986. *How to Write and Publish Engineering Papers and Reports*. Philadelphia: ISI Press.

13. Naisbitt, John. 1984. *Megatrends*. New York: Warner Books.

14. Pirsig, Robert M. 1976. *Zen and the Art of Motorcycle Maintenance*. New York: Bantam Books.

15. Porat, Marc Uri. 1978. "Global Implications of the Information Society." *Journal of Communication*, Winter 1978. Philadelphia: University of Pennsylvania Press: 70-80.

16. Saar, Doreen Alvarez. 1986. "A Technical Writing Teacher Becomes a Technical Writer: Reflections on an IBM Experience." *Linking Technology and Users, IEEE Professional Communication Society Conference Record* Charlotte, NC, October 22-24. New York: The Institute of Electrical and Electronic Engineers, Inc.: 131-134.

17. Stohrer, Freda F. 1984. "New Roles for the Technical Communicator." *Proceedings of 31st International Technical Communication Conference*, Seattle, Washington. Washington, DC: Society for Technical Communication: WE-29

18. Vreeland, James J. as quoted by Thomas V. Connolly at the Technical Communication Education Symposium, Rensselaer Polytechnic Institute, Troy, New York, April 18-19, 1986.

19. Whitburn, Merrill D. 1984. "The Ideal Orator and Literary Critic as Technical Communicators: An Emerging Revolution in English Departments." *Essays on Classical Rhetoric and Modern Discourse*, eds. Robert J. Connors, Lisa S. Ede, and Andrea A. Lunsford. Carbondale and Edwardsville: Southern Illinois University Press: 226-247

9

Corporate Culture, Technical Documentation, and Organization Diagnosis[1]

Lawrence B. Levine

Harvard Business School
Boston MA   02163

Abstract

This paper extends the recent work on "expanding the role of the technical communicator." It brings together some observations about how technical writers can get more involved in the mainstream of product development activities; the literature of organizational behavior, organization development, and corporate culture; and some guidelines for how technical writers can use these ideas about human systems to effect positive change within their organizations. A senior management perspective is considered in which Documentation's role as an internal service group provides opportunities for linking tactical problems of coordination and communication with strategic thinking. In conclusion, by applying the concept of corporate culture to the process of managing change and resistance to change, documenters can expand their roles, increase their organizational effectiveness, and broaden the impact of their work.

Introduction

Since the early 1980s there has been a rapidly growing interest in how technical writers and their departments can have greater impact on their company's success. Beginning at the 31st and 32nd International Technical Communication Conferences (ITCCs) in 1983 and 1984, Melinda Thedens provided technical writers with a checklist for earning credibility with technical staff (Thedens, 1983), and Joan Knapp presented a paper on how to involve technical communicators in the technical design process (Knapp, 1984). The following year, Levine and Bosch presented a checklist of how writers could facilitate technical design meetings (Levine and Bosch, 1985), and Knapp suggested that writers should be addressing their concerns not only in communication journals but to readers of the Harvard Business Review (Knapp, 1985).

The approach of these people has been appropriately termed "expanding the role of the technical communicator." Grice and Weiss[2] have extended these early ideas at the Fourth Annual Writing for the Computer Industry Conference at MIT by emphasizing relationships between the "information development" process and hardware and software development (Grice), and by focussing on the entire business context in which the documentation is being developed (Weiss).

These previous works indicate an exciting growth in Documentation's self perception and its recognition that documenters' behavior and beliefs will have to change before Documentation can be more successful and appreciated.[3] The commonality in these works is primarily what they reject as the key "interventions" required to achieve the goals of documentation departments. These are graphic design, expensive production tools, and increased attention on the verbal presentation of technical information (what Weiss aptly calls the "wordsmith fallacy"). Instead, these writers correctly address the central problem in terms of roles, relationships, management, and the business context in which documenters work.

At best, their approaches have eloquently stated the goals and provided some useful techniques for improving the lot of Technical Documentation. However, no one has adequately addressed the process, the "How do I actually do it?" None have enlarged the scope of their work enough to include managing change and resistance to change. This paper incorporates these critical additions to the excellent work undertaken during the past five years; it applies the concept of corporate culture to the process of managing change and resistance to change as they pertain to documenters' struggles to increase their organizational effectiveness by changing their roles and relationships.

Common Problems and Barriers to Solving Them

Documentation professionals share some common problems. Typical ones are as follows:

- second-class status
- not feeling appreciated
- product developers not invested in documentation
- product developers do not use the documentation
- unrealistic time requests for publication turnaround
- last-minute product changes
- limited access to information sources, usually product developers.

The list clearly emphasizes information flow between documenters and developers, particularly in the direction of documenters' access to the technical information that developers possess. Gaining and maintaining that access is critical to doing successful documentation work, and information flow within a business environment is most effective when conceived not as isolated transactions but as communication channels that grow out of a network of relationships. Creating and developing the relationships that enable building and maintaining these channels to ensure continuous access to the primary sources of information is a fundamental goal of all documenters. Improving these relationships often requires changing the behavior, beliefs, and assumptions of your information sources.

Your own behavior, beliefs, and assumptions that may inhibit
changes in those relationships (such as feelings of antagonism,
anxiety, and powerlessness with regard to your organizational
environment and the people whose behavior and beliefs you would like
to change) may also need to be examined and changed. Corporate
culture is an extremely powerful tool to help you break through your
own resignation, empower yourselves, and overcome resistance to your
attempts at changing the behavior, beliefs, and assumptions of your
information sources.

Corporate Culture and Managing Resistance to Change

Since 1980 an enormous body of literature about corporate culture
has emerged. Beginning with the Businessweek article of October 1980
and peaking in two conferences and full-issue business journal editions
in 1983-84,* scholars and practitioners have disputed the nature and
utility of corporate culture.

The broadest and most fundamental distinction is between culture
as primarily shared doings and shared beliefs (Sathe, 1985:17).
The former emphasizes action; the latter emphasizes attitudes.
In Search of Excellence (1982) and Corporate Cultures (1982) often
refer to corporate culture as "the way we do things around here."
This commonly accepted definition connects with our intuitive sense of
culture, but it also tends to favor action over belief. Some writers
give greater emphasis to our motivation for action and "the thoughts
in our heads" that may influence our actions. They tend to emphasize
beliefs as exemplified by systems (such as rewards, accounting, and
performance appraisal) and statements of values made in corporate
mission documents, human resource brochures, and reports from
interviews by individuals at many organizational levels.

Some writers grant the importance of shared doings and statements
of beliefs and values, but assert that the core of a culture cannot
be assessed by either of these "visible" means. Rather, they argue
for the importance of tacit, taken-for-granted assumptions that have
worked so well for so long that they have become powerful enough to
disappear from conscious awareness (Schein, 1985:6).

Music provides an example of how actions, beliefs, and assumptions
inter-relate as follows:

Musical Part	Cultural Level
melody	shared doings
harmony	shared beliefs and values
bass	shared assumptions.

The most obvious musical part is the melody, the clearest (most
visible) manifestation; this part conforms with shared doings. The

assumptions are the bass part -- always present, but often _felt_ more
than _heard_. The bass drives the rhythm (the beat) and sets tempo (the
speed); it determines the harmonic structure of the music and is crucial
to musical analysis, but is primarily emotive and functions implicitly
for normal listening enjoyment. The harmony (the inner parts) are the
articulated beliefs and values which can be heard more clearly than the
bass but less clearly than the melody; they influence the melody in an
observable way, but are influenced by the bass primarily by implication.

Democracy in America offers another example. Independence Day
ceremonies are the shared doings; statements such as "All men are
created equal" are the shared beliefs; and one taken-for-granted
assumption might be that that groups (by direct vote or
representation) make better decisions than individuals.

The debate among theorists has many additional facits. Ed Schein
asserts that culture has different functions during different stages
of organizational development (Schein, 1985:270). Linda Smircich
poses the question -- Do organizations _have_ cultures; or _are_ they
cultures (Smircich, 1983)? Stanley Davis distinguishes between "daily
beliefs" and "guiding beliefs" (Davis, 1984). Craig Lundberg views
culture in terms of organizational learning (Lundberg, 1985:173);
Joanne Martin is interested in organizational stories (Martin, 1982);
and Alice Sapienza is conerned with corporate use of metaphors
(Sapienza, 1984, 1985). Many writers, notably Schein (1983, 1985) and
Martin and Siehl (1985), emphasize the importance of founders and
leaders in molding and transmitting cultural values.

Some feel that culture is approached too psychologically,
individually, and from a top management perspective. They argue for a
more sociological and political perspective that emphasizes a
bottom-up collection of conflicting subcultures rather than a single,
unified _corporate_ culture (Van Maanen and Barley, 1985; Louis, 1985).
Most recently in an article about organizational rites, Beyer and
Trice (1987), categorize the two camps as those that make culture too
complicated, and those that make it so vague and general as to render
it useless. But one well-known culture theorist describes what is
common in recent culture studies; he says, "They all reject the more
rational and quantitative approaches for their consistent failure to
account for fundamental aspects of organizational realities."▱

Of all the differences among culture theorists, perhaps the
largest concerns the question: "Can culture be managed?" Two volumes
of essays published in 1985 (Frost; Kilmann) each devote a large
section to this controversy. The two major positions tend to polarize
the practitioners and academics. Their basic positions are as
follows. The practitioners are accused of assuming that culture can
be changed relatively easily and of recommending culture change as a
panacea during the early 1980s. The academics tend to believe culture
change is nearly impossible and are extremely concerned with the
ethics of even attempting to "manage" culture. For my purpose,
managing culture is the most relevant question raised by the theorists.

I agree with writers like Schein and Deal and Kennedy that lasting culture change is possible, but requires a long time and is extremely difficult. The speed and likelihood of culture change depend on the change context. For example, writers have asserted that culture is more changeable in times of predictable oranizational transitions (Martin and Siehl, 1985), in concert with more tangible system changes such as the introduction of technology (Pava, 1983), in response to environmental or governmental policy changes as in the break-up of AT&T (Tunstall, Deal; both in Kilmann, 1985), and as a result of the acquisition and merger process (Mirvis, 1987; Tracy, 1985). The similarities among these change contexts may imply that culture is most likely to change when participants feel that change is unavoidable.

For Technical Documentation the most general and applicable area of research on managing corporate cultures is overcoming resistance to change. Two forms of resistance are prevalent: (1) lack of understanding of the change and (2) reluctance to give up power.[6] To harness corporate culture for addressing these two problems of resistance, documenters can benefit from some of the concepts about planned change developed by a long line of applied behavorial scientists whose work contributed to the Organization Development (OD) movement.

OD practitioners share a philosophy and techniques for viewing organizations as human systems and making third-party "interventions" designed to facilitate change in response to problems uncovered via early phases of data gathering and diagnosis.[7] Their work has a long and conflicted history, but three concepts are applicable to how documenters can use the concept of corporate culture to overcome resistance to their change efforts.

To effectively address the common problems discussed in the previous section, documenters need to think of themselves as CHANGE AGENTS and the people whose behavior and beliefs they want to change as CHANGE TARGETS. They also need to identify the LEVERS available for influencing behavior. To adopt these roles, tools, and objectives, writers need to evolve their roles in organizations from overly focussing on products and tasks to emphasizing processes and people. Making these changes means not only becoming change agents and identifying change targets, but also addressing the two primary resistances to change as follows: (1) lack of understanding, with the lever of education; and (2) loss of power, with the lever of service. Documenters may be uniquely situated to do this because they very often possess both the skills and the organizational opportunity to address resistance to their change efforts with education and with a service orientation.

Getting Involved

How can you make these changes in your roles? First, you must get involved. But getting involved is not easy because your involvement itself may represent the kinds of behavior and belief changes you seek in your target group. In our department at Atex, involvement throughout the product design, development, and delivery cycle was of paramount importance. In all recruiting advertisements during four years, our headline was -- "software writers get involved." That included office locations, inclusion at team meetings and informal lunches, staying informed about product changes, and becoming integral members of product development teams.

Why is getting involved so important? Job one in any work environment is earning credibility. That means knowing with whom you have to earn that credibility and how it is done with those people. Particularly with engineers, the most effective way I know is to do something useful quickly, or "identify and satisfy a felt need." To know what the needs are you must first be involved.

Senior management, technical management, and even writers and documentation managers themselves often fail to see how crucial their involvement is. They are all operating under the mistaken assumption that a writer's involvement in technical and product development at best merely yields a record (photograph or mirror image) of the decision process, but has no influence on the process or its outcomes. This is a classic error of applied positivism, and those who ignore its limitation for our purposes are likely to miss the full import of the approach presented here.

How many people could seriously claim, for example, that a wedding photographer "merely records" what is happening at a wedding but does not influence events or individuals' experiences of those events? Anyone who has participated in even a semiformal wedding knows that photographers interfere with the festivities in countless ways. Brides are blinded by lights as they walk down the aisle; family is crushed along the aisles as photographic crews angle for position; rituals like feeding each other cake and the first dance are often more for the pictures than the experience; and, of course, the entire wedding party is detained sometimes for hours after the ceremony to "capture" precious moments in picture.

An ironic example concerns how anthropologists influence the environments and the people they study (Schein, 1987; Van Maanen, 1987; Clifford and Marcus, 1986). Bringing cigarettes, chocolate, writing instruments, and cameras to native environments often influences the people in unpredictable ways. The ethics of anthropology advocates minimizing researchers' influence on the cultures they study, but clearly "avoiding" the problem is not enough. They are very sensitive to this imposition, but have done little to solve the problem. Contrary to our difficulty making positive, intentional changes in our work environments,[□] these "scientists" influence their research environments even when they bend over backwards to avoid doing so.

The conclusion to be drawn from these two examples is that mere recording of events or decisions without influencing the proceedings is an illusion. For writers, this means that "getting involved" is a significant "intervention" which in itself enables your most basic recording or reporting activities to influence decision processes and outcomes.

Capitalizing on initial involvement is a multi-stage process as Levine and Bosch (1985) showed with their checklist of specific actions writers can take to get involved and make an increasing contribution to technical design teams. That approach was the basis for the following more concise and more general set of stages that matches a writer's increasing involvement with his/her increasing acceptance of, understanding of, involvement in, and contribution to the cultural environment in which s/he seeks to be effective.

Figure 1 illustrates these stages. Item 1b is a crucial point that is often the stumbling block for people to understand and manage culture -- becoming aware of culture is in itself always the first step. This is largely an unconscious process that rarely be verbalized, at least at the early stage. Item 2b points out that verbalizing something about the culture to newcomers, for example, illustrates a truth that writers and teachers often advocate: You don't understand something until you can explain it. We often only realize that we experienced Stage 1, accepting that "there is a culture," _after_ we have already "understood and described it" in Stage 2.

Two comments about Stage 3 are appropriate. First, Ed Schein and other group process theorists[▼] explain the growth of groups and individuals' assimilation into groups as a two-dimensional process. They include both _tasks_ and _relationships_. Often, relationship management takes precedent early on, giving way to greater task focus when members know each other and have comfortable roles, and moving back toward focus on relationship issues as the group's task raises conflicts that may include personality clashes and revision of group goals. For the writer trying to get involved in the culture of developers, sensing this flow between task and relationship and believing that developing and managing relationships is "doing the work" is critical to success in your mission.

Second, the "steps" to getting involved parallel Nelson Bolles' four-stage hierarchy for becoming effective in any new work situation (Bolles, 1978). The stages are: (1) "What's Happening"; (2) Survival; (3) Meaning or Mission; and (4) Effectiveness. Bolles also emphasizes that growth in competence requires continual balancing of _mastery_ and _challenge_. I find his model extremely useful for pacing and measuring your increasing involvement.

	YOU		CULTURE

1a. THERE ARE NORMS AND RULES --   **1b.** THERE IS A CULTURE

A WAY TO DO THINGS, AND

NOT DO THINGS

2a. KNOW THE NORMS, RULES, "THE WAY"   **2b.** UNDERSTAND AND DESCRIBE

THE CULTURE

3a. GET INVOLVED (STEPS)   **3b.** ENTER THE CULTURE

    A. EARN CREDIBILITY   - RECOGNIZE THAT YOU

    B. STABLE INVOLVEMENT   ARE IN THE CULTURE

    C. INCREASE LEVEL   - SEEK AND GAIN

                             ACCEPTANCE

                             - PROVIDE A TASK FUNCTION

                             - BE A GROUP MEMBER

4a. EXPAND YOUR ROLE   **4b.** INFLUENCE, MODIFY, CHANGE

PRODUCT (DOCUMENT) --> PROCESS   THE CULTURE

                             YOUR CONTRIBUTION CHANGES

                             FROM TANGIBLE PRODUCT TO

                             ROLE OF COMMUNICATOR,

                             INTEGRATOR, FACILITATOR

          TASK/RESULT   PEOPLE/PROCESS

Figure 1. Four Steps to Getting Involved in a Workplace Culture

As you take on new challenges, whether documenting a single new command or an entire command language, growing from project leader to manager, installing one outlet in your home or rewiring an entire floor, your start over again in this hierarchy. You need to seek opportunities to increase your involvement, but also know your own need for balance between mastery and challenge because your effectiveness may drop to the "what's happening level" again as you act upon challenging opportunities. The important point is to know yourself, to understand that <u>increasing level</u> of involvement means <u>temporarily lowering effectivenss</u>, and to use the four-part structure as a guide for measuring your progress from confusion to competence in each new challenge.

Achieving "stable involvement" always precedes focussing on the ultimate level of involvement. Discover your strengths and the group's points of acceptance; these are the places to build a comfortable involvement first. Appropriate this territory and even teach newcomers to the group about your small area of learning. This shows group members that you have mastered something and want to share that learning as quickly as possible. Based on acceptance and credibility in these small areas of "mastery," you can seek greater involvement and influence in other, perhaps, more risky areas. What usually happens to writers who carefully build upon a sound base of contribution is that group members begin to initiate requests for greater involvement.

The result is illustrated in 4a and 4b. You have expanded your role from the clear task of "data gathering" (plus organizing and writing) to actively participating in and facilitating the process by which your "data comes into being" and is organized. The IBM people have taken a wonderful step in referring to documentation work as "information development" (Grice, this volume). However, the culture approach advocates even greater involvement in product development processes than IBM's concept of "parallel development." It contends that information development <u>affects</u> product development. If managed properly, it affects it in very positive ways. Achieving this level of involvement shifts the role of documenters from a task/result orientation to a process/people orientation that includes the new roles of communicator, integrator, and facilitator. Gaining this level of access and impact requires a sophisticated <u>understanding of the culture</u>; and changing the behavior and beliefs of the "target" group to allow and endorse this new role is itself a significant <u>change in the culture</u>.

Diagnosing Opportunities for Successful Involvement

Some organizational cultures are more receptive than others to such change efforts, and diagnosing how receptive yours is may be crucial to the success or even start of your efforts. In assessing an organization's readiness and identifying the obstacles to redefining the documentation role, some helpful generalizations may be possible.

Analyzing your organization in terms of the following criteria will help you assess how, when, and where to start your change effort; how much resistance you are likely to encounter; and what is your likelihood of success.

1.   Physical location of documenters relative to information sources

The concept "out of sight, out of mind" operates quite effectively in a business environment. The example I always use is that developers find it easier to miss review deadlines by three weeks if they do not bump into the documenter at the coffee machine in the morning as a unstated reminder that s/he has not reviewed the book. Informal daily contact reinforces that "they are people too," which applies equally to writers' attitudes toward developers. In short, physical proximity is a flat-out necessity.

Where corporate norms do not already include close proximity of writers to their information sources, use the other criteria (below) as guidelines for assessing the likelihood of moving writers' offices near the development teams with whom they work. Resistance to this sort of change may be unusually high, because it is very visible and semi-permanent, making "passive" resistance to, or silent boycott of, your changes impossible. In fact, you may discover more about how the development organization values documentation work by how it responds to the physical proximity issue than almost any other change you seek. This issue is an excellent diagnostic tool for drawing out a crucial underlying assumption.

Changing the physical proximity of writers to developers may require subtlety and some research, such as being extremely in tune with planned floor layout restructuring or building moves. In fast changing environments, the opportunities for taking advantage of upcoming building changes is enormous. Consider getting to know the facilities manager, and do some background reading on how office layout influences work team creativity and workplace productivity (Steele, 1973; Stone and Luchetti, 1985). By keeping informed about possible office changes and providing information as a resource on office layouts, you may be able to discover and capitalize on short windows of opportunity to relocate key writers with their development groups. In such cases, the general turbulence caused by office moves may draw less attention, and possibly less resistance, to this critical step in improving the relationships between writers and developers.

2.   Organizational alignment of documentation groups

Being a part of the organization which contains your information sources is the primary goal of close organizational alignment. In my experience, writers are happier and more effective as they move closer (both physically and organizationally) to their information sources, which in most cases means the product developers. Marketing organizations often view documentation as an extension of marketing

communications. Although marketing and sales organizations may be
"closer to the customer" than most engineering organizations, getting
customer feedback is easier to address than credibility with your
information sources. Referring to the IBM triumvirate of software,
hardware, and information development (Grice, this volume), documentation
is most effective if organizationally aligned with product development.

Some companies have decentralized, aligning most functions by
product or business unit. In the past 10 years reducing management
layers, pushing down decision making, and organizing to stress
interactions among participating groups has been a common trend (Porter,
1985:414; Mintzberg, 1983:95-114). One growing software company just
reorganized itself to align human resources, quality assurance, and
documentation groups directly with its six business units. This makes
documentation closer to its product team, but potentially weakens the
overall cohesiveness of the department.

Where possible, the groups should be matrixed informally to the
product teams, while retaining centralized reporting. Decentralization
offers corporate-level legitimacy for placing all groups in closer
structural relationships. The disadvantage is that subgroups of
functions struggling to improve their credibility have more difficulty
helping each other and drawing on a common leadership vision about their
functional role.

Background reading on the advantages and disadvantages of
decentralization can help you recognize where difficulties are not those
of the documentation group alone. In companies that are not
decentralized, some reading can help you anticipate and predict when and
under what circumstances your company is likely to decentralize, enabling
you to plan for taking advantage of that reorganization. This awareness
may prove critical, especially under major organizational changes. Often
Documentation is fit in to the organization on the basis of expediency
rather than effectiveness. Thinking ahead and being informed may make
the difference between reporting to the senior manager in charge of the
business unit or having your group in corporate communications.

3.   History of the documentation department

In some circles history is a dirty word, because it implies dwelling
on the past, and companies are changing so fast that only the future and
today's brushfire often receive attention. The purpose of studying
history is much more enlightened than merely "preventing it from
repeating itself." From the perspective of cultural analysis, change,
and resistance to change, knowing the history of a documentation
department may be crucial to mounting any successful change effort.

For example, the history of criteria 1 and 2 above tell a story
about how documentation has fared throughout a corporate history.
Knowing how the documentation department first came into being may be
crucial. Consider these questions: Whose idea was it? When in the

company's history did it occur? Was it while business was good, or
perhaps a tool for improving business? What product(s) drew attention to
the importance of documentation? Which customers drew attention to the
need for improved documentation?

     Seeking out people who have transferred into or out of
Documentation, seaching out nondocumentation supporters both present and
past, and even contacting previous writers or managers about your
department's history are important tools for assessing how and where to
begin change efforts. In short, the past is significant because the
greatest lines of resistance are likely to come from people and around
issues that were stumbling blocks in the past. Like the issue of
physical proximity, historical study may uncover significant assumptions
about documentation work at your company that will help you in making the
changes you seek.

     At Atex my history work was extremely helpful in knowing where to
find support, what people to avoid, and what issues had been hot buttons
in the past. For example, I discovered that my boss had been extremely
hostile to a particular writer. This naturally concerned me. But I also
discovered that the writer's work was not well received, that he was
considered antagonistic, and that the poor relationship between my boss
and him had been more of a personality conflict than a reflection of the
department's perception of documentation. More generally, I discovered
that at one time the VP of Software explicitly told developers not to
spend time with writers; the president was against making any commitments
in writing, including job descriptions and product specifications; the
best writers had become developers; and Engineering was very unhappy with
Documentation's refusal to release final drafts for in-house use.

     At DEC, I once remarked to my supervisor that many policies seemed
unusually well-grounded and clear, such as use of active voice and second
person, requirements to run your own examples, physical proximity of
writers to developers, and inclusion of documentation managers and
documentation plans as part of the project planning process. His answer
is still a source of inspiration and reinforces many of the ideas in this
paper. It was about history. He smiled and said, "Well, we just won a
lot of our battles along the way." I never figured out what many of
those battles were, but thereafter I always thought about current
practices, policies, hostilities, and affinities as possibly results of
historical battles, alliances, and crises. This is why we study history.

4.   Writing of product specifications

     Who writes product specifications? Two prior questions are
necessary. First, are there any product specifications?. Second, how
seriously are they taken -- are they written before coding begins; are
they updated; are they merely for show, or do they actually function as a
vehicle for making and revisiting cross-departmental decisionmaking?
Having writers write specifications is one of the clearest signs of a
positive documentation environment. However, it is important that the
writer understand the job is much more than "writing." S/he needs to

believe in and be coached in the idea that his/her work includes
facilitating and documenting a social, decisionmaking process. That
means resistance and conflict should not be ignored or minimized, but
focussed and revisited.

In many companies, the writing and purpose of specifications are not
clearly defined. This is a giant problem, and is often a focal point for
tension between the technology and commercial sides of the business.
Specification writing poses an extraordinary opportunity for
documentation people to get involved and give something back to their
information sources during product development. However, assessing
readiness of the participating groups for this kind of "service" is of
critical importance. The key point is that a writer's reception and the
process for negotiating a contract with a project leader may have less to
do with "documentation" than with how the project is going and how the
key decisionmakers work together.

This is extremely high risk territory, only to be traversed by
writers who have the greatest confidence and interpersonal and political
skills. However, their success can benefit whole departments, but only
if perceived as models of work to be vigorously promoted by Documentation
management. Even without the skills or the organizational readiness for
this kind of participation, documenters will be served well by finding
out and staying on top of issues concerning the product specification
process.

5.   Documenter/Developer ratio

Because I advocate focussing on the people and the process more
than the product and the task, I think assessing how many busy,
independent software engineers a writer can possibly keep up with is a
useful measurement. When documenters are little more than editors on
military specifications, for example, it is not uncommon for the
writer-to-developer ratio to be about the same as the teacher-student
ratio in public schools. I think environments that show reasonable
respect for the work of documentation provide one writer for every 5-10
programmers.

Environments that get closer to one writer for two programmers are
the most advanced. This may seem somewhat inflated. But if information
development is as important as other product development activities, and
if writers can better develop those products by being involved early and
giving back services to the development group during product development,
then a ratio of writers-to-developers approaching 1:2 may be warranted.[10]

6.   Department composition and background of members

A few significant details about writers' backgrounds and the general
composition of the documentation department may be helpful in assessing
the group's readiness and the developers' receptiveness to making changes
in writer-developer relationships. These include writers' (and
developers') previous company experience, their skill sets, the

documentation management's background, and the history of transfers
between the documentation and development groups.

First, it is important to know **writers' previous companies**,
particularly where they where initiated into the business. Knowing this
for developers is also important. The culture of many large
documentation departments is well known and can serve as a predictor of
writer and developer attitudes about asserting and accepting new roles.
For writers who come to the field with training and/or experience in
other professions, such as journalism, literature, music, or pure
science, these backgrounds may also serve as partial predictors of their
ability and incentive to expand their roles.

Second, writers come to documentation with different skill sets
besides writing and technology. The most important of these might be
termed "behavioral skills," including listening, managing, influencing,
assertiveness, and group process. Another is teaching. As mentioned
earlier, the two most effective ways to overcome resistance to change
are with education and service. A third is skills related to library
science which help writers be information brokers and managers of
information flow. In short, writers who possess these skills in addition
to competencies in research, organization, composition, and technology
are most likely to have the organizational abilities to be change agents.
Writers ill-suited to these efforts are sometimes frustrated novelists
who are too attached to the end product -- their book -- and technology
buffs (the documentation equivalent of computer hackers) who prefer to
sit in a corner and play with neat software.

Third, the expertise, company history, and industry **background of
the documentation management** are critical elements. Managers from
outside the electronics industry may find it difficult to gain
credibility with very technical development managers and may be
disinclined to emphasize developer-writer relationships. Managers who
have been editors may focus on the writer-editor or writer-designer
relationships more than on writer-developer relationships. Those whose
primary expertise is production or design (which is extremely common)
may emphasize those areas as the real points of struggle in being
successful. A general management that chooses documentation managers
for their expertise in editing, graphics, or production shows an assumed
underlying emphasis on the product/task orientation to documentation
work, perhaps indicating a low likelihood that it will recognize the
critical importance of the people/process issues. In short, assessing a
documentation manager's ability and incentive to adopt the ideas
proposed in this paper is critical to making the proposed changes.

Fourth, instances of **transfers between the documentation and
development groups** may provide important data about potential
changes. This may appear to be of slight importance, but I think
transfers in both directions can be beneficial. There is a
double-edge to losing a writer to a development group. It may show that
your work environment does not enable writers to be happy being writers,
and others may be encouraged to transfer. It may also show that many of

the writers' loyalties are more with their development groups than with
the writing group as a whole. However, if writers are perceived as
technically competent enough to transfer, the entire department may
benefit from the vote of confidence implied by "one of yours" being
accepted as "one of theirs." The critical point is that group members
(particularly managers) can leverage the credibility earned by the few
to enhance the credibility of the whole group.

When a developer becomes a writer, the signal is even clearer that
documentation work is important, that the group is perceived as a real
part of the development process, and that both groups view each other
as partners. Second only to the importance of the physical proximity
of writers to their information sources, such transfers provide the
most concise and powerful combination of visible actions with the
symbolic significance of sending a positive signal on the levels of
beliefs and assumptions.

These guidelines for diagnosing a culture's readiness to expand the
role of documentation are important tools for entering and affecting the
culture of your organization. Without doing this work up front and
continuously, you risk making changes at the wrong times or in areas of
greatest resistance, or making inroads that do not persist. Most
important, you risk missing the most valuable benefit of your change
efforts -- gaining the positive attention of senior management.

Documentation as a Tool for Organization Diagnosis

The role of technical communication is changing. One reason is the
nature of the software business. No product has ever required so much
continuous learning by users and psycho-physical interaction as computer
software. As a result, the perceived importance of documentation by
organizational stakeholders has grown as processors have shrunk from
room-sized behemoths to desktop office appliances. The importance of
documentation has increased as nontechnical users become target markets,
as competition has increased, and as newer PC and workstation companies
learn from the mistakes of their mainframe and minicomputer
grandparents. Last but not least, the work of documentation pioneers
has helped raise the importance of Documentation in the eyes of
corporate decisionmakers.

These changes, however, amount to little more than acceptance of
Documentation as the proverbial "necessary evil." Developers would
still rather not spend time with writers; marketers still care more
about how a book looks and expect miracles of turnaround; customers
still complain about documentation accuracy and accessibility; and top
managment still views documentation work as little more than clerical
notetaking and packaging. With an expanded role based upon using
corporate culture to help you understand and manage change,
Documentation can do better than become a "necessary evil"; it can be
appreciated for its "strategic value."

Information Systems (IS) or Data Processing (DP) departments, for example, in large corporations are slowly succeeding in fighting a similar battle for credibility and impact within their organizations. Viewed largely as a backroom business of massaging numbers and generating stacks of paper, in the 1970s top management finally began to see IS as a requirement for doing business -- a necessary evil. In the mid-1980s, however, some changes have taken place that indicate a shift toward viewing the IS function as a strategic tool. Consulting firms are cropping up to train senior executives in the basics of IS technology. Harvard Business School instituted a required course in 1987 about managing information systems for strategic advantage. Most convincing, a new VP-level job in corporations -- the Chief Information Officer (CIO) -- is becoming more common (Mass High Tech, 1987).

I believe this illustrates a shift in how American business is understanding itself. The primary competences for business success in a rapidly changing environment are no longer just making product and selling product. Also included is the glue that coordinates these two primary activities -- the information flow between them. This is true not only for the growing service sector of the economy, often dubbed "the information economy," but even for the traditional "second wave" industrial sector (Naisbett, 1982; Toffler, 1980).

Writing about how companies make the transition from entrepreneurial to professional management, Mike Roberts (1986) addresses problems of coordination by drawing on a body of literature that approaches corporations less as producing and selling entities and more as information processing entities. Information processing, he argues, is the core activity of the decision-making and problem-solving behaviors that comprise coordination of specialized groups. He says information processing is the "key process underlying coordination" and quotes Herbert Simon's work of ten years earlier as follows:

> The decision-making process, rather than the processes contributing immediately and directly to the production of the organization's final output, will bulk larger and larger as the central activity in which the organization is engaged (Simon, 1976:10).

Ten years earlier than Simon, Paul Lawrence underscored the importance of coordination, in an article entitled "How to Deal with Resistance to Change" republished with his retrospective commentary in an updated version of his 1954 Harvard Business Review classic (Lawrence, 1969). Lawrence concluded:

> The gap that exists in outlook and orientation between specialized groups in industry has increased in the past 15 years....These larger gaps have in turn created ever more difficult problems of securing effective communication and problem solving between groups. Coordinating the groups is probably the number one problem of our modern corporations.

Perhaps Documentation can help fill this gap. The expanded role of Documentation for which I argue in this paper not only ensures greater access to technical information and raises credibility with organizational partners, it also places the Documentation function (along with other "service" functions like Quality Assurance, Training, Customer Service, Product Management, etc.) squarely into the "information flow" category. Documentation finds itself, therefore, at the center of an emerging nexus of management tasks and structures that increase the likelihood that Documentation work will be perceived by senior management for its strategic value.

A few examples explain how to benefit from the awkward position in the middle, between the making and selling functions. First, I have countless times seen a very competent writer struggle over manual definition. Using perhaps the simplest measurement, manual length, the writer's attempt to "do the right thing" and inquire upfront about what users really need is met with drastically different responses from Customer Service, Marketing, and Engineering reviewers. Is this a documentation problem? I think not, but rather an opportunity to head off conflict over product definition and user profile early in the product development cycle.

Second, is your documentation department shifting organizational alignment every 6-18 months? You can approach this instability as an issue of second-class citizenship that hurts the documentation function or as a larger problem in the company's organizational design. Viewed as the latter, a department that eludes a clear fit in the structure may offer the organizational designers an unusual opportunity for revising the structure to reflect and reinforce the company's competitive strengths.

Third, when developers and marketers are too busy to review documentation and cancel an appointment to go over a manual with you, this behavior may reflect the pressure they both feel to "get the product out the door"; it may say more about the hostility between marketers and engineers than it says about how they value your work.

Particularly in the current turbulent economic environment when the role of coordinating functions is increasing, Documentation offers senior management some headache remedies as well as the usual headaches.[11] These examples illustrate that if viewed in the greater organizational context, most of the problems documenters share are really problems of organizational design, communication, intergroup conflict, and coordination. I think it is the job of documentation managers to sensitize themselves and their writers to the positive advantages offered by these awkward situations: a changed perception of Documentation and the positive attention of senior management.

In achieving these goals, the role of culture is essential in helping you:

1. Step back from your narrowly focussed perception of your problems as being task- and product-oriented.

2. Understand why your change efforts are sometimes met with stiff resistance.

3. Make more lasting changes.

4. See that your daily, tactical dilemmas may have strategic value, offering access to precisely the kind of grounded, organizational problems which senior management always struggles to uncover.

The need for greater access to tactical problems and emphasis on their strategic value is underscored in the management literature and course development innovations of the 1980s. The practice of Management-By-Walking-Around (MBWA) described by many of the popular writers on corporate culture (Deal and Kennedy, 1982; Peters and Waterman, 1982) specifically addresses this linkage. The interaction between tactical and strategic issues is an explict goal of three new Harvard Business School courses.[12] Added to the school's required courses are Management Information Systems about planning and implementing information systems for strategic advantage, and Management Policies and Practices which stresses the role of top management in implementing strategy via the many levers of structure, systems, and culture.

A new marketing elective, Integrated Product Line Management, on the commercial-technical interface stresses lateral communication among functions and divisions as well as the interplay between strategy and tactics. Often, a single department, with employees whose salaries are fairly low and responsibilities seemingly narrow (such as order processing, inventory control, or customer service) struggle with difficulties in their daily work that have strategic implications. The business cases in this course illustrate this interaction and encourage students to diagnose these tactical problems with a strategic orientation.

Documentation can and should provide these opportunities for organization diagnosis. Documentation work is close enough to the product development and selling activities to give senior management unique access to both of those processes. In addition, Documentation is an integral part of the coordination and information flow process -- a set of tasks that management is struggling to understand and to make into a competitive advantage. Documenters have overlooked these implications largely because they were busy getting out yesterday's manual, chasing developers for crucial information, justifying costly production systems, and feeling resigned about their group's status and effectiveness.

Some ideas presented in this paper are highly abstract, but also speak directly to the realities experienced by documenters every day. The great opportunity for documenters, documentation departments, and senior management is the high potential for combining broad, abstract, strategic thinking with narrowly focussed, nitty-gritty, tactical problems of intergroup conflict, coordination, and information flow. Armed with a greater understanding of corporate culture, the Documentation function may be able to discover its true value to a corporation and thereby raise its own self image, enhance its organizational effectiveness, and make a contribution far beyond what anyone ever expected.

Notes

1. This paper is the outgrowth of three presentations and one workshop
I gave during the past three years. The first presentation was at the
33rd ITCC in Houston, in May 1985 about how technical communicators can
facilitate the process of technical design (Levine and Bosch, 1985).
The second was at the November 1985 Software Documentation Professionals
(SDP) monthly meeting about Documentation and Corporate Culture. The
third was a more concise version of the Documentation and Corporate
Culture presentation given at the 3rd Annual Conference on Writing for
the Computer Industry at Plymouth State College in June 1986. The
workshop, an embellishment and reorientation of the previous talks on
corporate culture, was held at the 4th Annual Conference on Writing for
the Computer Industry at MIT in August 1987.

These ideas and the connections among them are the result of my
business experience as a software writer and documentation manager at
Compugraphic, Digital Equipment Corporation, and Atex, Inc. (1979-1985),
and my academic work as a researcher and teacher at the Harvard Business
School (1985-1987).

At Compugraphic I learned that setting up a documentation
department required readiness on both my part and the part of the
organization. At DEC I learned about how a successful department
emphasized relationships among writers and product developers. At Atex,
Inc., armed with greater readiness on my part, an organization that was
more ready than Compugraphic had been, and the model of success at DEC,
I sought to achieve what I had not at Compugraphic.

I succeeded at Atex in developing a department of internal
communicators that grew rapidly, were paid equal to engineers, were
perceived as indispensible members of the technical staff, and
participated as integral members of product design and development
teams. Then, during the past two years as a teacher and researcher at
the Harvard Business School, I sought to understand -- in broader
management terms -- what I had done at Atex.

2. See their papers presented in this volume.

3. I use the following conventions throughout the paper. When
referred to as a generalized corporate function and as a department,
"Documentation" is capitalized. "Documenters" and "writers" are used
interchangeably. At times, the target audience will appear to be
writers as distinct from managers and vice versa; however, the
distinction is meant to be drawn much less often than the available
language would imply. Where appropriate I have also chosen to directly
address my audience as "you," in keeping with much of the thinking about
effective documentation. In part, this choice has been the source of my
seeming to suggest implications that separate the individual contributor
and managerial points of view. Finally, I have not chosen to refer to

documentation professionals as "we," because, although I count myself among you in spirit and prior experience, I cannot honestly now claim to be actively doing documentation work. I hope that the impact of my adopting a voice that includes the grammar of a compassionate outsider with the learning that comes only from the scars of the battlefield will help to present my purpose and role with greatest emphasis and objectivity.

4.   The two journals devoted to corporate culture were <u>Organizational Dynamics</u> and <u>Administrative Science Quarterly</u>, Autumn 1983. The two conferences were held in the spring and fall of 1984, one at the University of Pittsburgh and the other at the University of British Columbia. Collections of essays based on papers given at the conferences are listed in the Works Cited under Kilmann (1985) and Frost (1985).

5.   John Van Maanen, personal correspondence, March 1986.

6.   Based on Kotter and Schlesinger, 1979.

7.   Organization Development (OD) is a philosophy of planned organizational change and a set of technologies for achieving it. The beginning of Organizational Development theory and practice is commonly ascribed to Kurt Lewin's work in social psychology on change and the motivation theories of Douglas McGregor, particularly in <u>The Human Side of the Enterprise</u>, 1960. The Addison-Wesley series on Organizational Development is a comprehesive set of works tracing OD theory and practice since the 1960s. Edgar H. Schein is current editor of the series. For brief historical background, see Luke (1975); for more current trends and evaluation of OD research and practice, see Beer and Walton (1987). Both articles provide overviews, surveys of literature, excellent bibliographies, and also address the role of line managers in managing change efforts.

8.   The point is taken from Schein on how consultants and others who practice "the clinical approach" experience these difficulties (Schein, 1987).

9.   See Schein (1969), Chapter 4, and Schein (1985), pp. 65, 185, on tasks versus relationships and the stages of group development. See Blake (1969) on "grid" organizational development. See Hackman (1980) on work redesign and self-managing work teams.

10. This point is potentially controversial. However, recent work on the productivity and effectiveness of R&D work teams has been tied to human communication. Pava's work in a software development group (Pava, 1983), Ancona's work with many new development teams (Ancona, 1986, 1987), and Allen's many years of work on information flow in R&D labs (Allen, 1969, 1984, 1986) strongly underscore the importance of developing and managing information during product development. These works always assume that engineers or engineering managers do the

communication work. I believe that much of this communication activity can be handled by documenters in the normal course of information development.

11. This is even more true for companies during "the transition from entrepreneurial to professional management," when these intermediary, coordinating functions are just getting started.

12. Information about the three new Harvard courses comes from course descriptions, informal conversations, and my case development work for the Integrated Product Line Management course with Benson P. Shapiro.

Works Cited

Allen, Thomas J. and Stephen I. Cohen (1969). "Information Flow in R&D Laboratories," Administrative Science Quarterly, Volume 14, 12-19.

Allen, Thomas J. (1984). Managing the Flow of Technology. Cambridge MA: MIT Press.

_____ (1986). "Organizational Structure, Information Technology, and R&D Productivity," IEEE Transactions on Engineering Management, EM-33 (4), 212-217.

Ancona, Deborah G. and David Caldwell (1986). "Beyond the Boundary: Managing External Relationships in New Product Teams," MIT Sloan School Working Paper WP1805-86.

_____ (1987). "Beyond Task and Maintenance: Defining External Functions in Groups," MIT Sloan School Working Paper WP1918-87.

Beer, Michael and Anna Elise Walton (1987). "Organization Change and Development, American Review of Psychology, Volume 38, 339-67.

Beyer, Janice. M. and Harrison M. Trice (1987). "How an Organizations's Rites Reveal Its Culture," Organizational Dynamics, Spring 1987.

Blake, Robert R. and Jane S. Mouton (1969). Building a Dynamic Corporation Through Grid Organization Development. Reading MA: Addison-Wesley Publishing Company.

Bolles, Richard N. (1978). The Three Boxes of Life and How to Get Out of Them. Berkeley CA: Ten Speed Press.

Businessweek, October 27, 1980, "Corporate Culture: The hard-to-change values that spell success or failure."

Clifford, James and George. E. Marcus, editors (1986). Writing Culture, The Poetics and Politics of Ethnography. Berkeley CA: University of California Press.

Davis, Stanley M. (1984). Managing Corporate Culture. Cambridge MA: Ballinger Publishing Company.

Deal, Terrence E. and Allan A. Kennedy (1982). Corporate Cultures, The Rites and Rituals of Corporate Life. Reading MA: Addison-Wesley Publishing Company, Inc.

Frost, Peter, et. al., editors (1985). Organizational Culture. Beverly Hills CA: Sage Publications.

Knapp, Joan T. (1984). Proceedings of 32nd ITCC, Seattle WA, 1984, "A New Role for the Technical Communicator."

_____(1985). Proceedings of 33rd ITCC, Houston TX, 1985, "Getting Cinderella to the Ball: How We Can Improve the Status and Quality of In-House Documents."

Hackman, Richard J. and Greg R. Oldham (1980). Work Redesign. Reading MA: Addison-Wesleley Publishing Company.

Kilmann, Ralph H. et. al, editors (1985). Gaining Control of the Corporate Culture. San Francisco CA: Jossey-Bass Publishers.

Kotter, John P., and Leonard A. Schlesinger (1979). "Choosing Strategies for Change," Harvard Business Review, March-April 1979.

Lawrence, Paul R. (1969). "How to Deal with Resistance to Change," Harvard Business Review, January-February 1969.

Levine, Larry, and Tim Bosch (1985). Proceedings of the 33rd ITCC, Houston TX, 1985, "Technical Communicators and the Technical Design Process."

Louis, Meryl R. (1985). "An Investigator's Guide to Workplace Culture," in Frost (1985), Organizational Culture.

Luke, Robert A., Jr. (1975). "Matching the Individual and the Organization," Harvard Business Review, May-June 1975.

Lundberg, Craig. C. (1985). "On the Feasibility of Cultural Intervention in Organizations." In Frost (1985) Organizational Culture.

Martin, Joanne (1982). "Stories and Scripts in Organizational Settings," in Hastorf, Albert, and Alice Isen (Editors), Cognitive Social Psychology, Elsevier-North Holland, 1982.

Martin, Joanne and Caren Siehl (1985). "After the Founder: An Opportunity to Manage Culture," in Frost (1985) Organizational Culture.

Mass High Tech (1987). "The Making of the CIO," July 6, 1987.

Mintzberg, Henry (1983). Structure in Fives, Designing Effective Organizations. Englewood Cliffs NJ: Prentice-Hall, Inc.

Mirvis, Phillip H. and Mitchell Lee Marks (1987). A Guide to Managing the Merger and the Combination of Two Organizations. Presentation to the Greater Boston Organizational Development Network, May 1987.

Naisbett, John (1982). Megatrends. New York NY: Warner Books, Inc.

Pava, Calvin H. P. (1983). _Managing the New Office Technology, An Organizational Strategy_. New York, NY: The Free Press, A Division of Macmillan, Inc.

Peters, Thomas J. and Robert H. Waterman (1982). _In Search of Excellence: Lessons from America's Best-Run Companies_. New York NY: Harper & Row Publishers, Inc.

Porter, Michael E. (1985). _Competitive Advantage, Creating and ustaining Superior Performance_. New York NY: The Free Press, A Division of Macmillan, Inc.

Roberts, Michael J. (1986). _The Transition from Entrepreneurial to Professional Management: An Exploratory Study_. Unpublished doctoral dissertation, Harvard Business School, 1986.

Sapienza, Alice M. (1984). _Believing is Seeing_. Unpublished doctoral dissertation, Harvard Business School, 1984.

_____ (1985). "Believing Is Seeing," in Kilmann (1985), _Gaining Control of the Corporate Culture._

Sathe, Vijay (1985). _Culture and Related Corporate Realities_. Homewood IL: Richard D. Irwin Inc.

Schein, Edgar H. (1969). _Process Consultation: Its Role in Organization Development_. Reading MA: Addison-Wesley Publishing Company.

_____ (1983). "The Role of the Founder in Creating Organizational Culture," _Organizational Dynamics_, Summer 1983.

_____ (1985). _Organizational Culture and Leadership_. San Francisco CA: Jossey-Bass Publishers,

_____ (1987). _The Clinical Perspective in Fieldwork_. Qualitative Research Methods, Volume 5. Beverly Hills, CA: Sage Publications.

Simon, Herbert A. (1976). _Administrative Behavior_. New York NY: The Free Press, A Division of Macmillan, Inc.

Smircich, Linda (1983). "Concepts of Culture and Organizational Analysis," _Administrative Science Quarterly_, V. 28, N. 3, 339-358.

Steele, Fritz I. (1973). _Physical Settings and Organization Development_. Reading MA: Addison-Wesley Publishing Company.

Stone, Philip J. and Robert Luchetti (1985). "Your office is where you are," _Harvard Business Review_, March-April 1985.

Thedens, Melinda (1983). <u>Proceedings of 31st ITCC, St. Louis MO., 1983</u>, "Earning the Respect and Confidence of the Technical Staff."

Toffler, Alvin (1980). <u>The Third Wave</u>. New York NY: William Morrow & Co. Inc.

Tracy, Phelps K. and Barbara Perry (1982). "Mergers & Acquisitions published newsletter.

Van Maanen, John (1987). <u>Tales of the Field</u>. In press.

Van Maanen, John, and Stephen R. Barley (1985). "Cultural Organization: Fragments of a Theory," in Frost (1985), <u>Organizational Culture</u>.

10

USABILITY: Stereotypes and Traps

Edmond H. Weiss, Ph.D.

Crown Point Communications
1612 Crown Point Lane
Cherry Hill NJ 08003
(609)-795-5580

In very few years, the term <u>usability</u> has degenerated into a stereotype: "draft tested in a usability lab." Although such testing is an important part of usable documentation, it is not necessarily the essential part. Moreover, usability testing, as currently described in the professional literature, is powerless to eliminate the most intractable problems of user documentation: failures of analysis and design. There are two main flaws in the current stereotype. First, it is wrong to believe that usability can be substantially enhanced after the draft is complete; the most resistant and elusive usability flaws in a publication are <u>built into</u> a draft and are not likely to be ameliorated by after-the-fact testing. The second flaw is that usability testing of manuals seems prone to the same mistakes as the testing of program code: the "unit test" fallacy (failure to test interfaces); tester biases; and others. This paper argues that after-the-fact usability tests are best regarded as merely a late stage in a formal process that <u>engineers usability into a library of information products before-the-fact</u>.

Testing After-the-Fact

This paper offers a thesis that is bound to be unpopular. Despite the emergence of publication testing as the principal technique for achieving usable user manuals, I observe that the the term <u>usability</u> has degenerated very quickly into a cliche or stereotype: lab-tested before distribution. Although I am an ardent supporter of such testing, I must also argue that it is nearly impossible to increase substantially the usability of a publication that has reached a complete draft. Rather, I believe that the most intractable and frustrating problems in a manual are probably in the book for good by then. And, further, even if it were clear that widespread changes needed to be made at that stage, the parties involved would probably resist them.

Of course, the jury is unanimous: No responsible developer should distribute a publication until it has been tested rigorously. In an act of impressive humility, the editing profession has conceded that editing is not enough, that even the best editor/wordsmith cannot guarantee the understandability of a single procedure.

So, the rush is on. The more prosperous manufacturers of computers and communications equipment are setting up sophisticated laboratories. Draft manuals are crash-tested by appropriate subjects, who are interviewed before and after, and observed during. The statistical results are even bounced off significance tables.

All this is an extremely salutary development. At the very least, it raises the level of debate about publications and strengthens the link between manual-writing and human factors psychology. But it also raises new problems.

First, testing a manual only after it is a complete draft is much too late in the life of the publication. By the time a book has reached the draft, its most serious failings are deeply ingrained--"wired in." It is much too late, and probably much too expensive, to correct them.

Second, testing the pieces or "modules" of a larger publication does little to assure the usability of the publication as a whole. In just the way that successful "unit tests" of a computer program do not betoken an installed, functional system, neither do successful tests of the parts of a manual prove that the book will be usable.

Both of these observations, of course. derive from an analogy to software testing. Indeed, almost all of the improvements in the craft of user documentation are derived from the past twenty years of software engineering. Moreover, the criticism I offer in this paper is based largely on the traps and fallacies I have observed when programmers misapply notions of testing to their programs.

Usability: A Broader Perspective

Usability questions--like all questions of documentation policy-- are essentially business questions. We do not document out of moral necessity, but, rather, in pursuit of efficiency, success, and profit. And we do not make books easier to use out of altruistic regard for the readers, but, rather, to enhance the productivity of our organizations or to increase the loyalty of our customers.

If we pursue usability as though it were an abstract, technical imperative, then we confuse usability with perfection--the same mistake many quality enthusiasts make. Because there cannot be a "perfectly usable manual," we soon see that what is really meant by a usable manual is one <u>usable enough to meet our business or management objectives</u>. And a while later, when costs become an issue, <u>usable enough to please the particular readers and customers we most wish to please</u>.

For publications to be usable, they must not only pass the after-the-fact test of coherence and understandability. They must also contain the <u>right</u> material, selectively packaged to suit the convenience of favored audiences! They must present that material in a structure that makes it <u>accessible</u> to the favored audiences. And they must include material that <u>keeps pace with</u> users as their relationship with the system matures. Even though everyone these days is exceedingly worried about publishing technology and typesetting interfaces, we must not forget that the central technical question in user documentation is still <u>who needs to know what</u>.

What the testers should understand is that every sentence, procedure, and diagram in a manual could be clear, understandable, and correct--and that the book as a whole could be unusable. How? They could be the <u>wrong</u> sentences, procedures, and diagrams for the intended audience. Or they could be hard to find (though clear once you locate them). Or they could be suitable only for their first reading, but tiresome and unresponsive for later readings.

With a few conspicuous exceptions, after-the-fact usability tests do not address these issues. Nor do they deal with such problems as the interaction between information products (like books) and information services (like supervision). Or the degree to which manuals for versatile products, like spreadsheets or file managers, should explain specific "end uses."

The discussion below raises questions about the efficacy of usability tests when they are done well. That is, assuming that everyone pursues these tests as ambitiously as, say, IBM, what theoretical problems remain to be solved? (Later, I'll reflect on what will happen when usability testing becomes perfunctory--as is most software testing nowadays.)

Usability and Cost-Benefit

Making a document more usable is an upstream expense that should yield downstream benefits. Most of the organizations who feel driven to improve their user documentation are reacting to the heavy downstream expenses involved in supporting under- or badly-documented systems. It is not just that poor documents result in unproductive operations; the main complaint is the high cost of technical assistance, training, "hotlines," and other forms of expensive handholding. (Ultimately, the greatest cost can be lost business.)

But the organizations with these complaints do NOT have to improve their manuals. For a variety of reasons, they could choose to increase their supervision (like one of my military clients, who preferred more sergeants to better manuals), or provide a liberal hotline plan. One of my clients even said, half seriously, that there would be no point in making the manuals too clear when the company earned so much money from its training services.

In contrast, another of my clients wants "customer independence" through high-quality, usable user documentation...a policy with a high front-end expense.

How can an after-the-fact usability test address these and related questions of policy? How can we decide that a particular book is usable enough if we do not test it as part of a suite of information products and services? Is it economically justifiable, for example, to aim for a fully "independent" reader if the audience in question will never work independently?

And there are even thornier issues. Is the manual usable enough, given the extant delays in shipping the product? Is the manual usable enough, given the priority of the particular product, or even the priority of the particular audience? (Remember, in any genuine priority ranking, someone must be at the bottom of the list.) What are the opportunity costs of continuing to increase the usability of the publication? Would it be smarter to improve the user interface than to improve the user manuals?

Usability Testing and Document Overhead

A few months of working with the readers of user manuals reveals that the big problem is less one of understanding the instructions than of _finding_ the right instructions to read. Indeed, many of the technicians and entry-level employees who are presumed to be bad readers turn out to be adequate readers but _bad finders_.

The issue is document overhead: the effort expended by the reader in, first, locating the right starting-point and, then, jumping to the consecutive positions in the book. The overhead in a book is directly related to the frequency with which the reader must read something other than the next word or turn to something other than the next page. (Reversing directions is the most wasteful use of the reader's energy.)

Big books usually have more overhead than small ones. Books that address several functions, or attempt to serve diverse audiences, will have considerable branching, looping, and detours. The one-book-fits-all publication will often collapse under the weight of its own overhead. (The principal advantage of good online documentation, on the other hand, is that it has almost no overhead.)

Any usability test that tackles one component of the manual at a time will probably overlook the overhead problem. As I've written elsewhere, one of the main lessons that technical writers must learn from the history of programming is that, with complex entities, the trouble is in the interfaces. (See How To Write A Usable User Manual, ISI Press, 1985, Chapter 4.) That is, each of the small, well-defined components in a program (manual) may work beautifully, but the links between them may be such a hopeless tangle that the program (manual) fails as a whole.

All writers know from their own experience in learning to use word processing, graphics, and publishing software that, once you find the instructions, they are nearly always clear. Until then, though, nothing works. (As an experiment, read the IBM DOS 2.00 Reference Manual and find the instructions for putting a lable on a volume.)

An interesting irony is that many of the programmers who fall into this "unit test trap" claim that they are practising "top-down" devlopment. In fact, though, they have missed the main point; the essence of top-down design ("structured design") is defining the interfaces first, not last. The small processing units at the base of the design pyramid are coded last, after the really difficult design problems have been solved.

The fundamental design questions in assembling a user manual are: First, what topics (themes, tasks, procedures...) should be included, and, second, how they should be linked. Should the book be horizontal (reference) or vertical (procedural)? Should there be deliberate repetition (to reduce overhead) or austere economy? In engineering terms, should there be larger, less-cohesive modules, or greater interface complexity?

Although modern word processing and publishing tools have made it easier to reorganize a "finished" publication, it is still true that a complete draft has so much structural inertia--and so strong a commitment from its authors--that it makes little sense to raise these design questions after the fact. When we find structural flaws in a "finished" draft we tend to act like programmers who find structural flaws in a finished program: we patch and plug until the problem appears to go away.

Usability After the First Pass

Certain parts of a manual are read once or twice. Others are consulted repeatedly. Although the initial reaction of a reader to a manual may be an important predictor of its subsequent usability, it is hardly the whole story.

Usability tests, in the main, record first impressions. Typically, the subjects are exposed to a text and a task/problem for the first time. Usability is measured mainly in how well this first experience goes. (A small amount of excessive overhead, for example, will scarcely affect the novice, who often expects the first cut to be a little difficult.)

Again, although this maiden voyage is exceedingly important, it overlooks the inescapable fact that material which serves well on the first instructional passes becomes clumsy and unresponsive when the more-experienced reader consults it for reference or "quick reference." In my own consulting, I have found that users go through at least four stages in their relationships with their systems, with different documentation needs at each stage. At first, they need motivational material, meant to make them eager and to help them overcome their anxiety. Next, they need orientation, elemental tutorial material. Then, guidance, demonstrations and advice on how to string the elements into functions. And, finally, reference, material that jogs the memory of the competent user and reinforces what has been learned.

Diverse readers may join this process at various stages. Indeed, well-made software accelerates the progress to the reference stage. But it is wrong to believe that the same materials can be used to serve all these four functions.

In some ways, usability testing--which biases usability in behalf of better motivational and orientation documents--can be judged as correcting an earlier document bias. Another way of characterizing the "product-oriented" manuals of old is to say that they leapt directly to the reference stage, leaving the neophyte in the cold. Usability testing acts as a protector of the neophyte's rights--a principle dear to most technical writers.

The danger, though, is that usability will degenerate into a cliche--like "user-friendliness"--with its unmistakable bias toward ease-of-learning rather than ease-of-extended-use. Note that menu-drive software, especially when the choices are made with a mouse or light pen, produces a system that can be learned in a few minutes...but that often becomes cumbersome in three or four days.

Usable documentation, like usable systems, must serve both the
neophyte AND the competent user. What reads well in the usability
test may be painfully inappropriate after a only a week with the
system.

Usability Versus Maintainability

Manuals must be debugged, no matter how well they are tested.
Moreover, as systems change, manuals must be patched, supplemented,
enhanced....

The hardest engineering problem in developing manuals is choosing
between usability and maintainability. A usable manual has
conventional page numbers; many firms use no page numbers at all,
knowing that their publications will be updated so often that page
numbering would be a nightmare. A usable publication repeats certain
instructions, and even some figures, as a way of reducing the amount
of page-flipping and overhead; many firms will brook no repetition,
arguing that the problems of maintaining text and exhibits increase
exponentially with the repeated appearances of the items. A usable
set of manuals includes some overlap, so that the user will rarely
need to consult two books to perform one task; many firms will not
allow any overlap, fearful that the common material will be updated in
one volume but not the other.

Typically, large firms--especially those that manufacture
hardware--err heavily on the side of maintainability. (The most arch
example is probably the Bell System Technical Practices of the 60s and
70s.) As a result, my easiest consulting engagements are in firms
like these: in which the conventions of document maintenance are so
intrusive and overpowering to the reader that it takes only moments to
find a dozen ways to make the publications more attractive and
accessible to their human users.

But usability versus maintainability is too complicated an issue
to dismiss with a sermon about readers' rights. The fact is that out-
of-date, inaccurate documentation is at least as serious a problem as
a hard-to-use manual. And those firms that must work frantically to
keep their manuals current can be excused if they are somewhat
unreceptive to the usability theme. They argue, moreover, that it is
wrong to produce readable and accessible publications that are
inaccurate. And who would disagree?

The point, though, is that usability testing does not address at
all the issue of document maintainability. Indeed, the subject is
hardly ever raised either in technical writing courses or
documentation standards. But if the history of documentation
continues to lag the history of programming (as it has so far), I

expect document maintenance to become the key economic issue in the profession.

At least half of the students who attend my seminars, for example, are about to update or revise an existing book. I expect that by 1990 about 60 or 70% of the technical writers at work will be doing nothing else. Obviously, even though many technical writers call their chapters and sections "modules," most do not know what true modularity entails. Are their modules small enough? Are they self-contained entities that could be transported to other publications (without their links to the current publication)? Could the publications be updated simply by either the addition or replacement of a modules?

In short, is there anything in a typical usability test that tells the developer whether the book tested will be easy to revise, reuse, or cannibalize for later publications? And when a book is difficult to revise cannot we expect that it will remain unrevised or be revised poorly? Is it not fascinating how many new pieces of software are shipped with a "readme" file containing errors and omissions in the manual?

Usable Books Versus Unusable Systems

If a piece of software is hard to install, or if a peripheral device is hard to attach, is the fault in the instructions? Usually not. Clean documentation, as I have written often elsewhere, cannot improve messy systems.

Yet I am concerned that by the time a draft manual reaches a usability test, the system documented will be virtually beyond change. (That is, the politics and economics of the organization will resist any attempt to change the system itself.) How can a usability test discriminate between certain difficulties attributable to the book and those in the product the book explains. If, as is true with a certain popular "graphic interface," it takes nearly 15 minutes to change the printer in the setup configuration, is that the fault of the manual? (Note, further, that this particular interface is supposed to be so friendly that one does not need to use the manual!)

Further complicating things is the increasing tendency to conduct document usability tests along with the field test (beta test) of the new product or system. Even though this practice violates a precept of testing—one thing tested at a time—it is nevertheless becoming commonplace. The result is that, once again, defects in the design of the system will be blamed on on the manuals.

More than a few analysts believe that the typical user manual is little more than a compendium of flaws in the user interface. Although I do not subscribe entirely to this view, there is no denying that the hardest screens to document are <u>bad</u> screens, and the most challenging procedures to write up are <u>bad</u> procedures. If an organization runs its usability tests under the aegis of its publication or editing department, how will the real problem--the defect in the system--get action? Or will the new sophisticated era of documentation merely continue the tradition in which technical writers are expected to clean up the messes left by engineers and programmers, who, if they had been working correctly, would have produced a substantial part of the documentation as part of the development cycle?

In the long view, the best thing a writer can do for a system is to <u>eliminate</u> the need for documentation by insisting that the system is well-designed and by assuring that every sentence that appears on a screen is intelligible and well-written. (This policy can even have the effect of eliminating the need for most HELP screens as well.)

Usability is a characteristic of systems. While poor manuals detract from the usability of their associated systems, good manuals-- even those that pass muster in the testing labs--cannot compensate for awkward and unsound elements in the system. And manual writers, who know more about what makes systems hard to use than anyone, should assert themselves on this score. If the data from the usability test show that the screen is a loser, they should attack the screen, not the instructions for filling in the fields.

Toward A Theory Of Usability

Formal usability testing of "finished" drafts is best regarded as "power editing." It does what editors have traditionally been supposed to do: warrant the clarity of the document for the intended readers. All organizations need it, but especially those in which the writers and editors are drawn from the technical ranks. Those organizations who do it well, then, will accomplish what editing has always been supposed to accomplish: identification of troublesome sentences, passages, and illustrations--which are then revised and retested.

But what of those organizations who do it perfunctorily? Increasingly, the papers at the technical conferences are about quick and inexpensive ways to conduct usability tests. Today, the subjects used in the tests are sometimes members of the project team. There are even cases, I am sure, where the writers test their own books!

At its best, usability testing detects "tactical errors": problems of language and layout that used to be the object of editing. But at its worst, it could detect nothing. And the history of software testing and quality assurance gives us little cause for optimism. Every day, programmers test their own code; moreover, they test only its normal or intended uses; further, they correct its bugs with illegal and undocumented patches. Similarly, when there is a conflict between production and quality assurance, it is usually production that prevails.

How long will it be, then, before usability testing receives the same ill treatment that editing currently receives in most large firms?

Interestingly, the solution to the problem can also be found by exploring the analogy with software engineering. The firms who develop software well and test it responsibly are those with a theory of software/system quality. (Those are also usually the ones who document it best, too.)

The key to usable documentation is a theory and a set of associated heuristics. The theory, based both on philosophical analysis and hard scientific evidence, should address the broader problem of "user support technology," of which manuals are merely a component. It should help define the relationship between internal support (such as screen design) and external (such as manuals); it should clarify the relative costs and benefits, in a realistic marketplace, of information services (teaching, consulting...) and information products (manuals, tutorial disks...).

Although a presentation of this theory is beyond the scope of this article, it is possible to offer a few central ideas. The first principle is that

> Nearly every aspect of user support (including manuals) derives from the nature of the user interface.

Consequently, the nature of the user interface should be considered as part of the initial product conception. A system or product cannot be considered defined or specified until the main characteristics of the user interface are specified. The "user interface spec" is held as important as hardware or software specs. Thus, every new product or enhancement has a support strategy built in.

From this first principle comes the second:

> Manuals are merely a component in a fully-designed "user support envelope," which may include any information product or service made desirable or necessary by the user interface.

So, there can be no standard documentation complement used throughout
a company or across all its products. Each new product gets its own
support envelope, uniquely suited to its support strategy. And, in
some cases, there may be no manuals as at all!

This second principle leads us to a third:

Manuals are NOT the individual creations of individual writers or
artists.

In the next generation of manuals, each publication will be written to
an engineered spec, not created in private by an artisan. There will be
no unique authors; each page or module created will go into a data
base where it will be maintained and reused by other writers. The
systems analysts sometimes call this "egoless programming."

This emerging theory of user support (like the principles of
software engineering) will be applied before-the-fact in the
specification of needed documents (not only for neophyte but also
experienced users) and the design of particular information products.
Manuals will be developed through models and prototypes and tested
before they are drafted, by applying the principles to models.
Ultimately, when the essential strategic and structural choices have
been made, when the engineering tradeoffs have been argued and
settled, then, and only then, should the drafts be written and tested
on well-chosen subjects.

11

Investment in Computer-Product Documentation: Causes and Effects

John Kirsch

TechWriting Affiliates, Inc., Newton, MA 02159
Sloan School of Management, M.I.T., Cambridge, MA 02139

Investment in computer-product documentation tends to vary directly with projected sales volume and inversely with the unit price of the product. The relative size of the investment predicts attributes of the documentation, including the number of drafts that are prepared, the thoroughness with which they are edited, and the objectivity with which they are reviewed. These conclusions are drawn from case studies of typical documentation projects.

1. Introduction

Some computer companies spend $1,000 per camera-ready page of documentation, others as little as $100. The size of the expenditure expresses management's view of the relation between documentation and the product. At one extreme, documentation is treated as adding essential value; at the other, as adding little or no value. The first view leads to a large investment in technical writing and a resource-enriched environment for writers; the second, to a small investment and a resource-limited environment.

The terms "enriched" and "limited" imply strategic decisions rather than coincidence. Presumably, successful companies adapt to their markets and thus spend as much on documentation as necessary to maximize profits. It follows that both views of documentation reflect considered policies.

In this paper I examine causes and effects of these policies. I seek answers to the following questions:

- Why do companies make larger or smaller investments in documentation? Do specific business conditions predict whether the documentation environment will be enriched or limited? If so, what are those conditions?

- How does the investment decision affect the documentation itself? What attributes of the documentation vary predictably with the magnitude of the investment?

These topics should be of interest to managers of computer-product development and to documentation professionals. They should help managers evaluate the place of technical writing in development projects, and they should help documentation professionals understand factors that affect their jobs but that they do not control.

Method. This paper presents two case studies illustrating common but opposite approaches to documentation in the computer and telecommunications industries. The first case describes a resource-limited environment; the second, a resource-enriched environment. The cases are presented separately and then compared in order to shed light on the questions listed above. Thus the rest of the paper is organized as follows:

- ABC Hardware, Inc.: A Resource-Limited Environment
    - Company, Product, and Marketing
    - Narrative of the Documentation Project
    - Summary of Labor and Costs
- XYZ Software, Inc.: A Resource-Enriched Environment
    - Company, Product, and Marketing
    - Narrative of the Documentation Project
    - Summary of Labor and Costs
- Documentation Attributes Predicted by Level of Investment
- Business Conditions That Predict Investment in Documentation

The case studies are composites of many projects with which I have been familiar in my consulting practice. The companies and products are fictitious, but schedules, rates of work, types of documents, and levels

of staffing are based on observation. Quantitative summaries are
provided in order to facilitate comparison between the cases and to help
the reader assess their relevance to his or her own environment.

2. ABC Hardware, Inc.: A Resource-Limited Environment

Company, Product, and Marketing. ABC Hardware, Inc. manufactures
computer-controlled machine tools ranging in price from $10,000 to
$60,000. It is five years old and has about 100 employees. Since its
founding, it has been financed by its senior staff, a venture capital
company, and a revolving line of credit from a bank. After five years
of marginal financial results, ABC Hardware needs a major surge in
revenue and profits in order to pay off debt and attract new investment.

ABC Hardware's main assets are proprietary technology and
manufacturing skill. The technology has provided a temporary advantage
in various product lines, but other companies in the U.S. and Japan have
quickly brought out competing systems. Hence ABC Hardware's skill in
controlling manufacturing costs has been a major factor in its survival.

ABC Hardware does little selling to end-users. Its typical customer
is a company that repackages the product under its own brand name and
resells it to end-users. In the curious jargon of the computer
industry, both the manufacturer and the reseller are called "OEMs"
(although the abbreviation properly stands for "original equipment
manufacturer"). In an OEM relationship, the reseller usually buys in
quantity, sells unit-by-unit, and is responsible for training and
supporting the end-users.

ABC Hardware has signed a 3.5 year OEM contract with EFG
Distribution, Inc. ABC Hardware will design and manufacture the Model-
6000 Workstation to EFG Distribution's specifications, and EFG Distribution
will buy at least 200 units at $50,000. This is a major contract; if
successful, it will enable ABC Hardware to pay off debt and recapitalize.

Figure 1 shows the schedule in the contract. In months 1-12 a
prototype will be engineered and built; in months 13-18 EFG Distribution
will perform acceptance tests, while ABC Hardware debugs and creates the
production model. The test results will be fed back to ABC Hardware

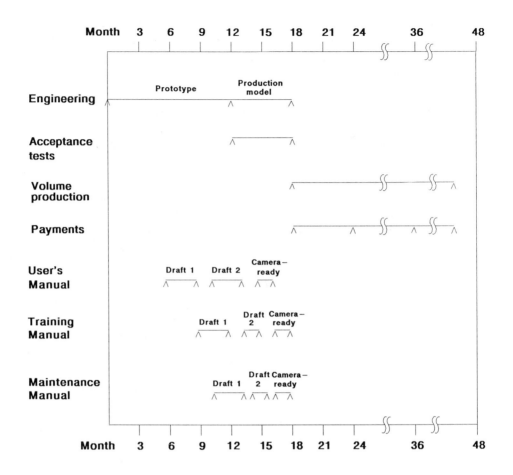

Figure 1. Model-6000 Project Schedule in Contract

progressively so that the production model will be ready by the end of month 18. In the debugging, ABC Hardware will be obliged to correct performance problems. In addition - and this is not mentioned in the contract - ABC Hardware will try to reduce the number of circuit boards, so that manufacturing costs can be kept down and profit objectives will be met.

When EFG Distribution has accepted the product, ABC Hardware will receive its first payment and will start volume production. In the following two years (months 19-42), EFG Distribution will take delivery of at least 200 units, paying for them upon delivery.

The Model-6000 is an enhanced version of an earlier product; it is faster (due to a more powerful microprocessor) and easier to use (due to extensive new software that provides a menu-driven interface). EFG Distribution will have exclusive rights to the product during the term of the contract. Since the machine is being custom-built and will not be modified in any way, the contract calls for ABC Hardware to deliver camera-ready documentation, ready for EFG Distribution to print and insert in its own binders.

Three manuals are specified in the contract. An *Operations Manual* will describe all hardware and software functions for the end-user. A *Training Manual* will enable EFG Distribution's salesmen to install the Model-6000 and to train three groups of end-users - operators, system administrators, and technicians. A *Maintenance Manual*, for EFG Distribution's field engineers, will document software diagnostics, and the removal and replacement of hardware components.

The contract does not give page estimates for these manuals but does stipulate illustration and production requirements. The *Operations Manual* must contain reproductions of computer screens showing menus, and the two other manuals must include "sufficient line art to illustrate the setting up of the workstation and the removal and replacement of parts." The camera-ready pages will be produced in multi-font proportional type on a laser printer; final text must also be delivered in ASCII files on diskette.

Documentation work is expected to begin in month 6. Two drafts of each manual will be prepared before camera-ready pages are delivered. The first draft is subject to internal review only; the second will be reviewed by EFG Distribution as part of the acceptance tests.

Narrative of the Documentation Project. The Documentation Department at ABC Hardware consists of a manager (who regularly spends half his time writing), a senior writer, and a secretary/production assistant. For illustrations the manager borrows the time of a draftsman who works for the Engineering Department. The writers enter and format text on an electronic publishing workstation; line art is prepared by hand and pasted up.

For the Model-6000 project, the manager outlined the three manuals, estimated page counts, and specified technical illustrations. For two manuals, *Operations* and *Training*, he followed outlines of documents about earlier ABC Hardware products; for the maintenance manual, he modeled his outline on a sample obtained from EFG Distribution.

The senior writer wrote the *Operations* and *Training* manuals; in all he spent seven months preparing two drafts of each manual and camera-ready final text. The manager wrote the *Maintenance Manual*, spending about two and a half months and producing a single draft and the final.

The writing was done under great time pressure, which was heightened by several factors. First, the writing started two months late because the software schedule had slipped. Second, the final page count turned out to be almost one-third higher than estimated (see Table 1). The overrun was due in part to the unavailability of complete specifications at the time of the estimate, and in part to inexperience with maintenance manuals. Third, access to the product was limited. For the *Operations Manual* the writer checked the software in a simulated (development) environment rather than on a working prototype. For the *Maintenance Manual* the manager could get only limited access to the prototype, and this slowed down the description of procedures for removing and replacing parts. Finally, the software and hardware continued to change throughout the writing period (months 8-18) and especially in the middle of the acceptance tests (months 15-16).

Table 1. Estimated and Actual Page Counts of Model-6000 Manuals

Manual	Estimated	Actual
Operations	130	160
Training	110	130
Maintenance	110	170
Total	350	460

Overrun as percentage of estimated total: 31%

Anticipating problems by the end of month 11, the documentation manager went to the vice president who was acting as product manager, and presented two options for temporarily increasing staff: hiring a contract writer to do the *Maintenance Manual*; or hiring a free-lance editor to copy-edit and coordinate production. The vice president turned down both requests while acknowledging that circumstances beyond the writers' control were adding to their work. However, there were cost overruns on the engineering side too, and priority had to be given to building a functioning product. Moreover, cash was tight because EFG Distribution would not start to pay for the product until it had been accepted (month 18 at the earliest).

Accordingly, the documentation manager and the senior writer faced difficult decisions. They did not have enough manpower to finish the manuals on time and in accordance with their own professional standards, but they could not reduce the scope of information to be covered. Therefore, they compromised various aspects of presentation and quality control. Here are the shortcuts they took in order to get the job done.

First, they did little editing. They reviewed each other's work in a cursory manner, focusing on consistency of terminology and format but bypassing problems that would require analysis and rewriting. Second, they did not provide indexes in the manuals. This omission troubled them particularly; although the inconvenience to readers would be partly offset by tabbed dividers between chapters (which EFG Distribution had told them would be present) and by the repetition of the table of contents for each chapter immediately after the tabbed divider.

Third, in reviewing each other's work they did not verify the text against the product. The burden of verifying content was left to the engineers at ABC Hardware and EFG Distribution, although at neither company did formal quality assurance procedures extend to documentation.

Finally, the manager wrote only one draft of the *Maintenance Manual* before delivering camera-ready copy. Lacking experience in this kind of manual, he had underestimated its length by a third. Also contributing to the time pressure, major changes in the circuit boards were made in month 16, just six weeks before the delivery deadline.

Throughout the project the manager and the senior writer felt embattled. So, in fact, did everyone working on the Model-6000, since the company's future depended on the project. The documentation manager was aware of a certain tension when he approached the engineering

manager to borrow the draftsman's time for the illustrations. There was
additional tension when he was scheduling use of the prototype and
interviews with the engineers. It was also difficult to get the
engineers to return written comments on the drafts on time.

Nevertheless, the manuals got written. During the acceptance
period, EFG Distribution asked for only minor changes. The camera-ready
pages were delivered on time; they *looked* good, thanks to the illustrations
and the writers' skill in using the publications workstation. The vice
president in charge of the product, who had been beset by engineering
problems and continual negotiations with EFG Distribution, went out of
his way to thank the documentation team for finishing the manuals on
time and within budget.

Summary of Labor and Cost. Table 2 summarizes the work that went
into the three Model-6000 manuals. "Management" covers the tasks of
outlining the text, specifying the illustrations, and continually
negotiating for illustration time, access to the prototype, extra staff,
and engineers' reviews. "Writing" includes entering and formatting the
text, since both tasks were performed in a single operation. "Editing"
refers to the two principals' reviews of each other's manuals.
"Composition and art" refers to the draftsman's tasks of drawing the
line art and pasting it up. The "pages per day" entries measure
productivity of total documentation labor and of the writing component

---

Table 2. Summary of Model-6000 Documentation Labor and Cost

Function	Man-months	Percentage
Management	1.4	11%
Writing (460 pages - see Table 1)	9.6	73
Editing	1.0	8
Composition and art	1.1	8
Total documentation labor	13.1	100

Pages per writing man-day: 2.1
Pages per documentation man-day: 1.5
Documentation as percentage of total product-development labor: 8.3%
Documentation as percentage of total product-development cost: 7.8%

---

alone. Finally, the two percentages compare documentation labor and cost with the respective totals for the whole product-development project.

3. XYZ Software, Inc.: A Resource-Enriched Environment

Company, Product, and Marketing. XYZ Media is a diversified communication and entertainment company with interests in trade and textbook publishing, newspapers, broadcasting, and motion pictures. A subsidiary called XYZ Software was created five years ago to leverage the expertise of the publishing subsidiaries. XYZ Media decided that the educational and editorial skills that go into textbooks could be applied to software for mass markets. In addition, XYZ Media saw possible synergism between trade book distribution and software marketing.

XYZ Software has been successful in publishing business programs for desktop computers. Of seven products marketed in the first five years, four have sold over 100,000 copies each. Instead of developing programs from scratch, XYZ Software buys or licenses them from small companies or individual authors. XYZ studies the potential market for each acquisition. If the research indicates sales of 20,000 copies or more in the first year, XYZ invests heavily in the product.

PC-IQ is the latest acquisition of XYZ Software. Designed for middle managers and other business professionals, PC-IQ is a desktop organizer with artificial intelligence. It provides the familiar desktop functions of notebook, appointment calendar, phone directory, and expense record. In addition, if the user learns to insert simple "flags" (codes) in his or her entries, PC-IQ can discern patterns or habits, and can make reasonable inferences about future actions based on past behavior. The program then informs the user of upcoming commitments as well as apparent inconsistencies or omissions in his or her office routine.

XYZ Software bought PC-IQ outright for $500,000. It plans to spend another $1.6 million on developing the product, plus substantial amounts on marketing. First-year sales are expected to be 40,000 copies at a wholesale price of $125.00. Eighty percent of all purchases are expected from users of earlier XYZ Software products.

The product plan for PC-IQ sets forth the company's traditional techniques for commercializing an acquisition. First, the user interface will be rewritten so that PC-IQ will have the same look and feel as the company's best-selling products and can readily exchange files with them. A standard interface is critical because existing customers are the primary market for the new product. Second, attractive, thorough documentation will be written; it must be accessible to users with varied styles of learning, making PC-IQ truly easy to learn and use. Documentation is critical because so many copies will be sold.

Table 3 lists the documentation specified in the product plan. A demo disk - the first thing a prospective buyer is likely to look at - will be a "grabber" that focuses attention on the easiest, most attractive features of the product. The *User's Manual* will describe the product completely. The *Reference Pamphlet* will repeat, in concise format, information on conventions and interfaces and will list all commands. The HELP screens will explain all commands, borrowing text from reference sections of the *User's Manual* but abbreviating and reformatting it for easier reading on the screen.

Table 3. PC-IQ Documentation Specified in Product Plan

Document	Function	Scope
Demo disk	Sales.	Attractive features.
User's Manual	Training. Complete reference.	How to install the software. Keyboard and other conventions. Interface with other products. All commands.
Reference Pamphlet	Quick reference.	Conventions. Interface with other products. All commands.
HELP screens	Quick reference.	All commands.

Figure 2 shows the development schedule in the PC-IQ product plan.

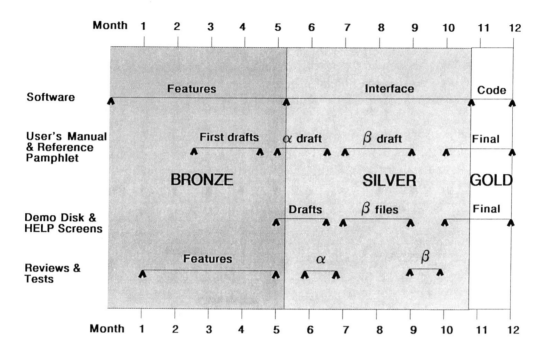

Figure 2. PC-IQ Project Schedule in Development Plan

Extending over 12 months, the project is organized in three phases - bronze, silver, gold - each culminating in a major software milestone. During the bronze phase, the acquired program will be redesigned and rewritten, several successive prototypes will be tested, and the manual and pamphlet will be outlined and drafted. The bronze phase will end with the freezing of software features and capabilities. During the silver phase, the demo disk and HELP files will be started, and there will be formal alpha and beta tests. The silver phase will end with the freezing of the product's interfaces: screens, commands, files, reports, and keyboard usage. In the gold phase the software will be optimized for size and speed; and the development group will release all items for manufacturing - code, demo and HELP files, camera-ready *User's Manual* and *Reference Pamphlet*.

Narrative of the Documentation Project. The PC-IQ team, headed by a product manager, represented all skills needed to develop, market, and support the product (see Figure 3). The team met weekly to coordinate all issues of design, development, testing, and marketing. Even before a department became active in the project, its representative attended the meetings, so that the potential impact of early decisions in any area would be considered by everyone.

The documentation representative on the team recruited staff from the Documentation Department for the PC-IQ project. At the beginning there was one writer, one editor, and one production coordinator. By the end of the project, there were three writers, three editors, and two production specialists.

The documentation was continuously reviewed and tested while being written. All reviews and tests were administered by the Quality Assurance (Q/A) Department in accordance with a well-established philosophy. The main tenet was that since the product consists of "everything that goes in the box," software and documentation must be reviewed as an entity.

Sample chapters of the *User's Manual* were repeatedly drafted during the bronze phase and reviewed by team members from Marketing, Q/A, and

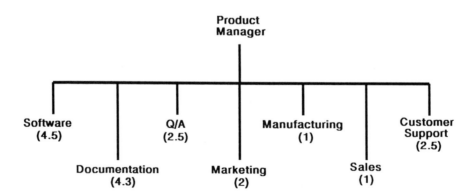

Figure 3. Product Team
Parenthesized numbers denote man-years of effort during the one-year development period.

Customer Support. The purpose was to experiment with stylistic approaches and to check the effectiveness of the outlines laid out in the project plan. As a result of the reviews, two "tabs" (major sections marked by tabbed dividers) were added to the *User's Manual*, increasing its length by about 60 pages.

In addition to receiving feedback from Marketing, Q/A, and Customer Support, the writers interacted directly with the Software Department. During the bronze phase the writers suggested new software features, and these were implemented. During the silver phase they suggested many improvements in the wording of commands and the layout of screens.

In the silver phase emphasis shifted from reviews to alpha and beta tests. In the alpha series the subjects were XYZ Software employees who had had no prior connection with the project; in the beta series they were customers recruited by the Sales Department. The alpha tests produced the last major change in the documentation plan. A new module was added to the demo disk, increasing its length by 40 screens.

In Table 4 the estimated length of PC-IQ documents, as set forth in the product plan, is compared with the final page counts. The 37% overrun required an increase in the PC-IQ documentation staff from two writers to three, as well as additional editorial and production help. When the product manager went to top management for a budget increase, she argued that the additional documentation would pay for itself in increased sales and fewer telephone calls to the Customer Support hot line.

Table 4. Estimated and Actual Page Counts of PC-IQ Documentation

Document	Estimated	Actual
User's Manual	165	230
Reference Pamphlet	15	20
HELP screens (page equivalents)	45	50
Demo disk (page equivalents)	75	115
Total	300	415

Overrun as percentage of estimated total: 37%

The customers who used the product in the beta test commented enthusiastically, thus confirming predictions of the original market studies. The tests resulted in many refinements in the software and documentation but no major changes. The programmers and the writers were pleased to receive positive feedback from "the real world."

Within the documentation group, the editors and production staff played roles of increasing importance during the silver and gold phases. Their mission was to assure maximum readability in style and layout. XYZ Software aimed for the same verbal and graphic polish in software documentation that its sister company, XYZ Textbooks, achieved in high school and college texts. However, the challenge at XYZ Software was greater because production schedules were tighter and there were two presentation media, the printed page and the computer screen.

To meet this challenge, the Documentation Department had developed resources and techniques which now helped the PC-IQ project. First, it had created a standards document that defined norms of readability, copy-editing, page layout, and screen layout; the readability norms comprised guidelines for sentence length and vocabulary as functions of readers' educational level. Second, Documentation had a policy of copy-editing all drafts starting with the alpha test; thus writers were alerted early to stylistic problems, and editors were exposed to the new product technology so that they could work with greater confidence as final deadlines drew near. Third, the beta manuals were produced in multi-font proportional type on a laser printer and then photocopied on both sides of the page. Thus beta tests yielded feedback on format as well as content.

Much production time was devoted to graphic elements of the *User's Manual* and *Reference Pamphlet*. On average, one page in three contained a table of reference information or the reproduction of a computer screen. Although the writers built the tables and captured the screens in their text files, the tables required additional format-coding and the screens required paste-up of call-outs. Further, hundreds of acetate overlays were affixed to the camera-ready copy so that screen reproductions would be printed with appropriate shading, and main titles and headings would be printed in a second color.

The product, both software and documentation, passed all tests and was released to Manufacturing on schedule. (The start of manufacturing

coincided with the first promotional mailing to XYZ Software's
customers.) As usual in a computer development project, the final weeks
were frantic. However, morale remained high, perhaps because each
participating group understood its own role and those of its colleagues.

Summary of Labor and Cost. Table 5 summarizes the work on the
PC-IQ documentation set. "Management" refers to the documentation
manager's tasks: meeting with the product team, estimating personnel
needs, obtaining staff from the Documentation Department, and
coordinating their work. "Writing" refers to the technical writers'
creation and revision of printed and electronic documentation.
"Editing" refers to the technical editors' tasks: substantive editing,
copy-editing, proofreading, and controlling the flow of drafts and
feedback. "Composition and art" refers to production specialists'
tasks: preparing the laser-printed beta manuals and the two-color final
manuals, and formatting the screens of the demo disk and HELP files.

Table 5. Summary of PC-IQ Documentation Labor and Cost

Function	Man-months	Percentage
Management	6	10%
Writing (415 pages - see Table 4)	18	30
Editing	24	40
Composition and art	12	20
Total documentation labor	60	100

Pages per writing man-day: 1.02
Pages per documentation man-day: 0.31
Documentation as percentage of total product-development labor: 25.6%
Documentation as percentage of total product-development cost: 18.9%

The "pages per day" entries measure productivity of the
documentation group as a whole and of the three writers alone. Finally,
the two percentages compare documentation labor and cost with the
respective totals for the whole product-development project. Total
product-development labor includes all members of the product team
(Figure 3). Total product-development cost includes acquisition of the
software but excludes advertising and manufacturing (printing,
duplicating disks, packaging).

4. Documentation Attributes Predicted by Level of Investment

How does the relative size of a company's investment in documentation affect the documentation itself? Each case study showed effects that may or may not depend on particular circumstances. Now the cases will be compared to see if they support general conclusions. In other words, do larger or smaller investments result in predictable differences in the documentation?

Table 6 collates data that were given separately for each project. "Total pages" and "total labor" show that the PC-IQ project produced 10% less output than the Model-6000 project but used four times more labor! If the personnel in the projects were of equal competence and had equivalent tools to work with, the disparity in labor should be reflected in quality of output.

Table 6. Page Counts and Labor in Two Case Studies

	Model-6000	PC-IQ
Total pages	460	415
Management	1.4 man-months	6 man-months
Writing	9.6 (Note)	18
Editing	1.0	16
Composition and art	1.1	12
Total labor	13.1	52

Note: Includes formatting the text files.

Figures 4 and 5 show the relative distribution of labor within each project. In the resource-limited Model-6000 project (Figure 4), writing was the overwhelming priority; all other functions were squeezed to the minimum. But note that writing included formatting, a composition and art task, which the writers performed while entering text.

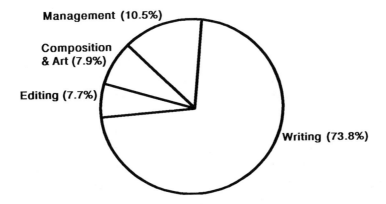

Figure 4.   Documentation Labor in Resource-Limited Case Study

In the resource-enriched PC-IQ project (Figure 5), the pie is split more evenly. Writing got a smaller relative share, and the extra resources were divided between editing, and composition and art. This allocation reflected the requirements of a mass product for simple language and attractive layout.

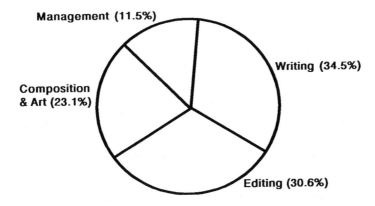

Figure 5.   Documentation Labor in Resource-Enriched Case Study

Again using the data of Table 6, Figure 6 compares the two projects with respect to rate of work in each labor category. The PC-IQ project spent much more time per page in all categories.

In the writing category, I infer not that the PC-IQ staff wrote more slowly but that they did more rewriting. They produced more drafts in response to continuous changes in the software, hands-on review and testing by readers other than programmers, and organizational and stylistic feedback from editors. The Model-6000 writers, on the other hand, were hard pressed to finish their work, which was reviewed but not rigorously tested. They received no feedback on the overall effectiveness of the writing, had no time for discretionary improvements, and were forced to omit the second draft of one manual.

Several factors contributed to the lopsided difference in editing rates shown in Figure 6. First, as in the case of writing, there were more drafts in the PC-IQ project, and each one was thoroughly edited before review or testing. Second, the PC-IQ documentation was polished for clarity and simplicity in accordance with readability standards developed in textbook publishing. Third, the PC-IQ typographic formats were more complex, and the formatting of electronic publications (demo

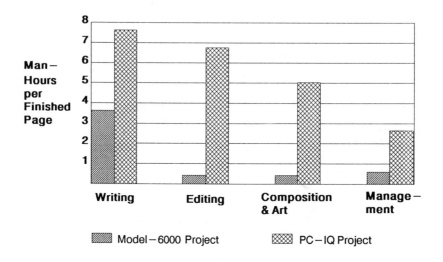

Figure 6. Rates of Work in Two Case Studies

disk, HELP screens) added another dimension of work. Fourth, the PC-IQ editors conferred with the writers, giving them general suggestions on organization and exposition. Finally, the editors helped control the flow of drafts and reviews. In contrast to this continuous editorial activity, the Model-6000 writers simply read each other's work once, checking for consistency of terminology and format.

With respect to composition and art, the difference shown in Figure 6 results from more attention being given to typography, graphics, and copy preparation in the PC-IQ project than in the Model-6000. The PC-IQ manuals had three times as many tables, four times as many computer-screen reproductions, shading of computer screens, call-outs labeling fields on every screen, and a second color of ink for main titles and headings. In addition, since the beta drafts were fully formatted, text changes resulting from the beta test entailed duplication of labor when the final camera-ready pages were prepared.

With respect to management, Figure 6 is misleading in showing that one project spent more management time *per page* than the other. The correct interpretation is that there were more people and tasks to be managed in the PC-IQ project than in the Model-6000. The management labor required in a writing project is probably a constant function of total labor, not of total pages. The two pie charts (Figures 4 and 5) suggest that this constant is roughly 10%.

In summary, when a company limits its investment in documentation, top priority will be given to producing a complete text, which will be reviewed but not rigorously verified. When a company makes more resources available, they will be allocated to rewriting in response to objective review and testing, to editing for readability, and to varied typography and graphics.

5. Business Conditions That Predict Investment in Documentation

The case studies illustrate common but opposite approaches to documentation in the computer and telecommunication industries. One company viewed documentation as adding little value to the product; the other, as adding a great deal. Now I would like to ask what business factors determine management's view of documentation in the first place.

Do the case studies suggest *general* reasons why one company should enrich its documentation environment while another should limit it?

Six variables that may explain the decision are listed in Table 7, with their respective values in the case studies. After discussing these six, I will comment on two more variables, competition and product liability, that are not operative in the case studies but may be important in other situations.

Table 7. Variables That May Predict Investment in Documentation

Candidate variable	ABC Hardware	XYZ Software
Sales volume (year 1)	100	40,000
Distribution channel	OEM	Retail
Unit price	$50,000	$125
Cash reserves	Tight	Ample
Hardware or software?	Both	Software
Number of user options (product complexity)	Many	Many

Note: Two more variables, which are not operative in the case studies, are considered in the text.

Sales volume is the strongest business reason for investing heavily in documentation. Targeting 40,000 buyers in the first year, XYZ Software sold through a large network of retailers who were not expected to explain the product to prospective buyers or to answer questions after sales were made. Hence the demo disk was an important sales tool, and the *User's Manual* and HELP screens were vital for assuring continuing satisfaction and favorable recommendations. XYZ Software could not afford a flood of telephone calls to its Customer Support hot line from users who did not understand the documentation. Still less could it afford customers to stop using the product without bothering to call.

Low sales volume reduces the importance of documentation in management's view. When fewer customers are expected, personal contact tends to be substituted for documentation both before and after the sale.

Distribution channel overlaps with sales volume in most instances. ABC Hardware invested in documentation to the minimum extent possible, since it was selling under contract to only one customer, EFG Distribution. EFG Distribution, in turn, did not impose stringent requirements on ABC Hardware, because EFG's salesmen visited all potential customers, and the customers' evaluation process included trial installation and training conducted by the salesmen. Thus personal contact superseded documentation in the critical early stages of the vendor-customer relationship. Only XYZ Software, with its large retail distribution network, was constrained to enforce high documentation standards.

The documentation investment seems to vary inversely with *unit price*. Inexpensive products, when sold in high volume like PC-IQ, require superior documentation. With high-priced products, on the other hand, a developer is likely to reduce the proportion of total development cost allocated to documentation and increase expenditures on various forms of personal contact with customers. I have just made this point with respect to product evaluation and sales; but personal contact, in the form of maintenance support, is equally important *after* the sale of a high-priced product. If the maintenance support is offered without charge, then the developer's documentation group competes with its maintenance group for internal funds. More often, however, the customer must pay for maintenance support; in this case, the developer's incentive to invest in documentation is reduced because documentation generates much less revenue and income than support. In general, then, computer companies tend to offer personal support for high-cost products, and such support tends to reduce the investment in documentation.

Cash reserves seem to determine a company's ability to make mid-course corrections of the kind that was needed in each case study. Recall that in both cases final page counts exceeded estimates by over 30%. ABC Hardware, pinched by the delayed payment schedule in its contract with EFG Distribution, could not allocate more resources; whereas XYZ Software could, thanks to cash reserves generated by successful previous products. However, underestimates of work and consequent cost overruns are extremely common in the computer industry due to the intrinsic difficulty of modeling and implementing intellectual processes in electronic products. Overruns should be anticipated in the development budget; they should not be allowed to become emergencies. Although cash-poor companies skimp on documentation, the need for a contingency fund is so predictable that a cash shortage is actually the result of a prior investment decision, not its cause or explanation.

Hardware versus software is no longer a clear distinction and thus does not help explain the documentation investment decision. Most computer products that seem to consist primarily of hardware are loaded with specialized software or firmware (read-only microcode, in many ways equivalent to software). ABC Hardware's Model-6000, with its menu-driven software interface, is an example of an integrated hardware-software system; smart modems for microcomputers and input/output controllers for minicomputers typify hardware-firmware products. In general, if a piece of hardware is marketed without software or firmware, it is likely to be a commodity rather than a product.

The case studies do not support a conclusion about the relative importance of *number of user options*, taken as a measure of *product complexity*. Although both products provided many options, the two companies made different decisions about documentation. It seems likely, however, that simple products attract relatively small investments in documentation.

Competition and product liability may be of independent importance in determining investment in documentation, although these variables were not operative in the case studies. *Competition* becomes relevant when a company feels that in order to gain market share for a new product it must match high-quality documentation of an established rival product. In this case, however, the newcomer tends to emulate the printing and binding of the rival manual, while ignoring the contents.

Liability is critical when the computer product has accessible moving parts (for example, an impact printer) or when it controls a physical operation (for example, a manufacturing system). However, if the product handles information only, liability does not in my opinion affect management's investment in documentation. Software publishers in particular count on boilerplate disclaimers of liability, prominently printed at the beginning of manuals. As far as I know, no law suit against a software publisher has been won because of alleged defects in documentation. Indeed, the most publicized suit on this or related issues - Cummings versus Lotus - was withdrawn (*New York Times,* December

10, 1986, page D8). However, in December 1985 the Internal Revenue Service ruled that if software provides "substantive instructions" for filing tax returns, the developer of the program is liable as a tax preparer (*Wall Street Journal*, August 4, 1986, page 17). This ruling stands as a warning to management concerning the liability of information-handling products and their documentation.

In summary, the case studies suggest that two variables dominate management's decision on the relative size of its investment in documentation. *High projected sales volume* seems to predict a relatively large investment, because high volume precludes personal contact with customers before and after sales. *High unit cost,* on the other hand, predicts a lower relative investment in documentation, because personal contact is more effective in influencing the purchase decision and competes with documentation as a means of delivering maintenance support.

Acknowledgments. The author gratefully acknowledges substantive comments on a draft of this paper from Sam Guckenheimer, Stephen G. Krug, David S. McNitt, Harold H. Wadleigh, and Howard G. Zaharoff, Esq.; and editorial suggestions from Edward Barrett, Jon Burrowes, Leslie Kirsch, James G. Paradis, and Robert R. Rathbone.

12

Preparing for a Successful Large-Scale Courseware Development Project

Richard Ziegfeld
Sverdrup Technology
16530 Commerce Court
Middleburg Heights, Ohio 44130

Ruth Hawkins
McDonnell Douglas Corporation

Wilson Judd
United Airlines

Robert Mahany
McDonnell Douglas Corporation

ABSTRACT

The McDonnell Douglas Computer-Based Training courseware team recently completed a large development project: it created software for 814 trainee hours in one curriculum. Based on that experience, we suggest six issues for project leaders to consider as they begin large-scale computer-assisted instruction (CAI) projects: project organization, production management, instructional design, editorial, graphics, and personnel. The project-organization section covers the division of labor and the relationships among the major courseware team components. The production-management section includes a description of the four control tools that the team used: pacing guide, time sheets, milestone recording, and automated reports. The instructional-design section indicates criteria for selecting a training design model. The editorial component reviews the need for an editor, a style manual, and rules on module completion. The graphic section covers team organization and standardization of the graphics development process. The personnel section outlines a six-stage search process (resume and cover letter, published sample, logic test, on-site writing sample, interview, and reference calls). It also offers a brief job description for authors.

INTRODUCTION

Rapidly changing technology has resulted in an urgent need for quality technical training programs in both government and industry. Consequently, large-scale training development projects are becoming more common. Trainers and training managers who are experienced with smaller courseware development efforts may underestimate the amount of planning and front-end organization required for the large-scale effort, so we think our experience on a large project may be valuable to you. As a result, we'll describe our experience and then offer some notes about what decisions you need to make as you begin your large-scale courseware project.

The McDonnell Douglas Computer-Based Training Systems Group (CBTSG) has had CAI courseware development experience ranging from small projects (1 or 2 student contact hours) to perhaps the largest single effort ever attempted (814 student contact hours). We learned (sometimes painfully) that the larger the development effort, the more important the planning phases. In this paper, we outline the major issues that you should consider before beginning development. For this discussion, we address the following areas:

- Project organization
- Production management
- The instructional design component
- The editorial component
- The graphics component
- Selecting personnel

Before we begin dispensing advice, we should describe the large-scale CAI courseware development project that taught us the importance of planning and preparation. Over a two-year period (1983-1985), we created 814 student-contact hours of first-line CF-18 maintenance training for the Canadian Forces. Our sister company, McDonnell Aircraft Company (MCAIR), which manufactures the F-18, performed the front-end analysis and developed the objectives. We created CAI lesson outlines and lessons that were reviewed by both MCAIR and Canadian Forces personnel. The final acceptance of each lesson was contingent upon that lesson passing a small group trial at the Canadian training facility (Cold Lake, Alberta).

PROJECT ORGANIZATION

Goals. Two program requirements shaped the organization of our courseware development project: a need for efficiency and a need to establish and maintain a standard of instructional quality.

Given the amount of courseware we had to develop and the time frame in which we had to develop it, it was obvious at the outset that we needed a large number of personnel: 40 to 60. In an attempt to avoid the inefficiencies that often accompany large group efforts, we divided the development group into a number of teams. While efficiency is not as dependent on group size as in software development, communications are more difficult and time consuming in larger courseware groups. As a secondary goal, we hoped smaller teams would increase the chances of new employees identifying with the team and, hence, with the project.

For a project of this size, it was imperative that we establish standards for many aspects of the courseware and that we apply these standards uniformly across courses. One major concern was, of course, standardization of instructional quality. Our previous experience with using instructional design personnel in staff positions strongly suggested that such an arrangement would not work here. Therefore, we placed the instructional designers in line positions as team supervisors, where they were responsible for both instructional quality control and production.

Organizational structure. We defined some teams by discipline (e.g., graphics, editing). However, we divided the basic authoring task among five teams of 5 to 8 members each, with each team responsible for either a single course or a group of courses with similar content. As we mentioned above, an instructional designer/team leader supervised each team. See Figure 1, Project Organization.

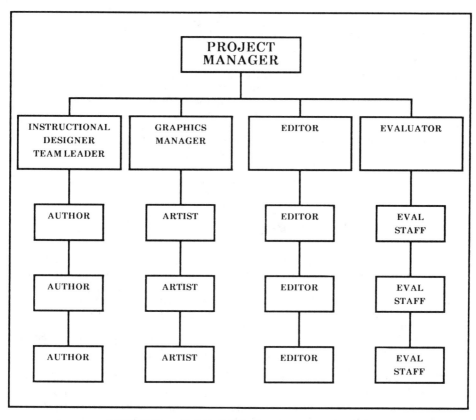

FIGURE 1 PROJECT ORGANIZATION

We could have placed graphics and editorial support within authoring teams. We decided, however, to provide these functions through separate teams, each with a team leader who was a peer with authoring team leaders. We did this partly because it was more efficient for consolidating editorial and graphics functions across the project. We also chose this approach so that the graphics manager and editor-in-chief would be independent to establish sound quality-assurance standards in their respective disciplines.

A third function which should have been kept separate was evaluation-- conduct of the small group trials at the customer's site. This was originally established as a separate function and as the responsibility of a single individual. As the project got underway, however, the Evaluation Manager was given additional duties that required more immediate attention and that eventually turned into a full-time job. As a result, preparation for the small group trials was put off until the last minute and then done in a much less efficient manner than should have been the case.

Hardware, software, administrative, and typing support came from personnel supervised from outside the courseware team. While this arrangement resulted in some communication and priority-setting problems, it is probably typical of most courseware efforts that take place within a larger organization. If we could make only one organizational change, it would probably have been to appoint one administrative person full time.

In addition to overall project responsibility, the Project Manager was also responsible for acquiring resources, for resolving conflicts among the various teams, and for handling program-level interactions with the customer, MCAIR, and supporting groups within our own company.

A group consisting of the project manager and the seven team leaders established the policies and standards that governed the complete courseware development process. The intent was to address the inevitable conflicts among the different groups (e.g., between graphics and an authoring team), establish a policy, and then evaluate the effectiveness of that policy. While policies evolved over the course of the project, each team leader was responsible for enforcing the current policy.

Key decision: for your content, how do you organize your writing team(s)?

PRODUCTION MANAGEMENT

Objectives. Two primary concerns led us to establish formal production management procedures. First, we needed an efficient system to keep track of over 600 modules as each module met 14 major milestones. Second, of course, was the ubiquitous limited budget. On a project of this size, even minor inefficiencies can result in major costs. We needed to monitor time allocation for development tasks *and* individual efficiency.

Tools. We created a tracking/time accounting system with four elements: (1) a development pacing guide, (2) weekly task-specific time reporting sheets, (3) milestone recording, and (4) an automated report program.

The project budget was predicated on teams producing CAI at a rate of "X" hours of effort per contact hour of CAI. The lesson specification for each module contained an estimate of that module's length. When we multiplied the estimated module length by the production rate, we could tell authors how many hours to budget for that module. For example, if the production rate were 200 hours per hour, a 1/2-hour lesson would get 100 hours of development, a 1-hour lesson would get 200, and a 2-hour lesson 400 hours. We refined length estimates (and budgeted hours) as development proceeded.

Pacing guide. The pacing guide divided the module development process into approximately 50 steps. See Figure 2, Module Writing Pacing Guide.

Module Writing Pacing Guide

MODULE IDENTIFIER: ESTIMATED CONTACT: 0.50 HOURS
MODULE TITLE:
AUTHOR   INSTRUCTIONAL DESIGNER:

	AUTHOR	ID	TYPING	GRAPHICS
PART I (33%) CORRECT THE OUTLINE				
1. Review Customer Comments	0.45			
2. Review Changes with Instr. Designer	0.14	0.14		
3. Correct the Outline	0.45			
4. Retype the Outline			0.23	
PART II (47%) CREATE THE GRAPHICS				
5. Attend Graphics Meeting	0.45	0.45		0.45
6. Develop Graphics				10.08
PART III (63%) WRITE MODULE SEGMENTS				
7. For Each Objective Segment, Write:	12.35			
Content structure diagram				
Statement support				
Examples				
Progress check				
8. Perform Preliminary Instr. Review		0.45		

FIGURE 2   MODULE WRITING PACING GUIDE

For each step, we allocated a certain percentage of the total development effort (to the right of the part number) and, thus, for a module of a given length, a certain number of person hours. The effort within each step was further distributed across the specialties involved. For example, the allocation for a single step might be one-half hour of the author's time and 15 minutes of instructional designer's time.

Time sheets. We developed time sheets that permitted us to track each person's time by task and module. Personnel recorded time allocation on a daily basis and we summarized it on a weekly basis. For example, during a particular week, an author might record that he had spent 6 hours reviewing lesson specifications for Modules A, B, and C; 12 hours developing an outline for Module D; 18 hours developing; and four hours revising Module F following customer review. The pacing-guide-percentage-complete figure was also updated each week for each module on which some effort was expended. All of this data was kept in a database that we will discuss later.

Milestone recording. Milestone status simply showed each module's position in the work cycle and how long it had been in that position, i.e., the date of its last milestone. See Figure 3, Milestone Reports--by Team. With this report, authors and team leaders could quickly scan the columns to determine which modules were incomplete or caught in bottlenecks.

MILESTONE REPORTS--BY TEAM
COURSE: 512.46 AIRFRAME

MOD	AUT	EST HRS	TITLE	LSD IN	COMM SENT	APPR CHG	COMM INC	LSD APPR	OUTL SENT
13.2.35	KW	.50	In/Ex In	04-22	04-29	05-12	05-13	05-18	05-21
13.2.36	JS	1.0	Pur Loc Ail	06-20	06-26	07-01			
13.2.37	JY	1.0	Hor/St--2	07-21	07-22	07-29	08-15	08-22	

KEY:

TERM	MEANING
MOD	Module number
AUT	Author of the module
EST HRS	Estimated hours that the trainee will spend on the module
TITLE	Title of the module
LSD SENT	Lesson specification document (LSD) received from customer
COMM SENT	Comments on LSD sent to customer
APPR CHG	Customer has approved changes
COMM INC	Customer's comments have been incorporated
LSD APPR	Customer has approved LSD
OUTL SENT	Outline has been sent to customer

FIGURE 3   MILESTONE REPORTS--BY TEAM

The second part of the report displayed, for each module, the number of hours spent by personnel in each specialty, the total number of hours expended on that module, the pacing guide percentage complete, the target number of hours budgeted for that module, percentage completion, and the percentage by which the module was over or under budget. See Figure 4, Automated Reports--for Authors. For example, on module 13.2.37, the author has put in 92 hours, the I.D. 9, the clerical 5, and the graphics artist 3. Total hours are 110, and the module is 95% complete. Scheduled hours for a 1.0 hour module are 117, so this module is running ahead of pace--at 107%.

AUTOMATED REPORTS--FOR AUTHORS

MOD	AUT	EST HRS	TITLE	AUT HR	ID HR	CMP HR	GRP HR	TTL HR	PACE PCT	SCH HR	RL RT PR
13.2.37	JY	1.00	Hr/St--2	92	9.0	5.0	3.0	110	95%	117	107%
14.1.52	JY	1.00	Hr/St--3	86	18	5.0	2.0	110	94%	116	105%
14.1.53	JY	1.60	In/St	102	9.0	6.0	8.0	126	95%	182	144%
14.2.21	JY	1.50	P/O Rd	29	10	3.0	43	285	94%	169	59%
Totals for JY	14.3			1057	94	54	138	1343	95%	1619	1159%
Average for JY	1.59			117	10	6.0	15	149	95%	180	129%
Av. for Airframe	1.17			108	20	8.0	17	153	94%	136	129%

KEY:

TERM	MEANING
MOD	Module number
AUT	Author of the module
EST HRS	Estimated hours that the trainee will spend on the module
TITLE	Title of the module
AUT HR	Author labor hours on the module
ID HR	Instructional designer labor hours on the module
CMP HR	Composer (clerical) labor hours on the module
GRP HR	Graphic labor hours on the module
TTL HR	Total labor hours on the module
SCH HR	Scheduled hours on the module according to pacing standards
RL RT PR	Author's relative rate of progress with respect to pacing standards
TOTALS FOR JY	Totals for this particular author
AVERAGE FOR JY	Averages for this particular author
AV. FOR AIRFRAME	Averages for the airframe writing team

FIGURE 4 AUTOMATED REPORTS--FOR AUTHORS

We also summarized these same data across modules for individual authors (toward the bottom of the figure) and for complete courses (last line in the figure). Thus, one could, for example, compare the percentage of development effort devoted to graphics in each of several courses, compare courses and individuals in terms of the total effort being expended, and track changes in any of these parameters over time.

Automated reports. We developed a tracking and time recording system using the DB Master (TM) database program for the Apple II. Once a week, we entered each person's reported time expenditures, the updated module percentages complete, and the dates on which they met any of the 14 milestones. We also printed a *weekly* report. The report consisted of two parts for each course: module milestone status and module status with respect to percentage complete and effort expended. Automated tracking of module status (which of the 14 milestones had been met and when) was essential for production control. A non-automated system would have been too cumbersome and slow to be of value.

Utility. The CAI development pacing guides were extremely important. While the division of effort across the 50 development steps was not at all optimal, the guides did provide a critical baseline for authors with respect to resource management. Authors knew that if, at a certain point in the process, they were 10 hours over budget, they had to make up those 10 hours later.

The time reports were useful but not necessarily in the ways that we anticipated. We assumed we would use the report data to refine the pacing guide. As mentioned above, however, we found pacing guide accuracy not to be that important and during the project, we didn't revise the guides on the basis of current data.

The reports' most valuable function was probably to alert team leaders to production problems quickly so they could take corrective action early enough to have an effect. That is, a team leader could efficiently check dozens of modules in a course and determine which were overrunning their budgets-- even when the modules were only a fraction complete. On the othe hand, we assumed that the report data would also reveal broader problem trends involving many modules, which could then be corrected. This was not the case. Involved individuals easily recognized general problems well before their data reflected the impact.

Rate-of-efficiency and development time were not the only factors used to evaluate the relative efficiency of the authors. Development-time data alone could not measure an author's effectiveness since it failed to account for a number of difficulty factors and since there were ways in which authors could manipulate it. The data did, however, serve to flag authors who were having difficulty and to track changes in their efficiency over time.

Finally, the weekly data accumulated across all courses measured how well the project as a whole was progressing relative to schedule and budget.

This permitted us to make quite accurate predictions about the number of people that we needed to finish the project on schedule and the rate at which authoring efficiency had to increase to complete the project under budget.

Key decisions: how much control do you need over the development process and how much labor can you afford to devote to providing reports?

THE INSTRUCTIONAL DESIGN COMPONENT

We developed these four production management tools for our project. Now let's look at the instructional design issues. Regardless of the instructional medium, it is difficult to create well structured, consistent, interesting instructional materials that actually prepare students to perform a job. However, when planning a courseware development effort, you can ensure the instructional quality of your product by carefully planning the instructional design component of your project.

Choosing an instructional design model. During planning, you need to make several important decisions. First, you should select and commit to a comprehensive instructional design philosophy. This overall instructional design philosophy or model will guide the development efforts of the authors and define the instructional quality-control criteria for the instructional designer during the review process.

There is no perfect instructional design theory. There are, however, some considerations to keep in mind when shopping for one to suit your particular courseware development situation. Look for a model that reflects the latest human learning theories, differentiates between various types of learning, is applicable to your particular situation (adult learners vs children, training vs education, etc.), and is readily applied (procedure-oriented).

Implementing the instructional design. After choosing a design philosophy, you will be faced with the more difficult task of persuading all parties involved that it is the best choice and that they should use it. If the instructional designer were to advocate one approach and the customer or user another, not only would the curriculum reflect this inconsistency but the potential for conflict during the review cycle would also increase. You want to avoid this kind of conflict. Either persuade the customer that your design philosophy merits adoption or adjust your approach to the customer's philosophy.

Once you choose the design philosphy, you must train authors, instructional designers, editors, and graphics artists to various levels so that they can use the model. During the training, it is important for authors and instructional designers to have ample opportunity to apply the design philosophy in actual courseware development situations and to receive feedback from the trainer.

When we planned the CF-18 courseware project, we created a set of design guidelines that guided authors through the development process for our project. We used *The Instructional Quality Inventory* (IQI) as the core and added guidelines of our own (Ellis, J. A., Wulfeck, W. H. II, Fredericks, P. S., *The Instructional Quality Inventory*, 1979). The IQI describes how to ensure the consistency and adequacy of objectives, test items, and instructional presentations, while our local guidelines dealt with lesson-level components such as advance organizers, refreshers, and reviews. We chose the IQI because it is prescriptive and procedure-oriented, based on recent learning theory, addresses a full range of learning categories, and was specifically developed for designing technical training materials. It assumes that objectives have been developed and sequenced; therefore, it is not appropriate as a guide for the pre-objective development steps in the Instructional Systems Design (ISD) process--task analysis.

Structured development process. In order for the development process to run smoothly, we created procedures as often as possible for the major tasks. By this, we mean that the steps in the process were carefully defined with review cycles and production goals specified. When we spelled out steps and production goals, authors had a job aid that helped them to avoid skipping steps; they also knew at which points their work would be reviewed by the instructional designer, editor, or graphics artist. Of course, these procedures reflected the overall instructional design philosophy for the project.

While planning the CF-18 project, we defined the development process in the form of step guides and pacing guides. The step guides provided detailed directions on how to develop a lesson; the pacing guides, as we noted earlier, provided approximate time that personnel should spend on a particular development stage for a specific lesson length. The pacing guides aided authors in setting time goals.

Establishing control policies and procedures to ensure instructional quality is a crucial step in your planning process. Unfortunately, far too many people believe that developing good instructional materials requires only "common sense" and that anyone can do it. A number of authors on the CF-18 project learned the hard way that this is simply not the case.

Key decision: what design philosophy best meets your content needs and customer desires?

THE EDITORIAL COMPONENT

A more subtle but equally important concern is the editorial component. When we first encounter the instructional capabilities of the computer, most of us get caught up in our excitement about the graphics, movement, color, interaction, and branching. It's easy to forget that our foremost goal is to communicate effectively. Precisely because of the distractions that the computer options cause, we need a good editorial process to ensure that our CAI teaches effectively.

The ideal editorial process requires three elements: an editor, a style manual, and rules about when modules are finished.

The editor. At the mention of the name "editor," many readers may conjure a tyrannical person attached to a blue (or red) pencil. Some editors, unfortunately, do fit this description. However, the editor can provide valuable services. The most useful is an objective, outside perspective on the lesson (an "other" set of eyes). Nearly as significant, an experienced CAI editor can help authors deal with the new writing issues in CAI. In a sense, writing is still writing; however, movement, color, and branching do raise writing problems that print authors haven't had to consider. Editors can often provide tips on how to work effectively with the new options.

Some editorial roles from the print medium also apply to CAI. The editor can help authors choose and troubleshoot an organizational strategy. Editors can also help authors with problem solving--*during* the composition process. Furthermore, they can suggest new variations because editors see samples from many writers. Then during the revision process, they can refine the presentation, to help authors reach their instructional goals. Editors can also do what most people think they do: copyedit for correctness and consistency.

One other issue to address: how to ensure technical accuracy. If your editor has technical expertise in the courseware subject, he or she can help refine the content. However, even if the editor knows the subject matter, it's still necessary to include a technical review by subject experts in your quality assurance process--preferably both internal (your own organization) and external (the customer's organization).

Style manual. The editor is important to the editorial process, but so is a style manual that provides a *written* record of decisions you make about laying out a module. We recommend using a manual for three reasons: it reduces production costs, raises the quality of your courseware, and improves morale. It may take a while to reach the consensus that you will lead cap the word "Radar" instead of using all caps or lower case, but reaching consensus once and writing it down requires much less time than it takes when 6 or 7 Subject Matter Experts (SMEs) sit around for hours several times a month arguing about capitalizing "Radar," only to have a succession of reviewers change the capping on the word two or three times. (We saw this happen regularly until we established and enforced style manual guidelines.)

Rules on module completion. After you obtain the first two elements, an editor and a style manual, you need to add a management fiat. In the print medium, when an author finishes writing, the publishing group physically takes possession of the manuscript and sees it through the production process. The delight in the CAI medium is that authors can do their own revisions in response to reviewer comments. The horror is that they can also continue rewriting and inserting errors, thereby precipitating an endless revision-and-review cycle. Almost every writing group has its inveterate "tinkerer," who *can't* let loose of a module. If you want the "tinkerers" to produce CAI in less than 1500 hours/hour, we invite you to establish management guidelines about what kind of changes are acceptable during the three revision stages: editorial, copyediting, and proofreading.

Editorial: here reviewers should have the power to require substantive revisions. This includes review for issues such as technical accuracy, clarity, organization, and writing style.

Copyediting: now *no one* should require changes in substance. Review here for issues such as house conventions, consistency, and typographical or mechanical errors. Allow rewrites only on content errors that you simply cannot ignore.

Proofreading: here you are checking to make sure that the fixes in response to copyediting were implemented and that you've caught all of the really noticeable errors. Don't release a module with serious errors, but also resist changing things at the proofreading stage. Proofread for these kinds of issues: spelling and typing errors and mechanical "missteps" with the computer.

Key decisions: do you appoint an editor; do you spend the money on a style manual, and how precisely do you control the rules on module completion?

THE GRAPHICS COMPONENT

Of the three courseware team components, the graphics component is the most immediately visible element in a CAI lesson. Well done, interesting, dynamic, color graphics enhance the instructional value of the lesson by visually conveying concepts and by motivating and interesting the student. A professionally organized computer graphics team is crucial to any large-scale CAI development effort.

Graphics team organization. Organizing the graphics development team for CAI development is much like organizing any graphics support group. The graphics team will generally be responsible for requirements analysis and the design, development, and quality control of all graphics information needed to support online and offline training and test materials. It is important for you to set up a team structure that works for your particular project. For example, the graphics development team for the CF-18 project was organized in a manner similar to that of the authoring teams with a graphics manager as the head of the team. The graphics manager was responsible for assigning work requests, setting deadlines, ensuring standardization of work within the graphics development group, scheduling graphics conferences between artists and authors, reviewing graphics requests, and providing graphics development status reports to all instructional designers and the courseware development manager. In addition to these responsibilities, the graphics manager interviewed and hired artists, provided their initial training, and monitored their on-the-job training experience.

During the planning process, you should carefully define responsibilities for each graphics team member. For instance, lead artists on the CF-18 graphics team were responsible for design and development of art, helping authors design the graphics component of their lessons including dynamic sequences and simulations, helping the newer artists assigned to them, and assisting the graphics manager in reviewing graphics requests. Less experienced artists designed and developed art and assisted authors in the graphics design of lessons.

Standardization of graphics development. When planning your graphics development component, you need to establish specific standards and control procedures to promote consistency and quality of the CAI materials. These devices permit another artist to take over an unfinished lesson, protecting the development group from being set back because an artist gets sick or leaves the project.

One area that requires attention during the planning process is the naming conventions for graphics. During a large-scale software development effort, an amazing proliferation of graphics and parts of graphics can occur. You must develop some scheme for designing and naming these graphics so that they are easy to locate and will display on the screen in a predictable fashion.

The most important step you can take to minimize unnecessary graphics development time is to create graphics request forms for both static graphics and simulations that require authors to give the artist the necessary information about the desired art. These forms will not alleviate the need for a face-to-face conference, but they should facilitate communication during the conference.

During the CF-18 project, we used these forms to present a prose description and a visual description of the presentation. We required the author to complete a form for each graphic, graphics sequence, or simulation used in the presentation.

Thus, your key decisions are these: do you hire artists; do you let authors create their own graphics; and how do you control your graphics library as you name and revise graphics?

COURSEWARE PERSONNEL SELECTION

The most important preparation for your courseware project is selecting courseware development personnel. The critical issue is to know who you want and how to make sound screening decisions. In this section, we review the selection of authors, instructional designers, graphics artists, and editors.

Ideal authors. Who are the ideal authors? Of course they are writers and teachers. And they have subject expertise or are bright enough to learn subjects quickly. We've found, though, that the following personal traits are very important. The ideal authors have a sense of humor and good judgment about priorities. They are also independent and receptive to constructive advice. Additionally, these multi-talented people exhibit certain "job" skills: they can meet deadlines, address varying audiences, draw inferences, plan well, and handle abstractions. Finally, they exhibit sound analytical skills.

Screening. You won't often find this "ideal" author, but your goal is always to use your screening process to unearth as many of these traits as you can. Once you've decided what kind of person you want, you need to set up a selection process. Our selection process reflects our painfully won belief that you seek out writers. In our six-stage screening process, we 1) review resumes and cover letters, 2) request an example of published writing, 3) administer a logic test, 4) ask candidates to sit for an on-site writing sample, 5) conduct interviews, and 6) make reference calls.

Resume and cover letter. We ask for both resumes and cover letters because so many people have resume services edit their resumes. With resumes, we watch for strong writing, and eliminate people who write poorly.

Example of published writing. We ask for a published writing sample, so we can weed out people who falsify their credentials or whose writing is so weak that even a good editor can't transform it. However, editors often "redo" weak documents, so we rely heavily on a logic test and writing sample.

Logic test. Here is an example of a test that we used--Figure 5, Logic Test.

LOGIC TEST

TIME: 20 Minutes. 20 Questions.

Each question consists of a series of letters which follow some definite order. Study each series to determine what the order is. Then look at the answer choices. Select the one answer that completes the pattern.

1. BACADAEAFAGA
   (A) HA (B) AH
   (C) KA(D) LA

2. ABDBBDCBDDBDEBDFB
   (A) HD (B) QX
   (C) DB(D) DG

FIGURE 5 LOGIC TEST

Logic tests let us check the candidate's ability to organize material and to envision long, complex sequences. Authors need the organizational ability for writing text and the sequencing skills for developing graphics and simulations.

On-site writing sample. For the writing sample, we give the writers a lesson plan and a small quantity of technical source material. Then we ask them to draft an outline and the opening 4-6 paragraphs of a CAI module. We watch for organizational skills, ability to work under pressure, and an ability to set a context for the reader (i.e., a WHOLE-PART-WHOLE structure or a variation on it).

Interview. During the interview, at least one writer and one instructional designer participate. We ask lots of "why" and "how" questions. For example, we'll ask: "Given Technical Order reference material, how would you transform this material into an effective instructional lesson?" We ask probing questions because we know that good writers can answer this kind of question for CAI readers and that weak writers don't or can't. We've learned that responses such as "That's a tough question" are definitely bad signs, particularly if they recur frequently.

Reference calls. We use reference calls for the obvious reason: they offer data points for making decisions. We ask about writing, teaching, and subject expertise (or potential to learn a subject).

How helpful is such a screening process? Before we went to this trouble, our author success rate was 1 in 3 (33%). After we initiated the process, our success rate jumped to 7 out of 8 (88%).

Requirements. We're looking for writer-teachers and use a six-stage screening process. Now, what requirements do we set? We look for candidates with two years' full-time experience in writing *and* two years in teaching. Subject expertise and experience with CAI, graphics, and a style guide are desirable. When we asked for experience in writing *and* teaching, we dramatically diminished the number of qualified candidates. Our experience, though, is that it's worth waiting for the right people.

Choosing between SME and technical writer. When selecting new authors for your project, it's very tempting to assume that you need to look for the best subject matter experts (SME). If the SME is also a solid instructor and writer, you have located your ideal courseware team member. Unfortunately, most courseware project managers eventually face a difficult dilemma. They can't locate the ideal writer, and they sometimes find themselves having to choose between strong subject experts and strong writers. Given the limited quantity of "ideal" candidates, what does our experience suggest about choosing technical writers and SMEs? That a mix of tech writers and SMEs works most effectively. Why? Because CAI development is primarily a writing job. The CAI lesson is about a technical subject, in the instructional mode, and on a computer, of course. Nevertheless CAI production is writing, so we chose writers.

Our recommendation on the mix? It depends heavily on how much source material, particularly written, is available. At one end of the spectrum, if you've got abundant written documentation, you might need only one SME for every 3 or 4 technical writers. If you have some written materials and access to articulate subject experts whom writers can interview, the ratio could be more balanced. If there is virtually no written material (the opposite end of the spectrum), you may need to reverse the ratio to 3 or 4 SMEs for every technical writer. We had abundant written source material, so we found that

1 SME for every 3 or 4 technical writers worked well. We'll probably raise some eyebrows with that ratio, but our experience was that when we exhausted the supply of ideal SMEs, our customer's representatives were happier with lessons from good and very bright writers than they were with material from technically sound SMEs who didn't write well. We hired most team members. Many of you will select team members from employees already on your staff. It remains important, though, to select staff carefully, even if they are already working in the organization.

Key decisions: do you test candidates, and what ratio of SMEs and technical writers will work best in your situation?

Choosing instructional designers. An instructional designer, above all, must have a thorough grasp of human learning theory and the ability to apply that theory in the production of instructional materials. This generally means that candidates should have at least a Master's Degree in instructional technology, educational psychology, cognitive psychology, instructional computing, or a related area.

Preferably, a candidate for the position of instructional designer will have at least two years of experience developing a curriculum and one year of teaching experience. He or she should also have writing experience. CAI development and management experience are desirable but not essential.

Choosing editors. CAI editors know sound writing practice, layout design, and teaching techniques. For this reason, we require experience in editing, writing, and teaching: two years each in editing and writing and four years in teaching. The following experience is desirable: layout, graphics, CAI, and management. We also ask for a B.A. or substantial experience.

Selecting graphics artists. Although menu-driven, graphics software makes creating graphics easier, you cannot bring in an individual without an art background and expect the graphics software editor to compensate for that person's lack of artistic ability. Careful consideration should be given to the artist candidate's experience, education, and personality traits. We require experience in composition, design, and layout (one year); computer graphics and teaching experience are desirable. We also require an associate degree in graphic/commercial art or substantial experience.

Graphics development for CAI differs from flat art in that it requires designing dynamic graphics sequences. Artists must be able to visualize and sequence changes to a display over time. We find that artists with experience in dynamic visual media (e.g., slide/tape, video tape or disk) more readily consider the temporal aspects of a CAI graphics sequence than others do.

SUMMARY

If you are about to embark on a large-scale courseware development project, resist the urge to dive right in and to begin development before you have completed all the necessary planning. Decisions you make during this planning phase--concerning selection and training of personnel and control policies and procedures--can make the difference between a smooth-running courseware development process and a management nightmare. Take the extra time and labor up front; it will pay off repeatedly during the course of your project, and the quality of your product will reflect your effort.

REFERENCE

1. Ellis, J. A. Wulfeck, W. H. II, Fredericks, P. S, *The Instructional Quality Inventory*, v. 2, User's Manual (NPRDC SR 79-24), San Diego, Navy Personnel Research and Development Center, August, 1979 (AD-A083 678).

13

The On-line Environment and In-House Training

Edward Barrett and James Paradis

Writing Program
Massachusetts Institute of Technology

Introduction

Electronic networks will create a supple environment for corporate and university training and management programs (Hiltz and Turoff; Johansen). An on-line, networked conferencing and instructional facility can provide a real-time "ecology" (Cooper) of extensible and interactive systems. Such a facility integrates various instructional and communications media, and, if properly designed, can become what Seymour Papert once called "an object to think with" (1980). A fluid and robust electronic framework facilitates such crucial processes as conferencing and problem-solving (Stefik, et al), document creation and review, in-house short-course training, and management of documentation groups.

The on-line environment is shaped by context. In industry it offers a conferencing system for problem-solving and an in-house training environment where people learn on the same system over which they routinely interact. In the university it becomes a seminar room and an out-of-class "virtual classroom" that extends the "text" of a class beyond scheduled class hours. Such a system, therefore, should carry with it no necessary methodological implications, so that it can be tailored to suit the needs of a particular constituency of users. Furthermore, an on-line conferencing and instructional system should not automate thinking and its related activity, documentation. We see networked systems ultimately as extensions of individuals in social settings. By modeling mechanisms such as document exchange and review, an on-line system can fundamentally transform the psychology of interaction in managerial and instructional settings.

In this chapter, we describe the Educational On-line System (EOS), developed at MIT for the Athena Writing Project. The design and implementation of this on-line instructional and conferencing system challenged and ultimately re-defined our assumptions about the uses of computers in training and management contexts. We will explore the key concepts behind the design of our system, describe a typical application of it to training writers and managing documentation cycles, and analyze its positive benefits in light of very real negative encumbrances. We offer this discussion as a way of formulating ideas for assessing the value of this technology to any training and management domain.

What Are The Functions An On-line System Must Model?

Any corporate or instructional conferencing environment can be defined as a set of functions that are carried out on a day-by-day basis. These activities are at the heart of problem solving, decision making, management, documentation, and instruction.

Text Creation

In any conferencing setting individuals interact socially to move to a consensus. This interaction is usually focused on some topic which we describe here as a "text": a problem to be solved, a decision to be made, or a document to be created or reviewed. Sometimes, the meeting itself is its own "text." For example, in a brainstorming session ideas may be recorded and achieve an historical projection, or they may just dazzle and fade like fireworks in air. Archived or not, a text is being created that may eventually take shape as a document, a policy, a plan to meet again. Thus by "creating a text" we mean either a literal one (a report, a manual, a writing exercise, some notes), or a metaphorical one (discussion, a vote, a sense of "getting things going," a cognition).

Text Presentation

Closely allied to this text-creating function is the presentation of texts in a conference or private setting. In the instructional domain this means the display of written text for study. Sometimes, a text is discussed and then dispensed with, or a text may be offered as a model for composition. Often, a text written by a student is presented for review, or a reference text is called up for information on a particular point. These texts are usually available for display both in-class and out-of-class (that is, in a social or private setting). Therefore, they are usually sorted and classified for ease-of-use and other pedagogical purposes. This ordering may be either chronological (order of presentation) or logical (how they cohere to construct knowledge). Usually, these two ordering schemes are interrelated. In the corporate realm the presentation of texts can have all of the above meanings in either of two settings--managerial or in-house training.

Text Exchange

The axis of text presentation may be "one screen-one user" or "one large screen projection device-many viewers" or "many screens-many users." However, this dynamic is further complicated by another related function, the exchange of texts among users. Exchange of texts may be vertical, from instructor-manager to student-employee, or from student-employee to instructor-manager. In this case the dynamic is one-to-many and many-to-one. The exchange of texts may also be horizontal as in peer review and discussion: a many-to-many dynamic. Horizontal exchange does not necessarily preclude direction by a manager or instructor. Every instructional setting is always threatened by the confusion engendered by the exchange of texts. This is especially true in writing instruction and documentation cycles: the welter of draft versions of reports, for example, places an enormous burden on the instructor or manager who must collect them in one place, order and store them in another place, and disseminate them again for another cycle of collection and review. Similarly, the student or trainee is expected to order and store a developing portfolio of work. The mechanical difficulty of text (draft) transmission and exchange is the single most limiting factor in managing a documentation cycle: it hobbles the peer review process by extending the feedback loop over a large span of time. As Christine Neuwirth in "Toward the Design of a Flexible, Computer-Based Writing Environment" (Wresch, 1984) points out, this time delay prevents writers from connecting problems in the final product with the process that created the problem.

Text Annotation

Finally, all of these processes converge in an annotation function. Texts are drafted, exchanged, and presented for review and comment, usually resulting in changes that engender another cycle of exchange. Thus, a dialogue is established in every documentation cycle. This dialogue may be actual, as in face-to-face meetings, or fixed within the matrix of a developing text by means of written marginalia, deletions and insertions, or a set of conventional shorthand symbols. Annotations, therefore, are either brief or extended. In certain instructional domains it may be important to keep a record of such comments in order to assess the development of a trainee or student: important both to the student who is "working on" certain problems, as well as for the instructor or manager who may have to keep an updated record of many individuals during a certain period of time.

In general, then, four processes define every instructional and conferencing environment: creation of texts, presentation of texts, exchange of texts, and annotation of texts. These processes rarely go on distinct from one another and are typically carried out in social and private settings. They extend the concept of "classroom" and "corporate meeting room" beyond the actual spatial and temporal boundaries denoted by such terms.

Modeling The Seminar Conferencing Room As A "Mechanism"

The key concept behind our design of EOS stems from this isolation of four processes that, we feel, define the conferencing-training environment. For our purposes, then, we conceived of a seminar meeting room and its associated dynamic of activities as a set of "mechanical" processes, and we sought to determine how the computer could support these traditional activities in real-time and whether that support would change the dynamic of instruction and conferencing. Also, as writing instructors committed to teaching writing as a process, we wanted to see how network technology could support writing instruction. Would it provide the interactive functionality that researchers into computers and writing were looking for (Bridwell and Ross; Catano, 1985; Daiute, 1983; Poore; Schwartz, 1982)?

The Cognitive Process Model

It is important to stress, however, that our decision to model the seminar room as a "mechanism" significantly departs from the model most other researchers into computer support for conferencing and instruction have adopted. As we demonstrate in a forthcoming article (Barrett and Paradis), most software developers in the domain of computers and writing instruction and conferencing use the computer to model a cognitive process which, they feel, goes on within the individual as she moves through the documentation cycle. Most typically, the computer is used to model the cognitive process theory expressed by Flower and Hayes (1981). For example, such popular software packages for teaching writing as *HBJ Writer* (Von Blum), and *HOMER* (Cohen and Lanham) are heuristic programs that reinforce the student throughout a well established "process" for writing by means of a series of programmed promptings.

Of course, the use of the computer to simulate cognitive processes in instructional and management contexts has a long history. Vannevar Bush in 1945 developed a computer program *memex*, to mimic the associational leaps of the mind (Bush); and Douglas Engelbart's work in the sixties on *NLS/Augment* (Engelbart) was meant to amplify native intelligence. Such programs are frequently cited as prototypes of another contemporary direction in computer research--hypertext, a term coined by Ted Nelson (1967) denoting programs for storing and accessing document databases by means of intricate associational linkages (Conklin). Hypertext, and the related concept of hypermedia (text, audio, video), is a key element of *Intermedia* at Brown (Garrett, et al), as well as Xerox PARC's *NoteCards* (Halasz, et al), CMU's *ZOG* (McCracken and Akscyn), University of Maryland's *Hyperties* (Schneiderman and Morariu), and University of North Carolina's *WE* (Smith et al). Christine Neuwirth's work on a hypertext note-taking facility at CMU is another application of this research to writing instruction (Neuwirth). A motivating principle in all this research is the move toward expert systems that will be able to engage a human user in a natural language "dialogue." Researchers in CAI see a useful application of this technology to their own fields (Quere).

Skinner

Sadler (1987), however, complicates this picture by suggesting that a behavioristic, Skinnerian model provides the real basis for educational software. And, indeed, Skinner (1961), in an article that originally appeared in the *Harvard Educational Review* was critical of "teaching machines" and complained of "a general neglect of educational method" in their conceptualization. He offered that "recent advances in the experimental analysis of behavior suggest that a true technology of education is feasible." Of course, the method he was talking about was his own, derived from experiments in reinforcing behavior in pigeons. Skinner felt that a simple machine could replace (a key concept) the instructor because a machine offered a more stable mechanism for reinforcement of selected behaviors. Also, a student working with such a machine could establish her own pace: faster if she were doing well, slower if the material was difficult. Most importantly, as presentation devices such a machine permitted material to be "chunked" into separate frames (still a key design strategy for on-line documentation) which the student could riffle through, step-by-step: the most important reinforcement strategy according to Skinner.

Limitations of the Cognitive Model

The cognitive model, therefore, is defined by these polar opposites: on the one hand, the cognitive process theories of Flower and Hayes, and on the other, the behaviorism of Skinner. Our own dissatisfaction with most contemporary educational software is that it ultimately tends to follow a Skinnerian methodology, no matter where it starts from. As Helen Schwartz, developer of *SEEN*, an electronic conferencing and heuristics program (Wresch, 1984; Schwartz, 1982), notes, the value of such popular software products for writing instruction referred to above is that the student eventually learns to internalize the programmed computer prompts; in essence, the user is being programmed, too (Schwartz,1984).

But as Bump (1987) notes, a program only flags down or prompts according to the lights of its programmer. The intervention of a mediator (instructor or manager) is, therefore, mandatory, as others have also stated (Rodrigues and Rodrigues; Earle). Furthermore, users do not internalize the programmed promptings of the machine if they are not motivated to use it (Nakamura, et al), or if access is restricted. The machine, then, becomes an intruder in the conferencing or educational process--it cannot "fit in" with the flow of instruction in the traditional classroom or the discourse of a meeting and is used, if at all, as an add-on (Wresch, 1982). Most importantly, computer models of cognitive processes necessarily entail certain methodological implications; the user is forced to accept a routine and its accompanying theory as well.

Research into artificial intelligence and related expert systems may in fact produce a computer program that closely models the way a human mind works, as Minsky has averred (1987). Yet, Weizenbaum (1976) is especially cautionary in pointing out how we tend to anthropomorphize the computer, ascribing to it functions that only a human can perform--an important admonition in the domain of instruction and management. In *Mindstorms* Seymour Paper argues against what he calls the "balkanization of teaching with computers" (180)--the use of computer technology in a way that atomizes true education into separate prescriptions for a pre-programmed method of performing a particular operation. He complains about educators who fall into the fallacy of using the computer to program the student rather than teaching the student to manipulate the computer in order to understand a concept or idea more richly--to facilitate thinking about thinking. Papert argues that we should use computer technology to create an "intellectual environment in which the emphasis is on process" in order to "give people with different skills something to talk about" (184). With this sort of syntonic learning the computer becomes an "object to think with" rather than a mere trope of a thinking object.

"An Object to Think With"

Aware of these limitations, then, we were skeptical of using a machine to model something as complex and difficult to study as the workings of a mind, especially when that mind is engaged in an activity as truly human as social discourse. We felt, however, that a machine could very effectively model another machine. As Papert says, the essence of the computer is simulation; he calls it "the Proteus of machines" (viii). And this protean ability is best displayed when the computer can provide us with an *object* to think *with*. Therefore, we extended Papert's discussion of computers in education to cover not only that domain, but any networked conferencing as well. We decided to trope the seminar conferencing room as a mechanism and model that, rather than attempt to model the cognitive processes of the mind operating within that context.

We believe, therefore, that our design rationale leads to a system in which computers support any individual's idiosyncratic problem-solving or instructional methodology--in any context. We offer a tool to think with, not a theory to be straightjacketed by. Ultimately, our system humanizes computer technology rather than automating human cognition and related activities such as writing.

Components of the Educational On-line System (EOS)

Although EOS was first tested in a university setting, it was designed for applications outside the university as well. A complete technical discussion of system design and components is given in three separate documents: *An Interim Report to Project Athena* (Paradis, Barrett, Bequaert), *User Documentation for File Exchange* (Shaw, Lewis, Cattey), and *Specifications for a User Interface* (Barrett, Bequaert, Paradis). An overview of components of EOS is shown in Figure 1.

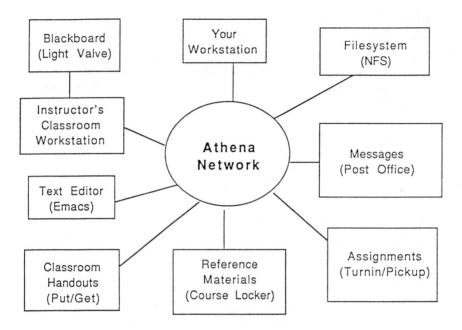

Figure 1. Overview of the Educational On-line System (EOS)

The Athena Network

The Athena network consists of 1,500 DEC Microvax 2000 workstations and IBM RT's connected campus-wide over an electronic network. Workstations run the UNIX operating system and X Window manager. Computing facilities are available in general-use clusters, classrooms, and living areas. Access to workstations and network software programs is available to any user anywhere at any time.

Network File System

A user logged on to the network has access to a network file system (NFS) which provides abundant on-line storage space for all user files (home directory), as well as a course locker where course-specific materials and software are kept. Figure 2 shows the specific software available to a user who has logged on to EOS.

"Turnin/Pickup" and Related Programs

A suite of programs was written to support the four processes we identified as central to any conferencing-instructional environment. "Turnin/pickup" allows exchange of texts vertically, from student to instructor and instructor to student for review and comment: a student turns in a document which is annotated and returned for pickup. "Put/get" is a program that permits files to be exchanged horizontally while a meeting is in progress, from instructor to all students, or from one student to everyone else. A user puts a file into a pickup bin; then others may get it from that bin for review and comment. All files are read-only while in a user's home directory. However, once they have been exchanged they are no longer write-protected. "Take" allows files to be stored ahead of time for general distribution later on. "Put/get" and "take" also permit files from the instructor/manager's workstation to be displayed in real-class-time via a large-screen projection device, in our case a Hughes light valve. Electronic mail is an ancillary file exchange program; "talk," a real-time conferencing program, allows users logged on to the system at different locations to type to each others' screens.

"Grade"

In addition to file creation, presentation, and exchange the program "Grade" permits storage, classification, and annotation of versions of docu-

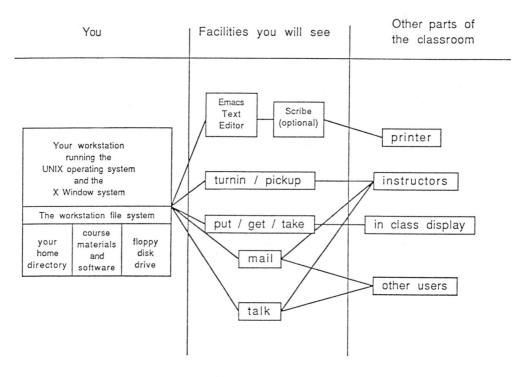

Figure 2. Facilities available to the user in EOS.

ments throughout a complete cycle of drafting and revising (see Figure 3). "Grade" contains two other programs, "admin" (for administration) and "hand" (for handout) that permit class lists to be set up and modified and class handouts to be organized and commented upon, respectively.

The "grade" program allows an instructor to collect a structured and easily accessible portfolio of an individual student's work over any set period of time. In our case, we organized files according to week number throughout the semester. These portfolios included not only the assignments themselves; all annotated versions of drafts were stored and classified. In addition, we could collect commentaries on individual papers throughout the semester in a separate file for use later on during mid-semester conferences with individual students.

Foundation and Classroom Emacs

Currently, two separate annotation programs are available within EOS. The first, *Foundation*, developed by Bill Cattey for this project, allows an instructor to highlight areas of text to be annotated. Pop-up annotation menus offer the instructor a choice of either standard, "quick" annotations (those comments that are made continually throughout a set of papers), or the option of creating a new type for more extended commentary. Both annotation types appear in windows to the side of the draft text, tied to those places in the original which have been highlighted for commentary; for annotations composed by the instructor these windows offer virtually infinite space to write in. Foundation is written in C.

The second annotation program operates within a special subset of GnuEmacs, called Classroom Emacs, developed by Dave Custer. Basically, this program allows an instructor to place comments directly into the original student assignment. These comments are demarcated by a special set of symbols and may be hidden or displayed for class discussions. This annotation program also gives the student access to an on-line style guide. This guide is basically a "middle-ground" hypertext document with cross-referenced help files containing instructional material on three levels. On the first level there are files containing simple examples of grammar and usage. From this first level, the student has access to a second-degree help file containing templates with formats for constructing technical documents within selected genres. From here the student can go to the next level where sample document texts are found (Custer).

```
Available 'grade requests:

help, ?                                      redisplay this menu
list, l                  [unam] [ass#]       list files turned in
whois, who               [unam]              find a student's real name
annotate, ann            [unam] [ass#]       annotate a file
duplicate, dup           [unam] [ass#]       keep a copy of a file
return, ret, r           [unam] [ass#]       return turned-in file to student
put, p                   [unam] [ass#]       return any file to student
purge, del, rm           [unam] [ass#]       remove turned-in file from bins
listp, lp                [unam] [ass#]       list files in pickup bin
purgep, delp, rmp        [unam] [ass#]       remove file from pickup bin
handout, hand, h                             go to the handout menu
admin, a                                     go to the administrative menu
quit, exit, q                                end this session
grade:   1 5
----------------------------------------------------------------------------
STUDENT    #  DATE                  STATUS      NAME          VERSION
crbiber    5  Thu Oct  8 17:03      returned    proposal      0
dnkato     5  Thu Oct  8 15:04      picked up   techd         0
drpepper   5  Thu Oct  8 17:09      picked up   proposal      0
furi       5  Thu Oct 15 16:27      new         prop          0
jazman     5  Thu Oct  8 17:04      picked up   techdes2.mss  0
mateo      5  Thu Oct  8 17:04      picked up   prop.rough    0
mateo      5  Thu Oct  8 17:03      picked up   research.des  0
myip       5  Thu Oct  8 17:11      picked up   proposal.txt  0
noster     5  Sun Oct 11 16:46      picked up   proposal      0
turntest   5  Thu Sep 24 13:29      new         Test3         0
wdc        5  Thu Oct  8 17:13      taken       init          0
```

Figure 3. The "grade" program menu showing a list of available commands (top). Below, is an example of the "list" command for the fifth week of a course: here an alphabetized class list showing date and time of submission of each student's draft. "Status" shows if the turnin is new or annotated ("returned" by instructor) and whether the student has picked up the annotated version. Assignment name and version (draft) number are also indicated.

These components of EOS comprise what we call a *virtual meeting room*: an invisible, dynamic set of interlocking systems that become the "mechanism" of any instructional or conferencing setting. In a sense, the software for EOS is inherently innocent: it supports, with no methodological implications, those functions that have traditionally defined instruction and problem-solving in both corporate and academic environments. It supports, in other words, human social interaction unmediated by theory or programmed heuristics. In the following section we describe how EOS was used in a typical instructional setting.

Corporate Training Programs: A Scenario for Using EOS

Typically, an in-house training course will draw upon the same functions as a conventional classroom. For example, two types of documents for instructional purposes are presented: models which an instructor has collected over the years and drafts of documents, or perhaps specific exercises, that trainees create during the course, or have created before the course and now wish to revise. Instructors meet with trainees and make presentations based on certain set models, which are usually in hardcopy book form or photocopied. Models are discussed in class, and course members are asked to write a sample of their own based on these models. These trainee texts are then collected, read through and annotated, copied, disseminated to the class, discussed, annotated again, and returned to trainees with comments--perhaps for another cycle of review.

In our first use of EOS, students met with us met once a week for two hours in a computer lab outfitted with twenty Microvax 2000 workstations and a Hughes light valve for large-screen projection. Handouts from our files collected over the years were stored on-line, readily accessible by means of brief commands or a set of keystrokes in class and outside class.

For the second meeting of our course, three sample documents from the on-line handout file were listed in a directory displayed on each course member's workstation. Each document in turn was viewed on the light valve while an instructor analyzed it for style and structure; students also had these files displayed on their monitors: they followed the instructor's comments and marked up their electronic copies. Students then engaged in a discussion of writing strategies based on these models. To illustrate various points in this discussion, we modified these texts in real-time at our workstation for immediate class display on the light valve. Once the discussion was over students saved these marked-up versions of the handouts to their own home directories for future reference--unmodified versions remained in the general handout bin for remainder of the course.

This presentation was followed by a short in-class writing exercise to practice key points from the discussion. Students were instructed to pick up from the "put/get" handout bin a text containing a description of an operation. Students were then asked to open up a new window for editing alongside this sample text already displayed on their screens. In this editing window they were told to write a set of operating instructions based on the text in the other window. During the next twenty minutes, as students wrote, both of us walked around the classroom to see how students were doing. Usually, we silently noted for discussion later on the various writing strategies students employed, although sometimes we stopped to help out a particularly pokey student.

We then asked the class to save their in-class exercises and turn them in on-line. From our pickup bin three student writing samples were chosen for immediate display in-class. The class then reviewed these examples, suggesting various revisions which were demonstrated on the light valve. We also had revisions to suggest, and our modifications of the originals were next displayed. This cycle of in-class writing, turnin and pick up, display and review took about forty minutes.

With their screens now clear again, we introduced the topic of paragraph development using an on-line handout displayed on the light valve and student workstations. Since the sample text exhibited several problems with paragraph structure, students were encouraged to identify these and to suggest ways of revising to eliminate them. The paragraphs were brief, and we instructed the class to revise them at their workstations for a few minutes. Then two students volunteered to show their versions of improved paragraph structure in-class; these files were turned in, picked up, and displayed on the light valve for further discussion and revision in class.

Students were then then asked to open another editing window. One of us reviewed key concepts from the presentation at the start of the class on technical descriptions. The other instructor then distributed a small binder clip to each student and asked the class to write a description of this object. He reminded the class that they could bring up another window on their screens to display any of the examples discussed earlier in the class, as well as any of

their own annotated versions that they had saved. These samples then served
as models for this in-class exercise. The class was given twenty minutes to
write their descriptions. Once again, both of us walked around the class to
answer any questions or resolve any technical difficulties. At the end of the
allotted time students saved their descriptions of the clip and turned them in
over the network using the turnin program. The following weekend, we
critiqued these in-class writing samples and returned them on-line to the class
with annotations and general comments.

As is clear from this brief description, the cycle of lecture, in-class exercise,
review, and feedback was much more immediate than in a conventional class.
More material could be efficiently displayed in class, and more examples of
student writing could be drafted and displayed for discussion. It was now
very easy to get students to practice what we had just been teaching and to go
through a cycle of presentation, in-class exercise, and review three times
during one two-hour class meeting.

An Initial Assessment of EOS as an Instructional Environment for Teaching Writing

We used EOS to teach an upper-level undergraduate course in scientific
and engineering writing at MIT during the spring, 1987 semester. The class
was composed of ten students: nine undergraduates working on theses in engineering and science courses, and one graduate student. Our initial assessment of the effectiveness of this environment for teaching writing, and by extension for electronic conferencing, was based on end-of-the semester student
evaluations, weekly committee reviews of each class, and instructor logs. It
should also be noted, however, that students were evaluating a first implementation of this system. We are currently in our third iteration of system
development.

Positive Student Comments

Exchange of Texts and the Process of Thinking

By far, the most positive student comments focused on the new dynamic
for exchanging papers in- and out-of-class created by EOS. One student felt
that on-line documentation allowed him greater freedom to concentrate on
composition and thinking: "the concept of turning in and picking up papers
electronically ... eliminates the hassles associated with formatting and obtain-

ing printed output, freeing more time to concentrate on the writing itself."
Another student wrote that this course was more effective in improving writing skills "mainly because of real-time feedback from instructors and students
and ease of exchange of files." He went on to say: "In-class review and feedback were useful for understanding the material since the concepts were still
fresh in my mind." This new dynamic for in-class exchange, one student felt,
was "more natural to the human mind" in learning situations. Part of that
"naturalness" may come from the fact that, as another student said, this environment allowed him "to put theories into practice immediately."

We were surprised, and pleased, to note this reaction to EOS. Our concept
was to model the on-line classroom as a "mechanism" involving dynamic, interlocking processes of text creation, presentation, exchange, and annotation.
Yet this troping of the class as machine lead to a system that supported and
enhanced the cognitive processes of learners in new ways. Most important of
these, to judge from student evaluations, was the transformation of classroom
psychology in this environment: it was now easier to integrate theory with
practice; students could close the loop of in-class writing, exchange, review,
revision much more quickly than ever before. Neither of us felt any loss of
focus when we shifted gears from lecture to workshop during a class. In fact,
students were eager to try out what we had lectured on. Class attention was
keenly focused on the task at hand; students wrote more and experimented
with different organizing strategies that had been demonstrated in class. Connecting workstations over a network permitted many parallel processes to be
carried out simultaneously; student were engaged in a sort of dialogue with
their material, themselves, and the composing process (Daiute, 1983).
Workstations were important focusing devices; students felt comfortable composing at them: as one wrote, the screen "forces the writer to focus ... and
results in longer concentration spans."

Storing and Classifying Files

Students also commented favorably that the on-line classroom imparted
greater order to the expanding portfolio of student work. One student felt that
the classification system of the "grade" program was "neat, clear, concise," and
that this "encouraged more re-writing." By one accounting over 1,400 files
were created during the course of the semester: student assignment files and
drafts of final papers, in-class exercises, and curricular files. Yet this proliferation of documentation never overwhelmed students or instructors.

In-Class Presentation

Most students thought that large-screen projection of on-line documentation was another positive element of this class. One student echoed a familiar response: "the ability to display a file on the large screen ... made discussion of writing easy." Real-time manipulation of text was now possible on a large scale: revisions were immediately displayed for discussion. Another student felt that the light valve was a "time-saving device" for students and instructors--documents did not have to be laboriously photocopied, and in-class display was virtually instantaneous. Since the process of display was quick and intuitive, discussion was more focused and intuitive also.

On-line Annotation

Student response to on-line annotation, however, was problematic. Only four students chose to comment on this facet of EOS: all were enthusiastic about the idea of on-line annotation, but three felt that its actual implementation was not effective. For them hardcopy was still the preferred format for commentary. One student liked the "manipulative capacity" of on-line annotation: the electronic medium permitted virtually infinite margins to write in; therefore, she felt, an instructor could focus and develop comments more fully than in hardcopy. Two students praised the concept of split-screen annotation windows in *Foundation* and lamented the fact that it was still in development and could not be used in this class.

Negative Student Comments

User Interface

All students felt that the first iteration of EOS was inherently too complex. The issue of interface was apparent to us from the start of the project and continued to exercise our thoughts throughout the semester. One student expressed the problem succinctly: "students should not have to worry about the information handling process." Another student suggested that "a menu-driven software interface would have been more useful than using Unix directly." Still another wanted better documentation, especially "quick reference cards" for in-class support. In fact, the system described in this chapter represents a second and third iteration of EOS which employs a simpler and more intuitive interface for in- and out-of-class procedures.

Students also complained that the physical layout of the room interfered with class discussion. Workstation tables were arranged in a severe grid pattern of three parallel rows down the length of the room. Students sometimes had difficult seeing over the monitors during discussions; they inevitably focused on the workstation screen rather than the light valve or the instructor. Three students commented on the noise-level in the room: the combination of light valve and workstations produced a rather insistent hum so that students and instructors could not easily be heard.

The Electronic Chalkboard

All students were critical of light valve technology. Images, they said, were neither sharp nor bright. Software related problems of typeface and font-size were also noted: any student more than ten feet from the large screen had difficulty reading text.

On-line Annotation

Finally, as noted above, students were either indifferent or actively opposed to on-line annotation. All students missed the bold symbology of red marks bleeding over a page as a quick method to assess an instructor's reaction. Three students had difficulty with our default system of annotation--using Emacs to insert comments directly into the text. Comments were hard to read, they felt, because we did not have a good method of demarcating them from the original. These students also felt that it was time-consuming to scroll through a long document, fishing for the inserted text.

We are not sure how to interpret this reaction to electronic annotation. Certainly, on-line comments are a new beast. We often missed the gestural efficacy of arrows, circles, and underlinings as much as our students. *Foundation*, with its text highlighting capabilities and annotation windows, may offer a supple mechanism for electronic commentary. We discovered, however, that we were really learning a new rhetoric of annotation. Hardcopy remarks rely on mutually accepted shorthand notations: marks, phrases, abbreviations. On-line annotation is far more dialogic: our sense was that we were talking to our students, not merely grading them--in essence, collaborating on documentation. Students, therefore, were required to read and digest comments that were more fully developed. This may, in fact, account for their resistance to on-line annotation: it changes the accepted power structure of student-instructor interaction; both now converse on the same plane of the text.

What are the Implications of this System?

EOS is currently in its third iteration of development. Major improvements in design have resulted from our initial assessment of the system as part of the Athena Writing Project. These improvements are reflected in a simpler and more intuitive user interface and in a more economical system design, as outlined above. The next phase of development will include wider testing of the system among diverse groups of users. Nevertheless, we feel confident that we can make certain statements about the value of EOS to other researchers into networked conferencing and instructional environments.

Our concept of using the computer to model the on-line classroom as a "mechanism" involving dynamic, interlocking processes of text creation, presentation, exchange, and annotation proved to be a valid and productive design choice. As student comments made clear, this "mechanism" supports learning and discovery. Yet, EOS carries with it no particular pedagogy or methodology. The system is essentially a tool to think with--a support for traditional human interaction in a conferencing and instructional situation. As a result, EOS transforms the psychology of in-class presentation, discussion, and review by narrowing the divide between theory and practice.

The on-line classroom also provides an ideal medium for integrating instructional software into the normal flow of any particular educational or conferencing setting. Since EOS is not defined by one cognitive model, it can be tailored to suit the needs of changing constituencies. EOS takes it shape from the place in which it resides and can model the typical interactions that define a unique context. We believe this capability alone represents a profound humanizing of computer technology.

Finally, the basic concept of EOS ultimately problematizes the thrust toward automating writing mechanisms. Writing is thinking, among other things, and no computer system can model the uniquely human and mysterious processes that go on when an individual is engaged in the act of composition. Nor should they: we must ask ourselves what is lost by diminishing the difficulty of writing. What complex of energies and cognitions are we sacrificing? Is there an organic relationship between engineering and thinking and writing and management? Where these forces intersect is the core of understanding.

Acknowledgements

Development of EOS was supported by a grant from Project Athena at MIT. Our thanks to Dave Custer for his comments on early drafts of this chapter.

References

Barrett, E., J. Paradis, and F. Bequaert. "On-line Classroom: Specification for a User Interface." *Athena Writing Project, MIT.* 1987.

Barrett, E. and J. Paradis. "Teaching Writing in an On-line Classroom." *Harvard Educational Review* (forthcoming).

Bridwell, L., and Ross, D. "Integrating Computers into a Writing Curriculum: Or, Buying, Begging, and Building." In *The Computer in Composition Instruction: A Writer's Tool*, William Wresch, ed. Urbana: NCTE, 1984.

Bump, J. "CAI in Writing at the University: Some recommendations." *Computers in Education* 11 (1987):121-133.

Bush, V. "As We May Think." *Atlantic Monthly* 7 (1945):101-108.

Catano, J.V. "Computer-Based Writing: Navigating the Fluid Text." *College Composition and Communication* 36 (1985):309-316.

Cohen, M. and Lanham, R.A. "HOMER: Teaching Style with a Microcomputer." In *The Computer in Composition Instruction.* See Wresch 1984.

Conklin. J. "Hypertext: An Introduction and Survey." *Computer* 20 (1987):17-41

Cooper, M. "The Ecology of Writing." *College English* 48 (1986):364-375.

Custer, D. "Classroom Emacs." (forthcoming, spring 1988).

Daiute, C. "The Computer as Stylus and Audience." *College Composition and Communication* 34 (1983):134-145.

_____. "Can the Computer Stimulate Writers' Inner Dialogues?" In Wresch 1984.

Earle, T. "Instructional Design and Course Implementation: a Case Study of an Integrated Approach Using Computers." In *Computers in Education*, Duncan, K.A. and Harris, D.L., ed. Amsterdam: Elsevier Science Publ, 1986.

Englebart, D.C. "A Conceptual Framework for the Augmentation of Man's Intellect." In *Vistas in Information Handling*. London: Spartan Books, 1963.

Flower, L. and Hayes, J.R. "A Cognitive Process Theory of Writing." *College Composition and Communication* 32 (1981):365-387.

Garrett, N.L., Smith, K.E., and Meyrowitz, N. "Intermedia: issues, strategies, and tactics in the design of a hypermedia document system." In *Proceedings of the Conference on Computer Supported Cooperative Work*. MCC Software Technology Program. Austin, Texas. 1986.

Halasz, F.G., Moran T.P., and Trigg, T.H. "NoteCards in a Nutshell." In *Proceedings on the ACM Conference on Human Factors in Computing Systems*. Toronto, Canada. 1987.

Hiltz, S.R. and Turoff, M. *The Network Nation*. Reading,MA: Addison-Wesley, 1978.

Johansen, R. *Teleconferencing and Beyond*. New York: McGraw Hill, 1984.

McCracken, D.M. and Akscyn, R.M. "Experience with the ZOG Human-Computer Interface." *International Journal of Man-Machine Studies* 21 (1984):293-310.

Minsky, Marvin. *The Society of Mind*. New York: Simon and Schuster, 1987.

Nakamura, T., Nakayama, Y., Fukagawa, Y., and Yanura, T. "A Methodology for Automatic Presentation of Exercise Problems Based on Related Text-Constructing Units." *IEEE Transactions on Education* 30 (1987):157-163.

Nelson, T.H. "Replacing the Printed Word: A Complete Literary System." *IFIP Proceedings*. October 1980:1013-1023.

Neuwirth, C.M. "Toward the Design of a Flexible, Computer-Based Writing Environment." In Wresch 1984.

Papert, Seymour. *Mindstorms: Children, Computers, and Powerful Ideas*. New York: Basic Books, 1980.

Paradis, J., Barrett, E., and Bequaert, F. "A Prototype On-line Classroom Using the MIT Athena Network to Teach Scientific and Engineering Writing: An Interim Report." *Athena Writing Project, MIT*, 1987.

Poore, J. "Computerization of Campuses." In *Computers in Education*, Karen Duncan and Diane Harris, ed. Amsterdam: Elsevier Science Publ, 1986.

Quere, M. "Expert Systems: Toward the CAI of the Future." In *Computers in Education*, Karen Duncan and Diane Harris, ed. Amsterdam: Elsevier Science Publ, 1986.

Rodrigues, D. and R. Rodrigues. "Computer-Based Creative Problem-Solving." In Wresch, 1984.

Sadler, L.V. "The Computers-and-Effective Writing Movement: Computer-Assisted Composition." *ADE Bulletin* 87 (1987):28-33.

Schneiderman, B. and Morariu, J. "The Interactive Encyclopedia System (TIES)." Department of Computer Science, University of Maryland, College Park, MD. 1986.

Schwartz, H.J. "Monsters and Mentors: Computer Applications for Humanistic Education." *College English* 44 (1982):141-152.

_____. "Teaching Writing with Computer Aids." *College English* 46 (1984):239-247.

Shaw, R., Lewis, B., and Cattey, W. "File Exchange for the Educational On-line System: User Specification." MIT Project Athena. 1987.

Skinner, B.F. "Why We Need Teaching Machines." *Harvard Educational Review* 3 (1961):377-398.

Smith, J.B. et al. "WE: a writing environment for professionals." *Technical Report 86-025*. Department of Computer Science, UNC, Chapel Hill, 1986.

Stefik, M., Foster, G., Bobrow, D.G., Kahn, K., Lanning, S., and Suchman,

L. "Beyond the chalkboard: computer support for collaboration and problem-solving in meetings." *Communications of the ACM* 30 (1987):32-47.

Von Blum, R. and Cohen, M. "WANDAH: Writing Aid and Author's Helper." In Wresch 1984.

Weizenbaum, J. *Computer Power and Human Reason: From Judgement to Calculation.* San Francisco: W.H. Freeman, 1976.

Wresch, W. "Computers in English Class: Finally Beyond Grammar and Spelling Drills." *College English* 44 (1982):483-490.

_____. *The Computer in Composition: A Writer's Tool.* Urbana: NCTE, 1984.

14

Technology + Design + Research = Information Design
Electronic Publishing Drives a New Approach to Design

Elizabeth Keyes, President
Watzman+Keyes, Inc.

David Sykes
Watzman+Keyes, Inc.

Elaine Lewis, Ph.D.
Boston University

"Think of the design process as involving first the **generation** of alternatives and then the **testing** of these alternatives against a whole array of requirements and constraints."
Herbert A.Simon, *A.I. Expert and Nobel Laureate*

Context

The arrival of electronic methods for developing and disseminating text-based materials has brought the need for fundamental changes in the process of document design. Designers must now shift their focus from the slow, reflective, evaluation of individual "products" to the efficient development of entire systems, specifications and software (which we call CoGSS, or Corporate Graphics Standards Systems) which others, such as writers, will later employ without ongoing professional guidance. Frequently, these specifications and systems are used by others to prepare vast numbers of documents over long periods of time (perhaps 5-10 years). Thus, the design of systems that must provide trouble-free, cost-effective operation may represent a significant investment by companies. To ensure a positive outcome from this investment, standards systems need to be rigorously tested, using legitimate social science methods, before organizations deploy them (Shubik, 1979). In other words, designers must now move beyond *styling* and become much more interested in how their work affects human *performance*.

Unfortunately, combining design and testing is not an easy process. Not only are design and research highly sensitive to changes in context, but designers and social scientists often have very different attitudes and vocabularies, and sometimes even strong prejudices against each others' orientations (Committee on Human Factors, 1983). These difficulties lead to inefficiency at best, or outright antagonism at worst. Both of these difficulties unjustifiably raise the cost of projects and the time required to execute them. Therefore, for designers and researchers to work together without compromising projects or each others' professional integrity–and in ways which truly improve the quality of the "products" they jointly produce–a new approach to the design process is absolutely necessary.

A New Approach: Information Design

Over the past two and a half years, based on our experience with a variety of projects for organizations ranging from Fortune 500's to high tech startups, we have developed a six-stage model for the design process which incorporates both design and social science perspectives. We call this new approach Information Design. The approach functions equally well for projects involving either print or electronic media formats. It has two parts: one is a project management procedure (See *figure 1*) and the other is a design development "philosophy" (See *figure 2*).

Figure 1: Six-Stage Project Management Procedure

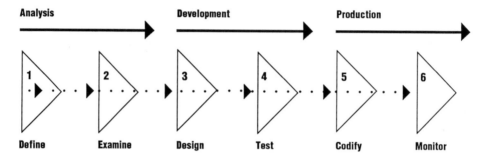

An Overview of the Design/Research Process:
An Overview of the Design/Research Process:
Six Steps to CoGSS (Corporate Graphic Standards Systems)

This six-stage model has two principle advantages: first, it expedites projects and second, it assures quality control. Design is a young "profession," so clients frequently have unrealistic expectations because they are unfamiliar with what designers do. As a result, they often come to us with inadequate budgets and time frames. In this circumstance, our model helps to clarify the process and leads to significantly improved communication between the firm and our clients. Furthermore, the development team uses this procedure to organize and focus projects. As explained below, the outcome of a clearly articulated process is that clients and people on the development team all work together comfortably toward a product that performs better.

Phase 1: Definition

Define the business problem: Who is sending the messages? For what purposes? Using what technologies? What constraints exist (budgets, staffing, etc.)? What degree of control or decentralization is advisable or realistic? Research applicable to this phase is most often in the form of content analysis (See *figure 5*). This phase ends in a *compilation and review*.

Phase 2: Examination

Understand the users: Who are they? How do they use information? What are their backgrounds and educational levels? Do they have unusual constraints? *Phases 1 and 2* form a complete *communication audit*.

Phase 3: Development

Brief the design team so they can develop design alternatives (several alternatives are necessary for valid testing). This results in a *presentation of alternatives* to the staff which will use the CoGSS system (see figure 2).

Phase 4: Testing

According to Nobel Laureate and A.I. expert Herbert Simon, "Design is both the development and testing of alternatives." In this phase, alternatives are subjected to various cognitive tests. Types of research appropriate to this phase are (See *figure 5*) *expert evaluation, panels,* and *controlled experimental testing.* The results are used to refine the CoGS System (see figure 2).

Phase 5: Codification

Once the CoGS System is developed it can be coded into software or a manual which is then used to train staff about the CoGS System. Electronic publishing fundamentally alters the way documents are produced and the way people work, so this phase includes training in teamwork as well as in basic system orientation. *Controlled observation* is a useful research approach in this phase.

Phase 6: Training, Monitoring and Trouble-Shooting

This phase ensures that the system does the two things it is supposed to do: i.e., it helps staff be productive and helps users learn complex equipment and tasks easily. In this phase, *survey research, focus groups, interviews* and *content analysis* are again useful research approaches.

The Heart of the Process

The core of the project management procedure occurs in stages three and four, where the design development "philosophy" which is modelled after Claude Shannon's Information Theory (1960), comes into play (see subsequent discussion). *Figure 2* highlights these phases.

Figure 2: Design Development Phase

Development

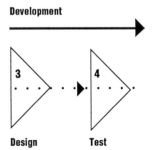

Design   **Test**

Variable Thresholds or "Tolerance Levels"

From an Information Theory point of view, humans have *physiological tolerance levels* or thresholds for information (Miller, 1981; Pearson, 1967; Shannon, 1960). But these levels are determined by the *structure* of information rather than solely by its *quantity*. For example, even though the tones, loudness, and texture of noise from a construction site may be similar in quantity to a symphony by Mahler, a listener finds the latter more tolerable and meaningful due to the *structure* of the sounds. In other words, much of what we see and hear is "noise" from which we actively extract the information we need or want. In this sense, information *which is carefully structured* before being presented to the senses assists readers in understanding more complex information. In some respects, this relationship between comprehension and structure is implicit in the very nature of information itself, for in philosophical terms, information *is* structure. Scientists like C.S. Smith (1981) and philosophers like Korzybski have been suggesting this relationship between information, structure and comprehension for many years in remarks like: "the only content of knowledge is structure," (Korzybski, 1936), and "Everything that we can see, everything that we can understand, is related to structure" (Smith, 1981).

Figure 3: Information Overload (based on Miller, 1981)

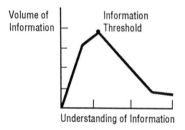

Figure 3 indicates that comprehension and quantity of information are positively correlated only to a certain point. Beyond that point, excess quantity (*or* insufficient structure) results in the rapid decline of comprehension. This view of the brain's response to information can be converted into a set of operations which designers can use to structure information into effective, "coherent" messages. In these terms information consists of structures of data, and "'understanding' (consists of) a set of processes performed on data structures" (Kosslyn, 1981). Designers who work from this perspective essentially "pre-process" information by structuring it coherently. Five relevant techniques drawn from cognitive science upon which information designers rely are: *chunking, queuing, filtering, mixing modes, and abstracting.* By using these techniques, designers "pre-process" information in ways which measurably influence a reader's attitude, speed of task performance, error rate and memory.

Figure 4: Five Pre-processing Techniques (based on Miller, 1981)

Chunking
Zoning or structuring the visual field by breaking information into manageable chunks according to their subject matter and then allocating them to various areas on a surface, screen or page.

Queuing
Ordering chunks of information in a spatial array *hierarchically*, that is, in an arrangement which suits the end user's sense of subject matter order and importance.

Filtering
Simplifying linguistic and visual order to "filter out" unnecessary "background noise" which interferes with the information being transmitted. Also, layering information, i.e., creating levels of depth and legibility through the use of visual metaphors, color, and tone, or by varying the sizes and weights of type.

Mixing Modes
People learn by using different cognitive modes or styles (Gardner, 1983). Some prefer or need text ("strings"); others need illustrations, photos, diagrams, or visual analogs ("images"); others demand formulae and other quantitative materials ("propositions") (Anderson, 1983). To suit these naturally varied styles, information must be "translated" into several different modes which are then arrayed in ways that provide everyone with equally straightforward, non-disruptive access.

Abstracting
Building effective visual information systems which work consistently over time on various media and in the hands of many users requires graphics systems which are characterized by simplicity, elegance and continuity. As in philosophy and mathematics, truly useful design systems can only be arrived at after considerable "abstraction." Appropriately abstracted rules must evolve from the needs of those the information system is being built to serve. They cannot be completely determined *a priori* and then used to dictate the system structure. On the other hand, a truly useful, flexible system provides a kind of "open architecture" which can be codified and converted into software. Such a system serves as a technology-based "visual language" which makes the process of communicating highly efficient–both for senders and receivers.

The Design Development Phase: an Iterative Process

The process of developing effective design involves the creation, evaluation, and refinement of design alternatives to achieve a finished product. Because several cycles are often needed, it is important to think of design as an iterative process. *Figure 5* illustrates how design professionals and research professionals who use our approach can combine their various disciplines to produce effective visual communication products or user-controlled systems of graphic standards (CoGSS).

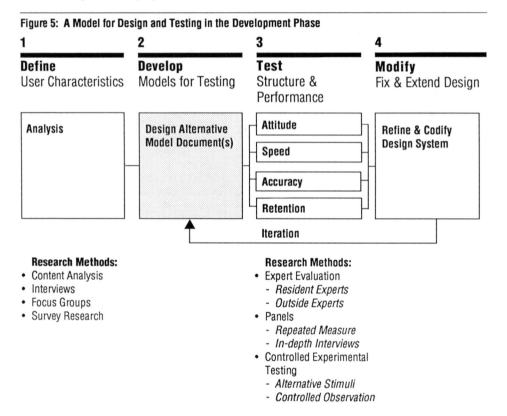

Figure 5: A Model for Design and Testing in the Development Phase

The model depicts four stages of design development: **analysis, development, testing and modification.** Research is an integral part of this process. Prior to the design phase, in **Stage 1: Analysis,** analysts collect information and carefully define the business problem. They may use any of four research techniques to gather the essential information: content analysis, interviews, focus groups or survey research.

In content analysis, teams collect and compile sample documents and other printed output. Much can be found from this analysis including typical production system characteristics, problems, constraints and expectations. Interviews can be used to supplement content analysis. In fact, they are particularly useful in determining attitudes and work processes, as well as the background and education of producers and users.

When it is important to know more about the end users of documents and communication materials, focus groups are an efficient way to obtain complex information rapidly. But when clients require quantitative bases for decision making, survey research is most useful. It is also desirable where the population of end-users is so diverse or widely distributed that neither focus groups nor interviews are practical.

Once data collection and analysis are completed, design development teams are briefed on the results. In **Stage 2: Development,** design teams begin developing alternative design strategies which will be tested later. Because designers usually employ intuitive processes–at which they are highly efficient–it is important for this phase to occur at its own pace without interference or active involvement by the analysis team. Nevertheless, designers do frequently confer with analysts. The purpose of this phase is to explore the wide range of possible alternatives without an analyst's bias. The outcome is a set of intuitively shaped designs that are ready for evaluation and testing.

In **Stage 3: Testing,** the three common testing methods are expert evaluations, panel studies, or controlled experimental tests. Design firms most often use their own internal experts to critique the aesthetics and potential effectiveness of a particular design concept or product. In the beginning phases of design this approach is the most efficient. After all, those who are involved in this kind of expert evaluation have a highly developed design sense, which is coordinated with cultural values and polished through their own experience. However, sometimes it is necessary to recruit external experts to supplement internal resources. Outside experts might include noted authorities on subjects ranging from cognitive psychology to management science, to various technology and engineering specialties.

In the final stage, **Stage 4: Modification,** designs are modified, extended and refined according to findings suggested by the testing stage. At this point, several alternative versions may again be tested and refined through subsequent cycles of the process.

Recently some designers, especially those who work with computer graphics and other electronic media, have begun to explore the use of computer-based expert systems for the evaluation of design *(Holynski, et al., 1986)*. However, such systems are still in the early development stages and although they successfully employ artificial intelligence techniques to discover formal graphic rules for abstract variables like complexity and color, the evaluation of content-related concepts, like queuing and data chunking, are still beyond their capacity.

During later cycles of design evaluation, social science research methods can be valuable tools for refining specific versions of the design for a system. Focus groups and interviews are useful techniques in this phase as well. Over time, panel studies can help to gather some performance data about the use of technical documents. In this case, representative users would be consulted before they have used the documentation and at regular intervals after they have begun to use it in the workplace. For more controlled performance data, experimental testing allows closer scrutiny of design formats.

Of course, the real advantage of experimental study is that is is conducted under controlled conditions and allows careful consideration of causality. For well designed studies with subjects who are representative of a target population, this technique allows comparative evaluation of different design alternatives or can even predict audience reactions to a particular format.

Experimental Research on Design

A wealth of published work exists aimed at evaluating design to discover general design principles. Unfortunately, most of these studies are confined to social science journals and thus, have never come to the attention of the vast majority of design professionals. Most of these research projects have employed experimental or quasi-experimental field techniques. A brief review of them suggests several of the the types of graphic variables and user variables which concern designers, so some of this work could have direct application to the design process.

In fact, researchers focusing on technical communciation issues have been reporting empirical work on design formats for at least three decades. Some of these studies have concentrated on styles and characteristics of type *(Foster and Coles, 1977; Haskins and Flynne, 1974)*, while others have examined the effects of arrangement and layout of text on readers' attitudes and perceptions *(Niekamp, 1981; Spencer, et al., 1974)*. More complex reader variables like comprehension and readability have been assessed as a function of text justification *(Campbell, et al., 1981; Fabrizio, et al., 1967)* and conceptual organization of the material *(Frase and Schwartz, 1978; Carver, 1970; Klare, et al., 1957)*. Overall resolution of printed documents has also been considered in terms of readers' speed, accuracy and satisfaction *(Lewis, et al., 1984; Snyder and Taylor, 1979)*. Although most of these studies relate to printed media, there is an increasing interest among researchers in examining electronic formats *(Tullis, 1981)*.

Recently, some technical communicators have summarized findings from this and other research to suggest guidelines for effective design *(Rubens, 1986; Jonassen, 1982)*. Indeed it may be possible to synthesize general design principles from work of this type. But the purpose of this chapter is to discuss how some of the evaluation methods used by communication researchers can be usefully incorporated into the day to day practice of design.

Variables for Design Research

Experimental testing in design is an examination of the relationship between two sets of variables: format variables and audience variables. Tasks for the researcher are to define (operationalize) variables in a clearly measurable way, to evaluate (measure) the variables in a particular case, and finally, to compare (analyze) the sets of variables in order to discover evidence of any causal effects. Identifying variables which are measurable, relevant to design issues and appropriate for the client's needs is a major challenge.

Design format variables encompass both graphic characteristics, and information structure. Graphic variables can concern typography (size, style, and placement of type), graphic elements (line, shape, color, value, texture), and composition (layout and sequence). Information structure can be defined as the use of alternative grid systems, methods of organizing content like branching and cueing techniques, or levels of realism and resolution.

Audience variables can relate to perception, comprehension and performance. Often general reaction to a particular design, such as its perceived clarity and professionalism, is of interest to a client. Certainly, a potential user's ability to comprehend the information conveyed by a particular design is crucial to that design's success. Performance can be measured as users' speed in reading a particular document, their ability to accurately apply presented facts or ideas, and, in some cases such as the design of computer documentation, whether or not the document design can aid successful completion of a particular task.

A Case Study of Information Design in Action: XYZ Corp.

In practice, the range of possibilities discussed above quickly becomes reduced by time and necessity to a limited set of discrete steps which we work with clients to tailor in order to meet the requirements of their individual projects. Because clients are different and, indeed, depend on differences between them and competitors to succeed, the processes described here are never allowed to become "cookie cutter-like." Following is a synopsis of how one such recent project for a Fortune 500 industrial/high-tech company (referred to here as XYZ Corp.) proceeded.

XYZ Corp. was in the process of purchasing and deploying electronic publishing technology, had already anticipated the problems that such "democratizing" technology might create, and had come to our firm in search of a solution. The solution (currently under development) is a Corporate Graphic Standards System (CoGSS), the evolution of which follows the process described above.

Phase 1: Definition

Senior analysts from Watzman+Keyes made several trips to XYZ Corp.'s midwestern headquarters to collect information about the organization, its staffing, needs, expectations, constraints, particularities, etc. Information was gathered from interviews and observation and then assembled by W+K staff into a report called a *compilation and review*. This report was then submitted to executives at XYZ Corp. who reviewed and approved it.

Phase 2: Examination

To further understand the implications of this project, our analysts next set about gathering information on XYZ Corp's customers–the end users of the information which the corporation's staff generates. This information was derived from interviews conducted with company executives, product managers and customer service personnel. Though focus groups involving customers or survey research would have been very helpful, time constraints prohibited the use of these research approaches, and no direct contact took place with actual XYZ Corp. customers. With the completion of this phase, our staff had finished its *communication audit*, and filed a second report. One of the most important outcomes of this audit phase was the preparation of an *Information Products Matrix* (IPM) which detailed the company's complete range of customer support information products and organized them by (a) audience and task definitions, and (b) media configuration (e.g., manual, audio tape, on-line tutorial, interactive video-disc, etc.). The availability of this matrix made it possible for the company to select specific pilot projects from the matrix for prototype development and testing. In this way, careful analysis enabled the company to save enormous amounts of money and time and to isolate particularly important policy and standards issues.

Phase 3: Development

Having jointly agreed upon an appropriate pilot project from the *Information Products Matrix*. The design team began *Phase 3*, the development of prototypes for testing. Designers rapidly developed half a dozen alternative approaches to the problem for purposes of internal discussion. This range of options was quickly narrowed to *one* solution with variables, a judgement arrived at using in-house experts. This one solution was then developed into a detailed prototype which was reviewed by an outside expert, an eminent cognitive psychologist at M.I.T. (the University is near our office). Based on this expert's comments, the prototype was revised and then presented to managers at XYZ Corp.

Phase 4: Testing

In the meantime, while our team had been focusing on design and cognitive issues as they arose in the context of the pilot project, a production team at the client company had–as a benchmark–been using the *same information* to produce an actual customer service product (a manual). Samples of this actual document were next pulled out and submitted to another office at XYZ Corp. for internal product testing. The client's objective at this time was to save money on research by performing it internally. Unfortunately, this process yielded three conclusions: (1) the documents (stimuli) which were submitted for testing were "invalid," or insufficiently developed to provide informative results; (2) the methodology employed by internal researchers was insufficiently rigorous to yield useful conclusions; and (3) the subject population used to test the documents was far too small to give valid research results, and asubjects were demographically and psychographically inappropriate. All of these problems, which were the result of an effort by the client to save money and time, ended up compromising the project and rendering that portion of it useless.

Phase 4b: Repeat Testing

At this point, XYZ Corp. returned the project to W+K for testing. During this stage of testing, we chose to evaluate design alternatives through a three-part research strategy. This provided both an overall evaluation and a detailed testing of specific design variables. The first part assessed the general design and some specific format variables (color and style of illustration) in terms of the attitude and performance of 100 people who were representative of the documentation's intended users. The second part examined the effect of information structure variables (branching and navigation/differentiation cues) with thirty potential users. Finally, ten subjects were asked to perform a specific installation task using the prototype documentation and components of XYZ Corp's computer system.

For part one, two dichotomous variables (color versus black-and-white and the use of photographs or line drawings for illustration) were evaluated for format effects through a 2 x 2 factorial research design. Twenty-five subjects were randomly assigned to each research cell (for a total of 100 subjects) to allow statistical comparison of the alternative documentation formats. Subjects were recruited from adult professional and clerical workers in the Boston area with limited computer experience.

First, they were asked to read one of the four versions of documentation and complete a written questionnaire. It included specific questions about the clarity, perceived professionalism and ease of use of the documentation, along with questions which evaluated the subjects' comprehension of the material. Some of the questions referred to a piece of system hardware available at the testing site. Length of time required to examine the documentation and complete the questionnaire was recorded.

In part two, thirty research participants were asked to review documentation which employs different methods of information structure (branching and clues to navigation). In-depth interviews explored users' facility with, and preference for, various types of content organization.

Finally, during part three, ten subjects were carefully observed as they used the documentation to perform an installation task. After they successfully completed the task, they filled out a written questionnaire and exit interview.

Data from all three parts was compiled and statistically analyzed where appropriate. Findings were used to modify and refine the documentation.

Phase 5: Codification

While the project for XYZ Corp. has not yet reached this phase, our purpose from the outset has been to develop and codify a useful, validated set of specifications for all subsequent information products of this type. When this phase is completed for this particular pilot project, we will select, jointly with XYZ Corp. executives, the *next* pilot project form the *Information Products Matrix* (IPM) for subsequent development and testing. This next project will most logically *not* be another print documentation product, but rather a project in another media, such as an *on-line tutorial*.

Phase 6: Training, Monitoring and Troubleshooting

Typically, as pilot projects are completed,the staffs which will employ them in their work must be carefully trained to use them in ways which preserve or improve standards of quality. None of our pilot projects for XYZ Corp. have yet reached this phase, but our experience in training other clients suggests that training can be usefully supplemented by focus groups and interviews which then provide results for fine-tuning systems and for improving subsequent products. However, the goal of our organization after the initial training phase is to recede from active involvement in the production of particular products and simply to monitor quality, and service the system when necessary. When a Graphic Standards System is complete, this quality control function is mostly accomplished through periodic reviews, although occasional panels, expert evaluations, focus groups, content analysis or survey research can provide useful information to production teams and managers. But the process of sustaining quality should be, by now, the responsibility of the properly equipped and trained production team.

Conclusion: Dealing with the "Sorcerer's Apprentice Problem"

Technology has changed, and is still changing the process of design. The nearly magical mechanization which the computer has introduced into the traditional process has also introduced a range of problems which can lead to chaos. First, design is no longer a slow, reflective process worked out by craftsmen using time-tested techniques. Second, the number of non-design users has increased. Third, this new class of users has a broad range of design options available but lacks the experience, education and informed decision-making capability necessary to discriminate among them. Fourth, the speed of the process has accelerated dramatically. Fifth, the demand for more output from organizations has also grown. Finally, tolerance for information among audiences is declining.

Because of all these changes, designers must move away from the traditional process of trial-and-error craftsmanship. Instead they must become professionals accustomed to working with other professionals and evaluation specialists, like researchers, in a team setting. Only by cooperating can these two frequently antagonistic professions overcome the context sensitivity of their work and begin to develop useful and socially beneficial results And only by working in such new ways can designers uphold the traditional standards of quality for which they are ultimately held responsible in a modern, automated information environment. Our model provides a useful production framework for the effective combination of design, technology and research.

Bibliography

Adams, Smelser, Treiman, eds., *Behavioral and Social Science Research, A National Resource*, Washington, DC, National Academy Press, 1982.

Anderson, John R., *The Architecture of Cognition*, Cambridge, MA, Harvard University Press, 1983.

Campbell, A.J., et al., "Reading Speed and Text Production: A Note on Right Justification Techniques," *Ergonomics*, 24:8, pp. 633-640, 1981.

Carver, R.P. "Effect of 'Chunked' Typography on Reading Rate and Comprehension," Journal of *Applied Psychology*, 54:3, pp. 388-396, 1970.

Committee on Human Factors, *Research Needs for Human Factors*, Washington, DC, National Academy Press, 1983.

Fabrizio, R., et al., "Readability as a Function of the Straightness of Right-Hand Margins," *Journal of Typographic Research*, 1, pp. 90-95, 1967.

Foster, J. and P. Coles, "An Experimental Study of Typographic Cueing in Printed Texts," *Ergonomics*, 20:1, pp. 57-66, 1977.

Frase, L.T., and B.J. Schwartz, "Typographic Clues that Facilitate Comprehension," *Journal of Applied Psychology,* 71:2, pp. 197-206, 1979.

Gardner, Howard, *Frames of Mind*, NY, Basic Books, 1983.

Gardner, Howard, *The Mind's New Science*, NY, Basic Books, 1985.

Haskins, J. and L. Flynne, "Effects of Headline Typeface Variation on Reader Interest," *Journalism Quarterly*, 51:4, pp. 677-682, 1974.

Holynski, M., R. Garneau, and E. Lewis, "An Adaptive Graphics Interface for Effective Visual Representation," *Eurographics '86*, A.A. Requicha, ed., Amsterdam: Elsevier Science Publishers, pp. 195-206, 1986.

Jonassen, D.H., editor, *The Technology of Text: Principles for Structuring, Designing, and Displaying Text*, Englewood Cliffs, New Jersey, Educational Technology Publications, 1982.

Klare, G.R., et al., "The Relationship of Typographic Arrangements to the Learning of Technical Training Material," *Journal of Applied Psychology*, 41:1, pp.41–45, 1957.

Korzybski, Alfred, *Science and Sanity*, 3rd Edition, Lakeville, Ct., International Non-Aristotelian Library Publishing Company, 1958.

Kosslyn, Stephen M., *Image and Mind*, Cambridge, MA, Harvard University Press, 1980.

Lewis, E., D. Sykes, and P.H. Lemieux, "An Empirical Comparison of the Effectiveness of Typeset, Typewritten, and Dot Matrix Business Documents," Wilmington, MA, Compugraphic Corporation, 1984.

Miller, J.G., *Living Systems*, McGraw Hill, NY, 1981.

Niekamp, W., "An Exploratory Investigation of Factors Affecting Visual Balance," *Educational Communication and Technology Journal*, 29:1, pp. 37-48, 1981.

Pearson, D., "A Realistic Model for Visual Communication Systems," Proceedings of IEEE, vol. 55, 1967, pp.381-392.

Pinker, Steven, *Visual Cognition*, Cambridge, MA, MIT Press, 1985.

Rubens, P.M., "A Reader's View of Text and Graphics: Implications for Transactional Text," *Journal of Technical Writing and Communication*, 16:1/2, pp.73-86, 1986.

Shannon, Claude E., "Coding Theorems for a Discrete Source with a Fidelity Criterion," R.E. Machel, ed., *Information and Decision Processes*, N.Y. McGraw-Hill, 1960, pp. 93-126.

Shubik, Martin, "Computers and Modelling," *The Computer Age*, Dertouzos and Moses, Cambridge, MA, MIT Press, 1979.

Simon, Herbert A., *The Sciences of the Artificial*, Cambridge, MA, MIT Press, 1981.

Smith, Cyril Stanley, *A Search for Structure*, Cambridge, MA, MIT Press, 1981.

Snyder, H.L. and G.B. Taylor, "The Sensitivity of Response Measures of Alphanumeric Legibility to Variations in Dot Matrix Display Parameters," *Human Factors*, 21:4, pp. 457-471, 1979.

Spencer, H.L., et al., "Typographic Coding in Lists and Bibliographies," *Applied Ergonomics*, 5:3, pp. 136-141, 1974.

Tullis, T.S., "An Evaluation of Alphanumeric, Graphic, and Color Information Displays," *Human Factors*, 23:5, pp. 541-550, 1981.

15

Writers as Total Desktop Publishers: Developing a Conceptual Approach to Training

Patricia Sullivan

Department of English
Purdue University
West Lafayette, Indiana 47907

This chapter explores a conceptually-based answer to the question of training total desktop publishers, focusing initial attention on the training of writers. It argues for developing a conceptual approach to training new users of desktop publishing and identifies some fundamental components that are related both to the process of publishing and to the quality of the document produced -- computer technology skills, problem-solving process skills, verbal skills, visual skills, and visual and verbal integration skills. The chapter then reports an observation of five writers learning to use desktop publishing and finds that the writers share problems with the computer technology, the visual skills, and the integration of the visual and verbal elements of a document. A discussion of developing conceptually-based training for desktop publishers closes the chapter.

1. Introduction

Desktop publishing merges writing, graphic design, art, instructional text design, and publication production in an entirely new way. Because the entire work of a publication can be mapped onto a single electronic file, desktop publishing creates a multi-disciplinary melting pot that encourages us to rethink the relationships of the allied publishing disciplines. This new technology allows any one of the professionals involved -- a writer, a designer, or a production specialist -- to become the total desktop publisher. Yet we expect that, at least initially, any one of these professionals who tries to be the total desktop publisher will conform to John Coltrane's observation about playing the saxophone: "The saxophone is an instrument that anyone can play. . . badly." The challenge of teaching desktop publishing comes when we try to move beyond simple procedural training in operating a particular desktop package and we ask: Can we teach people with diverse skills how to become total desktop publishers?

An anecdote fueled my initial interest in desktop publishing and focused my attention on the training needs of writers. My writer friend "George" witnessed a demonstration of desktop publishing on the Macintosh using Pagemaker and immediately bought a desktop publishing unit. He was sure that he would be turning out "publication quality" documents in hours and was disappointed at how hard it was for him to layout the simplest newsletter on his new system. I watched his frustration mount as he struggled to teach himself how to use a program he was convinced was easy-to-use, never realizing that he was learning a new system at the same time as he was trying to use that system on a task he had not done before (i.e., page layout).

George assumed the desktop publishing was simple and utterly transparent; any problems he had must be due to his clumsiness with computers. To make a long story short, had George not sought professional help he would have abandoned his machine or hired a person to be the desktop publishing specialist. Two months later the technical problems were solved but the documents were slightly comical in their excesses: George had reached the second stage and could now publish the way that anyone can play Coltrane's sax. . . badly. While he had mastered the capabilities of the desktop publishing program, he had not become a competent desktop publisher.

Technology has often quite suddenly remade the ways of the world. Walter Ong reminds us of this when he speaks about the impact of technological changes on communication. Comparing the way that information is accessed in manuscript and print cultures, Ong argues that print gave us the ability to fix words on particular pages, enabling standard references and indexes. Though manuscripts still existed past the invention of printing, indeed they actually increased in numbers, print transformed our understanding of writing from a notetaking used to "generally" preserve speech into a way to fix meaning on a page. Ong goes on to comment that the electronic media revolution is having as important an impact as the printing press:

> And so in the present and future, as we live with the electronic
> media, we are finding and will find that we have not wiped out
> anything but simply complicated everything endlessly [11].

And in desktop publishing, the media transformation has made it necessary for everyone (writer, designer, et.al.) to know something about everything.

Ong's point is that the new electronic media changes communication modes and also changes the ways in which we think of them, reinforcing the old modes but also reconfiguring them. This is true generally of the electronic media and specifically in the arena of the current discussion -- electronic publishing. Ong also stresses that we fool ourselves if we think the changes are limited to introducing a new machine with new procedures. In other words, doing the new media (i.e., desktop publishing) is not simply a matter of doing all the old things plus all the new things; instead it calls for doing the old things in a new way.

Thus, a change in the technology of producing communication interestingly complicates the way we think about what a particular communication requires. For whatever reasons we have embraced desktop publishing and its electronic publishing relatives, the fact is that desktop publishing is quickly finding its way into everyday use. In the next three years, DataQuest projects that more than a million desktop publishing packages will be sold.[1] As these desktop programs infiltrate the offices under the auspices of saving money, improving productivity, decreasing turn-around time, or just keeping pace with the quality of documents demanded, they are changing the look of our documents. Desktop publishing is also complicating our communications process and reconfiguring the ways in which we write and publish. It stands to reason, then, that we should treat the emergence of desktop publishing with respect and that we should consider the problem of training people to become desktop publishers as a worthy adversary. To the extent that theorists like Ong are correct, technological innovations such as desktop publishing are not innocent. They cannot be fully taught by introducing people to the procedures for running a program, nor can they be "handled" by training in the use of a set of templates.

In suggesting that the education of the total desktop publisher extends beyond the current training widely offered, I am not critical of the procedural training for particular desktop programs provided by companies or other groups, as I am not critical of template distribution.[2] Both of these training efforts are appropriate initial training responses and are useful, if not sufficient. An analogy taken from another technological innovation, one that has remade a basic process of research, can clarify my point. A few years ago, university libraries started using computerized card catalogs in place of the manual card catalog. Initial training on the computers focused on the procedural aspects of using the catalog to find books. The educators quickly realized, however, that knowing how to operate the catalog and "how to find a book by its title" did not translate into knowing how to search the catalog for books on a subject of interest. Further, giving the users searching templates, while it helped them with routine tasks, did not teach them how to search for many of the books they wanted. Conceptual training both in how the system worked and also in strategies for searching was necessary [3,8,13]. Those initial training efforts focusing on how to search were not wrong, nor were they abandoned as the training developed. Instead, the more sophisticated approach to educating searchers was added to the earlier efforts.

Educators training users of online catalogs found that they had to give new searchers a conceptual view of the system and how it operated, a mental model of searching for books on the computerized catalog, practice searching for books via computer, and strategies for dealing with problems that arise during an online search. The training that developed in association with the automation of library card catalogs can offer suggestions for training in desktop publishing, since it demonstrates how educators came to grips with a technology that remade a fundamental part of library research. The library experience suggests that in addition to the procedural training being given in "how to operate package or system X," and in addition to packages of templates we can purchase to help us produce newsletters and other documents, we need to develop a conceptually sophisticated training that helps people develop a mental model of the new activity and strategies useful in, to borrow a phrase from Jerome Bruner [4], going beyond the information given.

This chapter pursues the goal of developing conceptual training for desktop publishers by discussing the component skills that contribute to the desktop publishing effort and by focusing on how to train writers as total desktop publishers. Because desktop publishing reorganizes the complex task of low-end publishing, it is important to analyze the components of the new process and to determine the skills that are needed for a competent use of desktop publishing. Once that analysis is in place, the educator must assess what a particular group needs to be taught. In this chapter I propose several components of conceptually-based training and examine the needs of writers vis-a-vis these desktop publishing skills. Although the training of other professionals is not focal, I expect that this approach can be adapted to graphic artists and production specialists after an analysis of their needs has been conducted. The value of this conceptual approach arises both from its focus on basic skills that are used by the total desktop publisher and also from its acceptance of the integrity of desktop publishing as a new communication technology rather than seeking to patch together a publisher by educating a writer, and a designer, and a production specialist. After all, we cannot expect that any one potential desktop publisher has time, aptitude, and aesthetic breadth to learn everything about all three disciplines.

2. The Components of the Total Desktop Publisher

Several obvious components of desktop publishing can be targeted in an effort to improve the new desktop publisher's ability to manage the entire publishing process. When a person becomes a total desktop publisher, those parts of document production that were previously mysterious lose their magic. Because the purchaser of the system normally expects the system to cut down production time, cut printing costs, and improve productivity, the desktop publisher must import information (words and pictures), lay it out, edit it, prepare a master copy, and arrange for printing or copying in an expeditious manner. The basic computer technology problems of inputting, formatting, outputting, and debugging must be anticipated and solved. Further, the document changes that are caused by production problems, system limits, or human ability limits must not result in a document that fails to communicate or that loo ks unattractive. The total desktop publisher gains control over the publishing process, but at the cost of taking responsibility for that process.

Audience responses to the finished document offer two further components to desktop publishing -- the quality of the writing and the quality of the visual design. In the finished document, success will be determined by its ability to convey to appropriate readers the message intended, and that success will be a product of the document's verbal message and visual design.

Thus, obvious components of total desktop publishing can be drawn from both the production process and the finished product:

* The Process of Publishing

Ability to schedule work and solve problems in such a way that everything gets finished in a timely fashion.

Adequate knowledge of the technology to enable its use.

* The Document Produced

Ability to produce a document that communicates the intent.

Ability to produce a visually attractive document.

2.1 The process of publishing: Using basic problem-solving techniques

The process of desktop publishing combines the traditional elements of the publication production process with the new computer technology. In essence, most of the steps of the traditional production get handled during the process of making the document, but not in the same ways as before. Further, as the technology improves, the process is continually being massaged. The changes play out in one of two ways: if the new users of a desktop publishing system are knowledgeable of the production process, then a discussion of how a document is produced can lean on how the current technology reshapes the process; but if the new users do not already know how to "publish" a document, constructing a platform of previous production process techniques as a teaching basis would be counterproductive.

Instead of teaching the traditional publishing process, and then adding the computer publishing process, and then discussing how desktop publishing changes the production process, it makes more sense for the general new user to learn an approach specific to the computerized production of documents. This approach to the production process should be general enough to be flexible. Flexibility will allow it to be responsive to the continual changes in the computerized document production process.

What is called for is a problem-solving approach to the production process. By teaching the basic process of using a desktop package and then adapting that to particular kinds of document projects (producing a newsletter or developing a technical report series), the basics of planning a project can be molded to the particular, if diverse, task of producing a desktop publication. The basics of this process can be constructed by adapting general problem-solving methods to the tasks facing desktop publishers [7, 12]. New users who are unfamiliar with production can be taught to:

1. Analyze the Project.

2. Search for Workable Solutions.

3. Implement the Solutions Systematically.

4. Evaluate the Progress During the Project.

5. Accept Satisfactory Solutions.

6. Learn from Each Project.

Such an approach can be particularly helpful to people without production experience because it de-mystifies production. Problem solving begins by taking stock of what is called for and setting goals that are workable within the system being used. It then searches for solutions, but does so within the framework of what is feasible given the system, and also does so within a frame of continually asking, "Is this working?" Problem solving also stresses "satisficing," or accepting a reasonable answer, and reviewing each completed project for the purpose of learning from its successes and failures. The basic tactics of problem solving, then, are general, flexible, and systematic. When added to a basic introduction to the process of using a computerized publishing program, problem-solving techniques can help the new desktop publisher manage the production process.

2.2 The document produced: Integrating words and pictures on a page

The finished document combines the words and pictures into a communication. Both words and pictures contribute to the meaning of the document, yet usually a person is trained in either the making of verbal meaning or the making of visual meaning. Recently theorists in technical communication have begun to recognize the importance of visual meaning. Some have begun to develop vocabularies for talking about visual meaning in documents [2,9]. An integrated theory of document meaning will emerge as their work is merged with a vocabulary and aesthetic for talking about graphics in technical documents, as is available from Edward Tufte [14], and a reader-oriented concept of page design, as the work of James Hartley [6] suggests is possible. Currently, though, the work is preliminary. In fact, desktop publishing actually offers incentive for improving our understanding of how words and images interact on a page. Why? Because the page can now be much more complex than it was when it was simply typed.

The basic elements of a document are its words, its sharing of conventions with other documents of its type, its placement of words and images on a page, and the integration of words and images that it manages. We can consider the page as a basic unit of this meaning and the place where integration most commonly occurs. The integration can be usefully viewed as a continuum of meaning from text-based to image-based, with the visual-verbal integration a fulcrum point that moves along the continuum in concert with the type of document being produced.

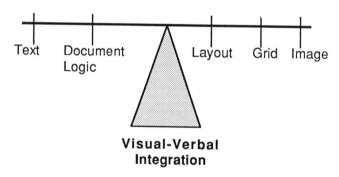

**Visual-Verbal
Integration**

As I see it, the Visual-Verbal Integration Point acts as the balancing point for documents, a fulcrum that shifts according to the nature of the document (who the audience is, how it will be used, what the textual and visual conventions are, the nature of the content to be conveyed, etc.). To suggest dramatic examples, the grid becomes more prominent in an advertisement, the text more prominent in a traditional essay. In computer documentation, the grid becomes more prominent in texts meant for quick reference, the text more prominent in texts aimed at learning a system's architecture. But text and image work together to create meaning on each page, and the document is coherent if they also work across the pages to create logical patterns.

On the conceptual level, the challenges of desktop publishing are tied to the user's ability to see the page as a unit of meaning that integrates the visual and verbal meaning in an appropriate way for the document. On the skill level, the challenges of desktop publishing are tied to the abilities of the desktop publisher to understand the points along that continuum well enough to function as a total publisher. That is, the user must be able to write text, develop a global logic for a document, devise layout, draw (or procure) suitable artwork, and see the grid. And all of that is in addition to the challenges of mastering the computer technology and production process problems.

3. Developing Conceptual Training for Desktop Publishing: Understanding the Needs of Writers

The training of a particular desktop publisher must take into account the previous history of the new user as well as the fact that desktop publishing merges communication, aesthetics, and production technology into a new publishing formula. The writer has been trained as a weaver of words into a communication, the graphic artist or designer has been trained as a visual aesthetician, and the printer has been trained in the previous generation's technology of production. Of course, these qualities bleed between the professions as people gain experience in producing published texts. The writer at work in the profession learns some visual conventions and production knowledge; the graphic artist some verbal communication and production skills; the printer some skills with words and pictures. Forward-looking writing programs are beginning to include courses in graphic fundamentals and document production.[3] But the training of the future professionals generally remains focused on one of the three major elements of the published book -- words, pictures, or production. This means that both the student and the publishing professional who are learning to employ desktop publishing will know one aspect of the process very thoroughly and the other aspects quite cursorily. If we operate from the perspective that education normally takes -- that you move from what is known to what is unknown, from the familiar to the unfamiliar -- our training should assume writing knowledge for writers, graphic knowledge for graphic artists, and production knowledge for production specialists and our training should be structured to build on those divergent skills with the goals of mastering the merger of the fields and also tuning in to the aesthetics and technology of the other two fields.

A commonplace from problem-solving theory is useful to keep in mind as we contemplate how to train desktop publishers -- the goals you can reach within a given time period will depend on where you are when you start and how rocky the path. A commonplace about education is useful as well -- new knowledge is built on the foundations of what we already know. New desktop publishers do not come to the task with the same background and skills nor do they come *tabula rasa*. Training goals with regard to new users, then, need to take into account what the users probably know when they approach desktop publishing and work around what they do not know.

Initially, I was intrigued by George's responses to desktop publishing and wondered whether his experience is typical of the many writers learning to use desktop programs. Do most writers tend to experience the two stages of learning that George exhibited -- first focusing on learning the basic procedures for operating a particular desktop system and second on using the power of the system on all documents? If so, what are the advantages of this natural movement and in what ways does it handicap the writer-turned-desktop-publisher? Further, what means are needed to redress the problems caused by the "natural" training people structure for themselves? To answer these questions I examined several cases of students and professional writers learning to use desktop publishing programs and systems.

3.1 The cases of five writers learning desktop publishing

I kept case histories of five writers learning to use desktop publishing -- three students enrolled in a class at Purdue University entitled "Computer-aided Publishing" and two professionals using desktop publishing for their work. Their stories suggest that writers share many similar problems as they start using desktop publishing, but also that writers are not totally homogeneous in their needs. The three students, chosen from a class of twenty, were selected to represent the types of interests and backgrounds students brought to the class: one was a political science major interested in producing an occasional newsletter for a student organization and lacking in any computer knowledge, one was a technical writing major with background in computers, and one was a journalism major with some newspaper layout experience but little computer experience. Neither of the two professionals had much computer savvy, but the ways they employed writing in their work varied: one was a grant writer whose primary job was writing and publishing while the other was a video trainer who had to produce an occasional script, a brochure, or advertising for workshops.

The students underwent procedural training on the Macintosh, learning the operating system, MacWrite, MacPaint, and MacDraw. They then produced job-finding materials (a business card, a resume, and a letterhead for stationery). Both professionals were familiar with using the Macintosh, so they were not trained in its use. All of these people were given two procedural training sessions on Ready-Set-Go (chosen because the machines being used did not have a hard drive), the students in a classroom setting and the professionals individually. Everyone then began work on either a newsletter or brochure; students were producing an issue of the newsletter of the local STC chapter, the grant writer was producing an alumni newsletter, and the video producer was producing a brochure to advertise a video fair. During this project I served as an archivist of their moves and as a resource person for their questions.

The writers had various problems as they completed the orientation and first project (see Table 1 for a list). All the writers observed shared some problems with the component skills related to desktop publishing. In addition, students shared some problems, the computer inexperienced shared some problems, those who view the system as something they will use occasionally shared some problems, and those without publishing experience shared some problems.

The shared problems could be characterized as follows:

All five writers had some problems obeying the conventions of the document: some misapplied layout conventions from magazines or newspapers; others did not use headings and captions properly; and others did not make the important information visually prominent. All the writers had a tendency to overuse visual devices useful in making information prominent -- the rules, boxes, typeface variations, and other effects -- and this was consonant with their lack of basic knowledge about two dimensional layout. Further, all writers had trouble keeping to the their schedule and keeping electronic copies of their work (in case of disaster).

The three student writers had trouble with the process of publication. They did not adequately plan their work, had trouble breaking the larger project into manageable units, and did not start subtasks in a manner that would allow them to complete the entire project on time. The students also had trouble making the information they deemed important stand out on the page and had modest problems trouble with the logic of typefaces.

Table 1: A Summary of the Problems of Five Desktop Publishing Users

The Problems	Total	Students			Professionals	
		Poli Sci	Tech Writing	Jour-nalism	Grant Writer	Video Trainer
Computer Technology Problems						
Computer Knowledge	4	X		X	X	X
Using Operating System	4	X		X	X	X
Manipulating Files	4	X		X	X	X
Revising Scanned Images	3	X			X	X
Fixing Minor Problems	3	X		X		X
Creating Simple Graphics in Macdraw or Macpaint	4	X	X		X	X
Entering/Saving Text	2			X		X
Backing up Text	4	X		X	X	X
Printing	2	X				X
Process Problems						
Planning Project	3	X	X	X		
Identifying Subtasks	3	X	X	X		
Starting Subtasks on Time	3	X	X	X		
Finishing Subtasks on Time	5	X	X	X	X	X
Keeping Alternative Versions	5	X	X	X	X	X
Trying More than One Idea	3	X	X			X
Doing Math for Layout Specs	4	X		X	X	X
Using a Grid or Mock-up	3	X	X			X
Visual Document Problems						
Obeying Conventions of Document	5	X	X	X	X	X
Misapplying Newspaper or Magazine layout	2			X	X	
Logic of headings	2	X				X
Labeling of Images	3	X		X		X
Making Important Info Prominent	4	X	X	X		X
Knowledge of 2-d Layout	5	X	X	X	X	X
Knowledge of Typefaces	4	X	X	X		X
Overusing						
lines and rules	5	X	X	X	X	X
boxes	4	X	X	X	X	
typefaces	4	X	X	X		X
images	5	X	X	X	X	X
effects (e.g., shadow)	4	X	X	X		X

The two professional writers did not share a pattern of problems that were unique to them alone. They were considerably better than the students at handling publication process problems that arose during the project, and they dealt with typeface decisions well.

Those with little computer experience (the political science major, the journalism major, and the two professionals) had problems with the basic computer tasks. In addition to dealing with producing the document they had to contend with basic problems in entering and saving text, importing and fixing images, backing up text, and printing it. They also admitted a lack of knowledge of operating systems in computers, and this seemed to exacerbate their problems.

Those who viewed the system as something they will use occasionally (the political science major and the video trainer) had more persistent problems than any other group, perhaps because they were less seriously invested in the learning. Their computer technology problems were particularly pronounced and long-lived.

Those with publishing experience (the journalism major and the grant writer) had fewer layout problems than those without publishing experience (the political science major, the technical writing major, and the video trainer) because they adopted the conventions of layout that they knew. However, they also had a tendency to use what they knew in all cases, and thus they misapplied the newspaper or magazine conventions to other documents.

3.2 Developing the conceptual training writers need

The problems shared by the five writers I observed suggest some obvious training needs of writers who are learning to be desktop publishers. What should we teach them? They need structured exercises that help them master the software, and they need conceptual understanding of the desktop publishing process. They need to understand how visual and verbal meaning work together on the page of a particular type of document. And, they need to learn how to use aids such as templates and click art, particularly if they are appropriate to the documents under construction. Put in terms of the conceptual needs addressed earlier -- those related to production process and those related to the document produced -- all writers who are learning desktop publishing must be assessed for relevant computer knowledge, ability to negotiate the production process, ability to solve problems that occur, understanding of document conventions, knowledge of visual layout, and knowledge of writing (with the expectation that this skill will be strong).

But the new users need to be assessed rather than simply handed a packaged training program. The writers observed above, while they could be grouped (see Table 2), could not be reduced to a formulaic set of training needs. For example, the student writers displayed problems with the computer technology, with solving the production process problems, and with creating documents that integrated the visual dimensions successfully; their strength was a proficiency with the writing tasks. The occasional users had problems with almost all aspects of the publishing, though they also showed writing strength. The professionals had the least trouble managing the production process and solving problems that occured during production. The approach to training writers such as these, while it can assume some shared starting points, needs also to be alert to the potential differences among new users.

	Production Process		Document Quality		
	Computer Technology	Problem-solving Process	Visual Design	Verbal Skill	Visual & Verbal
All writers	low	varies	low	high	low
Student writers	low	low	low	high	low
Professional writers	low	medium	varies	high	low
Occasional writer/publishers	low	low	low	varies	low
Total Desktop Publishers	medium	medium	medium	medium	medium

Table 2:   Expectations of Writers' Knowledge of Desktop Publishing Compared with the Total Desktop Publishers' Knowledge

We can use the observations of these five new desktop publishing users to propose a set of predictions about what writers may know. Suppose we assume that the total desktop publisher will need to have a moderate competence of the components I identified earlier -- computer technology, problem-solving processes as they relate to production, visual design of documents, verbal statement of meaning in text, and integration of visual and verbal into a successful document.   If we were developing training, we would need to determine which components need the most emphasis. The writers above, grouped according to shared problems, would compare to that Total Desktop Publisher as Table 2 suggests. The groupings indicate that work with computer technology and with visual and verbal integration is consistently called for, while a further examination of the group should dictate whether the training focuses much effort on problem-solving techniques or on visual design. The groupings also indicate that it would be easier to train students than professionals, as the students are more homogeneous than the professionals.

If we were to develop a training scenario that included all these writers, we would use their knowledge of writing as the keystone and expect at least some of the writers to need basic information about the other components. Thus, training for these writers would need to cover every basic component but writing, paying particular attention to giving them

An overview
* At least a black box understanding of the technological process.
* A conceptual vision of the document possibilities offered by the publishing.

An understanding of the desktop production process
* A functional understanding of key tasks.
* Problem-solving techniques for dealing with problems.

An understanding of the desktop document that builds from their knowledge of writing
* The appropriate conventions.
* The integration of visual and verbal.

By beginning with an overview of system, process, and document, the training could evaluate the level of the writers being trained in order to adjust the more specific training to their level of sophistication. The overview could also serve as an reference umbrella that ties the more specific discussion to the principles. That way, writers who got lost in the specific training could at least leave the training with a general idea of what is going on and teachers might recapture lost students through a series of recaps. By linking the technology to the process and the visual and verbal to each other, the training could suggest the logical linkings that writers need to have stressed. This hypothetical training plan can be extended to other writers (and even other types of professionals entering desktop publishing) as long as the educator is willing to assess the starting point of a particular group before developing the specific focus and level of example used in the training sessions. While writing knowledge is the staple for groups like the writers I observed, we might expect that this approach, when applied to a group of text designers would lean on page design and give basic instruction in writing. Simply stated, the approach I'm suggesting stresses training in basic components and how they are linked together in the desktop publishing, building on the strength of the group, and assessing the group for variance in expected knowledge before determining the bulk of the training being delivered.

4. Conclusion

In this article I have argued that desktop publishing offers a technological advance in publishing that profoundly affects the way that low-end publishing proceeds. Because the shift affects the way that communication and meaning is conceived, the changes are not innocent. We need to treat the education of the desktop publisher with respect. As a start toward assembling a conceptual approach to training the total desktop publisher, I have advanced several components for the training -- problem- solving techniques for managing the publishing process, general understanding of the relevant computer technology, general knowledge of the conventions of verbal communication and visual aesthetics appropriate to a particular document, and an ability to integrate appropriate visual and verbal elements of meaning on a page. While I do not suppose these components exhaust a classification of the components of desktop publishing, I do contend that they identify needed starting points in the development of conceptual training for total desktop publishers. These components are not missing elements from writers lives that educators will supply. When I observed five writers learning a desktop publishing system, they shared problems with several of the components, excelled at the verbal component, and had varied needs related to other components. The similarities and differences in the writers' knowledge and skill suggest the contours of their experience and urge us not to oversimplify our approach to training the Total Desktop Publisher. A conceptual approach to training can help us resist the urge to oversimplify the desktop publisher's education.

Notes

[1] Sales figures and projections [5] from DataQuest in San Jose show that sales of PC-based desktop publishing programs have grown from 4,000 in 1986 to 53,000 in 1987, and are expected to hit 300,000 by 1990, while Mac-based publishing programs have grown from 59,000 in 1986 to 92,000 in 1987, and are expected to be 534,000 in 1990.

[2] Current training in desktop publishing is focused on "hands on" seminars and on the distribution of templates. The seminars generally focus on a particular program and are so widely attended that they are booked well in advance [5]. Independent training centers such as Electronic Directions report a call from customers for more than time on the package; their customers have asked for training in DOS, in graphic design, in typography, in Postscript programming, and in output to typesetters (*Infoworld*, 29 June 1987, p. 27). Regarding the template approach, Aldus Corporation sells a set of templates (primarily newsletters) to accompany Pagemaker. And some experts expect templates that keyed to the document and the publishing software will replace "hands on" training in the future [1].

[3] Many schools offering technical writing degrees offer/require a class in the fundamentals of graphic design [10]. Purdue University, for example, advises its professional writing majors to take "Computer-aided Publishing," "Graphic Design Fundamentals," or "Magazine Layout and Production."

References

1.   Antonoff, M. (1987, July). Setting up for desktop publishing. *Personal Computing*, pp. 75-82.

2.   Bernhardt, S. (1986). Seeing the text. *College Composition and Communication, 32*, 66-78.

3.   Borgman, C. L. (1983). Performance effects of a user's mental model of an information retrieval system. *Proceedings of the American Society for Information Science, 20*, 121-123.

4.   Bruner, J. S. (1973). *Beyond the information given*. New York: Norton.

5.   Burns, D. & Venit, S. (1987, October 13). PC desktop publishing comes of age. *PC Magazine, 6*, pp. 93ff.

6.   Hartley, J. (1985). *Designing instructional text*. 2nd ed. London: Kogan Page.

7.   Hayes, J. R. (1981). *The complete problem solver*. Philadelphia: Franklin Institute
      Press, pp. 1 - 23.

8.   McClintock, M. H. (ed.) (1983). *Training users of online public access catalogs*.
      Washington, DC: Council on Library Resources.

9.   Mathes, J. C. & Stevenson, D. W. (1976). *Designing technical reports*.
      Indianapolis: Bobbs-Merrill.

10.   Nelson, R. J. (1986). Beyond the basic technical writing course: A status report -- Part
      I. *The Technical Writing Teacher*, *13*, 140-147.

11.   Ong, W. J., S.J. (1977).   Media transformation: The talked book. In *Interfaces of the
      word: Studies in the evolution of consciousness and culture* . Ithaca: Cornell
      University Press, pp. 82-91.

12.   Perkins, D. N. (1981). *The mind's best work*. Cambridge: Harvard, pp. 190-219.

13.   Sullivan, P. & Seiden, P. (1985).   Assessing educational needs for OPACS (Online
      Public Access Catalogs): A case study. *Library HiTech*, *3*, 10, 31-39.

14.   Tufte, E. R. (1983). *The visual display of quantitative information*. Cheshire, CT:
      Graphics Press.

16

Are Writers Obsolete in the Computer Industry?

Muriel Zimmerman

Interdisciplinary Writing Program
University of California
Santa Barbara, California 93106

Writing as a discrete act may be obsolete in the computer industry. In the past, writers have served as speechmakers for engineers and as representatives of users. They made technology accessible by means of printed books and on-line documentation. Now many of the functions of writers have been taken up by software developers and by users. The definition of "support" for users has expanded beyond providing documentation to include building products that do not need much documentation. By way of prototyping, developers build products with the active participation of users, and in a further extension, users write the documentation they need. These shifts in job responsibilities have already had substantial impact on the profession of technical communication.

1. Prologue

For the occasion of a conference on writing in the computer industry, I studied the ways that user documentation gets written in work environments that contain no employees known as <u>writers</u> or <u>editors</u>. In these settings, all user documentation is prepared by systems analysts, systems designers, and programmers. How do they do it?

My hypothesis was that I would find many strategies—both formal and informal—by which styles and standards for user documentation get established, modified, enforced, and passed on. It seemed

likely that these non-professional-writers would develop their writing skills in the following ways:

*By taking academic courses in writing for computer users;

*By taking writing courses offered by consultants;

*By subscribing to journals such as <u>IEEE Transactions on Professional Communication</u>;

*By attending conferences organized by groups like IEEE Professional Communication Society or the Society for Technical Communication;

*By studying what seemed to them good documentation supplied with commercial software products;

*By following precedents established in the organization for which they are presently working;

*By bringing to the present work situation precedents from other places in which they have designed and developed software and worked with others to prepare user documentation.

Over a six-month period in spring and summer of 1987, in an effort to study how employees in work settings without writers get user documentation written, I studied several software development settings:

* The first, here called L&S, is concerned primarily with accounting, budget, payroll, and other administrative management issues for a college with 541 permanent faculty, 500 part-time faculty, and 288 support staff. Software is developed by five full-time employees and one half-timer—not a writer among them.

*The second, here called IS&D, is concerned primarily with managing information in a student data base in a university of approximately 18,500 students. Concerns include admissions, quarterly registration, transcripts, and billing. This unit has 17 employees—understaffed from the usual 25 because of budgetary problems—not a writer among them.

2. Conclusion

I went looking for <u>writing</u>, for a conscious deliberation among my informants about the writing of good user documentation, either paper or on-line. I did not find what I was looking for. I also expected to hear from the systems analysts and programmers I interviewed that much would be improved about their products if they did, in fact, have writers on their staff. I did not hear any such sentiment. Though in these environments much that an observer would call "writing" goes on, the people doing it do not feel the activity of writing to be separate enough from the activity of software development to describe it as such.

I remembered the paper by James Paradis, David Dobrin, and Richard
Miller about writing at Exxon ITD (4). What surprised these three
researchers is that though written communication takes up a
considerable part of the time of employees at Exxon ITD and thus
represents a major financial investment, the in-house writing and
editing activities remain, in their word, submerged: "Given the
scale and importance of writing activities at ITD, we were
surprised that writing was neither commonly discussed as a
technique nor widely recognized as a key work activity (p.286)."
Among their interesting conclusions is this one: that writing and
editing cycles belong to the "nonrationalized domains of most
industrial operations"; that "writing proceeds underwater, so to
speak"(p.305).

My primary conclusion is this: that in the settings I studied,
developers of software are not focusing on writing anything but
rather, they are focusing on discovering ways that users can learn
from software they have developed. In the course of software
development, they do not write varied and multiple drafts of paper
or on-line documentation to support a product, but, instead, they
build varied interfaces, with the active participation of potential
users. Rather than involving personnel called writers to represent
the interests of potential users, they involve users at every stage
of product development.

When the software product is ready for distribution, these users
serve as trainers for additional users in their own departments,
and the software development site continues to answer questions
from users and to modify programs as necessary. Some amount of
what we have previously called documentation emerges in this
process--system documentation, written by programmers for
programmers; and some form of reference manual. But at no point is
the emphasis on the preparation of user documentation. The
emphasis is on user-based product development and on the training
of some users to be trainers of others.

In one of the settings I studied, the director of information
systems is advocating the next step: Departments themselves--units
that use the software product--would take it as among their
administrative responsibilities to write customized user manuals
tailored to their own needs, habits, and procedures. For now, his
ideas have landed him in moderately hot water. Many departments
feel that documentation must be written by those who hold a job
title "documenter." Though users at the office level have often
created their own remarkably relevant documentation in the form of
crib sheets, home-made reference cards, and internal memos, they do
not want to accept responsibility for writing their own.

3. Methodology

My method was interview. I went to each site, and met systems
analysts and programmers with my list of questions. Did you ever
take any classes in technical writing? What about classes in
writing for the computer industry? Did you write user
documentation in any of the university classes you took in
computer science? The answer to these questions was invariably
"no." Have you ever read a book about how to prepare user
documentation? Two of my informants had read and profited from
Jonathan Price's How to Write a Computer Manual (5). The rest had
never read a book--or even an article. Have you ever attended a
conference or workshop on the subject of writing user
documentation? No. Do you prepare varied documentation products
keyed to beginning, novice, and advanced users? Sounds like a good
idea, but no. Do you separate documentation that explains what the
system does from documentation that explains what the user can do
with the system? Huh? Oh, that sounds like a good idea too, but we
don't have time to do things like that. And so forth.

My revised method became listening.   I had always believed that it
was we--the writers--who saved the users from the programmers, who
made technology accessible.   In the course of my interviews, I
came to wonder if I had been somewhat provincial, not to say short-
sighted and narrow-minded.

4.   Case 1: L&S

The director of Administrative Computing Services in L&S has read
Jonathan Price's book about writing software documentation (5) and
passed it on to others in his department. One programmer found the
book so useful that she made an outline of its key points for her
own use. The L&S department, though, doesn't do much that they
call writing. If they were to get relief from their short-staffed
situation, they would add programmers, not writers.

The director has always been a student of other people's written
and on-line documentation, noting what looks good to him and what
doesn't. But he doesn't think that people want to read
documentation (he himself doesn't want to read documentation), and
his goal is not to produce better books--paper or on-line--to help
users with the products his division produces.

The director's major concern is to develop a repertoire of ways for
users to learn. He is presently involved in a rewrite of a major
accounting system, this time involving representative users in the
planning and testing stages of the rewrite. He actively
encourages users to call in their questions by phone. Because of
his concern that some users may be embarrassed to call so often, he
is trying to establish an electronic bulletin board on which users

can ask questions anonymously, see the answers to other people's
questions, and share ideas. He issues a <u>Technical Bulletin</u> each
month, with questions and answers related to widely-used software.
His concern in the <u>Bulletin</u> is again with teaching and learning:
many users do not know how to ask questions about what bothers
them, so he answers questions in a problem/solution format with the
intent of teaching users how to phrase questions about software
problems. He believes that user documentation problems being are
taken care of when the number of phone inquiries decreases and the
number of expert users in remote departments increases.

L&S does not supply users with tutorials or with reference cards.
Though the reference manuals it supplies to users are typically a
cumbersome mix of information about how the system works and
information about how users can use the system, L&S gets few
complaints. One user directed a complaint to me: Though she had
been involved in the development of a new product and was herself
well-trained in how to use it, she felt the reference manual
supplied with it by L&S to be impenetrable. She wrote a simple and
successful procedures manual for the use of those temporary data
entry personnel who were hired to establish the new data base.
She felt, though, that writing such a manual was not in her job
description and that a software development group should supply
user documentation.

5. Case 2: IS&D

The 19 information developers at IS&D have attended a week-long
workshop run by a team of outside consultants. They have learned
a systems development methodology* which they hope some day to be
able to follow scrupulously. New employees who missed the earlier
workshop are sent to other cities to learn the method.

A major feature of the methodology is this: actual users of
systems under design sit with developers. Developers ask
questions like: is this the type of screen you want? is this the
type of file you want? is this the format you want? is this the
connection you want between files? These users are involved at
every stage of product development. When the product is completed,
they go back to their own sites and train others. The IS&D
director feels that the natural extension of this methodology is
for users themselves to write the documentation they want.

---

*For a useful discussion of prototyping as a method of
producing software and developing documentation, see Guillemette
(1).

As the director sees it, documentation should not be produced by professional software developers or writers; it is important to discourage an "unnatural" dependency relationship between the user and the developer. User documentation is more appropriately prepared by users: it is their responsibility to train themselves and to provide documentation for future systems users. Users are not, however, at this time, "energized by this prospect," in the director's words. More discouraging to the department, users are not always even energized by the opportunity to be involved in development stages. Such involvement challenges traditional job descriptions and has significant political, psychological, and sociological implications in the workplace.

For now, IS&D continues to rely heavily on the technique of literally sitting with people and showing them how to use a system. They try to train a trainer in each department, encouraging the trainer to train others. And, like L&S, they encourage the use of phone inquiries: "It is easier," said one programmer, to answer telephone questions than to rewrite a program or to write documentation."

6. Adapting Technology to Users

As a writer in software development settings, it appeared to me that it was writers who made computer technology accessible to users. Improved access could be achieved by training and hiring more of us to provide the support that users need. Writers for the computer industry are unusually and richly multidisciplinary. We know about technical communication; rhetorical theory; communication theory; educational psychology; information science; linguistics; computer science; screen design; database design; human factors analysis; artificial intelligence; software psychology; document design; publications technology; marketing; and product development cycles. Programmers, in contrast, are only slightly maligned in the satire of Geoffrey James' Tao of Programming: "Those programmers live beyond the physical world. They consider life absurd, an accidental coincidence. They come and go without knowing limitations. Without a care, they live only for their programs" (2, p.23).

What has clearly happened in the business environments I studied is that the distinction between writers as friends of users and programmers as enemies has been blurred. Writers in the computer industry have, for many years, had a primary function of attempting to write right what has been designed wrong. They have served to counter relative insensitivity, even indifference, on the part of designers and programmers to the difficulties of learning to use their product. Now, however, many designers have taken to themselves the teaching functions formerly relegated to writers.

The systems analysts and programmers I interviewed were not

concerned with throwing more writing on troubled waters, but with learning more about how people learn. Their at-work conclusions seem generally to match the conclusions of the two MIT artificial intelligence giants, Patrick Winston (7) and Marvin Minsky (3).

Winston offers a learning hierarchy illustrated in the figure below:

> According to the view offered [here], no piece of apparatus is abandoned as one moves up the learning hierarchy. At each step something is added to those mechanisms already in hand. Learning by being told is simpler than learning by seeing samples since there is no need to decide what difference is most important and what to do about it. But on both levels there is a need for a data structure into which information about what is important can be assimilated. To learn by being told, there is a need to match descriptions that constitute the telling with the model as so far evolved in order to determine where to make a change. . . . Learning by discovery requires all of the talents of learning by seeing samples with the additional requirement that some new procedure must take on the burden of generating near misses. The progression is one in which the student assumes more and more of the work from the teacher (p.43).

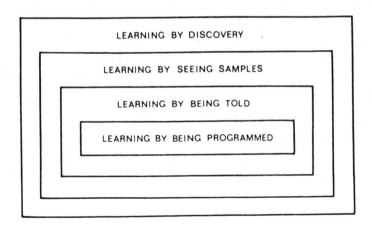

In Winston's general theory of learning, no piece of apparatus is abandoned as a student moves up the learning hierarchy.

In The Society of Mind (##), Marvin Minsky concludes that there is
no magic trick that makes us intelligent: Intelligence does not
stem from a single mechanism, and when any system fails, we have
alternative ways to proceed. Among our methods are the following:

*We learn many different ways to achieve each kind of goal.

*When one viewpoint fails to solve a problem, we can adopt
other perspectives.

*We embody different kinds of organizations for achieving many
kinds of goals.

*When simple methods fail, we can build new levels of
organization.

*We do not need perfect methods, since we can remember how
imperfect methods fail (p.308).

Learning about systems from printed books was part of the early
history of the widespread use of computers. Early users were more
familiar with books than with computers, and some preferred the
activity of reading to the activity of using the machine. But as
the machine becomes more familiar, the population of computer users
changes to people who have mostly used computers before. Reading
books about using computers now seems a cumbersome way to learn.
On-line assistance is perhaps part of a more recent history.
Nevertheless neither of these ways to teach and to learn is
necessarily the most effective way to provide support for users.

In 1985, Edmond Weiss identified the "next wave" of user
documentation, an era in which the definition of support for users
includes "all the activities that bridge the gap between the wishes
and abilities of the user on the one hand and the capabilities and
dispositions of the system on the other" (6, p.18). The settings I
describe seem clearly to fit what Weiss foresaw. Productive use of
technology does not need to depend on books; it can derive from
internal design features, and from the "merging of documentation,
quality control, training, implementation and customer service into
one enterprise" (p. 17). Designing away the need for an excellent
user manual is preferable to writing one, and such an option now
seems within reach.

7. Toward Holistic Technology

I went looking for writers; I went looking for writing; I went
looking for people who thought about writing. I couldn't find what

I was looking for, because what I was looking for was everywhere. What, then, is a writer? If a writer is that multidisciplinary specialist I referred to earlier, perhaps everyone working in a "next wave" software development environment is a writer. And if the next revolution happens, and users take responsibility for creating and maintaining their own documentation, then all users will be writers, too.

The user as writer is a particularly exciting possibility. We know that users have always made crib sheets and written notes to themselves about systems, answered questions for each other, and so forth. We have typically, though, seen these activities as signs of failure--failure of the writers for the computer industry to provide good-enough documentation and failure of the systems designers to avert the need for such documentation. Another way to look at it is that such activities are the real successes in documentation. They work: the crib sheets, notes, and prompts people write for themselves and each other are relevant, trenchant, useful, pointed. Who knows better than users do what they need to learn and to remember? Encouraging users to become systems documenters is a way of capitalizing on successful learning and teaching. What we saw as a failure may not have been failure: perhaps we only weren't seeing how to succeed--blinded, at least partially, as some of my informants were, by worn-out job descriptions.

Is the writer obsolete in the computer industry? Or, in fact, is it job descriptions within the computer industry that are obsolete? We no longer need writers who are only speechmakers for engineers; or engineers who develop products that do not account for users; or users who are passive receivers of products and books about products. Instead of the fragmentation that characterized recent years in computer product development--the engineer as developer, the writer as stand-in for the user, and the user as passive victim of both engineer and writer--we now see new roles for all parties.

Acknowledgments: Steve Cook, Gail Johnson, and Mike Stevenson of the University of California, Santa Barbara, let me in on their departments. Jack Falk of Servio Logic, Portland, Oregon, talked me through the implications for professional writers of what I had observed; the phrase "holistic technology" is his.

References

(1) R.A. Guillemette, "Prototyping: An Alternate Method for Developing Documentation," Technical Communication, Vol. 34, 1987, pp. 135–141.

(2) G. James, The Tao of Programming, Info Books, Santa Monica, 1987.

(3) M. Minsky, The Society of Mind, Simon and Schuster, New York, 1986.

(4) J. Paradis, D. Dobrin, and R. Miller, "Writing at Exxon ITD: Notes on the Writing Environment of an R&D Organization," Writing in Nonacademic Settings, L.Odell and D. Goswami, editors, Guilford Press, New York, 1985.

(5) J. Price, How to Write a Computer Manual: A Handbook of Software Documentation, Benjamin/Cummings, Menlo Park, 1984.

(6) E. Weiss, "The Next Wave of User Documentation," Computerworld, September 9, 1985, pp. 15–23.

(7) P.H. Winston, Artificial Intelligence, Addison-Wesley, Reading, 1977.

III

Designing On-line Information

17

Designing Online Information

Philip Rubens
Robert Krull

Communication Research Laboratory
Rensselaer Polytechnic Institute
Troy, NY 12180-3590

Preparing texts to support computer mediated tasks has evolved from a paper-based media to an electronic one that relies on the screen itself as the basic theatre for interaction. Tasks are typically supported concurrently by information resident within the host machine or application. Understanding the limitations and capabilities of such a medium will help information developers meet the needs of current users and create novel and useful interactions, based on more sophisticated equipment and programming techniques, for future generations.

A relatively new innovation in information can be seen in the developing area of online information. While information of various kinds has been readily available in electronic form for some time, online information can be distinguished from these routine classes of information by their usage patterns and the interaction capabilities found in their typical applications. Although it would be difficult to offer a definition of online information that would be inclusive of the entire range of this new media, it is possible to outline some of its basic characteristics. In preparation for a more detailed discussion of the design and development of online information, the next section provides a description of eight major types of online information. Following these descriptions, relevant observations on user characteristics will be offered. After suggesting possible models for designing online information, we conclude with some additional comments on those aspects of computing not used in creating online information and a discussion of the transitory nature of interface problems.

1. Major Types of Online Information

Support for interactive tasks. When someone deals with an essentially invisible process, a mediator or informant must be present. That is, when we work within the typical electronic environment we cannot physically "see" the activities that occur to make the task we have selected succeed. We, in essence, work within a "black box." Online information can play the very significant role of providing the means for the user to follow the action of a specific task or to find information about ways of performing tasks. Thus, we might find, at a very basic level, system messages that inform the user about the status of a process. Some of these might simply indicate that a process is underway, while others might present error messages that indicate unsuccessful operations. The range of supportive information will be explored in more detail later.

Reference material. Often users need to discover how to perform a specific task. This usually occurs in situations where the task is unique or infrequent in the typical operation path. For instance, a user might append one file to the end of another often, but might rarely add the contents of one file to a random location in another file. This less frequent task might require reference material. For those of us who have grown up with paper documentation this may seem like a novel but perhaps trivial method for gathering information. Wouldn't it simply be easier to locate the material in a paper text and then return to the task? Admittedly, this is a valid argument. However, there are two important reasons for providing online information of any sort.

First, offering information as an integral part of the product creates the impression of a consistent and integrated work situation. Second, most corporations need desperately to reduce their page counts — literally the number of times they pass a piece of paper through a printing press. They need to save both the money and the time needed to produce paper documentation.

Tutorial. In the past we have relied on human informants to act as trainers for introducing new products into the workplace. However, since most of this training is ad hoc, labor intensive (the informant leaves their own work and the trainee isn't performing productive work), and riddled with conceptual complications (will the informant show a new user how to use a product right or how to use it as they do?), such training is too costly and imprecise. Although training can be accomplished in a variety of media — video, cassette recordings, textbooks, etc. — corporations often depend on online tutorials. They have elected to use this media because it reinforces the integrated "feel" of products and introduces the new user to the product in the environment in which the actual product will operate. Some companies have gone so far as to link the tutorial directly into the "live" product so that users really do experience the actual product.

Data Entry and Retrieval Prompts. One major class of tasks centers on the ways in which a user enters and retrieves information electronically. In the past, when the same tasks were accomplished with paper, the user filled out a form that was normally stored in its initial shape and retrieved by using a filing system and a copier. These tasks have now been assumed by electronic devices. For instance, accounting spread sheets, mailing lists, sales reports, inventories, library holdings, and the like all share common characteristics that make them amenable to electronic storage. That is, they all have information fields that remain identical across records. For instance, a spread sheet might have a field for employee state taxes, and that field would be identical for all employees and for all pay periods. The electronic device housing this information provides a consistent method of data entry and retrieval. Usually this is presented in the shape of an online version of the more typical paper form. Retrieval is often also mediated by the same process. Searches can be initiated for specific characters in any field. For instance, in searching a library, the user would be given a blank form and allowed to enter the search terms in any field in that form [2]. Such consistency in interface design and operation is typical of online information.

Canned Demonstrations. Showing people how products operate is both time consuming and rife with error possibilities that will not present the product to its best advantage. To reduce the potential for error and to provide a stand-alone demonstration that prospective buyers can view, many companies have created electronic slide shows that depict the basic operation of the product as it would be seen under actual conditions.

Error and System Messages. Earlier we spoke of system messages that provided information about ongoing processes. In that context we had in mind those messages that were supportive of the task at hand. That is, we expect such messages to offer operational information about progress and assistance. In contrast, some products provide online information that is simply messages about the state of the process and do not try to mediate between that state and the users need to intervene in that state. For instance, an error message that indicates that a process has been unsuccessful — perhaps in sending a file with a telecommunication product — does little to help the user identify why the process failed. However, a supportive message, of the kind envisioned as supportive, would inform the user of the specific problem that prevented the completion of the task — perhaps the characteristics of the file are incompatible with the host machine. Error and system messages of the former type do little to help the user and are very low level online information [6].

Full Text. Ideally, text to support any product would be best if it did not have to exist at all. That is, if products were sufficiently easy to use, common enough in our culture, and free of any safety problems or bizarre operating characteristics, we would not need to explain anything to a user. However, since these goals are currently unattainable, we must document products even if we are only documenting design errors. Online documentation is seen as a method for reducing the amount of printing a company must do, and it also provides the user with a sense that the product and its supporting information are part of a consistent environment. The sense of integration, a powerful feature in defusing new user anxiety, promotes the perception that online information is a trusted informant as the user becomes more accustomed to the product. Thus, online information is sometimes provided that essentially duplicates the older printed text and displays that text only on the screen (with the added possibility that users can print on demand at their own sites, on their own printers, and with their own idiosyncratic binders).

We do not want to leave you with the impression that placing text online is either problematic or advantageous. For most display devices, full page displays are not possible; thus, text does have to be re-formatted to fit on the screen [14,11,8]. In addition, interaction methods — ranging from sophisticated indices, to relational databases, to hypertext — need to be created and implemented to provide adequate user interaction techniques. Some very sophisticated products allow additional interactions with newer storage media such as compact disks which provide incredible storage capacity for both texts and graphics (about 60,000-100,000 pages of text per disk depending on the material stored). Similar advantages have been realized with video technologies. Thus, full text online is not beyond the realm of contemporary possibilities.

Full Graphics. A more recent development in online information is the use of a graphic interface to mediate the same processes originally supported by words. Given the increasing dependence on visual information and the power of graphics to depict information across cultures, it is hardly surprising that such an innovation has occurred. In this type of online information icons depict many of the details of operation. Some of these iconic representations are more mimetic, bear a closer relationship to the actual objects, than others, but their key feature and source of power is that they allow the user to envision an object upon which they can act. The "black box" of the machine opens and we glimpse a tangible representation of the contents of that box. For instance, files can be depicted as either individual documents or as part of a file folder. Both of these icons are familiar in the work place and as such have a high degree of identification with the tasks people normally perform with these objects. For instance, we can save a file in a typical computing task by typing in a string of characters representing a "save" command, or we can do so by selecting a save command from a menu, or we could simply put the icon representing our file back into its folder. The latter bears a striking resemblance to the actions we have used for years in working with paper files.

Of course, it would be silly of me to suggest that a pure state of any of these varieties of online information exists. As in any information, the various kinds of information typically exist as mixtures of all of these types and many products include several kinds of information as well as a variety of techniques, selected by the end user, for ways to interact with the information. It is not uncommon to find graphics and text in the same product, nor to find reference, tutorial, and interactive support in the same product. Given this brief introduction to online information, we should like to turn our attention to ways of designing specific classes of online information. This discussion will be presented in two parts. First, we will offer some comments on design teams for online information and on authoring tools. Second, we will follow the typical design and development process for one variety of online information.

2. Nature of Users

In performing tasks all users are at risk. That is, when we are confronted with a problem we must all come to an understanding of that problem and seek a valid response to resolve that problem. Thus, in a major sense, tasks are both problem-setting and problem-solving activities and, as such, create anxiety behaviors in users. Our expectation has been that users encounter a problem and try to resolve it. Such a simplistic view ignores two major points. One, problems are not givens; they must be analyzed and posited in an answerable form before they can be resolved. Two, these activities are iterative processes; we do not simply look at a task or problem and comprehend or apprehend all of its implications at a glance. Understanding an activity or the information support- ing it occurs through a negotiated process. We read, consider, question, probe, assimilate, argue, and, hopefully, come to our understanding of an activity.

What this process means for users is that they must climb a learning curve. But that learning curve is not a stable structure. Learners do not move in some nice neat movement from ignorance to knowledge. In fact, they enter any intellectual event — even one that is task-oriented — at varying levels and with varying abilities, backgrounds, and expectations. At the lowest possible level a new user will know something about keyboards and screens, but may not know about disk drives. Typically, they will try to make something happen if only by pressing random keys. The point is that they will not be wholly ignorant of the machine or its interface and they will attempt to incorporate old knowledge into the event in which they are participating.

Beyond this simplistic level it is anyone's guess how users will react. For instance, a microbiologist may know laboratory procedures but will need to know how to implement these procedures when they are mediated by a computer. For this user the problems will not be related to the tasks but to the functions that perform the tasks. However, if the user finds the interface trivial, then the learning curve will be of little consequence. Similar examples can be found in learning to use accounting programs, CAD/CAM applications, and the like.

The point to all of this discussion is that users do not remain intellectually static during an intellectual event. They enter into the event with a certain repertoire, they change at varying rates during the event, and they exhibit idiosyncratic problem-setting/solving patterns that influence their ability to perform. They are, in short, highly volatile and mutable over time, over the duration of a task or intellectual event.

Combined with this volatile nature is a view of the ways in which people want to interact with information. Based on any number of studies it is obvious that the best form of information is that information that does not have to exist. That is, the product or process is so straightforward or error-free that it does not require supporting information. Aside from hand tools and toasters, there are few such devices. However, when we encounter a difficult to perform task, we are still likely to want to work our way through that task without assistance. We want to guess, to roam around, and to manipulate the task. If we succeed we move on; if we fail, we will probably seek a human informant to try to resolve our problem, usually someone who has already conquered the task. Texts, usually searched randomly, are our last choice for assistance, and we tend to be very intolerant of their deficiencies [9].

Online information can act as a surrogate informant. Since we are already working with a process that is being mediated by an intelligence, it is likely that we will view online information as an extension of that intelligence. The online information becomes the manipulator, the interlocutor, and the informant. In this sense, we begin to accept the illusion that we are commanding an intelligence to undertake specific tasks, that that intelligence is capable of informing us about the state of these tasks, and that it can offer additional information to assist us in understanding these tasks. That is, indeed, a powerful concept that completely overthrows the division between tasks and supporting information, especially in the form of paper documentation.

3. Design Teams and Authoring Tools

As in any information development process, there are ideal and practical ways of producing information. Online information presents some unique problems (and possibilities) because it demands the cooperation of so many talents. Since this information is not destined for a typical page, the development team must consider how users want to interact with both the product and information and under what circumstances they are likely to use the information. They must also consider where the information load will be imposed. That is, will the product expect the user to remember many operating details or will those details be part of the system? Typically, the memory load has been relegated to the user. Along these same lines, designers must also recognize the limits on user memory. How much information must be presented on single panels to reduce losing detail across a series of panels? Will graphics help reduce the need for memory overload by providing iconic representations of objects that can be acted upon?

Another aspect of development is the design of screen areas to establish a functional hierarchy. What elements of paper texts do readers use to discover information? How do they combine information to formulate a unique response to problems? How do they move through a text? How do they change during the course of a reading or intellectual event? How do they construct a cognitive map of a useful critical path through a text? How, or do, they remember specific details that are functional in nature? What is the effect of frequency of use on memory? When does an action move out of cognitive memory and into "muscle" memory? How do readers construct maps of objects explained in texts? All of these questions impose restrictions on the ways in which information can be presented on a screen.

For instance, if readers typically rely on headers as retrieval aids, then these same text devices will assist them in using online information. Thus, we can begin to parse up the screen and assign functional areas. Where will their major focal point be? Where will they expect certain kinds of information to be available? All of these considerations help structure the ways in which screens can be designed. Once the basic screen layout is established then the design team needs to consider how this layout restricts (or perhaps enhances) the writing possibilities. For instance, if the screen is a typical industrial monitor it will be restricted from the outset to displaying slightly under 2000 characters. If the screen layout reduces the major text area to say 30 percent, that means that any one idea or concept must be presented very tersely [3,4,13]. This may indicate that words are inappropriate for this product and may mediate for graphics (if, indeed, such a system supports graphics!).

4. Design and Development of Online Information

Online information, unlike paper documentation, has to be developed as an integral part of the product's operating system to be most effective. That is, it must create at least the illusion that the online information and the product interact simultaneously in time. This provides the user with two perspectives. First, it seems that the product and its supporting information are of a piece; that they were planned and executed with user support in mind. Second, it creates the sensation that work is going on in a unified system; that nothing was tacked on as an afterthought. Both of these are, in fact, valid observations and add to the difficulty of developing online information since it must be accessible from within the parent program or application. For information development this means that the supporting information must be planned as part of the product from the earliest stages and that it must develop concurrently with the product. Such a perspective is fraught with difficulties. It is these difficulties and their possible resolutions that will be the subject of the remainder of this section.

Early involvement. Since the online information and the product must eventually interact, it will be necessary for information developers to have a direct role in the product design from the outset. In this manner they can provide input about desirable ways in which users interact with information and machines and offer advice on ways to implement these perspectives in a program. Admittedly, this will be a highly political situation in which ego-involvement and subject area specialties will feel threatened. It will be equally threatening for those writers who have not had to consider these issues in the past and have not been expected to convince technical personnel about communication strategies. The need to do so may mediate for assigning writers to online projects who have some background in programming.

The composition of a typical design team should include writers, product developers, marketing personnel, graphic artists, and human factors specialists. It would be most helpful if certain members of the team possessed skills in at least two of these areas; these people should serve as referees and focal points for information exchange and they should mediate the negotiation process.

Programming the interaction techniques. The core of online information is the ways in which users can interact with that material. At the lowest level, provisions need to be made to allow users to access and view the information. Beyond that level varying degrees of sophistication can be used to provide truly powerful ways of interacting with the material. For instance, it might be possible to access the material in a manner that emulates a relational database. Such a technique would allow the user to capture closely related functions or information in a single search pass. Similarly, providing methods for moving, copying, or storing pertinent information makes a system even more useful, especially if such interactions provide "passback" techniques that reduce keystroke errors while performing tasks.

Early in the development process agreement must be reached about time and memory allocations for the online information. It is these decisions that will either foster or inhibit the development of certain interaction techniques. If the product requires a significant allocation of memory simply to operate, then the online information may have to be reduced considerably. If the idea behind the information is to introduce users to task functions and achieve rapid diffusion into the workplace, then a tutorial that simulates (or is tied directly to) the actual product will provide a faster entree to productivity. Once the basic decision about the purpose of the online information and the resources available for its creation are reached, then the programming effort can be directed by those decisions.

Several companies have developed online authoring tools that work somewhat like word processors and do not require programming skills. This is, indeed, a useful approach and one that will likely diffuse through the computing field as online information becomes more common. For now, however, it is a novel and highly idiosyncratic development that is often jealously guarded by individual corporations. As a consequence, the use and development of such tools are not discussed in depth in this essay and the assumption remains that the implementation of online information in a "typical" corporation will still require a design team.

Screen design. Once the programming interactions and support have been planned, then screen design must be completed. The basic design considerations must be made at this point because they control both the programming and the information preparation. Screen design focuses on how to prepare screen areas to perform specific functions and to hold certain classes of information. It also, if there are any options present, considers typographic variations and the use of color as design features [10,5,7].

The process begins with establishing the major screen areas. For instance, the first consideration is: where can we reasonably expect users to look when they first encounter a screen? That question responds to the fact that readers exhibit predictable patterns for reading pages and, at least for today's transitional audience, we must consider those patterns and their consequences for effective information transfer. Given the history of reading strategies, and some basic design geometries, we can establish a primary viewing area and begin to consider potential uses for remaining areas.

For instance, on a typical industrial-grade monitor that is restricted to an 80 column by 24 row matrix for displaying characters, a common design geometry would indicate that the primary viewing area should be from columns 10 to 60 (interestingly this produces a 50 character line, the optimal line width most frequently cited in the research literature) and from row 4 through 21. This yields a typical "C" shaped screen that has a left cueing area 10 characters wide, top and bottom margins each three rows deep, and a 20 character wide right area [12]. Anyone who has observed the development of online information screens realizes that this is a typical pattern.

Establishing such a screen design provides considerable guidance to both the programmers and the writers. For the programmers it means that they can reduce the placement of screen images to an algorithm. Major text will always appear in one area, secondary menus in other areas, illustrations in still other locations. Writers will be aware of the limits on text size — in characters — and the emphasis techniques available and can plan their work accordingly.

Once these preliminary strategies have been resolved — programming effort and screen design — the writers can begin planning the text. This division of effort is suggested because it allows the programming to proceed without the actual text in hand and to test the operation of that program on a simulated text. It also allows the writers to test the usefulness of the text in a paper simulation before combining the text into the program it will support.

Storyboarding. Since the medium used to display online information is dynamic, it is advisable to borrow the technique of storyboarding from film and advertising. Developing a storyboard requires the design team to create a paper representation (or electronic if you have a modeling product) that illustrates all of the techniques, interactions, and typical "text" envisioned for the final product. This will also include simulations of the ways in which a user could be employing the actual product and the anticipated relationships of the online information to that product. Such questions as:

- Will the online information overwrite (obscure) the work area when the user asks to see this information or will some of the work area remain visible?
- Will the user be provided with a method of moving information from the online information to other areas — a scratchpad or the work area itself?

will need to be considered because they have implications for the effectiveness of the online information to support the product and the ways in which people can successfully use information of a<u>ny</u> type. Storyboards should show exactly what developers expect to provide on the screen and should include a note area that describes any operational details that define the ways in which the product is expected to work.

<u>Preparing the information</u>. Now that the interaction techniques and the screen design have been developed, the writers can turn to the task of selecting an appropriate method for fulfilling these information needs. We use the terms appropriate method because there are a range of possibilities. One aspect of information development often overlooked is that one answer to information needs may be that the product needs to be redesigned to make the function work better. Often, information simply catalogs design errors; a fact that is underscored by the complexity of the explanations offered for some functions in manuals. While it is probable that the most frequent media selection will be text, it is possible to consider some reductionist text form, graphics, or composite information.

Text reductionist techniques and truncated texts.   While it is possible to simply place a document online and have that "work," most companies have had difficulty implementing such a plan.   For the most part, online information is reduced or truncated in some manner.   Sentence combining techniques, for instance, have been used to shorten text passages (although they typically increase the readability score). Other techniques such as information mapping have also been used.   However, the primary concern with "text" should be: how much human memory is required to use this information? Let me explain.

In using a book readers have the privilege of moving around in that book and comparing and sorting information in novel ways. It may be that they need to consider information that appears on widely separated, or many, pages and to integrate that information to solve a problem or perform a task. In addressing the same problem while using online information they do not have the same capabilities. Thus, either they must remember a considerable amount of information or they must find tasks supported by information that appears on only a few closely related screens. All of this is tied to "chunking" theory in which information is developed based on a concern for how much a reader can be provided and expected to retain successfully. To address the needs for reduced mental overhead on the human memory and continued support for tasks, some reductionist techniques need to be adopted, even if they only re-format existing material into screensful rather than pagesful of information.

Readers also have highly sedimented expectations about the ways in which they can use texts. They want tables of contents, indices, glossaries, typographic cues, illustrations, and the like. They want to be able to highlight and annotate their texts, as well as dog-ear pages. In short, they want to be able to depend on their highly developed methods for dealing with books. Thus, successful interactions will allow users to interact with online information in similar ways. While this, at first, looks like an array of potent techniques, they are actually quite easy to provide from a programming standpoint. The basic premise should be to use what we can of reader abilities and to reduce the amount of memory, oftentimes flawed memory, and redundant keystrokes, oftentimes equally flawed by simple typographic errors, required to use online information.

Graphic information. Text is not the only option for online information. Just as it is possible to develop wordless instructions, so too can online information provide only graphics. Most often this is in the form of iconic representations of objects. While this at first appears somewhat simplistic, it does give users the impression that they have the ability to manipulate objects within the electronic black box that is mediating their work. That is a powerful illusion.

While graphic interfaces have proven highly versatile in use, it is still too early to assess their long term vitality. Some early signs of disgruntlement and confusion have occurred. In addition, there are definite limits to graphic vocabularies and some attempts at developing a graphic set for any one product often borders on the absurd [1].

Composite information. As in any information context it is also possible to create hybrids of information types. Thus, it is probable that text, graphics, and illustrations will co-habit the same online information pool. The sole limitation on such hybrids is, once again, those imposed by rationale expectations for user interactions. Illustrations cannot be referenced to text that appears on other screens if your expectation is that readers must make comparisons to complete tasks.

Testing the information. Storyboarding the information will provide the writer with a complete set of expected screens. Writing code with simulated text also provides the programmer with a complete version of expected interactions. Both of these aspects can be tested at varying times, with various audiences, and without reference to each other. Thus, the development process can move at varying rates and does not require expensive programming updates as the text progresses through subsequent changes. It also provides the opportunity for the entire design team to examine all details of operation and support before incorporating them into the final product.

Ideally, testing should be formalized and carried out in a controlled testing atmosphere by trained professionals other than the product developers. These personnel lack ego-involvement in the success of the product and will provide an objective overview of problems and successes inherent in the product. Testing, given the two part development process, can proceed at varying rates and can be reiterated on demand with little planning time. If formal testing is impossible, anecdotal testing with a subject audience of expected users will suffice.

Combining with program. Once the program interactions and supporting text have been completed and tested, they can be combined in the actual working product. Some additional modifications may be required at this point, though they should be minimal. Further testing — both alpha and beta site — should be undertaken at this point. However, the product itself will be probably on a testing cycle by this time and the online information will simply be seen as a part of that testing.

Online information maintenance. Online information requires maintenance just like paper documentation. However, since it is integrated with a product it is more difficult to provide updates. It is unlikely, for example, that a product manufacturer would issue an update to a product simply to update the online information. It is more likely that an update will be issued when the product evolves.

In mainframes, online information will likely change more often than in disk based computer products. This is problematic because users typically employ certain information without further reference to supporting online information. Thus, if the product changes as well as its supporting information, it is unlikely that users will try to discover why their system doesn't work in an expected manner by examining the online information. In instances like this, it is necessary to provide "pointers" into the product to flag operational changes and advise the user to see the online information for an explanation. Further problems with online information maintenance occur when some of the information is stored on "read-only" media such as videotape or compact disks. In these instances, it is necessary to alter the entire product to change any single piece of information (though technological changes will obviate this problem).

5. Computing Capabilities Not Applied to Online Information

It is all well and good to be able to catalog major online information types, to be able to describe the characteristics of users, to suggest possible structures for design teams, and to offer a development plan; however, a considerable number of computing capabilities still remain unexploited. For the most part, online information relies on those elements and functions of computing that we have learned to provide to support typical computing activities. That is, it is likely that interactions will be command driven, that they will rely on verbal syntax and structure, and that information will be much reduced in nature and content. This is hardly a surprising synopsis of typical techniques; programmers know how to provide these techniques and feel comfortable offering them as solutions. Writers and other information specialists feel defeated by the lack of vitality to these options and only reluctantly develop online information for such impoverished systems.

The level beyond such simplistic interactions characterizes most of the contemporary online information. We have begun to experiment with graphic interfaces, with iconic representations, with direct manipulation capabilities, and with hybrids of command driven and graphic systems. We have seen common applications of windowed and tiled products, of pull-down and pop-up windows, of dialogue and decision boxes, and of function keys. We have also seen the emergence of considerable user control from immediate mode screen manipulation to application program configuration. All of these represent significant changes in attitude on the part of product manufacturers.

Many areas still remain that have not been adequately exploited. Basically, we have tried, quite correctly we believe, to use the computer, its display device, and its manipulative capabilities to create online information that retains as many characteristics of a book as possible. Given the nature of our current transitional audience that makes perfect sense. However, the real potential of the computer to provide online information will not be fully realized until some of its novel features have been incorporated into the communication process. Among the most potent are sound, voice, motion, and time, as well as compact disk technologies. In addition to these five, it is also possible to provide sophisticated interaction techniques in the forms of notebooks, scratchpads, passback features, and multi-tasking. The remainder of this section will examine each of these features.

Sound. When sound was first considered as a potential part of programming it usually was relegated to a simple bell that indicated a warning. The reaction to this feature was, understandably, negative. Simply indicating that something was happening did not provide the user with any information to help manipulate the event. More substantial use of sound involved music or extended audible signals to indicate conditions. Still, not much information was attached to those sounds or their intent was obscure.

It is now possible to interface a computing device with a range of sound producing devices. At the lowest level, a tape recorder can simply play messages. This is often used for mass telephone calling programs. It is also used to announce error conditions to flight crews in most commercial aircraft. The computer can also use its internal speaker and produce sounds comparable to a tape player. This, of course, requires a considerable commitment of memory.

Voice. Until now we have been concerned with sound as a means of communicating information to the user. However, it is equally likely that voice input will soon become possible. At that point users will begin to take the idea of online information as an expert informant seriously.

Motion. Little thought has been given to the use of motion in online information. Motion has the ability to attract attention and to make the user consider the purpose for the addition of motion. What are the likely candidates for the use of motion? For the most part it is likely that processes can be illustrated by motion. Some newer programs do add motion to show the flow of activities but these represent only a small fraction of all of the online information produced.

Time. Closely allied to the idea of motion is the use of time in terms of controlling the display rate. Computers allow control for location, rotation, movement, and display rate for anything imposed on the screen. Thus, a program can toggle among a set of pictures and achieve the effect of a cartoon. Similarly, graphics can be built on the screen through successive wipes to show the structural features of a device or process. Or, text can be displayed at slower rates — rather than using blinking or flashing, both of which users find obnoxious — to elicit the user's attention to a warning or caution. At present these simple, yet effective, techniques are conspicuously absent from online information.

Compact Disk (CD-ROM) Technology. More interesting advances in sound, motion, and time depend on the use of the CD player and its ability to store digital signals with incredible fidelity to their source. Several possibilities for online information depend on this technology. First, the digital signals can represent text, graphics, sound, or video. Thus, online information can include all or any of these media in unique combinations. That such a possibility exists is without doubt. Over a decade ago educators at a major university linked a mainframe computer to a videotape to provide demonstrations of physics principles for students using the system as a tutorial. Today's computing devices possess significantly more sophisticated and elegant programming functions and memory than that earlier system.

Second, the compact disk has tremendous storage capacity. One corporation that presently uses this technology as a storage media for its online information typically places 100,000 pages of information on a single disk; they have placed about 60,000 pages of mixed text and graphics on the same disk. Such a figure is probably equal to the total paper output of some corporations and far beyond the page count of many small companies. As a storage media CD-ROM provides incredible storage capacity in a very small package. A corollary to this capacity is that the reading devices that process these signals are also very fast and reliable. Read speeds across considerable distances are extremely fast and the integrity of the recovered data is excellent. In fact, both of these aspects of CD operation represent a significant technological leap beyond present storage and retrieval capabilities. Further advances will allow CDs to be used in the same manner as current oxide (floppy disk) media; that is, we will be able to read and write to the same media.

Notebooks, Scratchpads, and Passbacks. Readers have a highly sedimented set of strategies for using texts. They want to be able to interact with texts. One way that they achieve this interaction is to write notes, either in the text or on note cards. Often the purpose of this writing, particularly in text that support tasks, is to help them solve a problem related to their work. They want to find that information and be able to act on it as quickly as possible. Encountering a problem, establishing a context for that problem, following an information path to a possible resolution, constructing a response, and using that response to resolve the problem constitutes a considerable set of operations to ask a person to perform, especially when one considers that moving from the task to the supporting, external, paper documentation asks the user to shift from the computing environment to a book. If online information can create a consistent work context, then the user should be able to locate information while observing the task itself residing in the background. Given such conditions the user should also be able to roam through that information to discover a response and be able to take that response directly back into the task without rekeying it. This reduces errors and adds to the impression of unity and consistency in the interface and its supporting information. Any method that allows the free movement of information across boundaries in the electronic workplace, whether it is called a scratchpad, notebook, passback feature, or sticky yellow pad, will make online information more useful.

Multi-tasking. Closely allied to free movement within the task or computing environment is the concept of multi-tasking. Basically this term indicates that the user has the ability to access a variety of programs or applications simultaneously while working without closing a file or opening a new one. One way to envision this situation is to think of programs arranged on a carousel, as in a slide projector. To access any one program you simply move to the location on the carousel that contains that program and begin using it. Coupled with this ability to migrate through an electronic workplace is the ability to carry work from one program into another. This portability is similar to that suggested in the previous section. The only difficulty in providing such a feature is that all applications must treat their stored data in an identical manner or a translation routine must massage the data during any transfers.

6. Transitory Nature of Interface Problems

Given a choice of ways to interact with machines, we would like the machine to be transparent and allow us to focus on the tasks the machine supports. Given a choice of information sources, we would prefer a live, expert informant. These opinions, admittedly, are based on current technology and an understanding of typical, contemporary human behaviors. The problem with that observation is that both of these aspects undergo continuous changes, some subtle, some more radical. What do these changes portend?

First, the contemporary audience is fairly new to the technology underlying online information. In terms of diffusion of innovation, they represent early innovators who can be characterized as more tolerant and adventuresome than the population as a whole. But, these people are either predominantly word-oriented and inclined to manipulate tasks directly or are older users transferring their previous interaction expectations into the new computing environments. Thus, we have a number of tensions within the early innovator user group. While they represent a range of skills and backgrounds, they are still highly verbal and adventuresome. They also want to get on with their work without considering the tools that allow them to perform this work; they want some measure of control over their working conditions; and they want the combination of technology, task, and supporting information to present a consistent, supportive, and useful context for their work.

While it is important to address the expectations, needs, and capabilities of this audience, we need to recognize that it is a transitional audience. Younger users do not seem to possess the same characteristics as these early innovators. For the most part, younger users come from a richer visual culture and they have worked with computing equipment — of one kind or another — since early childhood. This group seems eminently more comfortable with graphic interfaces and direct manipulation than the early innovators.

Second, the current technology continues to alter the ways in which interfaces can be created and in which we can interact with computers. Consider, for example, that most of the interactions discussed thus far depend on visual and tactile capabilities. We must observe whatever appears on a display device and act upon that information in specific ways. Given the characteristics of most display devices this is not an easy task. Typical industrial monitors, those usually found in the workplace, are highly restricted by their hardware and the level of available programming support. More sophisticated devices are expensive and often unstable. Many users do not have access to such sophisticated systems.

Change in both audience and technology will be considerable. Regardless of the current problems or demands inherent in developing online information, regardless of the technological leaps that could influence the field, writers and others must begin to recognize that the tail end of this century provides an exciting opportunity for us to test our assumptions about communication. Online information is a communication medium as exciting in its own right as the invention of printing itself. We have a long history of text use to build upon and new ways to present information unheard of even a decade ago. Approaching and using these changes rationally to develop information that supports tasks presents all communication professionals with an exciting challenge.

References

[1]   Lynda A. Archer, "Blissymbolics — a nonverbal communication system," J. of Speech and Hearing Disorders, Vol. 42, 1977, pp. 568-579.

[2]   Diane Basara, et al, "A Case Study of Online Information: Second Generation System Design," IEEE Transactions on Professional Communication, Vol. PC-29, December 1986, pp. 81-86.

[3]   A. Bork, "A Preliminary Taxonomy of Ways of Displaying Text on Screens," Information Design Journal, Vol. 3, 1983, pp. 206-214.

[4]   A. Bork, et al, "Graphics and Screen Design for Interactive Learning," ACM Sigcue Bulletin, Vol. 17, 1983, pp. 19-23.

[5]   J. Durrett and J. Trezona, "How to Use Color Displays Effectively," Byte, Vol. 7, 1982, pp. 50-53.

[6]   D. M. Gilfoil, "Warming up to computers: A study of cognitive and affective interaction over time," Proceedings of Human Factors in Computer Systems Conference, 1982, pp. 245-250.

[7]   J. M. Heines, Screen Design Strategies for CAI. Digital Press, 1984.

[8]   R. Jackson, "Television Text: First Experience in a New Medium," in Kolers, et al., Processing of Visible Language, Vol. 1, 1979, pp. 479-490.

[9]   C. Lewis and R. Mack, "Learning to use a text processing system: Evidence from 'thinking aloud' protocols," Proceedings of Human Factors in Computer Systems Conference, 1982, pp. 387-392.

[10]   P. F. Merrill, "Displaying Text on Microcomputers," in The Technology of Texts: Principles for Structuring, Designing, and Displaying Text, ed. D. H. Jonassen, 1982, pp. 401-414.

[11]   L. Reynolds, "Display Problems for Teletext," in The Technology of Texts: Principles for Structuring, Designing, and Displaying Text, ed. D. H. Jonassen, 1982, pp. 415-438.

[12]   P. Rubens, "Online Information, Traditional Page Design, and Reader Expectation," IEEE Transactions on Professional Communication, Vol. PC-29, December 1986, pp. 75-80.

[13]   P. Rubens and R. Krull, Application of Research on Document Design to Online Displays," Technical Communication, Vol. 32, 1985, pp. 29-34.

18

Technical Writers as Computer Scientists: The Challenges of Online Documentation

Henrietta Nickels Shirk

Department of English
Northeastern University
Boston, Massachusetts 02115

Writing online documentation requires several significant departures from the writing techniques traditionally used to create paper documents. Although there are many useful transfers from the "paper side" of writing for the computer industry, some of the commonly accepted standards for writing paper documentation must be modified to create successful online documentation. This paper covers: (1) a definition of online documentation, including its various genres; (2) an exploration of the differences between paper and online documentation and their impact on technical writing tasks; (3) an overview of a structure for evolving a set of standards for designing and writing online documentation; and (4) an examination of the implications of the cross-disciplinary knowledge required for successful online documenters. It proposes that the technical writer who creates online documentation must become a special kind of computer scientist, with skills drawn from many fields.

1. Introduction

The increasing growth of online documentation requires several significant departures from the writing techniques traditionally used to create paper documents. Although there are many useful transfers from the "paper-based" approach to writing for the computer industry, some of the commonly accepted techniques for writing paper documentation are actually unsuitable for creating successful online documentation.

The issue is not so much that of destroying the powerful "paper tiger" of existing techniques (or mental processes) required for writing effective documentation, but rather that of re-examining these techniques in terms of the requirements of the emerging online technologies and then redefining them. In his book, *The Society of Mind*, Marvin Minsky presents the hypothesis that "many steps in mental growth are based less on the acquisition of new skills than on building new administrative systems for managing already established abilities" [9, p. 330]. This paper presents suggestions for developing the groundwork for a new mental "administrative system" to assist technical communicators with the task of writing online documentation.

It is only through understanding the writing requirements of the various online documentation genres, as well as their organizational and rhetorical differences, that the technical communicator can begin to redefine currently held theories about the qualities of "good" documentation. This process naturally evolves to thinking about standards for online documentation, as well as to rethinking the role and background required for the online documenter.

2. Defining Online Genres

Definitions for online documentation are numerous. R. John Brockmann defines online documentation as "communication designed to be presented on VDT [video display terminal] screens in order to ease interactions between computer software and the individuals who manage, audit, operate, or maintain it" [2, p. 206]. Judith Ramey, in her excellent article on "Developing a Theoretical Basis for On-Line Documentation," defines it broadly as "every aspect of computer software (the sets of instructions that run the computer) that guides users in putting that software to work" [11, p. 148]. Both of these typical definitions for online documentation stress the relationships between software and communication about how to use software.

While these definitions accurately represent several categories of online documentation, they do not include other types of documents which are presented exclusively through the medium of the computer (for example, computer-based training). The term "electronic" documentation would perhaps be more accurate than "online," since it is broad enough to encompass not only the different kinds of online documentation (with content that is both software and non-software related), but also the additional technologies (like interactive video) which are increasingly used in conjunction with documentation that resides in the computer and is accessed through a computer display terminal. Probably the term "online" is here to stay through common usage, rather than through technical accuracy.

However one choses to label it, online documentation is **not** paper-based documentation placed on the computer for access through a computer terminal. Rather, it is documentation written **specifically** for access **only** by means of a computer terminal. As such, it includes many different genres than paper-based documentation. The successful online documenter must understand these genres and their relationship to each other.

A useful way of categorizing these various genres of online documents is to view them as moving from relatively simple to complex writing. The "Taxonomy of Online Documentation" presented in Figure 1 shows this hierarchy of increasing writing difficulty.

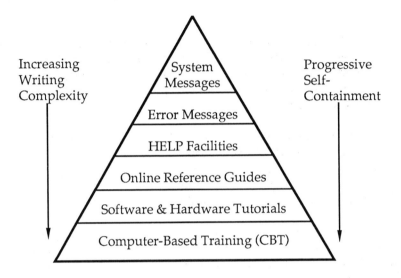

Fig. 1 Taxonomy of online documentation.

The components of this taxonomy may be defined as follows, in order of increasing writing complexity [5]:

System Messages: Information, instructions and problem indicators that can appear during the operation of software packages, including informationals (status and orientation information, prompts and menus) and warnings (alert and caution messages).

Error Messages: Information within software systems which indicates that a situation took place that threatens the integrity of the data, file, system or storage device, or that a given instruction cannot be executed. Included with the message that the specified problem exists can also be an explanation about why or how it occurred, where it occurred, the extent of the damage, and options available and methodology to recover from the situation and/or minimize the damage.

HELP Facilities: Directions within software systems for solving problems the user may experience with software which resides within the system or software application it supports and are viewed during their operation. They may contain both information and guidance which assist in identifying the problem, assessing the damage (if and), and developing a solution.

Online Reference Guides: Comprehensive, detailed compilations of information about software or hardware that are structured like dictionaries or encyclopedias and accessed through various indexing schemes. They are organized for quick access by users who are knowledgeable about the basics of their subject-matter.

Software and Hardware Tutorials: Online sets of instructions consisting of step-by-step procedural information and amply illustrated with examples and graphics. They are designed for first-time (or beginning-level) users, and they may be either without user interaction or with user interaction in which the system gives feedback about the user's performance.

Computer-Based Training (CBT): Instruction on any subject-matter which is delivered by a computer. It is not necessarily limited to tutorials about software and hardware, and it may include other media such as audiotapes and video-discs. In its general sense, CBT includes all forms of the use of computers in the support of learning. It has been defined as "anytime a person and a computer come together and one of them learns something" [13, p. 18]. Although there are numerous synonyms for CBT, this term (like "online") is becoming standard through common usage.

The "Taxonomy of Online Documentation" exhibits the additional dimension of possible progressive self-containment. As one moves from simple to more complex writing, each item on the list can (if the writer desires) contain some or all of the previous genres. Writers must think of these genres as related to each other, rather than as distinct entities.

Finally, the taxonomy itself is flexible. Some technical writers would choose to add the writing of actual program comments to the top of the pyramid, although the assumption of this task by writers would certainly be challenged by many programmers. However, the bottom of the pyramid will, without doubt, expand as new computer technologies are developed.

3. Exploring Paper and Online Differences

Understanding the framework of online genres in which technical writers can communicate is useful, but the more difficult issues revolve around the question of **how** that writing should be done. Most technical writing textbooks and publications professionals advocate adherence to five basic characteristics of technical writing: "clarity, accuracy, accessibility, conciseness, and correctness" [8, pp. 5–8].

While no one would dispute the fact that these criteria result in good technical writing, the mental model which is usually brought to their implementation is "paper-based" rather than "online-based." However, it is only by beginning with what is familiar that the differences required by the unfamiliar can be assimilated and effectively implemented. The following sections address each of the five criteria for good technical writing in terms of the unique requirements of online documentation.

(1) Clarity:

Clarity usually means that the text has only one meaning, which can easily be understood by the reader. While this is a sound principle in any medium, when writing online documentation it becomes focused in a special way.

A major difference between paper and online documentation is that paper has a tangible and permanent quality which the transitory images of the computer screen cannot match. For this reason, it is important that readers of online documentation are not only given clear messages but that these messages are written and presented in such a way to make them **memorable**. While an online message many be clearly expressed, have only one meaning, and be easily understood, it may not be easily retained in the reader's memory.

This problem occurs because readers bring paper-based habits to their reading of online documents. They may expect movement among screens to be as easy as flipping through pages in a book, especially when it comes to browsing for material that may be imperfectly remembered. However, it is never quite as quick or easy to move through several computer screens as it is to look back and forth between paper pages. Readers therefore become less patient with finding and rereading online what they did not understand the first time.

Research needs to be done on how readers' paper-based mental models affect their use and understanding of online documentation. For the online writer, clarity must also include the goal of being "clearly remembered."

This means not only writing unambiguously, but also writing in a style that captures attention and assures memory retention.

(2) Accuracy:

All the problems that might result from unclear writing can also be caused by inaccurate writing. No one would disagree that technical writers should record facts so that they do not confuse and annoy the reader, and so that they are valid and not slanted in any particular direction. But online documenters should also be especially concerned about wanting their readers to **perform accurately.** This means that audience analysis must be considered from a more focused and sophisticated perspective, and that there must be an even greater concern for logical consistency or accuracy in the presentation of online information.

Because of their physical and organizational limitations, paper documents are usually not addressed to a wide variety of audiences (a primary and a secondary audience are typical). However, online documentation is not so limited, because it is really a software database. As Geoffrey James explains: "A database is by its nature fluid and can be dynamically updated quite quickly"—as quickly as a software product can be modified. A database is multipurpose, because the reader, not the writer, decides what he wants to read [6, p. 10]. The flexibility of online databases allows the online documenter to write for as many different audiences as desired, tailoring the information to each group's particular needs—and thereby assuring accurate performance. Online writers must be able to identify, analyze, and write for the different requirements of a wide variety of audiences.

The logical accuracy of online information poses an even greater challenge for the writer. A paper document has a built-in organizational structure that is readily understood, because people are familiar with obtaining information from paper sources. Everyone knows that books move from beginning to end and that they have sections, page numbers, indexes, and other mechanisms that assist in locating one's place within their structures. However, because the reader (user) can access database information in any order desired, there is the tendency to become lost much more easily and to misunderstand information or to perform inaccurately. The online documenter must be sensitive to these issues and assure that enough information is given on screens to result in accurate comprehension. In some instances, this may mean extensive use of repetition.

(3) Conciseness:

It is generally assumed that the longer a paper document is, the more difficult it is to use. In paper documentation, the characteristic of conciseness appears to work against the notion of completeness. The paper documenter writes within the conflicting dualism of striving for ease of use by being concise, while attempting to achieve clarity by being complete. Online documentation resolves this issue, and places a different emphasis on both conciseness and completeness.

As previously mentioned, a document database can include as much information as the writer desires. This means that the writer does not have to worry about conciseness in terms of the overall document—everything can be included for the sake of clarity, because each user will create an individualized path through the information. On a "macro" (or system) level, conciseness is not an issue for online documentation.

However, on a "micro" (or screen) level, conciseness becomes a measure of success or failure for online documentation. It has been suggested that users of online documentation "expect the same type of rhetorical structure, closure, and organization from a screen as from a paragraph" and therefore information should be broken into discrete screens which do not require scrolling for understanding of a single segment of information [2, pp. 213 and 229]. From a writing perspective, this means that the online documenter must work with the smallest possible organizational "chunks" of information—something like writing "in miniature." The small space available on a screen (usually only 24 lines of 80 characters each) seems even smaller than the concept of a paragraph. Conciseness indeed takes on a more restrictive meaning on a computer screen than it ever could on paper. This is especially true when one considers other items which must appear on a computer screen to enhance accessibility.

(4) Accessibility:

Readers should be able to easily locate information which they are seeking. Two basic techniques to accomplish accessibility in paper-based documentation are headings and lists. Additionally, indexes, tables of contents, page headers and footers, and tabs are user support mechanisms which help readers find their way around paper documents. These mechanisms are part of the visually-oriented mental model which readers bring to paper documents. Online documentation requires a very different mental model.

While the accessibility aspects of paper documentation are immediate and physical, online documentation's accessibility must (because of its transitory quality) be a logically-oriented mental model for the reader to use in creating paths through the information. This means not only creating useful menus and hierarchies of information, but it also means including information on all screens which provides directions as to where the user is in the system and how forward or backward movement can be accomplished. For example, on-screen information which identifies the number of each screen in a sequence of screens ("Screen 12 of 24 on Data Inquiry"), and "Press the X Key to Move Backward," are necessary but repetitious instructions. Including this standard information leaves a minimal amount of space for information or data entry. In the trade-off between conciseness and accessibility, the latter must take precedence.

Several other features of online documentation have been identified as creating barriers to readers easily accessing information. Apparently, it is more difficult to read and comprehend information on the computer screen than it is on paper [2, pp. 209-211]. In order to overcome this shortcoming, online documenters must employ professional graphics and screen design techniques. It has been suggested that the test for effective screen design is to ask whether all screen elements can be identified through cues independent of their content (that is, without reading the words that make them up) [4, p. 41]. In order to achieve accessibility in online documentation, writers must not only create useful mental models, but they must also know how to present these models with visual effectiveness.

(5) Correctness:

Good technical writers usually pride themselves on the quality of correctness—using the language correctly by observing commonly accepted conventions of grammar, spelling, and punctuation and following format standards. While accessibility of online documentation demands strict adherence to format standards, the issue of language correctness can assume a different perspective in the online medium.

The necessity for conciseness imposed by the spatial limitations of the computer screen occasionally requires an abbreviated use of language. Although individual applications and organizations differ in this area, the tendency seems to be to leave out articles and other elements of "correct" grammar, as long as the screen message communicates effectively. This is an area that requires extreme thoughtfulness on the part of the writer, to assure that proper communication does indeed occur.

All these differences which online documentation brings to the "rules" of good technical writing require creativity and imagination on the part of online documenters. As clarity, accuracy, conciseness, accessibility, and correctness take on new meanings, it is important that the changes be implemented consistently.

4. Building Online Documentation Standards

Documentation guidelines for online communication are necessary tools for successfully implementing this new kind of writing.

Without standard ways of presenting information, online communication efforts possess the potential for failure. Readers may have learned to fumble their way through faulty paper documentation, but it is not always possible or easy to do this in the online medium, because most audiences have not developed habitual mental models for comprehending online information.

A list of suggested topics that should be included in a set of online documentation standards is presented in Figure 2. This list is only a beginning, and it is intended to provide a topical framework upon which one could develop detailed guidelines.

Writing Style:	**Screen Design:**
Computer "Persona"	Types of Screens (Menus,etc.)
Degree of Friendliness	Format (Constant Information)
Audience Levels	Line Length
Non-Standard Grammar	Depth of Queries
User Control Devices:	**Emphasis Device:**
Access Methods	Blinking
Paging (Hierarchy)	Color
Exiting	Reverse Video
Bookmarking	Graphics (Icons)
Scrolling	Animation
Error Recovery	Sound

Fig. 2—Topics for online documentation standards.

It is not within the scope of this paper to cover all these topics suggested for inclusion in a set of online documentation standards. The *Handbook of Screen Format Design* by Wilbert O. Galitz (see the Appendix at the end of this paper) is currently used widely in industry as a source for recommendations on many of these subjects. While this book is an extremely useful resource for information on the physical aspects of online documentation, it does not address some of the more general issues mentioned under "Writing Style."

The categories of information covered under "User Control Devices," "Screen Design," and "Emphasis Devices" are, however, important aspects of the technology involved in online documentation. They are the foundation upon which issues of "Writing Style" must be built. Specifications must be developed in these areas in much the same manner that paper-based documenters have formulated standards for packaging manuals, for designing page formats and layouts, and for using color and graphics.

Galitz' handbook is especially helpful in establishing a foundation upon which to build specific standards. In addition to hardware and software considerations, he covers the human side of screen design. Like the users of paper documentation, online readers want simplicity, clarity, and understandability. Galitz suggests several ways to fulfill these requirements, including where and how to place information on the screen. He discusses fonts, text and illustrations, field captions and data fields, and messages, recommending specific approaches for data entry, inquiry, multipurpose, question-and-answer, and menu screens. A final area of assistance is a chapter covering the steps involved in screen design. This book should be required reading for any technical writer working in the field of online documentation.

The importance of multi-leveled audience definitions and the potential for non-standard grammar have already been identified. However, the area of writing style relating to the tonal qualities of online communication requires intense focus.

Because of the interactive quality of most online documentation, it is important for online documenters to be especially sensitive to the "voice" or "persona" projected by their writing style. Although there is some dispute among software critics concerning the advisability of having "personalities" in computer programs, their presence seems unavoidable. Any time there is communication between a computer and a human, the information presented by the computer has a certain style, diction, and tone of voice which impact the human's attitude and response toward the software.

Although online documenters are usually advised against the extremes of excessively positive and negative feedback, there are a wide variety of conversational and learning styles between these two poles. It has been observed that "the manner in which that dialogue promotes or interferes with the person's cognitive style and affective disposition influences the human/machine interaction" [7, p. 29]. These variations in style must be identified (based on many different user audiences) and addressed in terms of writing styles.

From a standards perspective, a consistent image should be presented on behalf of the organization publishing the online documentation. This consistency may possibly differ for various audience levels, but it should remain constant within each group. Online documenters must then write within the stylistic guidelines established by the computer personas which their organizations wish to project to readers. This difficult task requires preparation beyond that usually required for technical writers.

5. Preparing for the Future

The shift of technical writing from the medium of paper to that of online documentation does not only require changes to commonly held beliefs about writing and writing standards. It also requires changes in how technical communicators function in organizations that produce successful online documentation and perhaps even in how these organizations are internally structured. These changes in turn raise important issues about the professional preparation and development of online documenters.

It is significant that most literature about online documentation quickly moves from the term "writer" to that of "designer." When creating online documentation, the writing process becomes part of a larger function called "design." The products of online documentation are, in reality, software products. And this means that these writers are software designers, who happen to specialize in creating (both verbally and visually) information which appears on the computer screens of software products. This shift in perspective has far-reaching implications for organizational structures.

Software design (or engineering) is typically a team process involving a "system life cycle" (the various phases which are undertaken during the creation of software). As designers, writers must not only understand this process, but they must also function as an integral part of it. This means that many existing publications departments will become extinct, as writer/designers directly and permanently join the ranks of software development teams. The paper-based practice of producing documentation after the software design has been completed is not practical for online documentation. Designers responsible for system, error, and HELP online information especially must be part of the software design process from its beginning. In a well-designed software system, these items are not after-thoughts.

Some online documentation designers are additionally responsible for the content and appearance of all the screens in software systems. Although job titles for these individuals vary, their responsibilities have the common factor of being focused on the "human-computer interface." Indeed, there is a whole new field emerging which is concerned with human information-processing psychology applied to computers. Various names (associating the topic in different ways) have been suggested: "user sciences, artificial psycholinguistics, cognitive ergonomics, software psychology, user psychology, and cognitive engineering" [3, p. 2]. Whatever title is finally granted to this developing discipline, it clearly includes areas of study important for the success of online documenters/designers.

Many recommendations have been made for the writers of paper-based computer documents to be "advocates for the end user." For example, one text on writing software computer manuals suggests that writers are stand-ins for users, who can (and should) "help revise the program itself, particularly the part the users actually see, known as the user interface" [10, p. 233]. Creators of online documentation must not only perform this user advocacy task, but they must also know how to implement the design for their own recommendations. In short, they must become computer scientists with a specialty in communication and psychology along with an understanding of a wide variety of related disciplines.

An important question is that of how technical communicators can best prepare themselves for their new role as online documenters/designers. Formal academic and on-the-job training in Computer Science and Technical Communication must be supplemented by wide reading in the topics mentioned above. A useful list of related books appears in the Appendix at the end of this paper. An excellent "Annotated Bibliography of Training and Technology Periodicals" appears in a recent publication of the American Society for Training and Development [1, pp. 4–10]. Affiliation with a variety of professional organizations can also be helpful. Groups like the Human Factors Society, the Association for Computing Machinery's SIGCHI (Special Interest Group in Computer-Human Interaction), and the Association for the Development of Computer Instructional Systems (ADCIS) provide excellent resources.

Successful online documentation design depends on creativity and breadth of knowledge which can only be developed through a cross-disciplinary approach. The individual implementing the human-computer interface must not only be interested in a variety of intellectual disciplines, but must also remain abreast of the current computer technologies. This occupation may provide one of the few remaining career opportunities to become a truly "Renaissance person."

6. Conclusion

Online documentation is a recent development in the technical communications field. Principles and practices regarding its successful implementation are still in the process of being formulated. As Judith Ramey has suggested, much more research needs to be accomplished [12, p. 311].

Those who would create online documentation must continually re-examine their assumptions about paper-based documentation from the perspective of the emerging computer technologies. It is important to understand the rhetorical and organizational requirements of the growing list of online genres, as well as to continually expand on the paper-based assumptions about good writing. It is not so much a matter of "slaying" the powerful "paper tiger" of past practices, but rather continually re-examining them for possible revision. Online documentation standards, and even the preparation of online documenters, are areas that must continually grow in response to technological development.

Finally, technical communicators in the computer industry must become agents for their own change. Anticipation rather than reaction is the key to creating successful online documentation. Online documenters are computer scientists and designers. Their role must be an active rather than a passive one. It is only through ongoing critical analysis of the past that there will evolve a new mental "administrative system" capable of reacting flexibly to the online documentation challenges of the future.

APPENDIX:
RECOMMENDED READING LIST FOR ONLINE DOCUMENTATION

American Society for Training and Development, *Computer-Based Training Today: A Guide to Research, Specialized Terms and Publications in the Field*, Alexandria, Virginia: ASTD Instructional Technology Professional Practice Area (ITPPA), 1987.

Brockmann, R. John, *Writing Better Computer User Documentation: From Paper to Online*, New York: John Wiley & Sons, Inc., 1986.

Card, Stuart K.; Moran, Thomas P.; and Newell, Allen, *The Psychology of Human-Computer Interaction*, Hillsdale, New Jersey: Lawrence Erlbaum Associates, Publishers, 1983.

Galitz, Wilbert O., *Handbook of Screen Format Design*, 2nd Edn. Wellesley, Massachusetts: Q.E.D. Information Systems, Inc., 1986.

Heines, Jesse M., *Screen Design Strategies for Computer-Assisted Instruction*, Bedford, Massachusetts: Digital Press, 1984.

Hunt, Morton, *The Universe Within: A New Science Explores the Human Mind*, New York: Simon and Schuster, 1982.

James, Geoffrey, *Document Databases*, New York: Van Nostrand Reinhold Co., 1985.

Monk, Andrew, ed., *Fundamentals of Human-Computer Interaction, New York: Academic Press*, 1985.

Norman, Donald A. and Draper, Stephen W., eds., *User Centered System Design: New Perspectives on Human-Computer Interaction*, Hillsdale, New Jersey: Lawrence Erlbaum Associates, Publishers, 1986.

Ramey, Judith, "Developing a Theoretical Base for On-Line Documentation, Part I: Building the Theory," *The Technical Writing Teacher*, Vol. XIII, No. 2 (Spring, 1986), pp. 148–159; and "Part II: Applying the Theory," Vol. XIII, No. 3(Fall, 1986), pp. 302–315.

Romiszowski, A. J., *Developing Auto-Instructional Materials: From Programmed Texts to CAL and Interactive Video*, New York: Nichols Publishing, 1986.

Schneiderman, Ben, *Designing the User Interface: Strategies for Effective Human-Computer Interaction*, Reading, Massachusetts: Addison-Wesley Publishing Company, 1987.

Schneiderman, Ben, *Software Psychology: Human Factors in Computer and Information Systems*, Cambridge, Massachusetts: Winthrop Publishers, 1980.

Steinberg, Esther R., *Teaching Computers to Teach*, Hillsdale, New Jersey: Lawrence Erlbaum Associates, Publishers, 1984.

References

[1] American Society for Training and Development, *Computer-Based Training Today: A Guide to Research, Specialized Terms, and Publications in the Field*, ASTD, Alexandria, Virginia, 1987.

[2] R. John Brockmann, *Writing Better Computer User Documentation: From Paper to Online*, John Wiley & Sons, New York, 1986.

[3] Stuart K. Card, Thomas P. Moran, and Allen Newall, *The Psychology of Human-Computer Interaction*, Lawrence Erlbaum Associates, Publishers, Hillsdale, New Jersey, 1983.

[4] Wilbert O. Galitz, *Handbook of Screen Format Design*, 2nd Edn., QED Information Sciences, Inc., Wellesley Hills, Massachusetts, 1985.

[5] Phyllis S. Illyefalvi, "System Messages," in a 1987 draft by the American National Standards Institute (ANSI) X3K1 Committee on *User Documentation for Small Computer Software*. The first three definitions of types of online documentation in this paper are adapted from this draft.

[6] Geoffrey James, *Document Databases*, Van Nostrand Reinhold Company, New York, 1985.

[7] Stephen Marcus, "The Host in the Machine: Decorum in Computers Who Speak," in *IEEE Transactions on Professional Communication*, Vol. PC-28, No. 2, June 1985, pp. 29–33.

[8] Michael H. Markel, *Technical Writing: Situations and Strategies*, St. Martin's Press, New York, 1984. The definitions about good "paper-based" technical writing are paraphrased from Markel's text.

[9] Marvin Minsky, *The Society of Mind*, Simon and Schuster, New York, 1986.

[10] Jonathan Price, *How to Write a Computer Manual: A Handbook of Software Documentation*, The Benjamin/Cummings Publishing Company, Reading, Massachusetts, 1984.

[11] Judith Ramey, "Developing a Theoretical Base for On-Line Documentation, Part I: Building the Theory," in *The Technical Writing Teacher*, Vol. 13, No. 2, Spring 1986, pp. 148–159.

[12] Judith Ramey, "Developing a Theoretical Base for On-Line Documentation, Part II: Applying the Theory," in *The Technical Writing Teacher*, Vol. 13, No. 3, Fall 1986, pp. 302–315.

[13] Angus Reynolds, "A Computer-Based Learning Glossary for Human Resource Development Professionals," Version 5.0, in American Society for Training and Development, *Computer-Based Training Today: A Guide to Research, Specialized Terms, and Publications in the Field,* ASTD, Alexandria, Virginia, 1987, pp. 13–40.

19

Creating a Style for Online Help

Jonathan Price

WordPlay
6119 Canning Street
Oakland, California 94609

Now, with graphic displays, cheap mass storage, and hypertext software, we have an opportunity to develop a new kind of online help. But what style will it be? In this essay, I raise some of the questions we will need to answer as we create that style, questions that revolve around the materials we now have to work with— moving and still imagery, text, units of organization, viewer control, points of access, methods of navigation, and overall metaphor.

Online help began as a few comments added to programs to show the user how to navigate, fill in the blanks, or execute a transaction. Unfortunately, the style in which these remarks were presented was often quite compressed, very verbal, drastically limited in perspective, crushingly static—in a word, stiff. At the same time, the material was often inconsistent within itself, complex without sophistication, cryptic, and ambiguous. In general, to get any benefit from this so-called "help," you had to be a programmer.

In the last few years, as more companies have recognized that consumers want their software explained on the screen (rather than on paper), the quality of online help has improved somewhat. But with the advent of graphic displays, huge memories, cheap mass storage, and hypertext software, we have an opportunity that earlier writers and designers only dreamt of. The question I raise here is: what style will you use, when you create this new free-flowing, interactive, visual, and potentially very personal help?

The question of style

When you write a poem, style seems just an artefact—an almost accidental trace of personality left behind as you make a series of choices about language and design. Where a poet creates a world out of language alone, the creator of online help builds an artificial world out of words, pictures, paths, and the contributions of the audience, moulded together by some overarching metaphor. Online style accumulates as you make decisions about how you want to handle all these materials.

What are the choices you have, in each of these areas? I pose some of them here as a series of questions—questions to which there is no right answer, only a personal bias, a sense of where you stand, a feeling of where you'd like to go. Only after you've developed the online help can you look back and describe the style. But as you design and create the help, you may be able to speed up your work by asking yourself these questions, and, instead of wondering what is "right," just listening to that little voice inside you.

Style always begins with the medium. Clay, for instance, offers the potter innumerable possibilities—a set of choices she can make, between rough and smooth, between flat surfaces and glazes, between thousands of colors, shapes, and sizes. The creator chooses among these possibilities; the net result of those choices is what we call style.

Most of us grew up on print. Whether we were students, teachers, trainers, designers, editors, managers, or writers, we dreamt of words on paper. We knew our worth was measured by the printed page. And whenever we wrote, we relied on at least four centuries' worth of work by thousands of people, for we inherited conventions, techniques, concepts, and sensitivities that made our work easier. So we have become quite sophisticated in our stylistic decisions when we create printed materials.

But now our medium is changing. A device we thought of as our subject and our tool has become our page.

It's a screen. It is not silver, and it is not TV.

For online help, the _computer_ screen is our medium. At its best, it can display images brought in from many different sources—color slides, video, computer animation, film, digitized or scanned images, drawings, paintings, spreadsheet graphics, diagrams from project management or outliner applications, infrared photographs, and the results of a thousand-and-one scientific probes.

We come from a tradition that has kept each medium separate. During the Sixties, experimental theater brought us the idea of "multi-media" performances, but that depended on the separation of media for true counterpoint. What we are witnessing today is the synthesis of text and images from many different sources, all brought together and presented in the same medium—the computer screen.

Within that bright screen we have so many possible choices that the mind shortcircuits for a moment. We must keep asking ourselves: What decisions do we need to make to develop a style that is truly helpful, in this medium that can communicate so much information in so many visual forms?

Here, then, are a series of dilemmas you need to resolve as you develop your online help; your answers—the particular combination of choices you make—will shape the style and atmosphere of your online world.

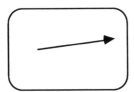

1. How widely are you going to refer to the world beyond the software?

Remember that some customers buy spreadsheets in the belief that the software will teach them how to develop a budget. (The salesman said so). Traditionally, manual writers have ignored this wish, but template makers and book writers have rushed in to help. You now have the opportunity to provide much more than definitions of commands. You can, for instance, teach basic economics to add value to your spreadsheet, or book design (with real illustrations) when you are supporting a page layout program. One way of rephrasing this question, then, is: to what extent are you going to take the viewer beyond the strict limits of your application?

In addition, when you bring in information from photographs, video sequences, data bases—from almost every medium—will you retouch the images and rewrite the words, so that a viewer can no longer guess where they came from? Or will every picture come trailing evidence of the brush or camera, the equipment and the person who made it? Such subtle echoes of other media widen the perspective of your work, enrich your texture, make the viewer aware of far more than just the subject. Is this what you want? How many earlier media will your screen echo?

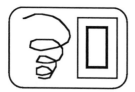

2. How mobile will your images be?

You may have nothing but still life's—precise diagrams, quiet models, motionless portraits. Or you may have the opportunity to include computer animation showing the way the cylinders move in a Buick engine (mobile, but repetitive); actual outtakes from a Kurosawa film (vivid, rapidly changing, quite formally beautiful); or clips from the ABC World News Tonight (talking heads, quick cuts, heavily edited).

How often and how dramatically will any one picture change within its frame? How quickly will you replace one picture with the next? A rule of thumb on American TV is that no shot should last longer than ten seconds; some McDonald's commercials pepper us with three or four distinct images a second—and we have learned to keep up.

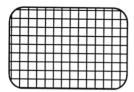

3. How much variety will your images provide?

Are they all going to be drawings done in the same style? Will they all have essentially the same subject? Or will they draw on different media, portray many different subjects, in many different styles? Will a series of pictures differ in contrast, color, resolution, and apparent depth? (The greater the contrast, the more we're aware that we have moved on). If we can navigate freely among images, then we may feel uncomfortably restricted if we can only find organization charts. It's like being given the keys to every cell in a prison, but not the front door.

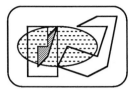

4. How much will your images blend together?

You're familiar with the slow fade in movies: as one scene darkens, another comes to life, and for a few seconds, we live in both. We can easily edit digital images so that they overlap, blur together, intermingle in odd ways, show through one another, pulsate. Such messy integration may seem to violate the austerity of our profession. But like video artists, we may find it helpful as a way of pointing out analogies, suggesting more than we can say, deliberately creating ambiguity where we have normally fought to get rid of it. Or we can ignore that possibility, and continue our almost professorial tradition, based on the best Bauhaus books, of keeping one image apart from another, as if to facilitate scientific comparison. These new tools draw us toward synthesis; the past pulls us back toward separation.

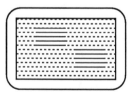

5. And to what extent will text be integrated with the images?

Will text live in a separate box, pointing to the pictures, but not able to put its finger on the spot it talks about? Or will you place labels over key parts of the picture, perhaps even adding a sentence or two of explanation, and a caption? Will you let the images carry the main theme, while text simply adds details? We all know how hard it is to read extended text on the screen; and we know our audiences don't much like to read anyhow. So the more we say in images, the more our audience will enjoy our help. But nothing computerized is ever far from words, and language will continue to be a necessary component of most online help. Some designers have created two parallel tracks: on the left, an image, on the right, numbered steps with written procedures. The viewer can glance back and forth, integrating them, but visually, each has its own realm. Personally, I believe this is only a transitional solution, as we outgrow pure text and edge toward procedures which are mostly pictures, with words serving only as brief comments.

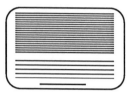

6. Speaking of text, how plain can it get?

As soon as you see a paragraph on screen, it looks too long. Writing the text of help messages usually means rewriting them to squeeze out the fat. The sentences become telegraphic. The ideal sometimes seems to be: more white space, less text. But there are limits. Below a certain number of words, your text becomes cryptic; instead of being concise, you find you're open to multiple interpretations. So how tight is your prose going to get?

Of course, your organization can make writing simpler. If you organize each unit (each screen of information for instance) in the same way—visually and logically—your prose can attain a similar simplicity. A multi-leveled hierarchical organization, in which I must proceed from general ideas through more specific topics to very particular facts, may leave me wondering where I am; if your layout does not tell me, your prose may have to take on that task, explaining that one fact in a hundred contexts—and that can make the writing twist like Laocoon. And if you completely lose track of your own structure, or have to apologize for someone else's impenetrable organization, your prose soon becomes a thicket of cautions, preambles, and reminders. And so...

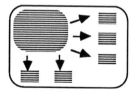

7. How sprawling can your organization be?

In printed prose, the basic unit is the paragraph; online, the basic unit of organization is the window—usually the same shape as the screen, but smaller. I conceive of online help as a series of these windows: one idea per frame. Like a page in a book, a window offers a retaining shape, a convenient unit; but unlike a book, online help doesn't show you what page you're on, how far you've read, where this page is in relation to a linear sequence of other pages. Your frame floats in imaginary space. That means it's more important as an organizing element, a unit of meaning, than a book page ordinarily is. It has to be more self-contained, since the context is so hard to see.

One way to carve up your material is to sort it into types of information—the different kinds of fact a customer might look up. So a general topic might be organized into a definition, a procedure, an example, advice, exceptions, and rules. Whatever types of information a customer might want, they form a set of questions you can ask—and answer—about any topic. In this way, you begin to work out the individual atoms of your material—what goes into each frame.

Whenever you find that an atom won't fit in a frame, no matter how you tease it, your organization begins to sprawl. I hate making someone scroll down for more information; it's a sign of poor structure. It makes the viewer uncertain whether the frame contains everything needed—or not. Where is the end of the information? How deep does it go? Are we getting a bland introduction, while the hideous details lurk several layers down? Or is there nothing there—no extra fact, no philosophic perspective, no electrons and ions whirling? Once you let information spill beyond the frame, you create anxiety, an emotion appropriate for art, but not for online help.

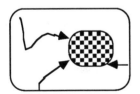

8. Are you going to have one path in—or many?

Some people make the customer go to a menu, choose help, choose a topic, and leaf through the information. Other folks are fancier: you can press a key combination, turning the cursor into a question mark, then click on an object you want to know about. Or you can choose help on the menu. Or you can hit one of the programmable keys to get a scrollable index of help topics; another key for a table of contents; another key for a glossary; and yet another for topics related to the object you have your question-mark on top of. All this gets a bit dizzying, and viewers have sometimes pleaded for less access, not more.

One path in is certainly easier to learn than five. But is it as flexible? Does it take too long for me to get straight to the fact I want? You and your programmers can and will debate these issues for hours. I'd just say: three ways in is plenty—a front door, a back door, and a window.

Whatever access methods you provide will have a big effect on the customer, making your help seem complicated or simple, slow or quick, multi-layered or flat. Similarly, the paths you offer a customer through your material also set the tone for the experience.

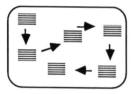

9. How long and flexible are the paths through your material?

By paths here I mean the trails that lead from one menu to another to another, or from a list of topics to the fact I want. In some programs I can only go down a series of staircases leading from the most general to the most specific information. For instance, with some forms of Videotex, I had to choose Entertainment, then choose Cinema, then East Bay, then Berkeley, then North Berkeley, then after 5pm, to get a list of local movies. Tortuous. In other programs I can jump happily from detail to detail, or go leaping all the way up to broad generalization, without having to retrace my steps. These moves establish an atmosphere: do I feel constricted, directed, forced into a few routes? Or do I feel as if I can drive almost anywhere? A stupidly designed hierarchical system can make me feel like a victim crying for escape, and a completely loose system may raise agoraphobia. That's why I raise the next question.

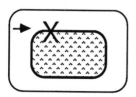

10. How carefully do you show me where I am?

So often when using an information service such as Dialog, people panic when they wonder where they are—how far down in the hierarchy are they? How can they get out? Do they have to climb back out of all the choices they made to get in? Or can they ride some escalator back to the top level menu? These people have entered hyperspace, that eerie limbo. They yearn for some sign (perhaps an indication of all the choices they made to get here), some map (a visual description of the route they've taken), some memory album (a collection of the last half dozen screens they've looked at). Backtracking is not enough: in fact, sometimes it only increases confusion. The point is people want to know where they stand, and the models they have ("where I am") are almost all based on paper. Once your online help gets complicated enough so someone can get lost in it, you need to provide a consistent indication of where they are (how they got here, and how they can get out). It's a little like Hansel and Gretel leaving a trail of pebbles.

Whatever method you use—a series of headings, for instance, or a map—you face the problem of reconciling that with the metaphor you use to explain where things are, in your help system.

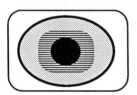

11. Do you provide an overarching metaphor?

For instance, do you show a map instead of a menu, and encourage people to imagine they are walking through a town, visiting various stores, the library, the post office, and the pachinko parlor? That geographical metaphor should then inform your individual frames of information (each is a "place") and the reassuring proof that they are not lost ("Here's the map!").

You're all familiar with the desktop metaphor. Once upon a time, someone thought that the screen resembled a desktop, and each application might be described by its real-life analogy (a data base is a Rolodex; a word processor is a typewriter, and so on). Well, we all know the limitations of that metaphor.

You can't expect one metaphor to cover every case. But it should arch over all activities as a general explanation, an imaginary environment. In this case, your work is like that of the science fiction writer. You must create another world. It might be a single room (an office, a kitchen, a garage, a factory), a city, a country, or an entire ocean. Remember that metaphor is another way of saying what is true—not just an advertising gimmick. To be helpful, your metaphor must express something accurate about the way you present your organization visually, about the way you let people move from one topic to another, from one level to another, from area to area.

Once you decide on a metaphor, you need to find some verbal and visual analogies from that world, to rename commands, objects, and experiences in online help. For instance, in the geographical metaphor, you may talk about driving to another place when you are actually just jumping to another node on a network of data. The point is not to achieve absolute consistency (few poems do), but to cast a spell over the whole—what the Scots used to call a "glamour," so that the whole experience seems somehow unified.

This is not lying. It is expressing what would otherwise remain hidden. It is, also, a way of providing a broad context within which many of the customer's decisions make sense. As we know from teaching, having such meaningful context accelerates learning.

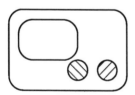

12. To what extent will <u>your viewer</u> have control over your imagery?

Interactivity wakes people up. Nothing's more hypnotic than leaning on the Return key to keep showing the next screen full of information, and the next, and the next. That isn't real interaction. It's waving a gold watch in front of a subject. The more you give the viewer control over the sequence and speed of presentation, the more alert your viewers will be.

You and your programming team may give the viewer the chance to get rid of one picture (or camera angle) and jump to another quickly and often, or you may not choose to offer that freedom. Can I zoom in for a closeup? Can I touch the screen, and get a completely different picture showing what lies inside that building? Can I affect the rhythm, or stop the show, to study one image for a while? The more I can tilt and tack through the imagery, the freer I'll feel. (What I think of that freedom, of course, depends largely on your overarching metaphor and your strategies for handling my anxiety).

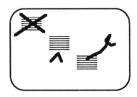

13. To what extent can the viewer modify the contents?

Once a customer enters your world, can he or she actually remake it, so it's more useful, more personal, more meaningful? Following your metaphor, how would you describe the changes a customer can make? Can they rewrite your text? Make new connections between various frames? Delete something? Revise a picture?

At first, most trainers balk at the idea that the student might be able to doodle on the training materials. But you could give the student the chance to make notes ("Watch out! This never works!") or redo your text in terms of her own office ("Use green letterhead for this.") The opportunity is not enough; you may need to show people how to take advantage of this chance to tame, modify, and localize your material. Saying "this space is for notes" is just teasing; if you are serious, you might show how a few previous customers have annotated some frames.

When you encourage the learner to adapt your material, to add to it, to improve it, you show your respect. Your online help becomes a well-led discussion, not a lecture.

At the moment, few online help systems go this far. At best, they let the customers define themselves as expert, intermediate, or beginner—so that whole hunks of material are hidden, as part of an effort to meet the particular needs of that customer. A few systems let the customer specify which types of information he wants to appear first; and which he'd like never to bother with. In this way, the customer tailors his own help. But it's a long way from that to a collaborative venture in which the customer is invited to make notes in the margin, or even rewrite the textbook.

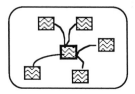

14. How sociable is your help?

Can an entire workgroup pitch in to revise your help, making it more useful for them? To what extent do you set it up to encourage people to talk to each other, asking questions, responding with their own helpful comments, so that gradually the help contains a collection of shared solutions, a little library of that group's solutions. Online help exists on local area networks. It's possible to make help like an electronic bulletin board, where you set up a discussion topic, and encourage everyone to add their ideas, tricks, tips, creating a shared body of lore. So: are you going to help folks talk to each other, or are you going to maintain your awful authority by preventing them from talking in class? I exaggerate the dilemma. But another metaphor for online help could be a conversation. A chat between friends. (And friends never call each other "user.")

Conclusions

You can see how far we've come from the rather simple editorial decisions needed to put out a reference guide. We have not, of course, abandoned the questions of organization and approach that we must answer as we create books. But creating onscreen help in hypermedia has multiplied the questions, and made style an even more complex web.

Now that it has the ability to produce text in any font, to import images from almost any source, to make those images dance to real music, the computer screen has become a medium capable of real art. The artist's job is to push the medium to the limit; to see what it does best; to put it to the test. In that effort, style is just the evidence left behind, the splattering of paint.

But the creators of online help are not artists. Our job is not to follow the medium wherever it leads us, but to tame it to our rather limited purpose. And to be really helpful for a broad range of viewers, we must be conscious of our stylistic choices, asking ourselves always: is this style really helpful? Is it friendly? Is it intelligent, informative, and coherent? As Bernard Shaw would have said, does the style do the job?

20

HOW "FRIENDLY" IS YOUR WRITING FOR READERS AROUND THE WORLD?

John Kirkman
Consultant on technical communication

(Formerly Director of the Communication Studies Unit,
University of Wales Institute of Science and Technology,
Cardiff, Wales)

> "Until you mentioned it, I'd never really
> thought about people for whom English is
> a foreign language."

These words were uttered by a professional technical
writer in the USA, who had just told me that the text we
were discussing would be distributed in Europe. She was
a conscientious and able writer, with a good command of
English and of her topic: she simply had not thought
about the difficulties her text might present to readers
using English as a foreign language.

I think it is fair to characterise her attitude as
"unthinking" or "unmindful" rather than as "unfriendly".
She had tried hard to make the text accurate and
comfortable for readers. For example, to relieve the
forbidding tone of computer jargon, she had written:

... software is a fancy name for a computer program ...

Unfortunately, she did not recognise that such comments
increase difficulty for many overseas readers. To
comprehend the meaning and tone of "is a fancy name"
requires a substantial command of English vocabulary and
idiom.

Regrettably, it is becoming common for writers to cause
difficulties and spoil tone in their efforts to be
"user-friendly". Here is an extract from a training
manual, a two-inch-thick book issued to be read before a
training course, sent for use in Europe. The extract
comes from the beginning of Module 2:

... Now that Module 1 has turned you against
computers forever, let us make matters worse
by giving you the bum's rush through the
technical details of the XXXX workstation ...

Four points must be made about this extract. First,
the whimsical tone would be considered patronising by many
readers. Humorous tone does not travel easily across
national boundaries[1]. Second, the intended tone would
probably not be detected by many readers using English as
a foreign language. Third, the idiom "... giving you the
bum's rush ..." would not be readily understood outside
the USA, even in Great Britain (my invaluable Webster's
Ninth New Collegiate Dictionary gave me no help under bum
or rush). Fourth, it is an inappropriate colloquialism
anyway, because - so my American friends have told me - it
implies very rapid removal of a troublemaking reader from
the scene, which is scarcely what the writer wanted to
imply.

The writers of these two examples were making conscious
efforts to be "friendly", for which they deserve credit;
but their thinking was insufficiently international. They
were not taking account of the many ways in which
"unthinking" writing causes difficulties for readers using
English as a foreign language.

Shouldn't text for foreign countries be translated?

In this paper, I shall discuss a dozen ways in which
"unthinking" writing causes difficulty for readers using
English as a foreign language. But before I do, I must
deal with a question that always arises when I encourage
writers to "think internationally": "Is it really up to
us to write in a way that overseas readers can understand?
Isn't it the job of translators to convert text into a
form that will be easily comprehensible to audiences in
foreign countries? If readers overseas cannot understand
the jargon, or if they cannot cope with a natural flow of
ordinary language, then texts must be translated".

I accept that translation is desirable; but my answer
emphasises three points:

1. whatever may be desirable in theory, manufacturers
   in the USA and Britain frequently, in practice, try
   to get away with using only English in their

support documents, on-screen "help" information,
hands-on training packages, and on-screen
error-messages;

2. even if writers know that their manuals and
   on-screen materials will be translated for
   distribution overseas, they still have a
   professional responsibility to write thoughtfully, to minimise the difficulties they
   create for translators;

3. it is not usually specialist jargon that
   causes most difficulty for overseas readers:
   difficulty stems more frequently from
   thoughtless use of "ordinary" language
   in between the specialist terms.

Accordingly, when we evaluate written material that is
to be distributed around the world in book form or on
screen, we must ask two broad questions:

- will the text as it stands be easily
  comprehensible to the whole audience –
  that is, both to native speakers of English
  and to people for whom English is a
  foreign language;

- if the text is to be translated, will it be
  easily translatable (by translators who
  frequently do not have a technical
  background)?

Inconsistent use of terms

"Unthinking" writing causes difficulties for all
foreign-language readers (from this point onwards, for
economy, I shall use the contrasting terms
"native-language readers" and "foreign-language readers").
However, the first two points I want to make are about
aspects of unthinking writing that pose particular
problems in the daily lives of translators. I have
chosen two points that illustrate the wide variety of
matters that writers must consider: inconsistent use of
terms, and failure to recognise the space required for
translated text.

Imagine that you have been asked to translate a text. In
the text, you find that the writer has used all the
following expressions:

```
... the VDU ...
... the CRT ...
... the monitor ...
... the screen ...
```

How should you translate those four words?   Do they all
mean the same thing?   Certainly, in the text they have
all been used to denote the object on which pictures
appear; yet it would seem reasonable to argue that the
screen is not quite the same as the monitor.   Should you
clarify the writer's fuzzy thinking?   Should you struggle
to find four different words in your own language ... or
should you be consistent and use just two ... or perhaps
just one?

   Also in the text, the writer has used:

```
... key in the data ...
... input the data ...
... type in the data ...
... enter the data ...
```

And sometimes enter means "type in"; sometimes it means
"press a key, to transmit to a program file the data you
have just typed in"; sometimes it means "both type in and
transmit the data"; and sometimes it means "move into"
(as in "enter Program A from System X").   How should you
deal with these confusions?

   Elsewhere, the writer has written:

... The logic board runs with zero wait states ...

Two lines later, you find:

... The XXXMEM runs with no wait states ...

Should you translate zero and no with the same word in
your own language? Perhaps the writer wished to indicate
a significant difference by the use of zero in one case
and no in the other (in fact, he did not).   What should
you do?

   All these confusions could have been avoided if the
writer of the original text had been consistent in the use
of terms.   Consistency is desirable even if texts are not
scheduled for translation: when texts are to be
translated, consistency is a basic professional courtesy
that writers should extend to their colleagues, the
translators.

Failure to recognise the space required for translated text

Consideration of the space needed for a translation is becoming increasingly important as more and more information is presented on screen.

A text may expand by as much as 40% when it is translated from English into another language. This can wreck the careful design of a manual, a brochure, a quick-reference card, or a series of "help" screens. The originator of the text in English, the designer of the document, and the developer of the program (or whoever is responsible for creating on-screen messages or forms to be filled in) must all foresee problems of accommodating translated text within limits of book lay-out, coding and/or file-structure, and screen design. If they do not, they cause great problems for translators, designers and programmers responsible for "internationalisation" or "localisation" of books and on-screen material.

Common features of incompetent technical writing

Now for the ways in which unthinking writing causes trouble for all foreign-language readers, even for translators who have a good command of English.

Of course, foreign-language readers have particular trouble when confronted by the common features of incompetent technical writing, such as:

- long and complex sentence structures;
- long-winded and grandiose expression;
- assertion of false links by slovenly use of logical signals such as <u>therefore</u> and <u>hence</u>;
- confusion of tenses;
- unexplained use of jargon with which the specified audience is not familiar;
- excessive nominalisation, and unnecessary use of passive constructions.

Every book on technical writing describes how these features cause difficulty for <u>all</u> readers, and gives advice on how to write more readably. I assume that I need not give further discussion of sheer incompetence. I shall focus on writing that is unthinking rather than basically incompetent - on writing that causes special difficulties for foreign-language readers.

Culture-bound references

First, I want to draw attention to "culture-bound references" - allusions to ideas or entities that exist in some countries or cultures but not in others.

I have seen a text that introduces the term "April Fools" in an example illustrating an application. Such a term presents readers with a problem in countries where there is no tradition of April foolery.

Similarly, it puzzled me (a reader with a reasonable command of English) to receive, during my progress through a self-teaching program, the on-screen message "Close, but no cigar!". That idiom is not current in British English, let alone in other languages.

Some trade-names have become household words in Britain and the USA (for example, in Britain to hoover = to vacuum-clean; in the USA, to xerox = to photocopy): but for foreign-language readers, such terms are substantial obstacles. We should therefore refrain from writing:

> ... you may need a Pozidriv screwdriver to
> loosen ...

Colloquial expression

Colloquial expression causes major problems for foreign-language readers. A technical leaflet, designed to promote sales of computer-based equipment internationally, claimed:

> ... At Company X, we understand your needs,
> because we've been there.   ...

Been where? Apparently, this expression meant "because we have been confronted by the same problems as now confront you". It requires a substantial experience of the allusive style of advertising English to pick up that meaning - experience that few foreign-language readers have had.

A similar problem is presented by this caution:

CAUTION

Watch Out for Static Zap!

XXXXXXX COMPUTERS AND PERIPHERALS CONTAIN
ASSEMBLIES AND COMPONENTS THAT ARE SENSITIVE
TO ELECTROSTATIC DISCHARGE. CAREFULLY OBSERVE
THE PRECAUTIONS AND RECOMMENDED PROCEDURES IN
THIS NOTE TO ENSURE THAT YOU DO NOT COMPROMISE
YOUR SYSTEM'S RELIABILITY BECAUSE OF COMPONENT
DAMAGE FROM STATIC ELECTRICITY.

The phrase static zap may be familiar in American
English (my Webster's Ninth gives zap as a verb meaning
"to strike with or as if with an electric charge"); but
it is not common in British English. Foreign-language
readers with a shaky command of either American English or
British English would probably find static discharge
easier to comprehend.

You may object that I am being unduly fussy, because the
subsequent text makes clear what the caution is about.   I
accept that the text does explain the meaning of static
zap, but I would suggest that it would have been wiser
writing to use the term static discharge in both the
heading and the text.

I would also point out that the text goes on to use
another colloquial expression that would puzzle many
foreign-language readers:

   ... ensure that you do not compromise your system's
      reliability because of ...

Native-language readers recognise compromise as a weasel
word ("a word used in order to evade or retreat from a
direct or forthright statement or position", says
Webster's Ninth).   It is the type of word a Legal
Department or a Sales Department tells a writer to use in
order to avoid the unfavourable image created by a caution
such as "... otherwise you will damage the components in
the system ...".

If we use such weasel words in documents for
international audiences, we do so at the expense of
immediate and accurate communication with our
foreign-language readers.

American English and British English

In Close, but no cigar! and static zap, we have seen
already two examples of American English that would not be
immediately comprehensible to most British readers.   It
is important for writers on both sides of the Atlantic to
recognise that American English (AE) and British English
(BE) have many differences.   (Had you noticed that this
text is written in British English?   If so, what features
of my writing had brought that to your attention?)

The most obvious differences, such as differences in
spelling or in the conventions of punctuation, are
probably the least important from the point of view of
break-down in communication.   Much more important are
differences in meaning attached to individual words, and
different usage of some grammatical structures.

I read in a text that computer equipment would function
satisfactorily provided the power supply was:

   ... subjected to regular interruptions only ...

To me, as a BE reader, the meaning seemed to be that
evenly spaced and consistent interruptions would not be
troublesome: but the writer was writing in AE, and
intended regular to mean "normal" or "usual" - a very
different idea.

A BE reader who was not familiar with AE might
misunderstand this extract from an AE text:

   ... packet switching allows alternate routing ...

In BE, to use alternate routing would be to use first
route A, then route B, and then route A again, and so on.
The AE writer wanted alternate to mean "alternative,
allowing a choice between two (or more) possibilities".

When I first read the statement that follows, I thought
I understood it:

   ... most software bugs have been eliminated, and
       preliminary results are quite encouraging ...

I took quite encouraging to mean "giving some
encouragement, but not very much".   But then I saw the
results, which were excellent.   So I checked with the AE
writer, and learned that the intended meaning of quite was
"very".   The writer was using quite in a way that is

becoming common in AE usage - as an intensifier. ("You're
quite welcome" does <u>not</u> imply that the speaker is only
half-hearted, as it <u>does</u> to the British ear!)

A grammatical point to be aware of is that the AE
practice of beginning an instruction with <u>have</u> seems
peremptory to the British ear:

... Have the recycle systems regenerated.   Then, ...

In BE, an instruction beginning with <u>have</u> usually has a
bossy or overbearing tone: "Have the recycle systems
regenerated <u>at once, or you'll be in trouble!</u>".   The more
normal BE expression would be "Regenerate the recycle
systems ..." or, in speech, "Get the recycle systems
regenerated ...".   Also, it is very likely that a BE
reader would wonder if a question mark was missing: "Have
the recycle systems regenerated?   Then, ...".

Let me emphasise that I am not suggesting that the BE
expression is right and the AE wrong.   Neither is right
or wrong: they are simply different common forms in the
two languages.   My point is that professional writers
need to be aware of differences such as these, and to
avoid vocabulary or grammar that might cause mis-readings
among native speakers of "other" Englishes.

It is essential, too, to recognise that readers for whom
English is a foreign language will usually have learned
just one form of English, and will be as puzzled as
native-language readers if they are confronted by a text
in another form of English.

Is it really necessary to take the trouble to learn the
differences between AE and BE?   A considerable effort is
required to learn which items of vocabulary and which
grammatical structures might be misunderstood.   Isn't it
reasonable to rely on the fact that readers will recognise
which language the text is written in, and will interpret
accordingly?

If you are tempted to produce this argument, stop and
think.   You are asking the foreign-language reader to
develop the sensitivity to different Englishes that <u>you</u> do
not want to bother to develop.   Certainly, it is
important to write consistently in either AE or BE: the
worst case of all for foreign-language readers is to be
confronted by a text written in "mid-Atlantic" English,
which requires interpretation sometimes according to AE
norms and sometimes according to BE norms.   But I would

argue that simple consistency is not enough.   When
required to write a text for international distribution, a
writer with a proper professional attitude should aim to
remove as many as possible of the foreseeable obstacles to
comprehension.

Doesn't this produce texts that seem distorted to native
speakers of either AE or BE, or to both?   Not usually. It
is usually possible to find a form of words that is
accurate and comfortable for both groups of readers.   In
the example above, the form: "Regenerate the recycle
systems.   Then, ..." would have seemed entirely natural
expression on both sides of the Atlantic.

Faux amis

Another obstacle the thoughtful writer must try to
remove is any faux ami, "false friend" - any word that
looks the same in two or more languages, but which
actually carries different meanings in the different
languages.

The word actually is a prime example.   In AE and BE,
the primary meaning of actual(ly) is "existing in fact,
not merely in theory or potential".   In most European
languages, its primary meaning is "current, present".   To
the French writer who produced this statement:

    ... le program ne le permet pas dans sa forme
        actuelle ...

it meant:

    ... the program does not permit this in its current
        form ...

A British or American reader, not recognising the "false
friend", might translate it as:

    ... the program does not permit this in its actual
        form ...

using actual to imply the program's form in reality as
distinct from its form in theory.

So, to reduce the likelihood of misinterpretation by
foreign-language readers, the thoughtful writer, using AE
or BE, will avoid expressions such as:

```
      ... though it is a single unit, the XYMEM actually
          comprises two memories ...
```

and will write instead:

```
      ... though it is a single unit, the XYMEM
          comprises two memories ...
```

or:

```
      ... though in theory the XYMEM is a single unit,
          in practice it comprises two memories ...
```

or:

```
      ... though the XYMEM is constructed as a single
          unit, it consists of two memories ...
```

Are you sceptical about the need to make the effort
required to write in this thoughtful way?   If so,
remember your own struggles with translation when you were
learning a foreign language.   Long ago, when I was just
setting out on a career in technical writing, an
experienced author gave me some valuable advice: "When
you think of your average readers overseas, imagine this:
that they have your text in front of them;   that they have
had a few years' study of English in a secondary school;
and that they may have the help of a technical glossary
and a concise English dictionary".

I would add to that the warning that <u>average</u> levels of
English vary considerably in European countries: general
levels are higher in Scandinavia than in Spain and Italy.
And even foreign-language readers with a good command of
English are prone to make mistakes.   Here is a Frenchman,
experienced in writing technical documents in English, who
nevertheless slips into the use of a false friend:

```
      ... Run the sub-tests eventually ...
```

He intended that instruction to mean "Run the sub-tests if
necessary";   but he overlooked the fact that
<u>eventuellement</u> in French (= possibly, perhaps, should the
occasion arise) cannot be translated directly to
<u>eventually</u> in English.   When we write texts for
international distribution, we should avoid <u>eventually</u>. It
is a false friend in most European languages.   We should
use instead an expression such as <u>ultimately</u>, <u>in the end</u>,
<u>at last</u>, or <u>after a time</u>.

Expressions that can have two or more meanings

We need, also, to avoid usages that are accurate and acceptable to native-language readers, but are difficult in various ways for foreign-language readers. I have space to mention just three elements of writing that are accurate and acceptable English, but can nevertheless be difficult:

- expressions that can have two or more interpretations (for example, while ... constructions);
- unnecessary "fillers" (for example, Go ahead and ... or Why don't you ...);
- words that can have varying tone (for example, grab).

In English, it is entirely acceptable to use while to indicate a time relationship, to introduce an opposition or contrast, to indicate a link, or to imply a concession:

... This is achieved by switching the ABC into each channel in turn while the XYZ feeds the other channel ...
(Intended meaning was: "during the same period")

... one XYZ port is used by the application while the other is used by the ABC system to route ...
(Intended meaning was: "whereas" or "and");

... system X controls six subsystems while system Y controls seven ...
(Intended meaning was: "but, in contrast").

... while the X procedure gives the fastest response, the Y procedure is the most cost-effective of the four ...
(Intended meaning was "Although")

When we write such statements, we rely on readers being able to infer from the context the intended meaning of while. Even for native-language readers, that is sometimes difficult: it is particularly difficult for readers whose command of English is not strong. It is wise for professional writers to develop the habit of reserving while for use in its most easily recognisable sense - to indicate a time relationship. To indicate a contrast, a link or a concession, it is best to use but, whereas, in contrast, and, or although.

"Fillers"

In an effort to be friendly, writers sometimes put into their texts "fillers" like <u>Go ahead and ...</u> or <u>Why don't you ...</u>. These expressions are not intended to be taken literally: readers are not expected to go in any particular direction; they are not being asked a question. The expressions are intended to give encouragement, to soften the tone of the instruction:

    ... is packed in a large box. Go ahead and
        remove the computer from the box ...

    ... (An on-screen message in a training program)
        You missed that time. Why don't you try again.

To foreign-language readers who do not have a strong command of English, these fillers present possible distractions: "Go where?". "There isn't any reason why ...". It is therefore desirable to reflect very carefully before including such expressions in a text for international distribution.

Words that can have varying tone

We need to be especially careful about our choice of verbs. Many verbs in English can have two or more meanings, or varying overtones:

- <u>manifests</u> can mean "shows" or simply "has";
- <u>locate</u> can mean "find" or "place precisely in position";
- <u>replace</u> can mean "put back the original where you found it" or "throw away the old and fit a new";
- <u>seize</u> can mean simply "take hold of" or "grasp in a vigorous or rough manner".

As we write for audiences around the world, we must be careful to avoid verbs such as these. Consider this extract:

    ... Remove the plastic cover from the rear of the
        display module base as follows (see Figure 2-17)

- Grab the plastic cover by its sides, pull
  slightly outward and then back and up to
  disengage it from the side catches.

- Lift the cover ...

Imagine that you are an Italian reader, with only a
modest command of English.   The verb grab is not familiar
to you, so you look it up in your dictionary.

If you have a Webster's Ninth New Collegiate Dictionary,
you find:

grab (vt,vi) 1. to take or seize by or as if
              by a sudden motion or grasp; 2. to obtain
              unscrupulously; 3. to take hastily;
              4. to forcefully engage the attention of.

If you have an Oxford Advanced Learner's Dictionary of
Current English, you find:

grab (vt,vi) take roughly; selfishly or
               eagerly snatch.

If, as is most likely, you have a small Italian-English,
English-Italian dictionary, you find something like the
entry in my pocket-size Collins Contemporary Italian
Dictionary:

grab (vt) afferare, impadronirsi con la
            violenza di.

The first definition, afferare, means "to seize, grasp,
comprehend".   The second definition, impadronirsi con la
violenza di means "to take possession of, seize, master
with the violence of".

Whichever dictionary you use, it is not your fault if
you go back to the technical text with the general idea
that the plastic cover should be handled with some vigour!

All of that difficulty could have been avoided if the
writer of the original text had more thoughtfully used the
verb hold:

... Hold the plastic cover by its sides, pull
    slightly outward ...

To hold is tenere in Italian, which would carry none of
the unfortunate overtones of grab.

Mis-relation of phrases and clauses

So far, I have been discussing aspects of writing that
would not normally cause trouble for native-language
readers, but which frequently cause trouble for
foreign-language readers.   In the remaining sections, I
shall discusss aspects of style that cause discomfort even
to native-language readers, and that cause substantial
trouble to foreign-language readers.

First among these aspects comes mis-relation of phrases
and clauses, especially of participial groups and <u>with ...</u>
groups.

Every course on technical writing warns about
mis-related participial constructions, or "dangling
modifiers"; yet we still read frequent statements such
as:

   ... When reporting internal errors to the Technical
       Assistance Center, the following documentation
       must be used ...

   ... After loading the test cassette, the loading
       menu gives a choice of entering one of four
       systems ...

   ... When using the system instructions are given
       to the remote terminal by means of the bit-pad
       or by typing ...

To a native-language reader, it is "obvious" that these
statements are not to be interpreted according to the
normal rule of proximity.   A moment's thought makes plain
that the first writer misled us by attempting to write
impersonally.   The intended meaning was:

   ... When you are reporting internal errors to the
       Technical Assistance Center, you must use
       the following documentation ...

The second writer misled us by attempting to compress
the statement too much.   The intended meaning was:

   ... After you have loaded the test cassette, the
       loading menu gives you a choice of entering
       one of four systems ...

The writer of the third extract compounded our confusion by omitting punctuation as well as by producing a mis-related clause. After discussion, I discovered that he had intended to put a comma after <u>system</u>:

> ... When using the system, instructions are ...

But, as he acknowledged, that still left a mis-relation. He should have written either:

> ... When the system is being used, instructions are given to the remote terminal by means of ...

or:

> ... When you are using the system, you give instructions to the remote terminal by means of ...

Mis-related phrases and clauses cause a definite but slight disturbance to native-language readers. To foreign-language readers, they are a substantial inconvenience. This is particularly true for the least experienced, who decode laboriously in accordance with a set of rules learned in a course on English as a foreign language. Those rules do not help much when the reader has to guess what the writer <u>probably</u> intended.

A similar source of confusion is the use of word-groups beginning with <u>having</u>, <u>being</u>, and <u>using</u>. In English, these word-groups can fulfil two roles: an adverbial role or an adjectival role. To understand which role is intended, we have to look at the position of the group in the sentence, and note how the sentence is punctuated. If the group is in the wrong position and/or the punctuation of the sentence is faulty, the reader is misled.

Consider the following example from a procedure for computerised banking:

> ... Report the anticipated expenditure to the counter clerk using Code 999 ...

Foreign-language readers will have been taught that a <u>using ...</u> group such as this is adjectival: it relates to the noun immediately preceding it; you know this because there is no comma separating the <u>using ...</u> group from the noun. If there is a comma, the <u>using ...</u> group functions as an adverbial construction.

In fact, the writer wanted the group read as an
adverbial construction, but his careless writing gave us a
false signal: he failed to recognise that the <u>absence</u> of
a comma is as significant as the presence of a comma in a
sentence like this.   He should have written either:

   ... Report the anticipated expenditure to the
       counter clerk, using Code 999 ...

or:

   ... Using Code 999, report the anticipated
       expenditure to the counter clerk ...

Similarly, an unthinking writer causes special trouble
for foreign-language readers by unpunctuated use of a <u>with</u>
<u>...</u> group:

   ... The full-duplex 8mbit link running at 4.5 mbit
       per second is likely to use 25.9% of an 1100/92
       with a bi-directional transfer time of about
       7 minutes ...

Native-language readers may recognise quickly that the
text as it stands has a peculiar meaning.   Foreign-
language readers may have more difficulty.   To them,
decoding laboriously according to the grammar rules they
have learned, the absence of a comma after <u>1100/92</u> signals
that they should interpret the <u>with ...</u> group as an
adjectival group qualifying <u>1100/92.</u>   It may take them
some time to recognise that the writer should have written
either:

   ... The full-duplex 8mbit link running at 4.5 mbit per
       second is likely to use 25.9% of an 1100/92, with a
       bi-directional transfer time of about 7 minutes ...

or:

   ... The full-duplex 8mbit link running at 4.5 mbit per
       second is likely to use 25.9% of an 1100/92, and
       the bi-directional transfer time will be about
       7 minutes ...

Faulty punctuation

Faulty punctuation and absence of punctuation are
constant sources of difficulty to struggling
foreign-language readers.

They should not have to pause to work out whether <u>two
channel translators</u> is intended to mean "two-channel
translators" or "two channel-translators" in:

> ... if you are connecting two channel translators
> to the unit, connect ...

They should not be led into mis-interpretation of this
extract by the omission of a comma:

> ... the section referring to installation in this
> manual deals only with the XXX software
> installation which you will carry out ...

The intended meaning was:

> ... the section referring to installation in this
> manual deals only with the XXX software
> installation, which you will carry out ...

They should not have to pause, even momentarily, to re-
assure themselves that this apostrophe is a false signal:

> ... this option can give rise to inconsistent
> read's because ...

And they should not have to pause to work out when there
<u>should have been</u> an apostrophe to signal a possessive. The
<u>current habit of</u> omitting both the apostrophe and the <u>s</u>
when writers want to indicate a possessive is a major
obstacle to quick comprehension for all readers. We do
not know if:

> ... to pass on the customer requests ...

refers to one or more customers. We do not know if:

> ... for use in a customer network ...

refers to "a customer's network" or "a network of
customers".

Why should any reader have to pause to work out that:

... are responsible for customer collections ...

is not meant to be a possessive or an <u>of ...</u> construction
of any sort?   The intended meaning was:

... are responsible for collections from customers ...

   Foreign-language readers in particular would have found
it easier to recognise the meaning of:

... check against customer records ...

if that meaning had been expressed in accurate English.
This confusing, fashionable use of a singular premodifier
could have meant:

... check against the customer's records ...
... check against the customers' records ...
... check against our records about the customer ...
... check against our records about the customers ...

In fact, it meant the third.

   My appeal is for explicit, accurate writing.   I want
writing that minimises the number of times
foreign-language readers have to stop and work out meaning
that has disappeared behind awkward expression.   Here is
an example of inaccurate writing that causes confusion in
two ways: by being inadequately punctuated, and by using
excessive premodification:

... can be configured to meet a wide range of
    user data communication requirements ...

Six possible interpretations of that extract occur to me:

... to meet the data-communication requirements
    of a wide range of users ...
... to meet a wide range of requirements for
    communicating users' data ...
... to meet the requirements for communicating
    data from a wide range of users ...
... to meet the requirements for communicating
    data to a wide range of users ...

```
... to meet the requirements for communicating
    a wide range of data about users ...
... to meet the requirements for communicating
    data about a wide range of users ...
```

If native-language readers cannot be certain, what chance
have foreign-language readers?

Compressed or elliptical style

To arrive at a round dozen of points about unthinking
writing, let me make a specific comment about
instruction-writing. Many writers use a "compressed" or
elliptical style – omitting "small" words like the, a,
all, some, and other specifying words – when they write
instructions. For example:

```
... Connect cables to proper boards on chassis ...
```

How many cables?   Which cables?   To which boards?   On
which chassis?   Are there some improper boards?

This elliptical style is particularly difficult for
foreign-language readers to follow, especially when it is
allied to a general vagueness in instruction-writing. Of
course, the context often supplies clarifying information.
Perhaps there were only two cables and one chassis.
Perhaps a previous part of the text had defined which
cable and board comprised a "proper" pairing. If that
was the case, the writer could still have been more
explicit:

```
... Connect each cable to its specified board
    on the chassis ...
```

In fact, there was no such clarifying information.
Readers were left to work out for themselves the meaning
of proper and to decide what words would be relevant in
the ellipses in the statement.

It is the writer's responsibility to make it possible
for me to move smoothly along the lines of a text, with
minimum need to go back and adjust my interpretation of
the words I have read previously. As my eye and mind set
off along the lines of a text, I have no idea what is
coming. I am equipped with an understanding of the
normal conventions of English. I attempt to decode the
message piece by piece, relying on the signals on the page
before me, and gradually accumulating in my mind a

coherent over-all statement.   I resent having the
accumulation-assimilation process disturbed by elliptical
writing such as:

   ... Adjustments

        Voltage values are seen through small windows
        in panel.   Switch ranges from 100 to 240 in
        six steps, and is positioned by turning ...

Decoding this text according to the normal conventions
of English, I first had to adjust my interpretation at
<u>small windows in panel</u>.   Normal expectation is that a
word-group like <u>in panel</u> will be followed by at least one
other word, usually an identifier, such as <u>in panel A</u>.
But in the text above, I arrived at a full stop, not at an
A or other identifier;   so I had to adjust my
interpretation, and guess that a <u>the</u> had been omitted from
in front of the noun <u>panel</u>:   I guessed that the intended
meaning was "in <u>the</u> panel".

I was obliged to adjust again at <u>, and is positioned</u>.
Decoding according to normal English, I assumed that
<u>Switch</u> was an imperative verb.   If there had been another
signal, such as <u>the</u>, in front of <u>switch</u>, I should have
started with a different interpretation;   but there was no
<u>the</u>;   so I did the best I could with the group up to the
comma.   I assumed that the writer had done the same as he
had in the previous sentence - omitted a <u>the</u> from in front
of a noun, from in front of <u>ranges</u>:   "... Switch the
ranges...".

However, when I arrived at <u>, and is positioned</u>, it
became clear that I was accumulating in my mind a
completely wrong idea. So I had to review the whole
sentence, and build a new interpretation of what the
writer wanted to say.

To describe (even very roughly) the psycholinguistic
process of reading that example has taken me far longer
than the reading itself;   but I wanted to emphasise the
nature of the process, in order to make plain why
compressed/elliptical writing is difficult for foreign-
language readers.   Most of us, when we are reading in a
foreign language, are desperately dependent on the framework of rules we have learned (more or less efficiently!)
in our lessons on the foreign language.   It is hard
enough to decode a foreign-language text that <u>is</u> written
according to the rules: it is a disaster to be confronted
by one that seems to change the rules as it goes along!

The cost of unthinking writing

Most companies in the computer industry would like to establish contacts and markets world-wide. "Thoughtful" writing, in English, can help them do so: it makes information accessible without translation to the largest possible number of readers; it makes translation quicker and more accurate; it creates confidence by its manageability. "Unthinking" writing costs money because readers lose time as they seek clarification of meaning; it costs money because it makes translation necessary where a better-written text would not: it slows the translation process; it erodes goodwill because it causes irritation.

Without doubt, thoughtful writing calls for a greater investment of effort by writers; but that investment is more than counterbalanced by the time saved for readers, and the greater efficiency of communication.

REFERENCE

1. Kirkman, John   That's Not Writing, That's Typing, Proceedings of the First Conference on Writing for the Computer Industry, Department of English, Plymouth State College, Plymouth, New Hampshire 03264.

Index